D1350040

SPEED OF INFORMATION-PROCESSING AND INTELLIGENCE

Speed of Information-Processing and Intelligence

Edited by:

PHILIP A. VERNON

Department of Psychology
University of Western Ontario
London, Ontario, Canada

Ablex Publishing Corporation
Norwood, New Jersey 07648

Copyright © 1987 by Ablex Publishing Corporation.

All rights reserved. No part of this publication may be reproduced, stored in a
retrieval system, or transmitted, in any form or by any means, electronic, mechanical,
photocopying, microfilming, recording, or otherwise, without permission of the
publisher.

Printed in the United States of America.

Library of Congress Cataloging-in-Publication Data

Speed of information-processing and intelligence.

   Bibliography: p.
   Includes indexes.
   1. Human information processing.   2. Speed.
3. Intellect.   I. Vernon, Philip A.
BF444.S64   1987   153   87-14532
ISBN 0-89391-427-4

Ablex Publishing Corporation
355 Chestnut Street
Norwood, New Jersey 07648

LANCASTER UNIVERSITY
-8 OCT 1991
LIBRARY

90   09343

Contents

To M. L. and A. D.

Preface

Ten or fifteen years ago, a major problem that the writer of a review paper on reaction times and their relationship to intelligence would have encountered would have been the dearth of recent material pertaining to the topic. Indeed, given the lack of interest that most differential psychologists paid reaction times at this time, it is unlikely that it would have occurred to anyone to undertake such a project. Had they done so, with few exceptions, all of the references would have been pre-1930, and the majority of the discussion would have centered on the role of reaction times in the theories of such turn of the century luminaries as Sir Francis Galton and Charles Spearman.

Much has happened in the past decade, however, and it is now doubtful that a single review paper could do justice to the abundance of research and theorizing that exists on the contributions of reaction times, mental speed, and speed of information-processing to individual differences in intelligence and mental abilities. Much of this research is reviewed and discussed in the present volume, by contributors who either are actively involved in research on reaction times and intelligence or whose perspective on these topics provides a valuable commentary on the role of speed-of-processing in theories of intelligence.

In the first four chapters, attention is paid to recent reaction time research, including studies of the heritability of measures of speed of information-processing, neurophysiological correlates of reaction times, the role of attention in reaction time performance, and a comprehensive meta-analysis of reaction times in the Hick paradigm. Chapters five through eight provide critical commentaries on reaction time research and offer a number of interesting interpretations regarding the place of mental speed in intelligence theories. Chapter nine is devoted to research on inspection times and provides the most thorough treatment of this topic that has appeared to date. Finally, in chapter ten, the "last word" is reserved for "The Next Word on Verbal Ability": an exhaustive account of this topic by one of the leading contributors to the field. Regrettably, a chapter devoted to reaction times and mental retardation was not delivered in time to be included. This, however, is perhaps the only topic that has not received the attention it deserves.

Thanks are due, first and foremost, to the contributors to this volume, who devoted much time and effort to their respective topics. Thanks for her assistance and patience is well-earned by Barbara Bernstein of Ablex. Special thanks to my secretary, Carol Meyer, without whose skills and assistance this project would have been hard-pressed to meet its deadlines. And, finally, thanks to my father—Philip E. Vernon—for his many contributions and continued encouragement.

CHAPTER 1

New Developments in Reaction Time Research

Philip A. Vernon
Department of Psychology
University of Western Ontario
London, Ontario, Canada, N6A 5C2

Research on the relationship between reaction time (RT) and mental ability has had a checkered history. At first, it appeared to some that RTs and other simple perceptual and sensory discrimination measures held great promise as a means to revealing and elucidating the mysteries of human intelligence. As early as 1904, for example, Charles Spearman claimed that "general sensory discrimination" and "general intelligence" were essentially perfectly correlated. The optimism that this may have generated would be short-lived, however, as other workers failed to replicate Spearman's results or to support his conclusions (e.g., Thorndike, Lay, & Dean, 1909). Indeed, even before Spearman, Wissler's (1901) report of a correlation of only − .02 between RTs and estimates of ability anticipated the paradigm's impending desuetude.

Thereafter, for some 50 or 60 years, the use of RTs in the study of intelligence was an isolated practice (e.g., Lemmon, 1927; Peak & Boring, 1926), regarded by most to be of little interest or consequence. Introductory Psychology students by the thousands must have heard that Galton and Spearman were wrong — RTs and mental abilities had been proven to be unrelated. Given the prevalence of this belief, the recent attention that RTs have enjoyed, and the concomitant recognition that they are a potentially important correlate of intelligence, may be regarded as one of the great comebacks in psychology (only somewhat less modest, perhaps, than the rediscovery of the brain following the reign of Behaviorism!). Several aspects of this comeback are addressed in the present volume.

Following a brief introduction, this chapter will focus on three somewhat disparate issues: the relationship between RTs and intelligence test scores obtained under timed or untimed conditions; the heritability of RTs; and sex differences in RTs. Each of these has received some attention in the literature, although, with the exception of the first, their discussion here will center around previously unreported studies and results. Clearly, these topics will not provide an exhaustive account of all of the new developments and recent research on RTs and intelligence. To attempt such an account would, among other things, involve unnecessary duplication of material presented in some of the other chapters. The topics are, however, indicative of the sorts of issues that researchers in the area have found fruitful to explore and, hopefully, they will at least implicitly raise questions towards which further research may be directed.

THE "NEURAL-EFFICIENCY" MODEL

Reviews of research on RTs and intelligence, such as Jensen (1982) and Vernon (1985), have concluded that the two are moderately highly correlated—zero-order correlations range from about −.30 to −.50, though multiple Rs in the .70s have been reported—and have attempted to account for the relationship in terms of what might be called a model of "neural efficiency." The essence of this model is that the human short-term or working memory has a limited capacity to store and to process information, and that the information that it can hold is subject to fairly rapid decay or loss in the absence of continuous rehearsal. During problem-solving, or performance of any intellectual task sufficiently complex to result in individual differences, as information is taken into the system and the task's requisite component processes are carried out, there is some probability that the capacity of the system will reach its threshold. Presumably, were this to happen, the individual would be unable to solve the problem or, at least, would need to backtrack or to start again. The probability of this occurrence would be lowered, however, if the system had some way to overcome its limitations. Rapid execution of the requisite cognitive processes is proposed as one such way of "beating the system."

Information entering working memory would quickly fill up its limited storage capacity unless it could (at least) equally quickly be recoded and stored as a small number of chunks. Information retrieval from long-term memory (LTM), necessary for the task's solution, could, unless performed quickly, be accompanied by the decay or inaccessibility of the earlier-stored information. The retrieved information must itself be held in working memory, contributing to the bulk of the material being stored, while at the same time rehearsal processes and the component processes involved in the task's solution must be carried out. Speed may not be the only factor operating to reduce the probability that the system will be overloaded but a substantial amount of research—described in detail in the previously cited reviews by Jensen (1982) and Vernon (1985)—has demonstrated that it is an important factor.

SPEED OF INFORMATION-PROCESSING AND TIMED VS. UNTIMED MEASURES OF INTELLIGENCE

To what extent might the relationship between RT measures of speed of information-processing and intelligence be attributable to the fact that many tests of intelligence are themselves speeded or contain timed subtests? Some authors (e.g., Carroll, 1981; Schwartz, Griffin, & Brown, 1983; Sternberg, 1984) have suggested that the answer to this question is "quite a lot," while others (Vernon & Kantor, 1986; Vernon, Nador, & Kantor, 1985) have taken the contradictory and seemingly counterintuitive position that RTs might actually correlate more highly with untimed than with timed IQ scores. Fast information-processing is useful during a timed test because, in order to answer a large number of items in a short period of time, an individual must be able to "work"—that is, to perform the cognitive operations demanded by the items—quickly and efficiently. During an untimed test, the individual may no longer appear to have to work quickly but, according to the neural efficiency model described previously, speed of information-processing is still important. The reason is that items on intelligence tests are typically arranged in order of increasing difficulty, and that later items, which untimed individuals are more likely than timed individuals to reach and attempt, will, because they are more difficult, place increasing information-processing demands on the individual, an increasing burden on the individual's information-processing system, and thus result in an increasing need for fast speed of information-processing to ameliorate the situation.

Results supporting this position were reported by Vernon et al. (1985) and by Vernon and Kantor (1986). In the first of these studies, 81 subjects were given a multiple-choice, paper-and-pencil intelligence test (the Multidimensional Aptitude Battery [MAB]; Jackson, 1983) under both timed and untimed conditions. On each of the 10 subtests of the MAB, subjects were instructed to work as quickly as they could for 5 minutes, recording their answers with a blue pen. At the end of each 5-minute period, subjects switched to a red pen and continued working for as long as it took them to finish the subtest. Subsequently, each subject's timed score was computed as the number of correct answers marked in blue, while the total number of correct answers marked in blue or red became their untimed score. Multiple regression analyses, in which these timed and untimed scores were regressed on RTs, yielded multiple Rs of .605 and .504, respectively. These correlations are not significantly different from each other, and it was concluded that speed of information-processing is an approximately equally good predictor of untimed as of timed intelligence test performance.

This study has been criticized by Sternberg (1986), who points out that zero-order correlations between the MAB and RTs were consistently higher with the timed than with the untimed scores. In fact, of 21 RT measures, 20 correlated more highly with timed than with untimed MAB scores. Sternberg omitted to report, however, that the magnitudes of the differences between the correlations were mostly quite small: averaged across the 21 measures, the difference was only .06. Of more concern (as Sternberg, 1986, also points out) is the fact that the so-called "untimed score" is only partly untimed, since it was computed as the sum of subjects' timed and untimed scores. The effect that this may have had on the scores' correlations with RTs was investigated by Vernon and Kantor (1986).

In this study, 113 high school students were randomly assigned to one of two groups: one was allowed only 5 minutes to work on each subtest of the

TABLE 1

Zero-order correlations between reaction times[a] and Full-Scale, Verbal, and Performance MAB scores in each group

	SD2	DIGIT	DT2 Words	DT2 Digits	CATMATCH	SA2	DT3 Words
Full-Scale							
Timed	− .265	− .452	− .379	− .437	− .523	− .493	− .484
Untimed	− .336	− .353	− .230	− .161	− .440	− .508	− .541
Verbal							
Timed	− .184	− .351	− .295	− .353	− .391	− .446	− .461
Untimed	− .378	− .337	− .298	− .174	− .516	− .519	− .541
Performance							
Timed	− .282	− .434	− .362	− .402	− .521	− .395	− .360
Untimed	− .228	− .304	− .114	− .117	− .278	− .401	− .440

[a]Reaction time tests are described in detail in Vernon, Nador, and Kantor (1985). Briefly, they are: SD2: Same-different words
DIGIT: Sternberg probe-recognition
DT2: Same-different words + DIGIT
CATMATCH: Category matching
SA2: Synonyms and antonyms
DT3: Synonyms and antonyms + DIGIT
TRFAL: True/False sentence verification
DT4: Arithmetic problems + DIGIT

MAB; the other was given unlimited time. Subsequently, all subjects were administered the same battery of RT tests used by Vernon et al. (1985) under standard conditions. Regression analyses yielded multiple Rs of .559 and .662 when timed and untimed MAB scores, respectively, were regressed on RTs. Note that the untimed MAB yielded the larger correlation. This was reflected by the finding that zero-order correlations between the MAB subtests and individual RT tests were, on average, slightly larger in the untimed than in the timed group. As in Vernon et al. (1985), the differences are mostly quite small but, unlike the first study, the majority (61 of 110) of the correlations are higher with the untimed MAB.

Interestingly, Verbal and Performance subtests behaved quite differently in terms of the conditions under which they were administered and their resulting correlations with RTs. At the level of individual subtests, 38 of 55 correlations between Verbal subtests and RTs were higher in the untimed than in the timed group. In contrast, 32 of 55 correlations between Performance subtests and RTs were higher in the timed group. At the Scale level, as can be seen in Table 1, untimed Verbal Scale scores correlated more highly than timed scores with 8 of 11 RT tests, while untimed Performance Scale scores correlated more highly than timed scores with only 3 of the 11 RT tests. Per-

| | | | | | Correlations with: First Factor | |
DT3 Digits	TRFAL	DT4 Math	DT4 Digits	Average	Loadings	Mean RTs
− .410	− .370	− .369	− .376	− .414	.757	.166
− .350	− .482	− .339	− .353	− .372	.085	.332
− .355	− .300	− .206	− .273	− .329	.686	− .001
− .346	− .480	− .397	− .327	− .392	− .019	.507
− .348	− .338	− .454	− .384	− .389	.493	.372
− .287	− .393	− .214	− .313	− .281	.192	.105

haps some of the later Verbal items—those attempted more frequently by subjects in the untimed than in the timed group—are sufficiently complex to place a high premium on fast speed of information-processing. This might be true of Arithmetic items, for example, the later, more difficult of which would be expected to impose considerable information-processing demands even in the absence of a time-limit. Performance items, in contrast, may be relatively less complex and more amenable to solution when unlimited time is provided. This would be particularly true of Digit Symbol, in which subjects merely have to match increasingly lengthy strings of digits and associated symbols, and to a lesser extent, perhaps, of Spatial items. Inspection of the average zero-order correlations between each subtest and the 11 RT tests in Table 2 in fact reveals that Digit Symbol and Spatial are the two Performance subtests whose correlations with RTs are markedly larger in the timed than in the untimed group. For Picture Completion, the correlations are approximately equivalent in the two groups, while both Picture Arrangement and Object Assembly actually correlate somewhat higher, on average, with RTs in the untimed group. All of the Verbal subtests correlate more highly, on average, with RTs in the untimed than in the timed group but the difference is largest in the case of Arithmetic.

Referring back to Table 1, it is also evident that there is a not inconsiderable range in magnitude among the MAB and RT correlations within each group. The correlations with untimed Full-Scale scores, for example, range from $-.161$ to $-.541$; with timed Performance Scale scores, from $-.282$ to $-.521$. Furthermore, the variations that exist within the timed and the untimed tests appear to be attributable to quite different sources. Factor analysis of the intercorrelations among the 11 RT tests yielded a strong general factor, accounting for 75.6% of the variance. In the second column from the right in Table 1, the correlations between the RT tests' loadings on this general factor and their correlations with the MAB Scale scores are reported. As can be seen, these are all positive and quite high for the timed scores (.757, .686, and .493 for Full-Scale, Verbal, and Performance, respectively) but are negligible, and in one case negative, for the untimed scores. Evidently, the extent to which a RT test correlates with timed MAB scores is quite highly related to the test's loading on a general speed factor, but this loading is unrelated to the test's correlation with untimed scores.

Somewhat more important for untimed scores is the relative complexity of the RT tests, as operationally defined by their mean latency. In the far right column of Table 1, correlations between the means of the RT tests and their correlations with the MAB are reported. For untimed Full-Scale and Verbal scores, the correlations of .332 and .507, respectively, are positive and moderate in magnitude, while the corresponding correlations of .166 and $-.001$ with the timed tests are much smaller. For these tests, then, it appears that the relative complexity of a RT test is related to the degree to which it correlates

TABLE 2

Mean zero-order correlations between each MAB subtest[a] and 11 reaction time tests in the timed and untimed groups

	INFO	COMP	ARITH	SIMS	VOCAB	DGSYM	PICO	SPAT	PICARR	OBJASS
Timed Group	−.294	−.251	−.149	−.356	−.256	−.379	−.350	−.234	−.203	−.257
Untimed Group	−.364	−.285	−.291	−.390	−.265	−.204	−.315	−.141	−.296	−.304

[a]MAB subtests, in the order listed above, are: Information, Comprehension, Arithmetic, Similarities, Vocabulary, Digit Symbol, Picture Completion, Spatial, Picture Arrangement, and Object Assembly.

with untimed but not with timed tests. This pattern does not hold for Performance scores, however, which correlate more highly with the RT tests' means in the timed condition.

Taken together, these results indicate that timed and untimed tests of mental ability impose rather different information-processing demands on test-takers, but that the speed with which they can execute the different cognitive processes that each requires is related approximately equally highly to the probability that they will handle the demands successfully. Timed intelligence test performance appears to be most highly related to general speed of information-processing, reflecting the fact that a high timed-test scorer must be able to perform a wide variety of cognitive processes quickly and efficiently. A high score on an untimed test, however, is not related to this general speed factor but, reflecting its own reliance on the ability to answer later, more difficult items, is positively correlated with the relative complexity of the RT tests. The finding that this holds for Verbal but not for Performance Scale scores supports the earlier contention that later Performance items may — at least in some subtests — be relatively less complex than some later Verbal items.

THE HERITABILITY OF MEASURES
OF SPEED OF INFORMATION-PROCESSING

To what degree do RT tests tap what might be referred to as the "hardware" of the brain? That is, to what extent are individual differences in RTs attributable to differences in biological or neurophysiological properties of the brain that may be hypothesized to underlie both the speed with which persons can process information and their intelligence? One step (among several) that may be taken in an approach to this question is to obtain estimates of the heritabilities of different RT tests — i.e., to estimate the proportion of the total variance in RTs that is attributable to genetic variance — and to determine whether these heritabilities are sufficiently large to warrant the inference that individual differences in performance on the tests are in part determined by underlying biological processes or mechanisms.

The first, and, to my knowledge, only published study to investigate this was conducted by McGue, Bouchard, Lykken, and Feuer (1984). In this study, 34 pairs of monozygotic twins that had been reared apart (MZA) and 13 pairs of dizygotic twins reared apart (DZA) were administered three different RT tests and a battery of psychometric tests. The RT tests were factor analyzed to yield three factors — overall speed of response, speed of information-processing, and speed of spatial processing — and intraclass correlations between the MZA twins were computed. Briefly, none of the MZA correlations involving speed of specific cognitive processing was significant, whereas the correlation for overall speed of response ($r = .456$) was significant. The authors concluded: "the results reported here support the existence of a general speed component underlying performance on most experimental cognitive tasks which is strongly related to psychometric measures of 'G', and for which there are substantial genetic effects" (p. 256).

Over a period of approximately 10 months, I have collected RT and MAB data from 32 pairs of MZ twins and 35 pairs of DZ twins living in southwestern Ontario. With the exception of one of the MZ pairs who were separated at birth until 12 years of age, each of the twin-pairs had been raised together at least until the age of 15 years. The MZ twins ranged from 15 to 37 years of age (mean = 24.5, SD = 6.5). Twenty eight pairs were female, four male. The DZ twins ranged from 15 to 40 years of age (mean = 22.2, SD = 6.9). Fifteen pairs were female, 5 male, and 15 mixed-sex. The zygosity of the same-sex pairs was determined by means of a questionnaire developed by Nichols and Bilbro (1966). According to these authors, the questionnaire is 93% accurate relative to blood sample analyses, and may thus be considered a fairly valid tool for its purposes.

Table 3 presents the results of a series of multiple regression analyses, designed to show both the overall relationship between RTs and full scale MAB

TABLE 3
Summary of adjusted Rs obtained in regressions
of full-scale MAB scores on RTs within
MZ and DZ samples

Sample	R_{adj}	Average
Total Sample (n = 134)	.635	
All MZ subjects (n = 64)	.685	
All DZ subjects (n = 70)	.562	
Within MZ subjects[a]:		
Twin 1/Twin 1	.672	.700[b]
Twin 2/Twin 2	.727	
Twin 1/Twin2	.629	.647
Twin 2/Twin1	.664	
Within DZ subjects		
Twin 1/Twin 1	.561	.642
Twin 2/Twin 2	.723	
Twin 1/Twin 2	.296	.310
Twin 2/Twin 1	.324	

[a]Regressions performed in which each twin's MAB score was regressed on either his/her own (twin 1/twin 1 and twin 2/twin 2) RTs or on his/her twin's (twin 1/twin 2 and twin 2/twin 1) RTs.

[b]This correlation is the average of .672 and .727, i.e., the average R obtained when each twin's MAB is regressed on his/her own RTs.

scores in these twin samples, and to provide a preliminary indication of the degree of similarity that exists among MZ and among DZ twin-pairs in RTs and intelligence. The first correlation ($R = .635$) is the shrunken multiple R obtained from the regression of all subjects' MAB scores on their RTs. In other words, this correlation was obtained by ignoring the fact that the subjects were twins and treating them simply as a sample of 134 subjects. The magnitude of this correlation is similar to that obtained in previous studies that have used the same tests (e.g., Vernon et al., 1985; Vernon & Kantor, 1986). If age is controlled, all the zero-order RT/MAB correlations are increased and the resulting shrunken multiple R is .678. The next two correlations in Table 3 ($R = .685$ and .562) were obtained in the same manner as the first, but within the MZ (treated as $N = 64$ subjects) and DZ ($N = 70$) samples. For these samples, at least, the relationship between RTs and intelligence appears to be stronger among the MZ than among the DZ subjects.

The next set of four correlations was obtained by arbitrarily designating one member of each MZ twin-pair as "Twin 1" and the other as "Twin 2." Regressions were then performed in which each twin's MAB score was regressed on his or her *own* RTs (resulting in $R = .672$ and .727 for the 32 Twin 1 and Twin 2 subjects, respectively), and in which each twin's MAB score was regressed on his or her *twin's* RTs (resulting in $R = .629$ and .664). Note that each of these four analyses yields a correlation that is of approximately the same magnitude as those obtained from all 64 of the MZ subjects and from the total sample of 134 subjects. Among the MZ twins, then, approximately the same degree of relationship between MAB scores and RTs is found even when one twin is substituted for the other.

The final set of four correlations in Table 2 shows what happens when the DZ twin-pairs are treated in the same fashion. When each DZ twin's MAB score is regressed on his or her own RTs, correlations of .561 and .723 are obtained. The average of these ($R = .642$) is still approximately the same as those obtained in all the previous analyses. When each DZ twin's MAB scores is regressed on his or her twin's RTs, however, the resulting correlations ($R = .296$ and .324) are markedly lower. Unlike MZ twins, it is not possible to substitute one DZ twin for the other and observe the same degree of relationship between MAB scores and RTs. In fact, the correlations are only about half as large.

The greater similarity among MZ than among DZ twins, both in mental abilities and in speed of information-processing, is shown clearly in Table 4. Here, the intraclass correlations obtained from the MZ and the DZ samples are reported for each of the MAB subtests, the MAB Scale scores (Verbal, Performance, and Full-Scale), and for 11 RT measures. With only one exception, all of the intraclass correlations are larger in the MZ than in the DZ samples, and a simple estimate of heritability ($2[r_{I_{MZ}} - r_{I_{DZ}}]$) reveals that both the MAB and many of the RT measures have a substantial heritable

TABLE 4
Intraclass correlations obtained from MZ and DZ twins for MAB subtests, MAB Scale scores,[a] and RT variables, and heritability estimates (h^2) based on these correlations

Variables	MZ correlations	DZ correlations	h^2
INFO	.734	.588	.292
COMP	.750	.568	.364
ARITH	.638	.495	.286
SIMS	.717	.233	.968
VOCAB	.843	.523	.640
DGSYM	.729	−.019	—[b]
PICO	.471	.344	.254
SPAT	.710	.226	.968
PICARR	.630	.156	.948
OBJASS	.743	.345	.796
VERB	.905	.544	.722
PERF	.866	.254	—
FULL-SCALE	.923	.470	.906
SD2	.706	.298	.816
DIGIT	.578	.408	.340
DT2 Words	.550	.508	.084
DT2 Digits	.690	.256	.868
CATMATCH	.513	.156	.714
SA2	.688	.244	.888
DT3 Words	.720	.298	.844
DT3 Digits	.461	.321	.280
TRFAL	.610	.518	.184
DT4 Math	.379	.095	.568
DT4 Digits	.326	.365	—

[a]MAB subtests are as described in Table 2. The Scale scores are Verbal, Performance, and Full-Scale.
[b]h^2 estimates > 1 or < 0 are not reported.

component. In these samples, the heritability of the full-scale MAB is .906, and heritabilities of the RT measures range from .084 to .888, with a mean of .559.[1]

Within the MZ and DZ samples, correlations among the 11 RT tests referred to in Tables 1 and 4 were submitted to principal factor analysis. In each sample, a single factor with an eigenvalue greater than one was yielded, accounting for 74.1% and 66.9% of the variance among MZs and DZs respectively. All of the variables had high positive loadings, ranging from .734 to .923 among the MZs and from .677 to .889 among the DZs. The loadings for MZs and DZs were themselves correlated .872, and the factors are inter-

[1]This mean is based on the 10 RT tests for which heritabilities could be computed with this formula.

preted as representing general speed of information-processing.[2] Intraclass correlations between factor scores on these factors were .685 and .429, for MZ and DZ twins respectively, yielding a heritability estimate (applying the same formula as before) of .512.

Finally, intraclass correlations were computed for three speed-of-processing variables derived from the 11 RT tests. These variables include two estimates of speed of scanning information in STM; two estimates of speed of retrieval of information from LTM; and three estimates of storage-processing trade-off in STM. The way in which these variables are derived is described in Vernon et al. (1985; Table 3). The first two (STM scanning and LTM retrieval) represent processes that are similar to those tapped by McGue et al.'s (1984) speed of information-processing factor, and, as in their study, MZ (and DZ) intraclass correlations for these variables are small and nonsignificant. For the two STM scanning variables, the average MZ correlation in the present study was .267. The corresponding correlation for the DZs was .183. For LTM retrieval, the average intraclass correlations were .304 for MZs and .275 for DZs. In contrast, the storage-processing trade-off measures — which are hypothesized to measure the extent to which subjects can store one type of information (usually strings of digits) in STM while simultaneously processing other information (e.g., synonyms and antonyms or simple arithmetic problems) — yielded larger MZ and smaller DZ intraclass correlations (the average across the three estimates was .429 for MZs and .103 for DZs), which in turn yield a fairly substantial estimate of heritability: .652 using the average correlations.

In sum, the results of the present study support those of McGue et al. (1984) in showing that some measures of RT and speed of information-processing have a substantial heritable component, while others appear to be less influenced by genetic factors. Currently, I am continuing to collect twin (and other kinship) data and, as larger samples are obtained, more stable estimates of the variables' heritabilities will be provided. These, in turn, will allow other interesting questions to be addressed, such as what factors are related to the variability among the tests' heritabilities. Will the heritabilities be related, for example, to the tests' loadings on the general speed factor? Or to their correlations with measures of intelligence? For the moment, it will be sufficient to conclude that individual differences in the speed with which persons can perform certain cognitive operations are in part attributable to genetic differences, and to infer that RT measures of speed of information-processing are (albeit indirectly) tapping biological or neurophysiological properties of the brain.

---

[2]Despite their names, these factors are not directly comparable to the factor that McGue et al. (1984) labelled "speed of information-processing." Their factor was defined by three variables derived from the S. Sternberg and Posner tasks.

SEX DIFFERENCES IN
SPEED OF INFORMATION-PROCESSING

Sex differences in mental abilities have been subjected to extensive investigation, but studies in this area have yielded few unambiguous results. It is probably safe to say that representative samples of males and females will differ very little, if at all, on Full-Scale measures of general intelligence or, more importantly, since many of the tests themselves have been designed to minimize sex differences, on g factor scores derived from heterogeneous batteries of tests, but that females will tend to obtain higher scores than males, on average, on certain verbally-loaded tests and that males will tend to obtain higher scores than females, on average, on certain spatially- and/or numerically-loaded tests. These generalizations, which apply primarily after puberty, have been sufficiently well-replicated to be considered reliable empirical phenomena. The question of what factors are responsible for the phenomena is, however, an unresolved one that has generated much research but few uncontested answers. Cultural sex-role socialization practices, genetic factors, hormonal factors, and anatomical differences between the brains of males and females have all been proposed as possible sources of between-sex variance in abilities, but the conclusions that can be drawn from the research that each has generated are at best equivocal.

Sex differences in RTs have also received some attention in the literature, but the results of studies that have investigated these are even more inconclusive. Landauer, Armstrong, and Digwood (1980), for example, recently reported that females obtained significantly faster simple and choice RTs than did males, and Landauer (1981) suggested that this might indicate that females "have greater cognitive abilities" (p. 90). Similar results were reported by Fairweather and Hutt (1972), in which girls up to the age of 12 years performed faster than boys on choice RT tests. Results contrary to these, however, were reported by Hodgkins (1963), Coles, Porges, and Duncan-Johnson (1975), and Bell, Loomis, and Cervone (1982), each of which found males to have faster RTs than females. Finally, Botwinick and Thompson (1966), Crabbe and Johnson (1979), Yandell and Spirduso (1981), and Jensen (1984) have all reported no significant differences between males and females in RTs. Although there are plausible methodological reasons for these discrepancies — for example, the use of very small samples in some studies and the failure to differentiate between reaction time and reaction-time-plus-movement-time in others — it is nonetheless clear that the results are sufficiently inconsistent to warrant further investigation. In addition, rather than focussing on RTs to simple visual stimuli (e.g., lights on a panel), as many of the studies in this area have done, it would seem to be potentially more useful to measure RTs to verbal, spatial, and numerical stimuli and to vary the extent to which each RT test requires primarily short-term or long-term memory processes. If this were done, it might be possible to identify and isolate sex differences in speed of execution of specific cognitive processes applied to specific types of information.

In my own studies (e.g., Vernon, 1983; Vernon et al., 1985), sex differences have been rare both on psychometric measures of ability and in RTs. In Vernon (1983), for example, the mean WAIS Verbal IQ scores for males (n = 35) and females (n = 65) were 124.74 and 121.34, respectively. The corresponding Performance IQ scores were 119.34 and 118.34. Neither set of means is significantly different. The largest difference between the mean RTs of males and females on seven RT measures was 19.57 ms. (on a test requiring synonym/antonym judgments), which yields a t of .50! Marginally more interesting results were observed in Vernon et al. (1985), in which males obtained significantly higher untimed Performance Scale scores (on the MAB) than females and were consistently faster on RT tests involving scanning digit strings or performing simple arithmetic operations. Only the latter test yielded a significant difference, however, and interpretation of the results is muddied by the finding that males also obtained higher Verbal Scale scores than females but did not obtain significantly faster RTs on any of the RT tests involving verbal stimuli.

Further analyses of these data included inspecting the RTs of males and females who scored one standard deviation (*SD*) or more above or below the mean on either the Verbal or the Performance Scale of the MAB. Large differences were observed between the mean RTs of high and low Verbal and of high and low Performance females. Averaged across 11 RT tests, high Verbal females obtained a mean RT of 669.32 ms., compared to 1113.86 ms. for low Verbal females: a difference of 444.54 ms., or 1.67 *SD* units. The largest RT differences appeared on tests involving verbal stimuli. Similarly, the mean RT for high Performance females was 696.52, compared to 1019.41 for low Performance females: a difference of 322.89 ms., or 1.12 *SD* units. The largest difference here occurred on tests involving numerical stimuli. High and low Verbal males obtained mean RTs of 670.21 and 774.27, respectively, averaged across the 11 tests: a smaller difference than was observed for the females, but still amounting to .78 *SD* units. Again, the largest differences appeared on tests involving verbal stimuli. Finally, high and low Performance males obtained mean RTs of 749.28 and 726.26, respectively: a difference of − .19 *SD* units. These results, it must be noted, are based on small subsamples but, if replicated, have interesting implications. High verbal ability appears to be associated with faster RTs, particularly on tests involving verbal stimuli, for both males and females. High performance ability, however, is associated with faster RTs (particularly on tests involving numerical stimuli) for females but not for males. On the contrary, the high Performance males were actually very slightly slower, on average, than the low Performance males.

Pursuing this, and the issue of sex differences in speed of information-processing in general, one of my graduate students — Sue Nador — has administered a large battery of paper-and-pencil tests of verbal, numerical, and spatial abilities, and 10 RT tests involving verbal, numerical, and figural stimuli, to samples of male and female university undergraduate students. The paper-and-pencil measures included a vocabulary test, a test of arithmetic and mathematical reasoning, the space relations subtest (Form A) of the Differential Aptitude Test (Bennett, Seashore, & Wesman, 1947), and the Harshman Figures (Harshman & Harshman, 1983) — a measure of perceptual closure. The RT tests were designed to require subjects either to scan verbal, numerical, or figural stimuli in short-term memory or to access and to retrieve verbal or spatial information from long-term memory. Tests of the former included variants of S. Sternberg's (1966) probe-recognition test, and a test requiring subjects to recognize rotations or mirror images of abstract shapes and figures. Tests of the latter included variants of Posner's letter-matching task (Posner, Boies, Eichelman, & Taylor, 1969), and a test which required subjects to make true/false decisions about geographical-location statements of the form: "Canada is north of America" or "Ontario is west of Alberta" (all subjects were Canadians, to whom the information in these items was very familiar). The main hypotheses were that males and females would differ significantly, in the usual directions, on the paper-and-pencil tests, and that these differences would be reflected by differences in the speed with which they could process specific types of information. We also wished to explore the extent to which sex differences in RTs would occur on tests requiring primarily short-term or primarily long-term memory processes. Might it be the case, for example, that females can retrieve verbal information from LTM more quickly than can males, but perhaps are no different in their speed of scanning verbal stimuli in STM? Or that males can scan figural stimuli or perform mental rotations in STM more quickly than can females, but are no quicker in the speed with which they can retrieve spatial (geographical) information from LTM?

The first analyses — simple t tests between the males and females — yielded disappointing results, in that sex differences failed to appear on any of the variables, paper-and-pencil or reaction time. This may be attributable to the fact that all subjects were university students, although reliable sex differences have been observed on several of the same paper-and-pencil tests in similar samples (e.g., Harshman, Hampson, & Berenbaum, 1983). As before, then, further analyses were conducted within selected subsamples, to investigate the extent to which males and females of above or below average verbal, spatial, or mathematical ability might differ in RTs. Because the sample sizes were relatively small (50 males and 50 females), "high" and "low" ability subjects were operationally identified as those who scored half a standard deviation or more above or below their group mean. Thus, high and low ability subjects, so defined, differ by at least one *SD* unit on each paper-and-pencil measure.

First, within the female sample, high verbals obtained considerably faster mean RTs than low verbals on tests involving scanning verbal stimuli (letters) in STM, and retrieving verbal information (about synonyms and antonyms) from LTM. In *SD* units, the differences between their means on these tests were 1.17 and 1.09, respectively. In contrast, high verbal females were only slightly faster than low verbals (.34 *SD* units) in the speed with which they could make spatial rotation judgments. The reverse effect was observed for high and low spatial ability females, the former being .75 *SD* units faster than the latter, on average, on the rotations RT test but essentially no different (.07 *SD* units faster) on the synonyms test. Finally, females with high math scores were faster than low math-scorers, on average, in the speed with which they could scan figural stimuli (shapes) in STM (1.04 *SD* units), and retrieve spatial/geographical information from LTM (.88 *SD* units), but were hardly different (.11 *SD* units faster) on the verbal RT tests.

A very different pattern of results emerged within the male sample, the most marked discrepancy being that lower ability males were somewhat faster than higher ability males, on average, on several RT tests. In addition, while high verbal males were faster than low verbals in retrieving verbal information from LTM, the difference between their means was small (.33 *SD* units) and not much larger than the corresponding difference in their speed of scanning figural stimuli in STM (.26 *SD* units). Similarly, high spatial males were only very slightly faster than low spatials in scanning figural stimuli (.16 *SD* units), and showed a difference of similar magnitude (.10 *SD* units) in speed of retrieving verbal information from LTM. In one of the few instances in which males produced results comparable to those of the females, high math-scoring males were faster than low math-scoring males, on average, on the geography RT test (.69 *SD* units), and on the spatial-rotations RT test (.54 *SD* units), but were only very slightly faster (.15 *SD* units) on the verbal RT tests.

A final series of analyses compared the RTs of high ability females with those of low ability males, and of high ability males with those of low ability females. First, high verbal females were significantly faster than low verbal males on speed of retrieval of verbal information from LTM, but were no faster at scanning verbal (or figural) stimuli in STM. High spatial males, however, were no faster than low spatial females on any of the RT tests, and the largest difference between these groups' means, although appearing on the spatial-rotations RT test, amounted to only .37 *SD* units. High math males, in contrast, did show significantly faster mean RTs than low math females in retrieval of spatial/geographical information from LTM, and in scanning figural and numerical stimuli in STM. These groups did not differ on any of the RT tests involving verbal stimuli. Finally, to see what would happen if the typical sex-differences in abilities were reversed, high math and high spatial females were found to be no faster than low math or low spatial males, respectively, on any of the RT tests, and the only test on which high verbal males were found to be faster than low verbal females was the one that involved retrieval of geographical information from LTM.

In summary, while it is clear that the samples tested here were far from ideal as sources of information regarding sex differences in abilities, the observed results nonetheless indicate that RT studies involving a variety of tests may be able to shed some light on the issue. Specifically, insofar as the present results are generalizable, it appears that females who are above average in verbal, spatial, or mathematical ability will obtain faster RTs than lower ability females, on average, on tests involving the processing of verbal, spatial, or figural information or stimuli, respectively. High verbal females also obtain faster mean RTs than low verbal males on tests involving accessing and retrieving verbal information from LTM, but not on tests involving figural stimuli or the scanning of verbal stimuli in STM. High verbal and high spatial males do not consistently process verbal or spatial information faster than low verbal or low spatial males, respectively, although high math-scoring males are faster than low math-scoring males, on average, on RT tests involving geography recall and spatial-rotations. High math-scoring males are also faster on these RT tests than are low math-scoring females, on average, but are no different on RT tests involving verbal stimuli.

Again, the relatively small size of some of the subsamples of high and low ability males and females must be emphasized, but an interesting pattern of results appears to be emerging. Most salient are the differences that appear between high and low ability subjects within each of the sexes: the RT differences between these groups being considerably more pronounced among females than among males. Secondly, there are some notable consistencies in the data, such as the finding that high verbal or spatial or mathematical abilities are not associated with faster mental speed per se, but are associated (particularly within females) with faster RTs on tests that were designed with specific types of stimuli to tap specific types of cognitive operations. Thirdly, comparisons between the high and low subsamples of males and females (i.e., high male-low female and high female-low male) again indicate that high scores on specific ability tests tend to be associated with faster RTs on specific tests rather than with faster mental speed in general. Fourthly, high verbal males, and high spatial and mathematical females, do not differ from low verbal females, or low spatial or low mathematical males, respectively, in the same manner that high verbal females, and high spatial and high math-scoring males, differ from low verbal males, and low spatial and low math-scoring females, respectively. In other words, it appears that sex is an important mediating variable in terms of the degree to which differences in abilities will be reflected by differences in RTs.

SUMMARY

In conclusion, this chapter has focussed on three issues pertinent to the study of reaction times and their relationship to intelligence and mental abilities. The results generated by research into each of these issues may be summarized briefly as follows. First, RTs and speed of information-processing are reliably and quite highly correlated with measures of intelligence. Second, this correlation obtains, and to approximately the same degree, both when the measures of intelligence are administered under timed conditions and when they are administered under untimed conditions. Third, several RT tests and the general speed factor extracted from the tests' intercorrelations have a substantial heritable component. Only one of three specific speed of information-processing variables — STM storage-processing trade-off — was found to be heritable. Measures of speed of STM scanning of information, and of LTM retrieval of information, showed low MZ and DZ intraclass correlations, replicating the results of the only other study to have investigated this issue (McGue et al., 1984). Fourth, sex differences in mental abilities — specifically, verbal, spatial, and mathematical ability — may be related to differences in the speed with which males and females can perform specific cognitive operations on specific types of stimuli, but further research employing more representative samples is needed before any definitive conclusions can be drawn.

To repeat a point that was made in the introduction, RT research is enjoying increased recognition by researchers on intelligence. To be sure, not all researchers are equally enthusiastic about the potential of RT work in the study of intelligence; indeed, several of the authors in this volume are quite critical both of the work that has been done and of theoretical positions that place more importance on speed of information-processing than they believe is deserved. This notwithstanding, the results of recent research on RTs have challenged a number of long-standing "truths" about intelligence, and it is surely not unrealistic to suppose that future studies will continue to advance our understanding of the nature of individual differences in mental abilities.

REFERENCES

Bell, P. A., Loomis, R. J., & Cervone, J. C. (1982). Effects of heat, social facilitation, sex differences, and task difficulty on reaction time. *Human Factors, 24,* 19–24.

Bennett, G. K., Seashore, H. G., & Wesman, A. G. (1947). *Differential aptitude tests: Space Relations (Form A).* New York: The Psychological Corporation.

Botwinick, J., & Thompson, L. W. (1966). Components of reaction time in relation to age and sex. *The Journal of Genetic Psychology, 108,* 175–183.

Carroll, J. B. (1981). Ability and task difficulty in cognitive psychology. *Educational Researcher, 10,* 11–21.

Coles, M. G. H., Porges, S. W., & Duncan-Johnson, C. C. (1975). Sex differences in performance and associated cardiac activity during a reaction time task. *Physiological Psychology, 3,* 141–143.

Crabbe, J. M., & Johnson, G. O. (1979). Age group male and female choice reaction time performance during face to face competition. *International Journal of Sport Psychology, 10,* 231–238.

Fairweather, H., & Hutt, S. J. (1972). Gender differences in a perceptual motor skill in children. In C. Ounsted & D. C. Taylor (Eds.), *Gender Differences: Their Ontogeny and Significance.* Baltimore, MD: Williams & Wilkins.

Harshman, R. A., Hampson, E., & Berenbaum, S. A. (1983). Individual differences in cognitive abilities and brain organization, Part 1: Sex and handedness differences in ability. *Canadian Journal of Psychology, 37,* 144–192.

Harshman, R. A., & Harshman, L. (1983). Harshman Figures Test of Visual Closure. *Tests in microfiche.* Princeton, NJ: Educational Testing Service.

Hodgkins, J. (1963). Reaction time and speed of movement in males and females of various ages. *The Research Quarterly, 34,* 335–343.

Jackson, D. N. (1983). *Multidimensional Aptitude Battery.* Port Huron, MI: Research Psychologists Press.

Jensen, A. R. (1982). Reaction time and psychometric *g.* In H. J. Eysenck (Ed.) *A Model for Intelligence.* Berlin: Springer-Verlag.

Jensen, A. R. (1984). Methodological and statistical techniques for the chronometric study of mental abilities. In C. Reynolds & V. L. Willson (Eds.), *Methodological and Statistical Advances in the Study of Individual Differences.* New York: Plenum.

Landauer, A. A. (1981). Sex differences in decision and movement time. *Perceptual and Motor Skills, 52,* 90.

Landauer, A. A., Armstrong, S., & Digwood, J. (1980). Sex differences in choice reaction time. *British Journal of Psychology, 71,* 551–555.

Lemmon, V. W. (1927). The relation of reaction time to measures of intelligence, memory, and learning. *Archives of Psychology, 15,* 5–38.

McGue, M., Bouchard, T. J., Lykken, D. T., & Feuer, D. (1984). Information processing abilities in twins reared apart. *Intelligence, 8,* 239–258.

Nichols, R. C., & Bilbro, W. C., Jr. (1966). The diagnosis of twin zygosity. *Acta Genetica, 16,* 265–275.

Peak, H., & Boring, E. G. (1926). The factor of speed in intelligence. *Journal of Experimental Psychology, 9,* 71–94.

Posner, M., Boies, S., Eichelman, W., & Taylor, R. (1969). Retention of visual and name codes of single letters. *Journal of Experimental Psychology, 81,* 10–15.

Schwartz, S., Griffin, T. M., & Brown, J. (1983). Power and speed components of individual differences in letter matching. *Intelligence, 7,* 369–378.

Spearman, C. (1904). "General intelligence": Objectively determined and measured. *American Journal of Psychology, 15,* 201–292.

Sternberg, R. J. (1984). Toward a triarchic theory of human intelligence. *The Behavioral and Brain Sciences, 7,* 269–315.

Sternberg, R. J. (1986). Haste makes waste versus a stitch in time? A reply to Vernon, Nador, and Kantor. *Intelligence, 10,* 265–270.

Sternberg, S. (1966). High-speed memory scanning in human memory. *Science, 153,* 652–654.

Thorndike, E. L., Lay, W., & Dean, P. R. (1909). The relation of accuracy in sensory discrimination to general intelligence. *The American Journal of Psychology, 20,* 364–369.

Vernon, P. A. (1983). Speed of information-processing and general intelligence. *Intelligence, 7,* 53–70.

Vernon, P. A. (1985). Individual differences in general cognitive ability. In L. C. Hartlage & C. F. Telzrow (Eds.), *The Neuropsychology of Individual Differences: A Developmental Perspective.* New York: Plenum.

Vernon, P. A., & Kantor, L. (1986). Reaction time correlations with intelligence test scores obtained under either timed or untimed conditions. *Intelligence, 10,* 315–330.

Vernon, P. A., Nador, S., & Kantor, L. (1985). Reaction times and speed-of-processing: Their relationship to timed and untimed measures of intelligence. *Intelligence, 9,* 357–374.

Wissler, C. (1901). The correlation of mental and physical tests. *Psychological Review Monographs, 3,* No. 6 (Whole No. 16).

Yandell, K. M., & Spirduso, W. W. (1981). Sex and athletic status as factors in reaction latency and movement time. *Research Quarterly for Exercise and Sport, 52,* 459–504.

CHAPTER 2

Speed of Information Processing, Reaction Time, and the Theory of Intelligence

H. J. Eysenck
Institute of Psychiatry

THE TWO PARADIGMS OF "INTELLIGENCE" – GALTON VS. BINET

The theory that "mental speed" is fundamental to cognitive processes, and is correlated with intelligence, goes back to the very beginnings of modern empirical studies of intellectual processes, as is clearly indicated in Berger's review (1982). The debate centering upon this issue cannot be understood except with reference to two major points of view relating, respectively, to the existence of different definitions and conceptions of cognitive psychology, which require to be carefully distinguished, and the opposite attitudes taken by two great schools, namely those of Galton and of Binet, towards the conception and measurement of intelligence.

Hebb (1949) and Vernon (1979) have distinguished between Intelligence A, Intelligence B, and Intelligence C, referring, respectively, to *biological* intelligence, underlying all cognitive processes and differences therein; *social* intelligence, i.e., Intelligence A applied to everyday life affairs, and inevitably mixed up with a large number of different noncognitive factors, such as personality, socio-economic status, education, experience, etc.; and last, Intelligence C, which refers to the *psychometric* measurement of intelligence, i.e., the IQ.

Figure 1 shows the implications of these terms, and the relation between the three concepts. Additionally, the center part of the "Biological Intelligence" circle shows some of the measures used to define it, e.g., EEG, averaged evoked potentials, contingent negative variation, etc. Notations outside the circles suggest some of the variables which have been shown to influence and shape the various types of "intelligence." Sternberg (1982, 1985) may be taken as a representative of the very popular school which identifies "intelligence" with Intelligence B, and disregards Intelligence A completely. In the subject index of Sternberg's *Handbook of Human Intelligence,* there is no entry for reaction time, and none for evoked potentials which have been found to be good measures of Intelligence A (Eysenck & Barrett, 1985).

I would argue that the usual practice of science is to analyze complex concepts into their constituent parts, so that we should regard Intelligence B as the dependent variable, and study the influence on it of independent variables such as Intelligence A, neuroticism, extraversion, psychoticism, socioeconomic status, education, experience, age, learning, strategy, and the many other factors which may play a role in determining individual differences in this variable. While Intelligence B probably corresponds fairly closely to *popular* conceptions of intelligence, this can hardly be the criterion for a choice which should be based on scientific rather than popular considerations.

The role of IQ tests is interesting, because they seem to stand half-way between Intelligence A and Intelligence B, being intended for the most part as measures of Intelligence A, while being afflicted with some of the same difficulties as is the measurement of Intelligence B, namely the intrusion of unwanted environmental factors. Sternberg (1985) has mentioned the curious tendency of many psychologists to use IQ as a criterion of intelligence even though they are trying to supplement it, or even to substitute some other measure for it. This, however, is not as unreasonable as it sounds; there is

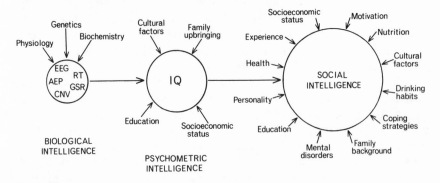

FIGURE 1.   Relations between biological, psychometric and social conceptions of intelligence.

good evidence that IQ, despite its imperfections, does measure general cognitive ability to a reasonable extent (Eysenck, 1979), so that it can be used as an admittedly imperfect criterion against which to test novel measures which are being suggested as being more closely related to Intelligence A. When Torricelli first produced a thermometer, he left the top open, thus leading to a measurement which was a mixture of temperature and barometric pressure. Pascal demonstrated that closing the top would give a better measure of temperature; yet, if the new thermometer had not shown high correlations with the old, it would have been very difficult to establish it as a proper index of temperature.

In this chapter we shall be mainly concerned with Intelligence A, and its relation to IQ; this is not to say that such investigations as those summarized in Sternberg's *Handbook* are not of interest and indeed of considerable value. The practical application of human intelligence (i.e., *biological* intelligence) to everyday life problems is obviously of considerable practical and theoretical interest, and as long as it is realized that we are not dealing here with Intelligence A, but with Intelligence B, such studies are obviously both scientifically and practically valuable, and add to the body of theory which is being built up around the concept of human intelligence.

Sir Francis Galton and Alfred Binet are essentially the originators of the two major streams of research and theory which have led to countless empirical investigations, and an understanding of the differences between them, and the resulting differences in attitude, conception, and investigation, is of fundamental importance. Galton, essentially, was concerned with Intelligence A (Galton, 1892, 1943), Binet, more with Intelligence B (Binet, 1903, 1907). Reeves (1965) has given a good sketch of their divergent approaches.

In the first place, Galton believed in the meaningful postulation of a general concept of "intelligence" which was fundamental to all cognitive processes, and which mediated differences between people in the degree to which these processes could be made to work successfully. Binet, on the other hand, thought of intelligence as a statistical artifact, namely a mere average of a number of independent or semi-independent faculties, such as memory, suggestibility, emotion, verbalization, etc. In other words, Binet really should not have used the term intelligence at all, as he considers the concept an artifact, but, of course, foolish consistency, as Emerson remarked, is the hobgoblin of little minds.

In the second place, for Galton differences in intelligence were almost entirely caused by *genetic* factors, whereas Binet was far more interested in *environmental* factors, which is not unnatural in an educationalist whose primary concern was the improvement of children's achievements.

The third major difference between Galton and Binet lies in the type of *measurement* which they suggested as being appropriate to the concept of intelligence. Galton, in line with this physiological and biological conception of

Intelligence A, advocated such rather primitive types of measures as reaction times, sensory discrimination, etc. Binet, in line with his conception of Intelligence B, suggested problem-solving, following directions, learning, and memorizing as being typical of the application of intelligence to scholastic and other problems shown by children.

It cannot be said that either Galton or Binet won this particular battle; indeed, in view of the fact that we are talking about different conceptions of intelligence, they were really not contradicting each other. There is little doubt now that the data almost force us to adopt the conception of a general factor of intelligence, labeled "*g*" by Spearman (1927), thus supporting Galton. However, it is also now necessary to recognize the existence of a number of group or "primary" factors, such as visuo-spatial ability, verbal ability, numerical ability, memory etc., closely resembling some of those put forward by Binet (Eysenck, 1979). Similarly, with respect to the genetics of IQ, the evidence strongly supports Galton in postulating that heredity plays a very important part, but the evidence is equally clear that environmental factors too have a powerful effect on individual differences in IQ (Eysenck, 1979). As far as the measurement of intelligence is concerned, it has been shown, and will be argued in detail in this chapter, that IQ and Galton-type measures of intelligence are indeed quite closely related, as indeed would be expected from the type of relationship suggested in our Figure 1. Thus, in a very real sense, both were right in what they asserted, and wrong in what they denied.

There does remain one interesting difference, however, which is of considerable importance. Galton and his successors insisted on an *experimental* approach to the problem of intelligence, i.e., the formulation of an explicit theory, and its testing by the use of specific types of tasks. Binet and his followers, on the other hand, essentially adopted the *psychometric* approach, i.e., relying on correlational studies to suggest theories, and to produce some kind of taxonomic order in what at first sight appeared to be chaos. This distinction is less absolute than it might appear at first, and some investigators appear on both sides of the fence. Spearman and Burt, as we shall see, started out on the experimental side, and then switched to psychometric studies. Nevertheless, the distinction is an important one, and, as it is very relevant to a consideration of speed as a fundamental variable in intelligence, it may be worth documenting, particulary as theories of mental speed were among those postulated by Galton and some of his early followers.

THE EARLY DEVELOPMENT OF RT-IQ RESEARCH

It has already been mentioned that Galton suggested the use of reaction time measures, sensory discrimination, and similar elementary investigations as useful measures of intelligence. Spearman (1904) has reviewed a number of early studies along these lines, and has contributed his own investigation of sensory discriminations in the fields of sound, light, and weight, using ratings as his criterion of intelligence. When properly corrected for attenuation, these correlations approach unity, thus suggesting the correctness of Galton's hypothesis. Work on the Seashore (1913) test of pitch discrimination has given significant correlations with IQ ranging from .14 to .58, and averaging around .35. More recent work by Stankov and Horn (1980), Buktenica (1971), Westphal, Lentenegger, & Wagner (1969), and others suggests that Spearman's hypothesis might have been along the right lines. Most important here is the recent work of Raz, Willerman, and Yama (1987), which is methodogically the most sophisticated, rules out alternative explanations and gives very positive results supporting the Galton-Spearman hypothesis.

Burt (1909) similarly used sensory tests such as touch discrimination, weight discrimination, sound discrimination, and comparison of lines, and motor tests such as tapping, card dealing, card sorting, and alphabet sorting; also used were association tests of immediate memory, a mirror drawing test, and an early version of the now popular "inspection time" (IT) type of measure, called by Burt "spot pattern." It is interesting to note that the "spot pattern" test has a correlation with intelligence of .83 (corrected for attenuation), but that the sensory tests appear relatively valueless. It is curious that neither Spearman nor Burt followed up these promising results, and that both turned to psychometric investigations, abandoning the experimental field entirely. In fairness to Binet, it should be added that he, too, in his earliest attempts at measuring intelligence, used tests of sensory discrimination, reaction times, and other factors in which rate of response was an important element (Peterson, 1925). He, too, just like Spearman and Burt, abandoned this type of elementary measure of individual capacity to switch over to the type of complex cognitive test which has become associated with his name.

Many other psychologists in those early days took seriously the "mental speed" hypothesis, and a good review of this early work is available in MacFarland (1928). Among these early studies were those of Gilbert (1894), Bagley (1901), Wissler (1901), Aikins, Thorndike, and Hubbell (1902), Brown (1910), Wyatt, (1913), McCall (1916), Anderson (1917), Gates (1924), Freeman (1923), Garrett (1922), Chapman (1924), Bernstein (1924), Highsmith (1925), Peak and Boring (1926), Sisk (1926), and Travis (1925).

There is little agreement in the results of these various studies, and Hunsicker (1925) is correct in drawing attention to the lack of methodological sophistication apparent in many of the reports. Nevertheless, McFarland (1928) concludes that: "In the six more recent studies of the past four years where investigations have been conducted under carefully controlled conditions, the evidence, although contradictory, decidedly tends to favour the existence of a positive relationship between rate and ability in mental tests" (p. 610). Of particular interest is a finding by Travis (1925) of a very high correlation between mental ability and rate of conduction of the nerve impulse in a reflex arc. It is worthwhile quoting the final statement by McFarland in full. "It should be clearly noted that the more refined and objective the investigation, the more convinced the experimenter becomes in each case . . . of a vital relationship between rate and mental abilities as tested by the intelligence test. . . . It is evident . . . that further research confined to laboratory techniques is necessary in order to clear the issue and to establish negative or positive significance of this important psychological problem" (p. 610.)

Unfortunately, interest in the experimental study of intelligence began to wane, and this recommendation was not followed. There was, indeed, a brief interest in the problem of speed as opposed to power in mental testing, exemplified by the early work of May (1921) and Ruch and Koerth (1923). These and many subsequent investigators correlated scores of groups of subjects on IQ tests when strict time limits were imposed, with scores obtained when these time limits were expanded, or unlimited time was allowed. The findings in general were that very high correlations were obtained between timed and untimed test scores, suggesting that speed was of the essence. These studies, too, can be subject to criticism (McFarland, 1928), but they did lead to the fundamental investigation of the problem by Thorndike, Bregman, Cobb, and Woodyard (1927), which may be said to constitute an important theoretical advance (Berger, 1976).

Thorndike suggested that ability should be analyzed into level, range, and speed. While acknowledging that IQ tests combining speed, level, and range in unknown amounts might be practically useful, "for rigorous measurements . . . it seems desirable to treat these three factors separately, and to know the exact amount of weight given to each when we combine them" (Thorndike et al., 1927, p. 75). He never really followed up these distinctions experimentally, but his incisive discussion of the problems involved in IQ measurement, combined with Spearman's (1927) criticism of the "hotch-potch" procedure employed in scoring intelligence tests, suggested to the writer the need for more careful dissection of intelligence test scores (Eysenck, 1967, 1973). The theoretical analysis he offered of the IQ was the result of over 10 years of empirical and theoretical work, carried out first in conjunction with Furneaux (1952, 1961) and later on with White (1973, 1982). Important contributions to the model were also made by Iseler (1970). The genesis of the model is explained in detail in Eysenck (1982).

A MODEL FOR MENTAL
SPEED–INTELLIGENCE REACTIONS

In essence, the model asserts that there are three major components to the concept of the IQ, all relatively independent of each other. The first of these, and probably the most fundamental, is *mental speed,* the speed with which cognitive functions are accomplished, and a conception possibly identical in nature with the speed of information processing. The second variable is *persistence,* i.e., the degree to which the search process assumed to be fundamental to problem solving is continued over time; this may be a personality variable interacting with mental speed. The third variable postulated is some process of *error checking* or error recognition, i.e., a tendency to eliminate errors from the final solution offered in the test. The studies quoted present some empirical evidence for the validity of this separation, but it should be noted that the independence of the factors depends very much on parameter values such as the difficulty level of the items; the instructions given to subjects, e.g., with reference to guessing; the mode of presentation, i.e., increasing difficulty level or randomized difficulty level; the time limits imposed (or not imposed, as the case might be); and so forth (Berger, 1976; Brierley, 1961.)

The major point to be noted about this model is the primacy given to *mental speed* as the most fundamental variable in accounting for individual differences in intelligence (Eysenck, 1967). This is a revival of the early work summarized by McFarland, and the theorizing of Galton and his successors, but it also presents many new features, both theoretical and experimental. Apart from the division of IQ into three major aspects, of which only one (mental speed) could be regarded as fundamentally cognitive in nature, both persistence and error checking being more closely related to personality, there are three major points which emerge from the research. In the first place, it gives rise to a "structure of intellect" model (Eysenck, 1953), which specifies a variety of mental processes, such as reasoning, memory, perception etc.; a variety of test materials, such as verbal, numerical, and spatial; and, finally, a quality dimension going from speed to power. Figure 2 illustrates this model, which of course bears some relation to the later Guilford model (Guilford & Hoepfner, 1971). The "quality" continuum is not intended to suggest a fundamental *qualitative* difference between speed and power; it is merely descriptive of the fact that some tests rely exclusively on the measurement of speed, all subjects being able to solve correctly all the problems in the test, whereas the so-called power tests contain items which some subjects could never solve, however long the time allowed. The inability of some subjects to solve some items in the power test was assumed to be due to differences in speed, as shown below; this was supposed to be the fundamental variable in all cognitive processes.

Furneaux (1961) took up the suggestion contained in some of the early material that the proper unit of analysis should be time spent on each item, and demonstrated a very important relationship between time taken to correctly solve an item and the difficulty level for that item. This observed relationship is shown in Figure 3, taken from Eysenck (1953). It shows the relation between difficulty level of test items and time (A) and log time (B) needed for

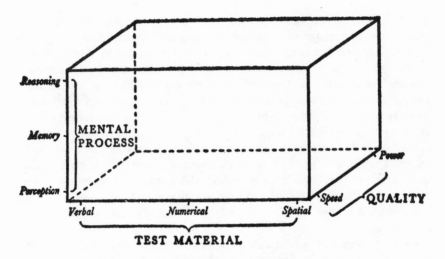

FIGURE 2.   Model of the structure of intellect. (Eysenck, 1953).

solution. Alpha, beta, and gamma are three imaginary subjects of high, medium, and low mental ability, respectively. The solid lines reflect the actual solution times; the stippled lines suggest how long solution times would have been for more difficult items had the individuals in fact succeeded in solving them (i.e., had greater persistence).

It will be seen that all three lines in B (log time) are in fact straight and parallel; this is an important empirical finding which explains why so-called speed and power tests are so highly correlated. If, indeed, all regression lines of log time on difficulty level are straight and parallel, then clearly the intercepts at the 100% solution level, i.e., the level of items having the lowest possible difficulty, would be sufficient to predict solution log times at all other difficulty levels. How long an individual continued to search for a solution would of course be a question of his or her persistence, not itself a cognitive variable. As only correctly solved items are used for the purpose of constructing these diagrams, error checking, while important for total number of successes, is irrelevant here. Later work (e.g., Berger, 1976; Brierley, 1961) has only partially confirmed these results, but, in the absence of any knowledge of the necessary parameter values to properly define the relations, partial success is all that is to be expected until we have a much better understanding of all the factors involved.

If there is any truth in this postulated relationship, then it should follow that choice reaction times, inspection times and similar measures should have high predictive value for much more complex problems and for IQ tests generally; such reaction time tests clearly lie at the 100% solution level of difficulty, i.e., near the intercept, and should therefore be highly predictive of so-

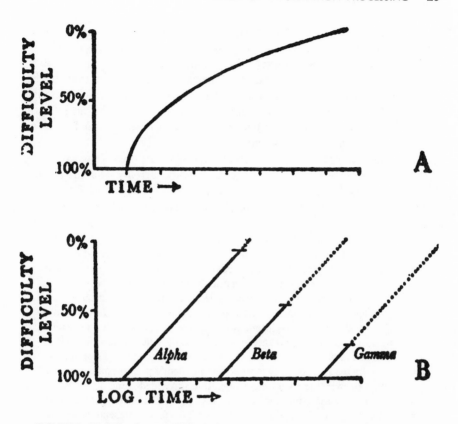

FIGURE 3.   Relation between difficulty level of test items and time (A) and log time (B) needed for correct solution. (Eysenck, 1953).

lution times for items of much higher difficulty level. This, at least, was the argument put forward by Eysenck (1967) for taking seriously work on reaction time such as that of Goldfarb (1941), Roth (1964), and others.

The third major point of the Eysenck-Furneaux model was the use of Hick's law (Hick, 1952) in postulating a search mechanism that would explain the observed relationships. Hick, in his paper, had shown that the relationship between the time taken to react in a multiple-choice situation and the complexity of the choice situation could be expressed in the following form:

$$RT = K \log M,$$

where RT is a choice reaction time, K is an individual constant, and M is a function of the complexity of the choice situation. According to Hick, this is the relationship one would expect to observe if multiple-choice activity involved successive binary classifications. As the brain seems to consist of a vast number of nearly identical units, he argued that it might be possible to posit that all its activities involved sequences of elementary operations of like kind and duration. Such a device might well function by carrying out successive binary switchings, with each "switch" taking the same time and involving the same sort of simple basic activity. Furneaux (1961) argued that this hypothesis of Hick's seemed to imply that multiple-choice reaction-time is a measure of the time required for a search to be completed in the brain for the set of "connections" which would initiate a required behavior. He further argued that problem-solving behavior should perhaps be regarded as a special case of a multiple-choice reaction, and that it would be possible to postulate, within problem-solving processes, the repeated occurrence of some elementary activity which requires a substantially constant time for completion.

The theory is best stated in Furneaux's own words (Furneaux, 1961, pp. 185–186).

The brain structure of any individual, P, includes a set of p^N neural elements which participate in problem-solving activities. It is not necessary at this stage to adopt any particular view as to the nature of these elements, which might be either single neurones or much more complex structures. The solution of a particular problem, h, of difficulty, D, involves bringing into association a particular set, $_DN_h$, of these elements, interconnected in some precise order. (The terms 'bringing into association' and 'inter-connected' should not necessarily be interpreted literally after the manner of, say, an electrical circuit. For example, the almost simultaneous firing of two otherwise independent units could constitute one method of bringing them into association, provided some device existed which could detect the simultaneity, while the exact order of firing might represent the mode of interconnection.) When problem h is first presented single elements are first selected, at random, from the total pool p^N and examined to see whether any one of them, alone, constitutes the required solution. A device must be postulated which carries out this examination—it must bring together the neural representations of the perceptual material embodying the problem, the rules according to which the problem has to be solved, and the particular organization of elements whose validity as a solution has to be examined. It must give rise to some sort of signal, which in the case of an acceptable organization will terminate the search process and will initiate the translation of the accepted neural organization into the activity which specifies the solution in behaviour terms. Alternatively, if the organization under examination proves to be unacceptable, a signal must result which will lead to the continuation of the search process. It will be useful to refer to this hypothetical device under the name of 'the comparator'.

If D $\neq$ 1, the comparator will reject each of the p^N trial solutions involving only a single element, which, when correctly interconnected, might constitute a valid solution. Suppose D $\neq$ 2, then all possible organizations of the p^N elements taken two at a time will also be examined and rejected, after which we can imagine that the search will continue among sets of three, four, five, etc. If $D = r$, then the comparator will reject in turn all the organizations involving from 1 to $(r-1)$ elements, so that there will be a time $\tau \sum_{r-1} E$ sec within which a solution cannot occur, where:

τ =   the time required for completing a single elementary operation within the search process.

$\tau \sum_{r-1} E$ =   the number of elementary operations involved in the search process up to the level of complexity $(r\text{-}1)$.

Similarly, after a time $\tau \sum_{r-1}^{1} E$ sec all possible organizations embodying r elements will have been examined, so that correct solutions to problems of difficulty r will always arise within the period defined by the two limiting times $\tau \sum_{r-1}^{1} E$ and $\tau \sum_{r}^{1} E$. In terms of such a hypothesis, therefore, $V\tau_r$ is in no sense a function of error of measurement but results mainly from the range of times required to set up all possible modes of neural organization at a particular level of complexity. It is perhaps worth noting, in passing, that within the framework of such a hypothesis, error would be accounted for by positing that during the search process organizations arise at levels of complexity $\tau - \sigma_1, r - \sigma_2 \ldots$, etc., which satisfy most, but not all, of the requirements of a true solution to a problem of difficulty r. If the comparator has characteristics analogous to those of "band-width" in electrical and mechanical discriminators, i.e., if its discriminating powers are such that neural organizations which closely resemble the organization representing a correct solution may be accepted as the required organization, then the possibility of error arises. The frequency of error, thus conceived, will be a function of the band-width of the comparator, and since the number of "nearly-correct" organizations will increase as D is increased, the likelihood of error will increase with D.
This probability is clearly dependent on the exact nature of the search process. Finally, continuance is easily defined in terms of such a "search" hypothesis; it is a measure of the length of time during which, following the initiation of search, the comparator remains "set" for a particular problem.

This theoretical conception links our theory with later AI (artificial intelligence) theories such as those popularized by Newell and Simon (1972) and the book on human problem solving by Winston (1984). Our model anticipated features of the computer which were to be used in AI theories, as, indeed, had Hick in his original model, and recent work on artificial intelligence in general, and the search process in particular (Barr & Feigenbaum, 1981, 1982; Cohen & Feigenbaum, 1982) has thrown much light on the properties of the search process, properties which could with advantage be transferred from computer models to the study of human intelligence.

THE ERLANGEN SCHOOL

It was thus, after 40 years of almost complete neglect (from 1925 to 1965, approximately) that reaction time began to enter again the field of intelligence measurement, and a great deal of important empirical and theoretical work was done by two major schools. One of these, the Erlangen school in Germany, has not received anything like the attention it deserves, probably because its findings were published in German and appeared in journals which, even in Germany, are not frequently and widely read by psychologists, such as the *Grundlagenstudien aus Kybernetik und Geisteswissenscharten,* or the *Kybernetische Pädagogik.* The other, much better known, school is that of Jensen (1982a, b). It is noteworthy that the two schools worked in complete independence of each other, but that they obtained strikingly similar results, and came to strikingly similar theoretical conclusions. We will begin our discussion with the Erlangen school, and then go on to the Jensen school. Thereafter, we shall consider the criticisms made of this work, in the light of our own investigations.

The work of the Erlangen School (Frank, 1960; Lehrl, 1983) takes its empirical grounding from the work of Roth (1964), who used the Hick paradigm to argue that what should correlate with IQ would be the slope of the Hick regression line (*b*). Lehrl (1983) illustrates Roth's findings in Figure 4, which shows the increase in reaction time with larger number of choices (bits), according to the IQ of the subjects, in a simplified diagrammatic fashion. Actually, the correlation of the angle of this regression line for Roth's 58 subjects is only − .39 with the Amthauer (1955) intelligence test; i.e., the less intelligent subjects showed a *greater* increase in reaction time compared with the more intelligent subjects. In this experiment, Roth used reaction time + movement time, rather than separating the two as Jensen and others have since done.

Bieger (1968) repeated the study on 50 university students, and obtained a correlation of − .21, which goes to − .33 on correcting for restriction of range. It thus seems that we have here a replicable phenomenon, although Amelang (1985) has pointed out a number of weaknesses in these studies.

Other studies of the Erlangen School have been reported by Oswald (1971) and Oswald and Roth (1978), using complex types of reaction tests, such as sorting playing cards according to different aspects such as color, number of points, or both together. As Burt (1909) had already found, sorting was highly correlated with intelligence. Oswald and Roth (1978) used the number sequence test, in which numbers are printed in a random manner on a sheet of paper and the subject has to connect them in sequence, i.e., drawing a line from 1 to 2, 2 to 3, 3 to 4, etc. This test has in the past been found to be a good measure of reminiscence (Eysenck & Frith, 1977), so that the possibility of irrelevant factors entering into the measurement cannot be ruled out. Lehrl

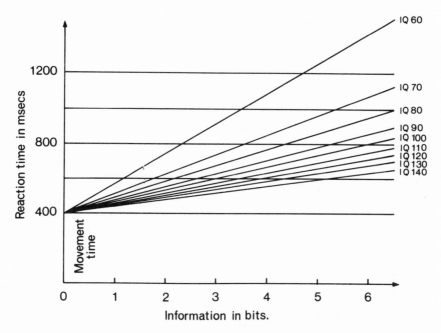

FIGURE 4.   Relationships between information in bits, reaction time in milliseconds, and IQ. Aafter Lehrl (1983).

(1980) has published a special *Kurztest für Allgemeine Intelligenz* (KAI), in which subjects are given series of 20 letters. Subjects are asked to speak the letters aloud in sequence as quickly as possible, and the time taken is the score on the test. Lehrl reports high correlations with intelligence, and Figure 5 is quoted from this study to show the relationship between IQ (ordinate) and the KAI score used by Lehrl on the abscissa.

This score is based on some arguments deriving from information-processing theory. He starts with the stochastic independence of the 20 letters used in the test, which means that the recognition of the single letter requires between 4.7 and 5 binary decisions (bits). Accordingly, the 20 letters contain approximately 100 bits of information, and, from the time taken to read the 20 letters, Lehrl calculates the duration of what he calls the *"Subjektive Zeitquant"* (SZQ), which, according to Frank (1960, 1971), corresponds to the duration of one psychological moment. Dividing these "psychological moments" by the number of seconds gives the values on the abscissa. If it takes a given person 5 seconds to read the 20 letters, that would give an individual SZQ of 1–20 bits divided by seconds, i.e., a duration of 50 milliseconds. For the average adult, the typical SZQ is 1/15 or 1/16 bit/sec, which corresponds to 57 to 63 milliseconds, respectively.

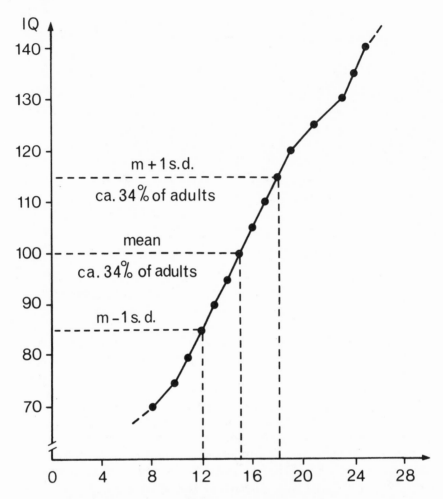

FIGURE 5. Relationship between IQ and Lehrls's Zeitquant. After Lehrl (1983).

On findings such as these, Lehrl (1983) has based the Erlangen model illustrated in Figure 6. Information about changes in the outer world, or in the body, reaches the cortex by the way of the sense organs and the sensory nerves, transmitting in each second between 10^9 and 10^{11} bits. Of these, of course, only a small proportion can be received by the cortex, and this flow of information (C_K) amounts to between 15 to 16 bits per second in the average adult. In other words, there is a maximum of 15 to 16 bits of information that can be consciously received by the cortex, giving information about the outer world or the body, or consisting of memory retrieval data. This capacity also forms the upper limit of the amount of information used in cognitive activities, such as changes of combination of items of information through think-

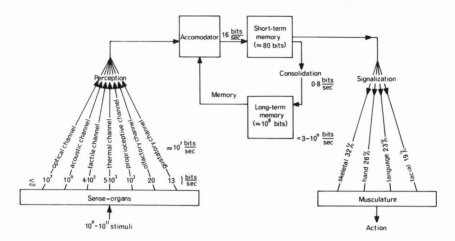

FIGURE 6.   The Frank-Lehrl model of intelligence as a function of the processing of information. After Lehrl (1983).

ing or creative activity, as in problem-solving. Part of this information finds a place in long-term memory, where it can be stored and can be accessed at any time.

In addition to the speed of information-processing, Frank and Lehrl recognized as important the duration of short-term memory (T_R), which corresponds to the time during which information is readily accessible before either being forgotten or being transferred through a consolidation process to long-term memory. On the average, T_R amounts to between 5 and 6 seconds, and information offered during the period of this duration would be available to the person concerned without effort.

According to the Erlangen theory, it is the *product* of T_R and C_K which is identified as a cause of differences in phenotypic intelligence, i.e., IQ scores. As Eysenck (1985) has pointed out, the great advantage of this new way of looking at the problem of individual differences in intelligence is that all the values entering into the equation can be measured directly in terms of objective and absolute units (bits and seconds), rather than, as in the case of IQ measurements, in terms of relative values and percentiles. Lehrl's theory of intelligence is clearly based on two elements, rather than on one single element. C_K, representing the speed of processing of information, is operationalized through the speed of reading 20 letters. T_R, representing the duration of short-term memory, is operationalized by through the number of letters or digits that can be correctly reproduced after intervals of 1 second.

What can be said in criticism of the theory? In the first place, the number of subjects used in these studies is not large enough to give one confidence that the correlations observed give an accurate value for the total population, apart from the fact that populations are not always clearly identified. In the second place, the methods used are not described in sufficient detail to make replication easy, or even possible. In the third place, factors of learning and experience are disregarded. Taking the measurement of T_R, it is known that unpracticed subjects are able to reproduce between 7 and 10 digits, respectively. Paul Baltes and his colleagues at the Max Planck Institute in Berlin have shown that, by using appropriate techniques of mnemonics, any adult of average intelligence can be taught to reproduce something like 90 letters or digits (Baltes & Kliegl, 1985.) Similarly, it is likely that the speed of reading 20 letters can be improved greatly by practice.

It is important to draw attention to the possibility of learning and environmental variables generally, because Lehrl (1983) has brought his information-processing theory of intelligence in direct contact with the rather novel genetic theory of intelligence recently advanced by Volkmar Weiss (1982; Weiss & Mehlhorn, 1982). According to this hypothesis, differences in intelligence are mediated by a single pair of alleles; one of these (M_1) is connected with a high level of intelligence, and has a frequency in the population of 20%, whereas the other (M_2) is connected with low levels of intelligence, and has a population frequency of 80%. Assuming assortative mating amounting to $r = .50$, the probability of an individual inheriting both the alleles favoring high intelligence would be 5%, i.e., producing a pure genotype of M_1M_1. The opposite pure genotype giving rise to low IQ (M_2M_2) would occur with a frequency of 68%. The remainder of the population, i.e., 27%, would form a mixed type (M_1M_2). Weiss argues that the M_1M_1 type processes twice as much information as the pure genotype M_2M_2, with the mixed type lying exactly between these two values.

The mean IQ of people with the genotype M_1M_1 would be around 130, whereas the other pure genotype, M_2M_2, would have a mean IQ of 94, with a mixed type of M_1M_2 averaging an IQ of 112. Weiss has pointed out that, because of the relative nature of the IQ measurement of intelligence, his hypothesis could only be tested by means of measures of information processing. This has been done (Lehrl & Frank, 1982), and their findings seemed to verify the Weiss hypothesis. According to their findings, the M_2M_2 type shows a short-term memory store amounting to 70 bits, the M_1M_2 type one of 105 bits, and the M_1M_1 type one of 140 bits. The simple relationships obtaining between these values (1:1.5:2) suggest, according to Lehrl, that the behavioral, genetic, and information-processing approaches to intelligence are on the point of discovering some very simple laws of nature.

Lehrl (1982) also attempts to demonstrate quantitative equivalence of SZQ and some measures derived from evoked potential determinations taken from Ertl (1971). He claims remarkable congruence between the SZQ values and the event-related potential, but it should be remembered that there is no rationale to allow us to identify intelligence with the measure of evoked potential taken from Ertl in what appears a rather arbitrary manner. In addition, the measures taken by Ertl showed only a low correlation between IQ and AEP, and there are many different choices that could be made within his measurement system, other than those used by Ertl and Lehrl. Lehrl does not give any particular reasons for his choice, and goes on to say that "attempts to explain the observed phenomena belong within the competence of neurophysiologists" (p. 182). Without some such explanatory hypothesis, it is difficult to accept the equivalence of Lehrl's SZQ and the evoked potential measures singled out by him. Lehrl (1983) also quotes Oswald and Seus (1975) as demonstrating correlations between IQ and averaged evoked potential, but this also does not seem to justify the particular choice or identity made by him.

THE JENSEN MODEL

Jensen bases his rationale of the importance of a time element in mental efficiency on a few well-established concepts and principles of cognitive psychology. The first of these is that the conscious brain acts as a one-channel or *limited capacity* information processing system. It can deal simultaneously with only very limited amounts of information, as also postulated by the Erlangen School. This limited capacity also restricts the number of operations that can be performed simultaneously on the information that enters the system, from external stimuli or from retrieval of information stored in short-term or long-term memory. As Jensen points out, speediness of mental operations is advantageous in that more operations per unit of time can be executed without overloading the system.

Secondly, there is *rapid decay* of stimulus traces of information, so that there is an advantage to speediness of any operations that must be performed on the information while it is still available. Thirdly, to compensate for limited capacity and rapid decay of incoming information, the individual may resort to *rehearsal and storage* of the information into intermediate or long-term memory (LTM), which has relatively unlimited capacity. However, the process of storing information in LTM also takes time, and therefore uses up channel capacity, so there is a trade-off between the storage and the processing of incoming information. The more complex the information and the operations required on it, the more time will be required, and consequently the greater the advantage of speediness in all the elemental processes involved. Loss of information due to overload, interference, and decay of traces that were inadequately encoded or rehearsed for storage or retrieval from LTM results in breakdown and failure to grasp all the essential relationships among the elements of a complex problem needed for its solution. The speed of information processing should, accordingly, be increasingly related to success in dealing with cognitive tasks to the extent that their information loads strain the individual's limited channel capacity. These hypotheses could easily be accommodated within the requirements of the Erlangen model.

The measurement of reaction time has not always been uniform, but, in recent years, it has become fairly standardized around the procedure used by Jensen (1982a, b). The subject sits in front of a panel in the center of which is a button which he or she is required to press down with his or her index finger. Around the perimeter are eight lights, arranged in the form of a semicircle; in front of each light is another button. When one of the lights lights up, the subject is required to remove his or her index finger from the button he or she is pushing down, and press down the button in front of the light that has gone on. Two times are recorded; one is the reaction time (RT), which is measured from the moment the light goes on to the moment the subject removes his finger from the button. The movement time (MT) is the time span from the moment the subject removes his or her finger from the original button, to the moment he or she depresses the button in front of the light that has gone on.

It is possible on this apparatus to measure simple and various types of choice reaction time. When simple reaction time is measured, a cover is placed over seven of the lights, so that only one is visible. When there is a choice between two lights, all the others are obscured by a cover. Similarly, when there is a choice between four lights, the remaining four are covered. It is only for the choice between eight lights that all the lights are uncovered.

Jensen (1982a, b) gives a thorough discussion of the literature to that date, including his own contributions, and formulates a number of conclusions. The most important of these are the following: (a) Simple reaction time shows some slight correlation with intelligence, usually around -0.2 to -0.3. (b) Simple movement time shows negligible correlation with intelligence. (c) Choice reaction time shows more substantial correlations with IQ than does simple reaction time. (d) Choice movement time shows significant correlations with IQ. (e) As the number of choices in the array (bits) increases, the correlation of RT with IQ increases. (f) The angle of the Hick slope (b) is negatively correlated with IQ. (g) The variability of RT measurements is negatively correlated with IQ, and this correlation is higher than that of any of the other RT or MT variables considered so far. This is an important finding, although of course there must be a statistical relationship between RT and variability; if variability is great, there clearly must be many long RTs, which would preclude a short mean or median RT. Nevertheless, if variability correlates more highly than RT with IQ, then this cannot be a simple artifact of the statistical relationship between them. (h) Reaction times involving STM, as in the Sternberg short-term memory paradigm (Sternberg, 1966), which measures the subject's speed of scanning his short-term memory for information, correlates significantly negatively with IQ. In this test, the subject is shown a series of between two to seven digits or letters (termed the "positive set") for several seconds. Then, a single "probe" digit is presented. In a random half of the trials, the probe digit is a member of the positive set, and the subject is required to respond as quickly as possible to the probe digit by pressing either a "yes" or a "no" button to indicate whether the probe was or was not a member of the positive set. (i) Long-term memory RT, as in the Posner LTM paradigm (Posner, 1969; Posner, Boies, Eichelman, & Taylor, 1969) correlates significantly negatively with IQ. This is a measure of the time it takes the subject to access a highly overlearned item of information stored in his or her LTM. This procedure is based on the comparison of the subject's discriminative RTs to pairs of stimuli which are the same or different, either physically or semantically (Hunt, 1976). Similar results have been found with children (Keating & Bobbitt 1978). (j) Inspection time (Nettelbeck & Lally, 1976) is negatively and significantly correlated with IQ. In this test, the time is measured which is required for a visual stimulus to be encoded in sufficient detail to permit discriminative judgment easy enough with sufficient time available to allow of no errors. By means of a tachistoscope, the subject is presented with a brief exposure of two vertical lines of markedly different length, followed by a backward masking stimulus. The subject is then required to report whether the long line appeared on the right or the left, the position varying randomly from trial to trial. Inspection time (IT) is the duration of stimulus exposure at which the subject's judgment is correct on at least 19 out of 20 trials. Positive results on this test, which can also be given in an auditory form, have been reported by Brand and Deary (1982). (k) Most recently, there has been added Eysenck's "odd-man-out" paradigm, in which the subject reacts to the one of 3 simultaneously illuminated lights on the Jensen apparatus which is farthest removed from the other two (Frearson & Eysenck, 1986). This paradigm gives correlations in excess of $-.60$ with IQ for random samples of the population, and shrunken Rs of a similar size even for range-restricted university student populations (Jensen, personal communication, 1986).

Jensen (1982a) has used the search model proposed by Hick, which also forms a fundamental part of the Eysenck-Furneaux model, as a possible mechanism that could account for the main features of the RT data, as well as for individual differences in these features. Figure 7 shows the dichotomizing or binary resolution of uncertainty, as measured in bits. The n choice alternatives in the physical stimulus array can be thought of as being isomorphically represented in the neural network of the cerebral cortex. The dots in Figure 7 represent focal points or nodes of excitation which will fire when a critical level of stimulation is reached. The number of aroused or prime nodes of the RT task corresponds with the number of alternatives in the array of reaction stimuli.

Jensen hypothesizes that the level of excitation at each node *oscillates,* so that half of the time the node is refractory. Above-threshhold stimulation of

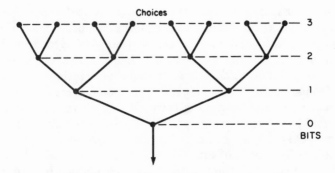

Choices

FIGURE 7. Hierarchical binary tree as used in Jensen's oscillation theory. (Jensen, 1982a).

a node at any given level of bits is transmitted downwards through the chain of nodes to the final common path for response. For example, a stimulus which contains only one element of eight possible alternatives will excite one of the eight nodes in the top row of the figure to discharge, and the discharge will be transmitted to the final common path by the three intervening nodes, at the levels of 2, 1, and 0 bits. When the stimulus is one of four alternatives, the excitation would be transmitted through only two intervening nodes, etc.

The amount of time taken to respond to the stimulus over and above the irreducible minimum RT, which is attributable to peripheral sensory and motor-mechanisms, will depend essentially on two factors: (a) the number of levels in the chain through which the excitation must be conducted, and (b) the average period of oscillation of the transmitting nodes. Excitation, of course, is not transmitted by a refractory node. Volleys of stimulation must persist until the node is excitable. The refractory phase of the oscillation at the node is the chief source of time delays in the system, and individual differences in the rate of oscillation would cause individual differences in RT (but presumably not in MT). Oscillation would also cause variability in RT from trial to trial, because the onset of the stimulus is random with respect to the refractory and excited phases of the oscillation, and Jensen assumes that the phase of oscillation of a node at any point in the chain is random with respect to the phase of any other mode. Stimulation of a node at one level thus may or may not be delayed by the phase of oscillation of every other node in the chain. The theory is described in much greater detail in Jensen (1982a), to which the reader is referred.

There are certain obvious physiological difficulties with this theory. Refractoriness in the CNS is normally regarded as the function of previous excitation, which produces the refractory phase. However, time intervals between one stimulus and another are so long that there is no question of previous neural currents causing refractoriness to subsequent ones. One would have to hypothesize a rather unphysiological picture of refractory phases occurring on a random basis, without reference to previous stimulation. This does not seem reasonable. In addition, there is no direct evidence for the model suggested by Jensen, and it would hardly account for such correlations between movement time and intelligence as have been observed. These objections do not rule out the possibility that the model may have explanatory value, but they do cause difficulties in regarding the model as being physiological in a meaningful sense.

CRITICISM OF THE JENSEN MODEL

Jensen's work has been criticized in detail by Longstreth (1984) and Carroll (1986), and many of the criticisms also apply to Jensen's predecessors, whose work he has summarized. The first three criticisms made by Longstreth relate to apparatus and procedures, and concern order effects, visual attention effects, and response bias effects. Order effects arise because set size is confounded with order of trials; in other words, single RTs precede 2-choice RTs which in turn are followed by 4-choice RTs and 8-choice RTs. If there are practice effects, then clearly this would reduce the expected reaction time on later trials, which would be confounded with set size. Jensen has repeatedly stated that there is no evidence of learning in his work, but studies such as those of Williams, Pottinger, and Shapcott (1985), as well as our own (Barrett, Eysenck and Lucking, 1986) do show that learning takes place, both for RT and MT. Longstreth (1984) also reports an experiment to demonstrate practice effects.

Visual attention effects relate to displacements made possible by the spatial layout of Jensen's apparatus, which would qualify as a possibly source of RT variation. Longstreth maintains that magnitude of retinal displacement is correlated with set size using Jensen's apparatus, and indeed it is not easy to find a way to modify the Jensen task to get around this problem. It may be that the stimulus lights are bright enough to produce no retinal displacement effect, but there is no direct evidence for such a suggestion, and there is much evidence for the retinal displacement effect.

The third criticism, that relating to response bias, is based on the fact that the response to each stimulus is not only different, but that some of the responses may require more time for programming or preparation than others; e.g., a left-moving response may take longer than a right-moving response. Longstreth reports an experiment which suggests that response bias may be a real problem with Jensen's apparatus. These three objections are no doubt well taken from the point of view of the experimentalist, but it is doubtful whether they by themselves would suffice to throw any doubt on the relationship between IQ and reaction time as such. They do throw some doubt on the precise data on slope correlations and increasing correlations with IQ when the number of items in the stimulus array is increased, and to these points we must turn next.

Longstreth and Carroll both argue, on the basis of a detailed examination of Jensen's own data, that the reported gradients of RT across set size obtained from diverse groups differing widely in mean IQ as well as on a wide variety of other factors "contradict the asserted negative correlations as much as they support it" (Longstreth, 1984, p. 153). Also queried is the RT-IQ-complexity relationship, a point also raised by Nettelbeck and Kirby (1983). They show that, when normal subjects only are considered, i.e., when the retarded groups used by them and omitted, correlations between choice RT and IQ show no hint of larger correlations with larger set size. Concerning Jensen's own data, Longstreth concludes that "when groups are examined separately, there is simply no supporting evidence for the claim" (p. 154).

Longstreth and Carroll make many other objections to Jensen's work, such as the sampling used. Altogether, sampling has been a weak point in the work done by most of the experimenters working in this field. Many have used range restricted samples, such as university students, or else they have used samples unduly extended in range, i.e., including retardates. Apart from the possibility that retardates may present qualitative differences from nonretarded subjects, their inclusion requires correction for range effects just as much as does the concentration on university students alone. Such corrections should always be included, whether they increase the observed correlations (as with the student samples), or whether they decrease it (as in samples with retardates included). Quite generally, one would advocate the use of normal samples having a mean and standard deviation similar to the standardization sample of the IQ test used. Jensen (1982a, b) prefers the use of contrasting groups, e.g., students versus nonstudents, or bright, average, and dull children, but this paradigm, while it gives us information on the significance of the differences observed, does not enable us to form an opinion on the degree of relationship observed.

It should be noted that Jensen has put forward a very convincing reply to the criticisms made, particularly by Longstreth (Jensen & Vernon, 1986). This reply contains numerous analyses of data collected over the years, and makes good many deficits of previous reporting.

Similar problems have arisen in relation to inspection time and its relation to intelligence (Irwin, 1984). While earlier workers have claimed very high correlations (e.g., the Adelaide group represented by Lally & Nettelbeck, 1977, and Nettelbeck & Lally, 1976, and the Edinburgh group, represented by Brand & Deary, 1982), Irwin (1984), using 50 children of normal IQ range, only found low and sometimes insignificant correlations with verbal and nonverbal intelligence. He criticizes the smallness of the groups tested by the Edinburgh experimenters, the inclusion of retardates in the Adelaide samples, and the risky practice of estimating inspection time by extrapolation. It is clearly important to study the task-relevant parameters in order to discover which are the best to choose for obtaining optimum correlations between IT and IQ.

A recent symposium of the International Society for the Study of Individual Differences considered the situation as far as the relation between IT and IQ is concerned, and many new data were reported which strengthened considerably the claims of IT to be considered a serious contender for objective IQ measurement (Brebner & Nettelbeck, 1986). These data are too numerous to be discussed here, but they leave little doubt that a substantial correlation exists between the two variables (see Chapter 9, this volume.)

RECENT INVESTIGATIONS OF THE RT-IQ RELATION

We will now turn to the task of looking at the most recent and best planned investigations to see to what extent they bear out Jensen's hypotheses and to what extent they contradict his findings. This will also give us the opportunity of estimating the actual size of correlations between RT and IQ to be observed when adequate methodology is being used on reasonable samples. The literature prior to these studies has been adequately surveyed by Jensen (1982a, b) and Eysenck (1986), and we will not refer to it except when occasion demands.

As a beginning, consider the study by Jensen and Munro (1979), which may be used to compare the replicability of data in this field, and as a kind of base line with which to compare other investigations. Using a sample of 39 schoolgirls, all of similar age, who had been given the Raven's Standard Progressive Matrices, Jensen and Munro found correlations of −.39 with total RT and −.31 with variance. The correlation between Raven and the regression of RT on *bits* was −.30, very similar to the correlations found by Bieger and Roth. Uncorrected correlations between Raven and RT were −.26 for 0 bits, −.33 for 1 bit, −.41 for 2 bits, and −.35 for 3 bits. There is no evidence for claimed increases with bits of information for choice reaction times — the difference between 1 bit (−.33) and 3 bits (−.35) is obviously completely insignificant.

For MT, the correlations are even higher, going up from −.38 to −.43, −.36, and −.36 as we go up to 1, 2, and 3 bits of information. (When correction is made for attenuation, these figures all reach the middle 40s, and one even goes up into the middle 50s).

Clearly, simple reaction time and movement time is about as good a measure of intelligence as is the regression of RT on bits, which means that neither is "good" or accounted for more than 10% of the variance. Correlations do not increase as we go from 1 to 2 to 3 bits of information, but the correlation with IQ of both RT and MT now becomes reasonable, going up into the 40s. Taking RT and MT together, the shrunken multiple $R = .45$, which is not very different from the median correlation between the Raven and the WISC (Sattler, 1974, p. 155). In other words, the Raven correlates much the same with the RT and the MT measures in their study as with other standard tests of intelligence reported in the literature. The major stress in this is on choice RT, regardless of number of bits involved, rather than on Hick's regression.

Smith and Stanley (1983) reported on a well-chosen sample of 137 12-year-old children with IQs ranging from 59 to 142. They use several measures of intelligence which give rise to a g factor as well as a spatial and a verbal factor. Correlations with g were higher than those with S or V, with the 8-choice RT and SD giving higher correlation than the 4-choice or the 2-choice paradigms. The correlations were $-.33$ and $-.41$, and that with the slope was $-.28$. Inspection time did not show any significant kind of correlation. Combining the 8-choice reaction time and standard deviation data gives a multiple R of .44 with g.

Smith and Stanley report some interesting data on the test-retest correlation over 1 year for the RT measures on 52 subjects from this sample. For SD8, RT8, and b, the slope constant, the values were .48, .52, and .35, respectively. Correcting for attenuation between g and SDRT and RTRI raises the values to about $-.60$. As the authors remark, "the results . . . add to the picture that is emerging of common variance between measured intelligence and RT measure tasks requiring low cognitive involvement . . . . While the measure b with its identifiable theoretical basis as an intelligence measure, does correlate moderately, once again, simple measures of RT from the higher choice task show more promise, in this study, and are some of the better measures in Jensen and Munro (1979)" (Smith & Stanley, 1983, p. 366).

Nettelbeck and Kirby (1983) reported new data from a sample of 182 adults, and a reanalysis of data involving 48 adults from previously published studies. They found by multiple regression analysis that measures of timed performance accounted for as much as 25% of IQ variance in the normal population, but that the inclusion of borderline and mildly retarded subjects resulted in much higher correlation coefficients because of the markedly less efficient performance of these persons in tasks of this kind. "This outcome raised questions about the validity of combining data from retarded and nonretarded subjects" (p. 39). The multiple R for IQ and the eight timed performance variables used in this study was .83 for a normally distributed sample, including subjects with IQs below 85 and above 117, which was reduced to .57 by excluding the former.

With respect to inspection time, Nettelbeck and Kirby come to an opposite conclusion to that of Smith and Stanley (1983). They maintain that "the inspection time measure, which is designed to reduce criterial influence is perhaps the most promising since it has consistently indicated a negative association and has achieved statistical significance in the greatest number of instances" (p. 50). Nettelbeck and Kirby also present some evidence that with larger numbers of choices, differential strategies may affect the outcome, e.g., some subjects making a movement after detecting only the presence of a signal, but then delaying movement so as to permit a further decision during movement about which alternative was involved.

In a study by Carlson and Jensen (1982), 20 9th-grade girls were tested, using the Raven test, as well as reading comprehension and performance on the California test of basic skills as measures of intellect. Mathematics and English grades were also correlated with RT and MT. The observed correlations were consistently higher in this study than in the Jensen and Munro one, going from $-.42$ for 1 bit to $-.60$ for 2 bits, and to $-.58$ for 3 bits. These values are for RT; for MT, they are $-.40$, $-.48$, and $-.31$. Corrected for attenuation, the values are, of course, much higher, going up to $-.89$ for RT, and $-.74$ for MT. Slope data, by contrast, are even lower than for Jensen and Munro, being quite insignificant ($-.20$). Correlations with variability, on the other hand, are higher than for Jensen and Munro, both for RT and MT, equalling $-.71$ and $-.64$, respectively.

Correlations with reading comprehension are also quite respectable, ranging up to $-.60$ for RT and up to $-.42$ for MT. It must of course be remembered that the data are taken on 20 subjects only, so that standard errors are quite high.

One of the most thorough studies on the relationship between IQ and RT was published recently by P. A. Vernon (1983). He used 100 university students who were given five measures of speed or efficiency of cognitive processing, and the Wechsler and Raven scales as measures of IQ. The speed measures were, respectively: (a) Inspection time (IT), (b) The Sternberg STM scanning task, (c) The Posner LTM information retrieval tasks, (d) An efficiency of STM storing and processing task, which is essentially a combination of the Sternberg and the Posner tasks, and (e) Simple and choice reaction times. The matrix of correlations between these speed of processing tests was calculated and factor analyzed, giving rise to a strong first principal factor.

Subtests of the Wechsler were intercorrelated with each other and with the Raven scores, and the first factor extracted. To relate IQ with speed of processing, subject's full-scale WAIS IQ scores were regressed on their mean reaction times and intraindividual SDs on the speed of processing tests. Seven predictor variables produced a maximum shrunken R with IQ of .46. Correction for attenuation due to the restricted range of IQ of the sample gave a corrected R of .67, which reflects more accurately the correlation that could be expected to be found in the general population. Inspection time scores did not add significantly to the multiple $R,$ and a zero-order correlation with IQ was only .10; it was the only speed-of-processing variable that correlated positively with IQ. IT correlated negatively or nonsignificantly with all other reaction times, and did not load to any appreciable extent on the first factor extracted from their intercorrelations.

Subjects' intraindividual variability had about the same degree of association with IQ as did their reaction times. The results of the factorial study showed that whatever general intelligence and reaction times have in common cannot be attributed to their shared verbal and numerical content, nor solely or even largely to the facts that parts of the WAIS are timed. Subjects obtained very low error rates on all the reaction time tests, indicating that it is not the test difficulty per se that accounts for the relationship. Vernon concludes:

> Rather, it is the *g* factor common to all the psychometric variables that accounts for the bulk of the relationship between IQ and reaction time. Further, given the degree of this relationship, it appears that a moderately large part of the variance in *g* is attributable to variance in speed and efficiency of execution of a small number of basic cognitive processes. If this is the case, it is contrary to the notion that IQ tests measure little more than the knowledge an individual has acquired, the problem-solving strategies he has developed, and the opportunities he has had to learn these. . . In terms of speed of processing . . . it is proposed that the individual with a larger knowledge base and strategy base has acquired these as a result of his or her basic information-processing capability. Over a period of time — the years of formal education, for example — faster cognitive processing may allow more information to be acquired. (p. 69)

Carlson, Jensen, and Widaman (1983) studied correlations between reaction time, Raven's Matrices scores, reading scores, academic achievement, and an attention test on 105 7th-grade children. Correlations were low throughout, being higher with the variability of RT and MT than with RT and MT themselves. Correlations were higher with the reading scores than with the Raven scores, and the attention test correlated significantly with RT and SD. RT slope correlated effectively zero with all the variables in question. It is not clear why, in this study, correlations are lower than in the others considered so far.

Two recent studies by Paul (1984) and Ananda (1985) used rather novel speed-of-information processing tests. Paul employed the semantic verification test, which is based on grammatical transformations; he also used straightforward RT tests and the Posner paradigm, as well as the advanced Raven Progressive Matrices, on 50 University students. Paul concluded that:

> The results of the different types of multiple regression analyses provide considerable support for the hypothesis that the speed with which individuals can perform different cognitive processes is highly related to their intelligence. Conservatively, one could say that RT can explain approximately 20%, and intraindividual variability accounts for approximately 25% of the variance, in

subjects' general intelligence. One should remember also that the present sample was extremely homogeneous in regards to intelligence and that in the population in general the percentage of explained variance would no doubt be considerably larger. It seems possible to conclude that the speed and efficiency with which individuals can execute basic cognitive operations like those measured in this study will determine to a large extent how well they will perform in tests of mental ability. (p. 70)

Ananda (1985) used 76 subjects, aged 51 to 87, who were given a vocabulary test, a reasoning test, and several speed-of-information processing tasks. Correlation and multiple regression analyses were used to investigate the relationship between psychometric intelligence and speed-of-information processing. Multiple regression analysis of intelligence on various information processing components produced a maximum shrunken R of .68. "It was concluded that speed-of-information processing and psychometric abilities are highly related. Indeed, the present findings lend support to theories that link speed of mental processing to the broader and more complex intellectual abilities measured by conventional psychometric tests" (p. 2).

It is important to ask whether these RT variables relate to the central core of intelligence, as measured, e.g., by the first or general factor extracted from the intercorrelations of Wechsler subtests. Hemmelgarn and Kehle (1984) found, in a group of 59 intellectually superior elementary school children, that the 12 subtests of the WISC-R were correlated negatively with Hick's slope to the degree that the subtests were loaded on the g factor of the WISC-R battery. They correlated individual differences in Hick's slope with scores on each of the 12 WISC-R subtests, partialling out chronological age. The profile of these 12 correlations shows a rank-order correlation of 0.83 with a profile of the 12 subtests' g loadings.

It is also important to note that RT does not correlate more highly with *timed* than with *untimed* IQ tests (Vernon & Kantor, 1986; Vernon, Nador, & Kantor, 1985). This important finding is in agreement with the outcome of the speed-power debate already mentioned, but it is nevertheless interesting to note that the common sense notion of RT speed predicting scores on speed tests better than scores on power tests is not borne out by the results of an actual experiment.

Another paper concerned with the relationship between RT and IQ contains some analyses of data originating in the Air Force Aviation Psychology Programme of World War Two (Guilford, 1947). In the appendix of the volume on paper-and-pencil tests of the aviation psychology programme reports, there is a 65-variable correlation matrix, composed of the classification test battery and 40-odd research tests. From this matrix, R. L. Thorndike (1987, in press) designated six 8-test batteries, composed of the research tests in the order in which they appeared. The remaining 17 tests, all members of the classification test battery, were inserted into each of the six batteries, one test at a time, and the resulting 9-test batteries were factor analyzed, and the g-loadings for each test and each battery calculated. The study demonstrated the stability of g-loadings when a given test is embedded in the context of different batteries, g-loadings across batteries correlating with a median value of 0.82, and demonstrating that there is a good deal of stability of loadings in different batteries.

Our interest here is in test 65, which is a discriminant reaction time test. This test had loadings on the six batteries with which it was factor analyzed of .52, .55, .61, .59, .60, and .61, averaging .58. This was the second highest factor loading of all the 17 tests, being exceeded only marginally by a spatial orientation test which has a mean g-loading of .60. Factor loadings of the choice reaction time test exceeded those for general information, arithmetic reasoning, number operations, and reading comprehension, all of which are known to be good measures of g. This study thus leaves little doubt about the independence of g-loadings of the specific battery used, or the high g-loading of discriminant reaction time.

PROBLEMS AND CONTRADICTIONS

Barrett, Eysenck, and Lucking (1986) used two samples of adult subjects of reasonably average intelligence, containing respectively 40 and 46 subjects, who were administered the WAIS and the Jensen-type RT test. Both groups showed negative correlations between IQ on the one hand, and RT and SDRT, on the other, confirming earlier work. On the other hand, there was no evidence of correlation between the Hick slope and IQ, and the correlation between IQ and RT or SDRT did not increase from 1 to 3 bits of information. In these respects, the study gives results similar to those reported by others. The study is of interest particularly in that it was found that the Hick paradigm did not apply to some 20% of subjects in the samples tested, and that correlations with IQ were significantly increased when they were calculated only on subjects conforming to the Hick Law.

This suggests a possible reason for differences in results obtained by different investigators; it seems, to judge from published material, that the number of subjects not obeying Hick's law may differ from one investigation to another. Jensen has reported that only very few subjects fall into this category, but Amelang (1985) found that Hick's law did not apply to the majority of his subjects. It is not known why some should disobey this law, but it is quite clear from the Barrett, Eysenck, and Lucking study that the reasons are not related to personality (which was measured) or to intelligence. It is clearly an urgent and important task to discover in what way subjects who do or do not obey Hick's law differ, and the reasons why these differences exist.

Jenkinson (1983) investigated the question of whether , as Jensen (1978) proposed, the speed of basic cognitive processes is fundamental to a general factor of intelligence which corresponds to Cattell's (1971; Horn, 1972) factor of fluid intelligence, or whether, as Hunt, Lunneborg, and Lewis (1975) found, speed of information processing is related to verbal ability as measured by tests of knowledge or hidden meanings, syntactic rules, and semantic relations which operationally define crystalized intelligence. Sixty 6th-grade children completed measures of fluid and crystalized ability, and three RT tasks; correlations were found in the expected direction, but these did not favor either fluid or crystalized intelligence, suggesting that the "Anlage" functions (Horn, 1968) represented by speed of cognitive processing underlie fluid and crystalized ability equally (Horn, 1968).

Another problem which has beset investigators in this field has been the problem of mental retardation. P. A. Vernon (1981) obtained scores on Raven's progressive matrices and the Figure Copying Test, as well as simple and choice reaction time scores from 46 mentally retarded adults. Correlations with the Raven test showed no increase with larger stimulus arrays; quite on the contrary. Going from 0 to 3 bits of information, correlations were $-.25$, $-.27$, $-.31$, and $-.06$. Slope of RT showed highest correlations with Raven of $-.35$. This study also compared results from this mildly retarded sample with normal, superior, and severely retarded subjects, and found the expected differences.

A more analytic study has been reported by Todman and Gibb (1985). They used a version of Sternberg's memory scanning task on 32 subjects, aged around 14 years, divided into IQ groups described as high, average, low, and mentally retarded. Interest was both in the slope of the regression line representing rate of scanning of the memory set, and the intercept of the regression line, taken to represent the duration of encoding of the probe item together with time taken to select and execute a response. Seymour and Moir (1980) had used these two measures on 36 children assigned to six groups of six subjects on the basis of their intelligence test scores. Correlating individual mean reaction times with intelligence test scores, they found a correlation of $-.47$ with positive RT and $-.53$ for negative RT. As they point out: "The findings are consistent with Eysenck's contention that individuals of varying intelligence will differ in the time they take to perform simple tasks which involve an element of choice" (p. 57). Intercept, too, was correlated with intelligence with values just below $-.40$. The slope parameter, however, was not found to be significantly related to intelligence. Seymour and Moir found that a few subjects in their sample produced *negative* values for the slope parameter, and also gave extremely high intercept values, suggesting the existence of a general tendency to trade a high intercept for a shallow slope, or vice versa. (There was a high negative correlation between these two values.) This very much complicates the interpretation of the data.

The argument of the Todman and Gibb study is in part based on the Seymour and Moir study, and also on others (Horning, Morim, & Konick, 1979; Harris & Fleer, 1974; Silverman, 1974; Maisto & Baumeister, 1975) which showed that, when IQ is held constant while chronological age and mental age are covaried, the general finding has been a developmental trend towards smaller intercept values, with no comparable effect of mental maturity on slope values. In the Harris and Fleer (1974) study, however, comparing retarded groups with normal children matched on either chronological or mental age, an effect of IQ on the slope as well as on the intercept parameter was found. Similar findings have been reported by Dugas and Kellas (1974) and Maisto and Jerome (1977).

As Todman and Gibb say:

> Taken together these results suggest a general developmental trend towards increased speed in one or more of the processes contributing to intercept values and, among retarded individuals, a speed decrement in the comparison (memory search) stage, which is otherwise unrelated to mental maturity over a broad age range. It appears, then, that speed of processing in the most distinctly "central" component of the Sternberg task, as indexed by the slope parameter, does not predict psychometric intelligence over the non-retarded IQ range. On the other hand, both the intercept parameter in the Sternberg task and the inspection time measure, each of which has been interpreted as reflecting relatively "peripheral" operations (i.e., perceptual encoding and, in the case of the intercept parameter, response initiation), appeared to be moderate to good predictors of intelligence over the IQ range for which the tasks seemed usable. (p. 50)

In the Todman and Gibb study, the slope parameter did not differ between the three non-retarded groups. Contrary to expectation, slope values for the retarded group also did not differ significantly from those of the non-retarded groups. The correlation between intercepts and IQ over all subjects was highly significant ($r = -.77$), with a correlation only slightly lower ($r = -.62$) for the three nonretarded groups. Slope and intercept scores were negatively correlated, but, as Valentine, Wilding, and Mohindra (1984) have shown, substantial negative correlations between slopes and intercepts are predictable on purely statistical grounds, and their predicted and observed correlations are very similar.

Todman and Gibb conclude that their results, taken in conjunction with rather similar ones published by Hulme and Turnbull (1983), "suggested that inspection time and intercept measures are differentially predictive of psychometric intelligence at different levels of ability. . . . Whatever processing characteristics underlie differences in the psychometrically sampled intellectual performances of individuals may not be the same in different regions of the IQ scale, and processing components that are relatively remote from strategic control functions seem among the least likely to be critical across a broad ability range" (p. 56). They also argue that, although encoding and response initiation are the components that have generally been assigned to the intercept parameter, it could also incorporate a strategic control component representing time for resource allocation and preparation (see Nettelbeck & Breuer, 1981). However that might be, it is clear that no study involving both normal and retarded subjects is acceptable for a study of the interrelationship between RT and IQ, unless it is accompanied and followed by specific analyses designed to throw light on the possible nonlinear relationships involved.

EVENT-RELATED POTENTIALS

A line of investigation which promises to be of considerable use in understanding theoretically and using practically the relationships between intelligence and speed of cognitive processing relates to the use of evoked brain potentials. The literature on this field is very large (Eysenck & Barrett, 1985), and will not here be reviewed. As already mentioned, the Erlangen School attempted to link their theories with event-related potentials, using measures pioneered in this respect by Ertl (1973) and Ertl and Schafer (1969). Unfortunately, latencies and amplitudes of evoked responses do not correlate very highly with IQ and alternative measures seem much better than this for the purpose. Jensen, Schafer, and Crinella (1981) wisely chose for their study an EEG measure of "neural adaptability" (Schafer, 1979, 1982; Schafer & Marcus, 1973). Neural adaptability (NA) is posited as a cause of a tendency in human subjects to produce cortical evoked potentials with large amplitude to *unexpected* inputs, and small amplitude to inputs whose nature or timings a person can foresee. The *difference* in amplitude to these two kinds of stimuli is predicted to correlate with IQ, being larger in brighter subjects.

Jensen, Shafer, and Crinella (1981) employed 54 severely retarded adults for their study, using a battery of 15 psychometric tests as well as RT, MT, and NA variables. On this group, they obtained a shrunken multiple R of .64 with psychometric g, despite the rather narrow range of IQ scores involved. Individually, the IQ correlated with the RT + MT composite − .46, and neural adaptability correlated with g + .31. Neural adaptability correlated insignificantly with RT and MT, but significantly negatively with SDRT and SDMT, as well as with the RT and MT composite. Clearly, this is a very promising combination of scores to predict individual IQ, and perhaps explain it by logical arguments.

One particularly interesting finding in this study was that the severely retarded group failed to obey Hick's law; there was no further increase in RT beyond 1 bit of information. Jensen, Schafer, and Crinella speculate that Hick's law is only approximately true for any group. The true function relating RT to bits of information they considered to be more probably a parabolic curve, tending towards an asymptote at the point of informational overload for a given subject. This, they consider, is probably between 1 and 2 bits of information for the severely retarded, and close to 7 bits for average adults. The hypothesis is certainly a tenable one, but it would not explain the findings reported by Barrett, Eysenck, and Lucking (1986) showing a breakdown in Hick's law even for normal adults in a large number of cases.

The Schafer neural adaptability paradigm has shown high correlations with normal adult subjects, but so have other paradigms quite different from his, e.g., that proposed by A. E. Hendrickson (1982), and given an empirical basis by D. E. Hendrickson (1982). This model, which has been worked out in great detail along biological lines, explains information processing through a logically related chain of pulse trains which transmit the information. Assume that, for each individual, there is a specific probability R that just one of the synaptic transmissions involved will succeed in correctly transmitting the pulse train in question. The probability of failure is, of course, $1-R$. If we assume that each synapse has the same value of R, and that the probabilities are independent, the probability that a chain of N events will succeed is R^N. The Hendricksons suggest that R is the underlying biological basis of intelligence, so that the larger the number of errors $(1-R)$, the lower will be the IQ of the subject. They have shown that evoked potential measures derived on the basis of this show a very high correlation of .83 with the total Wechsler scale, but this correlation, of course, does not necessarily prove the underlying theory to be correct. The theory has been introduced, not because it is necessarily true, but because it suggests that the observed correlation between IQ and speed of cognitive processing may have a quite different biological foundation from one that would normally be associated with speed, i.e., such things as speed of neural conduction, or transmission across synapses, etc. It is an alternative theory to Jensen's hypothesis of "oscillation," and explains many features of the paradigms we have considered.

It is well known that information is never transmitted singly and through a single channel; what normally occurs is multiple transmission through several channels. Accordingly, we must postulate some kind of *comparator* (Sokolov, 1963). This comparator would compare the incoming messages with each other, and issue the command to react if the messages agreed. If, now, during transmission of the message errors occur, then the resulting final messages would not agree and the comparator would have to wait before giving the instruction to initiate action until a larger number of messages has been received, making certain that the correct percept had been identified. This would inevitably delay reaction, and hence turn differences in errors in transmission into differences in speed of reaction. The theory is developed in more detail in Eysenck (1985), and will not here be developed in greater detail. Note, however, that it explains both the longer reaction time for lower IQ subjects, and also their greater variability. The theory is still, of course, highly speculative, as is Jensen's oscillation theory, but both suggest that underlying differences in speed of reaction there may be more fundamental physiological and biochemical brain processes related to the transmission of information.

There are of course many different biological theories relating to intelligence, ever since Spearman's (1927) early notion of "energy," and Thomson's (1948) notion of number of bonds. Both these notions are equally far removed from being testable, or relating intelligence to existing knowledge of psychophysiology; in principle, at least, the notions of oscillation and errors in transmission are testable, and some predictions can be made from them which have already been found to be verifiable. However, obviously, there is a long way still to go.

THE "ENERGY" THEORY OF INTELLIGENCE

Weiss (1982, 1984, 1986) has suggested, on the basis of a review of the literature, that there is now much evidence for a biochemical analogue of Spearman's "mental energy" hypothesis. Early work on such a hypothesis was cited by Zimmerman and Ross (1944), who reported that feeding of glutamic acid to dull young rats resulted in a considerable improvement in maze-learning ability. Another group of workers, also at Columbia University, reported beneficial effects on the performance of rats in complex reasoning problems (Albert & Warden, 1944). This work was extended to mentally retarded children, with results which suggested that glutamic acid might increase their IQ as measured by standard intelligence tests; however, not all investigations have given favorable results, as indicated in the review by Hughes and Zubek (1956). Many animal experiments, too, have given negative results, probably because positive results have only been achieved with dull rats (and dull humans!), so that experiments using average or bright organisms are strictly irrelevant to the theory.

These empirical data are supported by theoretical considerations. Zimmerman, Burgemeister, and Putnam (1949) have argued that the improvement in learning ability might be due to the facilitatory effect of glutamic acid upon certain metabolic processes underlying neural activity. Thus, it is known that glutamic acid is important in the synthesis of acetylcholine, a chemical substance necessary for the production of various electrical changes appearing during neural transmission. It has been found that the rate of acetylcholine formation could be increased four to five times by adding glutamic acid to dialyzed extracts in rat brain (Nachmansohn, John, & Walsh, 1943). In addition, Waelsch (1951) has shown that the concentration of glutamic acid in the brain is disproportionally high, as compared with the concentration of other amino-acids, and is capable of serving as a respiratory substrate in the brain in lieu of glucose. Finally, Sauri (1950), experimenting on rats, discovered that the acid exerts its main effect on the cerebral cortex, lowering its threshold of excitability.

All these results clearly point to the importance of glutamic acid in cerebral metabolism. Its effectiveness, in dull rats only, suggests that the cerebral metabolism of dull rats is defective in some way, while that of average and bright rats is normal, allowing glutamic acid to facilitate or improve the defective cerebral metabolism of the dull animals, while having no particular effect on the normal metabolism of the bright ones. This suggestion is strengthened by the fact that Himwich and Fazekas (1940), in a careful study of tissue preparations from the brains of mentally retarded persons, were able to show that these tissues were incapable of utilizing normal amounts of oxygen and carbohydrates. In other words, the cerebral metabolism in these mentally retarded patients was defective.

More recently, work along similar lines has been taken up again, and given very promising and important results. Thus, IQ has been found to be correlated with the activity of brain choline acetyltransferase to the extent of .81 (Perry et al., 1978), with brain acetylcholinesterase to the extent of .35 (Soininen et al., 1983), and erythrocyte glutathione peroxidase to the extent of .58 (Sinet, Lejenne, & Jerome, 1979). Cerebral glucose metabolism rates have also been found correlated with IQ to the extent of about .60 by de Leon et al. (1983), and Chase et al. (1984). These studies, admittedly, were not intended to clarify the physiological background of normal intelligence, but to throw light on the metabolic causes of premature senescence and cognitive losses in Alzheimer's disease, Down's syndrome and Parkinson's disease, and normal aging (Mann, Yates, & Marcynink, 1984), and this disease may be viewed as one tail of a continuous distribution. Furthermore, these correlations with IQ have also been confirmed in healthy comparison groups (Soinine et al., 1984; de Leon et al., 1983, Chase et al., 1984), and hence the results must be regarded with respect.

Mutatis mutandis, the theory offered by Weiss is not dissimilar to that of Zimmerman already referred to. As Weiss (1986) points out, the brain consumes glucose as a normally exclusive source of energy. Although the human brain represents only 2% of body weight, its energy consumption is about 20% of total energy requirement (Hoyer, 1982). Compared with the high rate of utilization, the energy stores in the brain are almost negligible, and the brain is consequently almost completely dependent on the continuous replenishment of its glucose supplies by the cerebral circulation (Reinis & Goldman, 1982). Weiss goes on to argue that it would defy most fundamental laws of thermodynamics if individual differences in brain power did not find their counterparts in individual differences of brain energy metabolism. This argument is powerfully strengthened by the fact that two research groups (de Leon et al., 1983; Chase et al., 1984) report significant correlations of around

SPEED OF INFORMATION PROCESSING   55

.60 between regional cerebral glucose metabolism rates and a number of IQ tests, including memory capacity and mental speed, in both the Alzheimer's and control groups (Chase et al., 1984). By positron emission topography of radioactive fluorine, it becomes possible to quantify glucose metabolism in milligrams per 100 grams of brain tissue per minute. Now, since both IQ and glucose metabolism grades are far from perfectly reliably measured, these correlations must be regarded as very high indeed, suggesting a strong degree of dependence of intelligence on cerebral glucose metabolism.

Weiss (1986) takes the argument a good deal further, but this is not the right place to follow a complex biochemical argument, or to indicate possible criticisms in detail. The small number of normal subjects tested, the unknown reliability of the biochemical assays, and the failure of the authors mentioned to address the central issues of Weiss's argument (understandable because of their orientation towards medical problems of aging) combine to make it desirable for a new, large scale investigation to be carried out along the same lines, but emphasizing proper large samples of normal adults covering the range of IQ. However that may be, the data are certainly impressive, suggesting that glucose, glutamic acid, and other biochemical agents responsible for the energy supply of the cortex, and connected with the production of neurotransmitter substances, have a vital causal role to play in Intelligence A, and may be the ultimate source of that "mental energy" which is the underlying biological substrate of Spearman's g (general intelligence). It cannot at the moment be claimed that the search has ended with these tantalizing findings, but it may be claimed that it has not only begun, but has already made possible the postulation of specific testable theories.

Another biochemical feature which has been related to mental retardation, and in particular Alzheimer's disease, Down's syndrome, and the Parkinson-dementia of Guam is chronic calcium deficiency (Abalan, 1984; Barlow, Sylvester, & Dickerson, 1981). In the three areas mentioned above, the diseases disappeared after access to calcium was increased (Gajdusek, 1985). There is strong evidence that these diseases share an aetiology in terms of mineral deficiency (Garruto et al., 1985), and Deary, Hendrickson, and Burns (1986) have suggested a possible mechanism whereby the process of decline and dementia may be alleviated, and the normal process of aging and the decline of intelligence retarded. This appears to be another line of research into the causal biological factors determining differences in intelligence which would be worth following up.

SUMMARY AND CONCLUSION

In attempting to come to some conclusions about the results so far achieved, we must first of all consider the great variability of results reported. Does this variability preclude any firm conclusions? The answer to this question is probably no. Many studies have been done on relatively few cases, and the probable errors of a product-moment correlation are of course quite high for small numbers. Let us consider a "true" correlation between RT and IQ of − .40, and let us assume that the number of cases involved is 25. Under those conditions, 50% of correlations found in replicated samples would lie between − .51 and − .29, and half would lie outside these limits. In other words, even differences as large as those between − .20 and − .60 would arise by chance quite frequently. Thus, variability of results is built into the design of the experiments by the small numbers of cases usually employed − and it should be remembered that an N of 25 is a good deal larger than the numbers sometimes reported!

There are many other reasons for variability, such as the use of different IQ tests, the use of different RT measures (mean, median, or mode), derived from varying numbers of observations, variously arranged and spaced, and the use of many different types of samples of varying range, age, and sex composition. It would be a miracle if with such a variety of conditions results would show greater agreement than they do.

We must also consider that, in discussing results, it would not be useful to use terms denoting the observed relationships as large or small, impressive or negligible, important or irrelevant. The size of correlations should always be seen in the context of expectations based on theory − if a correlation is expected to be in the neighborhood of − .40, then a correlation of − .20 would be small, one of − .60 would be large. If the expected correlation is around − .80, then one of − .60 would be small! Furthermore, correlations should never be compared unless corrected for range of ability; such corrections should always be reported. Finally, from the theoretical point of view, it is important that corrections for attenuation should be made, particularly in view of the low test-retest reliability of RT measures. Such corrections, of course, are not very relevant to the practical use of the test, but from the theoretical point of view they are all-important. After all, we are concerned with the "true" relationship between IQ and RT; these relationships are seriously underestimated if we use very unreliable measures of either or both.

Multiple Rs are reported by many authors, and it seems reasonable to combine different measures, such as RTs, MTs and variabilities. However, multiple Rs, even if shrunk to avoid capitalizing on chance errors, are inherently very unstable when based on small numbers of subjects, and may be quite misleading. Measures should only be combined if both the measures used and their weighting is determined beforehand, preferably on the basis of previously reported investigations. Otherwise, multiple Rs are probably not a good guide to the "true" relations obtaining between variables.

Finally, we should look at the observed relationships in terms of the correlations usually found between IQ tests. Clearly, it is unlikely that RT and IQ measures would correlate more highly than IQ measures do with each other; indeed, theory dictates that, because IQ measures share certain noncognitive elements, they should correlate more highly together than any of them would with an RT measure not influenced by these noncognitive factors. Using a very rough estimate, we might say that IQ tests intercorrelate around .75 when they are relatively similar in structure, such as the Binet and the Wechsler, but that the correlation drops to about .50 to .60 when they are rather dissimilar, such as the Wechsler and the Raven. If RT measures encapsulate the biological essence of g, then we could expect observed correlations on suitable samples, corrected for attenuation, to be around .5 to .6, no higher. If they are higher than this, then the difference should not be larger than twice the standard error of the correlation itself; otherwise, the observed correlation would be too high to be in accord with the theory. Equally, results would not be in accord with the theory if the correlation were more than two or three standard deviations below that value.

Granted these boundary conditions, we find that, on the whole, results are in good accord with theory, in that choice RT and MT measures, and variabilities of these measures, correlate with IQ around .4, where no correction is made for attenuation, and between .5 and .6 when such corrections are made. This is true also of such more complex measures as the Sternberg or Posner paradigms. For IT, results are more divergent than for RT, but this may be due to the fact that the experimental paradigms used are much more dissimilar. The low results reported by Irwin (1984) may be contrasted with the high correlations reported by Raz, Willerman, Ingmundson, and Hanlon (1983) and Raz and Willerman (1985). Irwin, using a visual inspection time task for 50 children, concluded that results "do not support earlier claims that inspection time is closely related to conventional measures of intelligence" (p. 47). Raz et al. (1983) reported correlations for auditory IT (pioneered by Deary, 1980) ranging from −.51 to −.74, and Raz and Willerman (1985) reported values of −.58 to −.59. These values are much more in line with those reported by Brand (1981; Brand & Deary, 1982). Even the values for auditory inspection time quoted by Irwin (−.32 and −.23 for verbal and nonverbal intelligence test respectively) are not significantly different from those reported by Raz and his colleagues, although those for visual IT are indeed very low.

Contrary to the expectations expressed by both Jensen and the Erlangen School, neither the Hick slope nor the increase in RT-IQ correlations with increase in the number of bits in the stimulus array can be said to have given very high correlations. For the slope parameter correlations of −.30 may be regarded as typical, and while there is an undoubted and marked increase as we go from simple to choice reaction time, increases from one to three bits of information are not paralleled by any marked increase in correlation between RT and IQ. These disappointing findings may be related to the fact that

Hick's law is not obeyed by all subjects, and as many as 20% or more may show widely differing regressions. When such subjects are removed, the remainder show higher relationships, but, of course, until and unless an explanation is found for the departure from Hick's law of the remaining subjects, such an omission would be arbitrary and of little theoretical interest.

Does the fact that the correlation between simple reaction time and IQ is not zero contradict our theory? It is true that simple reaction time according to Hick implies zero bits of information, but that, of course, is a highly artificial way of looking at the situation. The subject is not getting any information from the lighting up of the lamp as to which target is going to be lit, but he or she does receive information about *when* the target is being lit. In other words, even when there is only one light and no choice, some cognitive processing has to take place, representing the duration of encoding of the stimulus together with the time taken to decide on the execution of the response. Admittedly, these cognitive processes are very rudimentary, and hence correlations with IQ will be expected to be much lower than when choice is involved, but would not be likely to be reduced to zero.

If simple reaction time were *qualitatively* different from choice reaction time, and carried no traces of cognitive processing, then one would expect that taking the *difference* between simple and choice RT for a given person, and correlating this difference with IQ, would increase correlations because of the elimination of irrelevant material. Carrying out this process on the data presented by Barrett, Eysenck, and Lucking (1986) showed that correlations were reduced rather than increased, thus demonstrating that if we postulate cognitive processes in choice reaction time, we must also postulate similar processes, if at a more rudimentary level, in simple reaction time measurement.

On the whole, results are in reasonable agreement with the general theory outlined at the beginning of this chapter. As shown in Figure 8, we may equate Intelligence A (biological intelligence) with some such concept as error-free transmission of information through the cortex. It is not suggested that this is the only paradigm that fits the data, but at the moment we believe it has more evidence in favor of it than various alternatives, such as Jensen's oscillation model. Differences in error-free transmission lead to differences in IQ, mainly through the influence of error-free transmission on mental speed. Error-checking and continuance are noncognitive variables which influence IQ, but do not influence error-free transmission; hence, IQ (Intelligence C) is an impure measure of intelligence. More complex still than IQ is Intelligence B (social intelligence), which comprises a number of cognitive activities (reasoning, judgment, problem-solving, learning comprehension, use of strategies, eduction of relations and correlates, etc.) which are largely influenced by biological intelligence differences, but which are also determined in part by extraneous variables such as personality, education, knowledge,

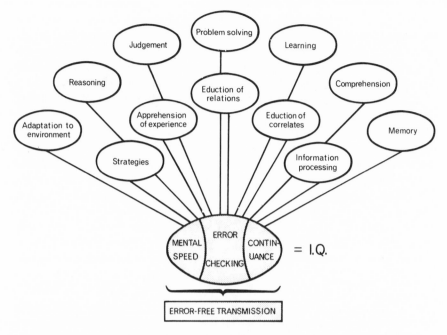

FIGURE 8.   Relation between biological and social intelligence, with tripartite division of IQ as intermediary.

socio-economic status, etc. Such a model, at the moment, seems in good accord with the facts, but it does, of course, need a great deal of detailed working out before it can be considered firmly established (Eysenck, 1986).

Can we regard a theory concentrating on speed of information processing as having explanatory value for such a concept as "intelligence" which, according to Spearman (1927), is essentially *noegenetic,* i.e., which produces *novel* concepts and solutions? Work on artificial intelligence suggests that this may be so (Winston, 1984; Lenat, 1977, 1982). In some way, obviously, this must indeed be so, as otherwise we would have to postulate some kind of problem-solving *homunculus* in the brain, which is all that most current theories of intelligence boil down to. Such a postulation would, of course, be useless, but it cannot be said that very much progress has been made in translating the simple processes of information processing into the creation of novel solutions. If this really entails nothing but the eduction of relations and correlates, then it should not prove too difficult to elaborate such a theory.

I have ventured to suggest that we are faced with a revolution in the theory and measurement of intelligence (Eysenck, 1983). This revolution, in essence, takes an important step further the theoretical foundations given to the experimental study of intelligence by Galton, Spearman, and Burt. Like all scientific revolutions, this one too confronts many anomalies, but it may be hoped that these will be eliminated in time by the process of "normal science," i.e., the puzzle-solving application of the scientific method to specific problems. It is also to be hoped that there will be a closer contact between investigators interested in individual differences, and those who study reaction time experimentally, and attempt to elaborate theoretical positions (Smith, 1968). The study of choice reaction time as a measure of intelligence has not paid much heed to the work done by experimentalists; it seems likely that only by doing so will we gain a better understanding of the way in which IQ and RT are linked, and the fundamental biological factors which determine speed of mental functioning.

REFERENCES

Abalan, F. (1984). Alzheimer's disease and malnutrition: A new aetiological hypothesis. *Medical Hypotheses, 15,* 385–393.

Aikins, H. A., Thorndike, E. L., & Hubbell, E. (1902). Correlations among perceptive and associative processes. *Psychological Review, 9,* 374–382.

Albert, K., & Warden, C. J. (1944). The level of performance in the white rat. *Science, 100,* 476.

Amelang, M. (1985). *Der Zusammenhang zwischen Intelligenz und der Geschwindigkeit von Informationsverarbeitung.* Unpublished TS, University of Heidelberg.

Amthauer, R. (1955). *Intelligenz-Struktur-Test (IST).* Gottingen, Germany: Hogrefe.

Ananda, S. M. (1985). *Speed of information processing and psychometric abilities in later adulthood.* Unpublished Ph.D. dissertation, University of California, Berkeley.

Anderson, M. (1917). An investigation into the rate of mental association. *Journal of Educational Psychology, 8,* 97–102.

Bagley, W. C. (1901). On the correlation of mental and motor ability in school children. *American Journal of Psychology, 12,* 193–205.

Baltes, P. B., & Kliegl, R. (1985). On the dynamics between growth and decline in the aging of intelligence and memory. In K. Preck (Ed.), *Proceedings of the XIIIth World Congress of Neurology.* Heidelberg, Germany: Springer.

Barlow, P. J., Sylvester, P. E., & Dickerson, J. W. T. (1981). Hairtrace metal levels in Downs Syndrome patients. *Journal of Mental Deficiency Research, 25,* 161–168.

Barr, A., & Feigenbaum, E. (1981). *The handbook of artificial intelligence* (Vol. 1). London: Pitman.

Barr, A., & Feigenbaum, E. (1982). *The handbook of artificial intelligence* (Vol. 2). Palo Alto, CA: Heuris Tech. Press.

Barrett, P., Eysenck, H. J., & Lucking, S. (1986). Reaction time and intelligence: A replicate study. *Intelligence, 10,* 9–40.

Berger, M. (1976). *A study of the Eysenck-Furneaux approach to the analysis of performance on intelligence tests.* Unpublished Ph.D. thesis, University of London.

Berger, M. (1982). The "scientific approach" to intelligence: An overview of its history with special reference to mental speed. In H. J. Eysenck (Ed.), *A model for intelligence.* New York: Springer.

Bernstein, E. (1924). Quickness and intelligence: An inquiry concerning the existence of a general speed factor. *British Journal of Psychology Monograph.* Cambridge University Press, vi + 55.

Bieger, H. J. (1968). *Uber den Zusammenhang zwischen Intelligenz und Geschwindigkeit der Informationsverarbeitung im Wahlreaktions-experiment*. Hamburg, Germany: Unpublished thesis.

Binet, A. (1903). *L'Etude experimentale de l'intelligence*. Paris: Schleicher, Frenes.

Binet, A. (1907). *La psychologie du raisonnement*. Paris: Alcan.

Brand, C. R. (1981). General intelligence and mental speed. In M. Friedman, J. Das, & N. O'Connor (Eds.), *Intelligence and learning*. New York: Plenum Press.

Brand, C. R., & Deary, I. J. (1982). Intelligence and "inspection time." In H. J. Eysenck (Ed.), *A model for intelligence*. New York: Springer.

Brebner, J., & Nettelbeck, T. (1986). Intelligence and inspection time. Special Issue, *Personality and Individual Differences, 7,* 603-729.

Brierley, H. (1961). The speed and accuracy characteristics of neurotics. *British Journal of Psychology, 52,* 273-280.

Brown, V. (1910). Some experimental results in the correlation of mental activities. *British Journal of Psychology, 3,* 296-322.

Buktenica, N. A. (1971). Auditory discrimination: A new assessment procedure. *Exceptional Children, 38,* 253-261.

Burt, C. (1909). Experimental tests of general intelligence. *British Journal of Psychology, 3,* 94-177.

Carlson, J. S., & Jensen, C. M. (1982). Reaction time, movement time and intelligence: A replication and extension. *Intelligence, 6,* 265-274.

Carlson, J. S., Jensen, C. M., & Widaman, K. (1983). Reaction time, intelligence and attention. *Intelligence, 7,* 329-344.

Carroll, J. B. (1986). Jensen's mental chronometry: Some comments and questions. In S. Modgil & C. Modgil (Eds.), *Arthur Jensen: Consensus and controversy*. Lewes, England: Falmer Press.

Cattell, R. B. (1971). *Abilities: Their structure, growth and action*. Boston, MA: Houghton-Mifflin.

Chapman, J. C. (1924). Persistence, success and speed in a mental test. *Pedagogical Summary, 31,* 276-284.

Chase, R. N., Foster, P., Brooks, N. L., Di Chiro, G., & Mausi, L. (1984). Wechsler adult intelligence scale performance: cortical localisation by flurodexoclucose F18-positron emission tomography. Archives of Neurology, 41, 1244-1247.

Cohen, P., & Feigenbaum, E. (1982). *The handbook of artificial intelligence* (Vol. 3). London: Pitman.

de Leon, M. J., Ferris, S. H., George, A. E., Christman, D. R., Fowler, J. S., Gentes, C., Reisburg, B., Gee, B., Emmerich, M. Yonekura, Y., Brodie, J., Kricheff, I. I., & Wolf, A. P. (1983). Positron emission tomographic: status of aging and Alzheimer's disease. American Journal of Neuroradiology, 4, 568-571.

Deary, I. J. (1980). *How general is the mental speed factor in "general" intelligence? An attempt to extend inspection time to the auditory modality*. Unpublished B.Sc. honours thesis, University of Edinburgh.

Deary, I. J., Hendrickson, A. E., & Burns, A. (1986, in press). Serum calcium levels in Alzheimer's disease: A finding and an aetiological hypothesis. *Personality and Individual Differences*.

Dugas, J. L., & Kellas, G. (1974). Encoding and retrieval processes in normal children and retarded adolescents. *Journal of Experimental Child Psychology, 17,* 177-185.

Ertl, J. (1971). Fourier analysis of evoked potential and human intelligence. Nature, 230, 525-526.

Ertl, J. (1973). IQ, evoked responses and Fourier analysis. *Nature, 241,* 209-210.

Ertl, J., & Schafer, E. (1969). Brain response correlates of psychometric intelligence. *Nature, 223,* 421-422.

Eysenck, H. J. (1953). *Uses and abuses of psychology.* London: Pelican.

Eysenck, H. J. (1967). Intelligence assessment: A theoretical and experimental approach. *British Journal of Educational Psychology, 37,* 81–98.

Eysenck, H. J. (1973). *The measurement of intelligence.* Lancaster, England: MTP Press.

Eysenck, H. J. (1979). *The structure and measurement of intelligence.* New York: Springer.

Eysenck, H. J. (Ed.), (1982). *A model for intelligence.* New York: Springer.

Eysenck, H. J. (1983). Revolution dans la theorie et la mesure de l'intelligence. *Revue Canadienne de Psycho-Education, 12,* 3–17.

Eysenck, H. J. (1985). The theory of intelligence and the psychophysiology of cognition. In R. J. Sternberg (Ed.), *Advances in the psychology of human intelligence* (Vol. 3). Hillsdale, NJ: Erlbaum.

Eysenck, H. J. (1986). Intelligence: The new look. *Psychologische Beiträge, 28,* 332–365.

Eysenck, H. J., & Barrett, P. (1985). Psychophysiology and the measurement of intelligence. In C. R. Reynolds & V. Willson (Eds.), *Methodological and statistical advances in the study of individual differences.* New York: Plenum Press.

Eysenck, H. J., & Frith, C. D. (1977). *Reminiscence, motivation, and personality.* New York: Plenum.

Frank, H. (1960). Uber grundliegende Sätze der Informations-psychologie. *Grundlagenstudien aus Kybernetik und Geisteswissenschaft, 1,* 25–32.

Frank, H. (1971). *Kybernetische Grundlagen der Pädagogik.* Stuttgart: Kohlhammer.

Frearson, W., & Eysenck, H. J. (1986). Intelligence, reaction time and a new "odd-man-out" R. T. paradigm. *Personality and Individual Differences, 7,* 807–817.

Freeman, F. N. (1923). Note on the relation between speed and accuracy or quality of work. *Journal of Educational Research, 7,* 87–89.

Furneaux, D. (1952). Some speed, error, and difficulty relationships within a problem solving situation. *Nature, 170,* 37.

Furneaux, D. (1961). Intellectual abilities and problem solving behaviour. In H. J. Eysenck (Ed.), *Handbook of abnormal psychology.* New York: Basic Books.

Gajdusek, D. C. (1985). Hypothesis: interference with axonal transport of neurofilament as a common pathogenic mechanism in certain diseases of the central nervous system. *New England Journal of Medicine, 312,* 714–719.

Galton, F. (1892). *Hereditary genius: An enquiry into its laws and consequences.* London: Macmillan.

Galton, F. (1943). *Inquiries into human faculty.* London: Dent.

Garrett, H. E. (1922). A study of the relation of accuracy to speed. *Archives of Psychology, 8* (No. 56), 104.

Garruto, R. M., Swyt, C., Fiori, C. E., Yanagihara, R., & Gajdusek, D. C. (1985, December). Interneuron deposition of calcium and aluminium in amyotrophic lateral sclerosis of Guam. *Lancet 14,* 1353.

Gates, A. I. (1924). Relation of quality and speed of performance. *Journal of Educational Psychology, 15,* 129–144.

Gilbert, J. A. (1894). Researches on the mental and physical development of school children. *Studies from the Yale Psychology Laboratory,* 40–100.

Goldfarb, W. (1941). An investigation of reaction time in older adults, and its relationship to certain observed mental test patterns. *Teachers College Contributions to Education, 941,* 831.

Guilford, J. P. (1947). *Air army forces aviation psychology program research reports: Printed classification tests. Report No. 5.* Washington, DC: U.S. Government Printing Office.

Guilford, J. P., & Hoepfner, R. (1971). *The analysis of intelligence.* New York: McGraw-Hill.

Harris, G., & Fleer, R. (1974). High speed memory scanning in mental retardates: Evidence for a central processing deficit. *Journal of Experimental Child Psychology, 17,* 452–459.

Hebb, D. (1949). *The organization of behaviour.* New York: Wiley.

Hemmelgarn, T. E., & Kehle, T. J. (1984). The relationships between reaction time and intelligence in children. *School Psychology International, 5,* 77–84.

Hendrickson, A. E. (1982). The biological basis of intelligence. Part 1: Theory. In H. J. Eysenck (Ed.), *A model for intelligence.* New York: Springer.

Hendrickson, D. E. (1982). The biological basis of intelligence. Part 2: Measurement. In H. J. Eysenck (Ed.), *A model for intelligence.* New York: Springer.

Hick, W. (1952). On the rate of gain of information. *Quarterly Journal of Experimental Psychology, 4,* 11–26.

Highsmith, J. A. (1925). Relation of the rate of response to intelligence. *Psychological Monogram, 34,* (No. 3), 1–33.

Himwich, H. E., & Fazekas, J. F. (1940). Cerebral metabolism in Mongolian idiocy and phenylpyruvic oligophrenia. *Archives of Neurology and Psychiatry, 44,* 1213–1218.

Horn, J. L. (1968). Organization of abilities and the development of intelligence. *Psychological Review, 75,* 242–259.

Horn, J. L. (1972). The structure of intellect: Primary abilities. In R. M. Breger (Ed.), *Multivariate personality research.* Baton Rouge, LA: Claitor's Publishing Division.

Horning, K., Morim, R., & Konick, D. (1970). Recognition reaction time and rate of memory set: A developmental study. *Psychonomic Science, 21,* 247–248.

Hoyer, G. (1982). The young adult and normally aged brain. Its blood flow and oridatial metabolism. A review–Part 1. *Archives of Gerontology and Geriatrics, 1,* 101–116.

Hughes, K. R., & Zubek, J. P. (1956). Effect of glutamic acid on the learning ability of bright and dull rats: 1. Administration during infancy. *Canadian Journal of Psychology, 10,* 132–138.

Hulme, C., & Turnbull, J. (1983). Intelligence and inspection time in normal and mentally retarded subjects. *British Journal of Psychology, 74,* 365–370.

Hunsicker, L. M. (1925). A study of the relationship between rate and ability. *Teachers College contribution to Education, No. 185.*

Hunt, E. (1976). Varieties of cognitive power. In L. B. Resnick (Ed.), *The nature of intelligence.* Hillsdale, NJ: Erlbaum.

Hunt, E., Lunneborg, C., & Lewis, J. (1975). What does it mean to be high verbal? *Cognitive Psychology, 7,* 194–227.

Irwin, R. J. (1984). Inspection time and its relation to intelligence. *Intelligence, 8,* 47–65.

Iseler, A. (1970). *Leistungsgeschwindigkeit und Leistungsgüte.* Weinheim: Beltz.

Jenkinson, J. C. (1983). Is speed of information processing related to fluid or to crystallized intelligence? *Intelligence, 7,* 91–106.

Jensen, A. R. (1982a). Reaction time and psychometric g. In H. J. Eysenck (Ed.), *A model for intelligence.* New York: Springer.

Jensen, A. R. (1982b). The chronometry of intelligence. In R. J. Sternberg (Ed.), *Advances in the psychology of human intelligence* (Vol. 1). London: Lawrence Erlbaum.

Jensen, A. R., & Munro, E. (1979). Reaction time, movement time, and intelligence. *Intelligence, 3,* 121–126.

Jensen, A. R., Schafer, E. W. P., & Crinella, F. M. (1981). Reaction time, evoked brain potentials, and psychometric g in the severely retarded. *Intelligence, 5,* 179–197.

Jensen, A. R., & Vernon, P. A. (1986). Jensen's reaction-time studies: A reply to Longstreth. *Intelligence, 10,* 153–179.

Keating, D. P., & Bobbitt, B. (1978). Individual and developmental differences in cognitive processing components of mental ability. *Child Development, 49,* 155–169.

Lally, M., & Nettelbeck, T. (1977). Intelligence, reaction time and inspection time. *American Journal of Mental Deficiency, 82,* 273–281.

Lehrl, S. (1980). Subjectives Zeitquant als missing link zwischen Intelligenz-Psychologie und Neuropsychologie. *Grundlagenstudien aus Kybernetik und Geisteswissenschaften, 21,* 107–116.

Lehrl, S. (1983). Intelligenz: Informationpsychologische Grundlagen. *Enzyklopädie der Naturwissenschaft und Technik.* Landsberg, Germany: Moderne Industrie.

Lehrl, S., & Frank, H. G. (1982). Zur humangenetischen Erklärung der Kurzspeicher-Kapazität als die zentrale individuelle Determinante von Spearman's Generalfaktor der Intelligenz. *Grundlagenstudien aus Kybernetik und Geisteswissenschaften, 23,* 177–186.

Lenat, D. B. (1977). The ubiquity of discovery. *Artificial Intelligence, 9,* 114–119.

Lenat, D. B. (1982). The nature of heuristics. *Artificial Intelligence, 19,* 87–94.

Longstreth, L. E. (1984). Jensen's reaction-time investigations of intelligence: A critique. *Intelligence, 8,* 139–160.

Mann, D. M., Yates, P. D., Marcynink, B. (1984). Relationship between pigment accumulation and age in Alzheimer's disease and Down's syndrome. *Acta Neuropathologica, 63,* 72–77.

Maisto, A., & Baumeister, A. (1975). A developmental study of choice reaction time: The effect of two forms of stimulus degradation on encoding. *Journal of Experimental Child Psychology, 20,* 456–464.

Maisto, A., & Jerome, M. (1977). Encoding and high speed memory scanning of retarded and non-retarded adolescents. *American Journal of Mental Deficiency, 82,* 282–286.

May, M. A. (1921). Psychological examination in the U.S. army. *National Academy of Science Members, 15,* 415ff.

McCall, W. A. (1916). Correlation of some psychological and educational measurements. *Teachers College Contribution to Education,* No. 79.

McFarland, R. A. (1928). The role of speed in mental ability. *Psychological Bulletin, 25,* 595–612.

Nachmansohn, D., & John, H. N., & Walsh, H. (1943). Effect of glutamic acid on the formation of acetyl choline. *Journal of Biological Chemistry, 150,* 485–486.

Nettelbeck, T., & Breuer, N. (1981). Studies of mild mental retardation and timed performance. In R. Ellis (Ed.), *International review of research in mental retardation* (vol. 10). New York: Academic Press.

Nettelbeck, T., & Kirby, N. H. (1983). Measures of timed performance and intelligence. *Intelligence, 7,* 39–52.

Nettelbeck, T., & Lally, M. (1976). Inspection time and measured intelligence. *British Journal of Psychology, 67,* 17–22.

Nettelbeck, T., Cheshire, F., & Lally, M. (1979). Intelligence, work performance, and inspection time. *Ergonomics, 22,* 291–297.

Newell, S., & Simon, H. A. (1972). *Human problem solving.* Englewood Cliffs, NJ: Prentice-Hall.

Oswald, D. W. (1971). Uber Zusammenhänge zwischen Informationsverarbeitung, Alter und Intelligenzstruktur beim Kartensortieren. Psychologische Rundschau, 27, 197–202.

Oswald, D. W., & Roth, E. (1978). *Der Zahlen-Verbindungs-Test (ZVT).* Göttingen, Germany: Hogrefe.

Oswald, D. W., & Seus, R. (1975). Zusammenhänge Zwischen Intelligenz, Informationsverarbeitungsgeschwindigkeit und evozierten Potentialen. In H. Tack (Ed.), *Bericht über den 29 Kongress der Deutschen Gesellschaft fur Psychologie.* Göttingen, Germany: Hogrefe.

Paul, S. M. (1984). *Speed of information processing: The semantic verification test and general mental ability.* Unpublished Ph.D. dissertation, University of California.

Peak, H., & Boring, E. G. (1926). The factor of speed in intelligence. *Journal of Experimental Psychology, 9,* 71–94.

Perry, E. K., Tomlinson, B. E., Blessed, G., Bergman, K., Ebson, P. N., & Perry, R. N. (1978). Correlates of cholinergic abnormalities with senile plaques and mental test scores in senile dementia. *British Medical Journal, 2,* 1457–1459.

Peterson, J. (1925). *Early conceptions and tests of intelligence.* Yonkers: World Books Company.

Posner, M. I. (1969). Abstractism and the process of recognition. In G. H. Bower and J. T. Spence (Eds.), *The psychology of Learning and Motivation, 3,* 43–100. New York: Academic Press.

Posner, M. I., Boies, S., Eichelman, W., & Taylor, R. (1969). Retention of visual and name codes of single letters. *Journal of Experimental Psychology, 81,* 10–15.

Raz, N., & Willerman, L. (1985). Aptitude-related differences in auditory information processing: Effects of selective attention and tone duration. *Personality and Individual Differences, 6,* 299–304.

Raz, N., & Willerman, L., & Yama, M. (1987). On sense and senses: Intelligence and auditory information processing. *Personality and Individual Differences, 8,* 201–210.

Raz, N., Willerman, L., Ingmundson, P., & Hanlan, M. (1983). Aptitude-related differences in auditory recognition masking. *Intelligence, 7,* 71–90.

Reeves, J. W. (1965). *Thinking about thinking.* London: Secker & Warburg.

Reinis, S., & Goldman, J. M. (1982). *The chemistry of behaviour.* New York: Plenum.

Roth, E. (1964). Die Geschwindigkeit der Verarbeitung von Information und ihr Zusammenhang mit Intelligenz. *Zeitschrift für angewandte und experimentelle Psychologie, 11,* 616–622.

Ruch, G. M., & Koerth, W. (1923). "Power" vs. "Speed" in Army Alpha. *Journal of Educational Psychology, 14,* 193–208.

Sattler, J. M. (1974). *Assessment of children's intelligence.* Philadelphia, PA: W. B. Saunders.

Sauri, J. J. (1950). Accion del acido glutamica en el sistema nerviosa central. *Neuropsiquiatrica, 1,* 148–158.

Schafer, E. (1979). Cognitive neural adaptability: A biological basis for individual differences in intelligence. *Psychophysiology, 16,* 199.

Schafer, E. (1982). Neural adaptability: A biological determinant of behavioural intelligence. *International Journal of Neuroscience, 17,* 183–191.

Schafer, E., & Marcus, M. (1973). Self-stimulation alters human memory brain responses. *Science, 181,* 175–177.

Seashore, C. E. (1913). *The psychology of musical talent.* New York: Silver Burdelt.

Seininen, H. S., Jolkken, J. T., Reinihainen, K. J., Holonen, T. O., & Riekkinenn, P. J. (1984). Reduced cholinesterase activity and somatostatics-like immuno reactivity in the cerebrospinal fluid of patients with dementia of the Alzheimer type. *Journal of Neurological Science, 63,* 167–172.

Seymour, P., & Moir, W. (1980). Intelligence and semantic judgment time. *British Journal of Psychology, 71,* 53–61.

Silverman, W. (1974). High speed scanning of non-alpha-numeric symbols in culturally-familialy retarded and non-retarded children. *American Journal of Mental Deficiency, 79,* 44–51.

Sinet, P. M., Lejenne, J., & Jerome, H. Trisomy 21 (Down's Syndrome), gluthathione perioxidase, hexose monosulphate shunt and IQ. *Life Sciences, 24,* 29–33.

Sisk, J. K. (1926). The inter-relations of speed in simple and complex responses *George Peabody College for Teachers Contribution to Education,* No. 23, 48.

Smith, E. E. (1968). Choice reaction time: An analysis of the major theoretical positions. *Psychological Bulletin, 69,* 77–110.

Smith, G. S., & Stanley, G. (1983). Clocking g: relating intelligence and measures of timed performance. *Intelligence, 7,* 353–368.

Sokolov, E. N. (1963). *Perception and the conditioned reflex.* Oxford, England: Pergamon Press.

Soininen, H. S., Jolkkonen, J. T., Reinikainen, K. J., Halonen, T. O., & Riekkinen, P. (1983). Reduced Cholinesterase activity and somatostatin-like immunoreactivity in the cerebroprimal fluid of patients with dementia of the Alzheimer type. *Journal of Neurological Science, 63,* 167–172.

Spearman, C. (1904). "General intelligence": objectively determined and measured. *American Journal of Psychology, 15,* 201–292.

Spearman, C. (1927). *The ability of man.* London: Macmillan.

Stankov, L., Horn, J. (1980). Human abilities revealed through auditory tests. *Journal of Educational Psychology, 15,* 21–44.

Sternberg, R. J. (Eds.) (1982). *Handbook of human intelligence.* Cambridge, MA: Cambridge University Press.

Sternberg, R. J. (1985). *Beyond IQ: A triarchic theory of human intelligence.* Cambridge, MA: Cambridge University Press.

Sternberg S. (1966). High speed scanning in human memory. *Science, 153,* 652–654.

Thompson, G. (1948). *The factorial analysis of human ability.* London: University of London Press.

Thorndike, R. L. (1987, in press). Stability of factor loadings. *Personality and Individual Differences.*

Thorndike, E. L., Bregman, E. O., Cobb, M. V., & Woodyard, E. (1927). *The measurement of intelligence.* New York: Teachers College of Columbia University.

Todman, J., & Gibb, C. M. (1985). High speed memory scanning in retarded and non-retarded adolescents. *British Journal of Psychology, 76,* 49–57.

Travis, L. E. (1925). The improvement of mental measurement. *Journal of Education Research, 11,* 1–11.

Valentine, J., Wilding, J., & Mohindra, N. (1984). Independence of slope and intercept in Sternberg's memory-scanning paradigm. *British Journal of Mathematical and Statistical Psychology, 37,* 122–127.

Vernon, P. A. (1981). Reaction time and intelligence in the mentally retarded. *Intelligence, 5,* 345–355.

Vernon, P. A. (1983). Speed of information processing and general intelligence. *Intelligence, 7,* 53–70.

Vernon, P. A., & Kantor, L. (1986). Reaction time correlations with intelligence test scores obtained under either timed or untimed conditions. *Intelligence, 10,* 315–330.

Vernon, P. A., Nador, S., & Kantor, L. (1985). Reaction time and speed of processing: Their relationship to timed and untimed measures of intelligence. *Intelligence, 9,* 357–374.

Vernon, P. E. (1979). *Intelligence, heredity and environment.* San Francisco, CA: Freeman.

Waelsch, H. (1951). Glutamic acid and cerebral functions. In M. L. Auson, J. T. Edsall, & K. Bailey, (Eds.), *Advances in Protein Chemistry* (pp. 301–339). New York: Academic Press.

Weiss, V. (1982). *Psychogenetik.* Jena, DDR: Gustav Fischer.

Weiss, V. (1984). Psychometric intelligence correlates with inter-individual different rates of lipid peroxidation. *Biomedical and Biochemical Acta, 43,* 755–763.

Weiss, V. (1986). From memory span and mental speed toward the quantum mechanics of intelligence. *Personality and Individual Differences, 7,* 737–749.

Weiss, V., & Mehlhorn, H. G. (1982). Spearmans Generalfaktor der Intelligenz: Genotypen mit ganzzahligen Unterschieden in der zentralen Informationsverarbeitungsgeschwindigkeit. *Zeitschrift für Psychologie, 190,* 78–92.

White, P. O. (1973). A mathematical model for individual differences in problem solving. In A. Elithorn & D. Jones (Eds.), *Artificial and human thinking.* Amsterdam, Netherlands: Elsevier.

White, P. O. (1982). Some major components in general intelligence. In H. J. Eysenck (Ed.), *A model for intelligence.* New York: Springer.

Williams, L., Pottinger, P., & Shapcott, P. (1985). Effects of exercise on choice reaction latency and movement speed. *Perceptual and Motor Skills, 60,* 67–71.

Winston, P. H. (1984). *Artificial intelligence* (2nd ed.). London: Addison-Wesley.

Wissler, C. (1901). The correlation of mental and physical tests. *Psychology Monogram,* No. 16, 62.

Wyatt, S. (1913). The quantitative investigation of higher mental processes. *British Journal of Psychology, 6,* 109–133.

Zimmerman, F. T., Burgemeister, B. B., & Putnam, T. Z. (1949). Effect of glutanic acid on the intelligence of patients with mongolism. *Archives of Neurology and Psychiatry, 61,* 275–287.

Zimmerman, F. I., & Ross, S. (1944). Effect of glutamic acid and other amino acids on maze learning in the white rat. *Archives of Neurology and Psychiatry, 51,* 446–451.

CHAPTER 3

Elementary Cognitive Correlates of *G:* Progress and Prospects

Jerry S. Carlson and Keith F. Widaman
The University of California, Riverside

The study of intelligence has occupied philosophers since the time of the ancient Greeks and is one of the most widely researched areas in contemporary psychology. However, despite the long history of interest in the construct, there is no unified concept of what intelligence is; rather, several alternative, though not necessarily mutually exclusive, theories compete. Theories of intelligence range from practical, ecological approaches that stress adaptation to the environment in which an individual lives, to statistically defined conceptions derived from individuals' performance on a variety of tests, to information processing approaches, which generally employ reaction time paradigms in which the dependent variable is speed of response to stimuli with differing cognitive demands. Each of these general approaches has several variants that differ both theoretically and methodologically.

In the present chapter, we will have occasion to refer to measures we term Galtonian and Spearmanian measures, because the types of measures resemble those used by Galton and Spearman, respectively, in their early and important programs of research. We use the term *Galtonian measures* to refer to measures such as reaction time, each observation of which is made on a highly differentiated scale. Galton used measures such as reaction time to different kinds of stimuli, various measures of strength and perceptual acuity, and so on, in his investigations of human capacities (Galton, 1885; see also Johnson, McClearn, Yuen, Nagoshi, Ahern, & Cole, 1985). Most of Galton's measures had a very low cognitive loading, but yielded data on highly differentiated quantitative scales.

We use the term *Spearmanian measures,* on the other hand, to refer to the types of items typically found on psychometric tests of ability. Each such item usually has only one correct answer and is scored in dichotomous fashion. A highly quantitative scale, allowing precise representation of individual differences, is obtainable only by summing across a large number of dichotomously-scored items. Because such items tend to have some cognitive loading, the summary score across a collection of items tends to predict important educational and academic criteria, such as success in school, quite well. Several historically important attempts to correlate performance on Galtonian measures with performance on Spearmanian measures led to notable, but disappointing results (Sharp, 1898–99; Wissler, 1901). However, more recent work (Jensen 1982, 1985, 1986; Vernon, 1985) has reported consistent, theoretically interesting patterns of correlation between the two types of measures.

In this chapter, we will first outline several major approaches to the study of intelligence, placing special emphasis on work done in the tradition of Spearman and Galton. Second, we will outline the major reaction time paradigms that have been used in correlational studies with psychometric measures of *g,* and summarize conclusions that we feel can be drawn from the relevant literature. In reviewing these paradigms, we will stress critical issues involved in the search for explanations of the relationships between Galtonian and Spearmanian measures. Third, we will present recent data from our laboratory that address several issues regarding observed correlations between measures of intelligence and reaction time, concentrating on the Hick paradigm. Fourth, and lastly, we will offer some suggestions for research that we feel will be useful for further exploration of the practical and theoretical meaning of the relationships between Spearmanian and Galtonian measures.

APPROACHES TO THE STUDY OF INTELLIGENCE

Ecological

The ecological approach to the study of intelligence is set within the framework of the naturalistic study of human behavior. Adherents of this approach are critical of the classical psychometric perspective, which assumes that intelligence is a trait possessed to a greater or lesser extent by individuals and measurable in controlled and standardized assessment situations. The study of limited relationships among test items that seem to have only peripheral usefulness in advancing our understanding of how intelligence develops and is manifested in everyday life situations is seen as potentially misleading, providing little information concerning how individuals interact with and adapt to their environments (Berry, 1980; Charlesworth, 1979).

The belief that the organism actively constructs its world is a fundamental epistemological assumption underlying theory and research guiding the ecological approach to the study of the development of intelligence (Elkind, 1981; Reese & Overton, 1970; Overton, 1984). The epistemological implication of constructivism is the conception that knowledge, and its correlate, intelligence, are created through interactions of the individual with his or her environment. Such individual–environment interactions begin with the activity of the individual, activity that is the sole avenue for the development of mental structures that are functionally more adaptive to the environment and its demands than previous forms of mental organization. The ecological research agenda are motivated by the attempt to assess the content of thought and the function of thought for individuals in their day-to-day interactions with their world. The preceding research agenda imply a larger sphere of research and theory than do approaches which attempt to measure single or multiple traits. They call for measurement approaches that include naturalistic observation as well as the adaptation of measurement techniques that take into account specific factors of the groups or individuals being tested. If insufficient care is taken to assess the person's fit to his or her environment, assessed performance levels may be quite unrepresentative of the cognitive competence of the individual or the group. Exemplary studies within the ecological approach are the work by cross-cultural psychologists such as Cole and Scribner (1974), Berry (1985), and Dasen (1985). Also stressing the need to ensure representativeness of assessed performance, and hence also within the ecological approach, are researchers, such as Day, French, and Hall (1985), Carlson and Wiedl (1980), and Arbitman-Smith, Haywood, and Bransford (1984), who apply dynamic assessment techniques to the study of individual and group differences.

Although the ecological approach involves both theory and method that appear to be at odds with the traditions of the classical psychometric approach, the bases for the two approaches may be more similar than is often thought. For example, it was the work of Sir Francis Galton that gave primary impetus to the study of intelligence in the modern era. Galton, consistent with the views of his cousin Charles Darwin, was convinced that the development of intelligence was the product of evolutionary processes and that intelligence could be understood fully only if one took a perspective appreciative of the view that intelligence, and its application to life situations, has primary adaptive and survival value for the species. For Galton, intelligence can only be understood fully in the context of phylogenetic processes and developments. Furthermore, Galton's (1869) classic work on the study of the English nobility, *Hereditary Genius,* was based on quasi-observational, historical methods.

The work of Binet and Simon was also largely motivated by practical concerns: those surrounding the real, everyday problem of educating subnormal and potentially subnormal children. The pragmatic concerns surrounding the use of performance on ability measures to predict which children were likely to profit from formal, public education were of great importance to Binet and Simon. In fact, it was the prediction of school performance that laid the basis for the claims of validity that Binet gave to the concept of intelligence.

In a similar, though more encompassing manner, David Wechsler (1939, 1975), the author of the currently most widely used intelligence scales, has emphasized the importance of viewing intelligence as primarily related to practical, life-relevant concerns. Wechsler has remained consistent in his view that intellence is "the aggregate or global capacity of the individual to act purposefully, to think rationally, and to deal effectively with his environment" (Wechsler, 1939, p. 3). More recently, Wechsler (1975) has suggested that abstract problem solving and the purely intellective aspects of intelligence constitute only a part of the definition of intelligence and intelligent behavior. Although the various Wechsler scales may fall short of his guiding, global definition of intelligence, the general views concerning intelligence voiced by Wechsler are consistent with an approach that appreciates the significance of the ability of the individual to adapt to his or her environment.

Psychometric

The psychometric approach to the study of intelligence is based largely on studies utilizing correlational and factor analytic techniques. The goal of the use of these statistical methods in the study of intelligence is to analyze and account for individual differences in patterns of response to tests that are made up of items meeting certain theoretical and practical criteria. Theoretical criteria can range from perspectives holding that tests and test items should be independent of particular cultural content and universally applicable, to perspectives recommending use of items that have particular cultural relevance and salience. Approaches consistent with the former perspective are represented by a host of workers in the field of intelligence. To name only a few, these include Cattell and Horn (1978), Spearman (1923), Raven (1960), Porteus (1965), and Vernon (1962). The latter perspective is less well represented, although culturally specific tests have been developed. The tests created by Binet and Wechsler are more difficult to classify, as they appear to lie somewhere between the culture-fair test approach and the approach that attempts to incorporate specific cultural factors into test development.

Although the history of the psychometric approach can be traced back to the pioneering efforts of Galton, factor analytic theories soon became the hallmarks of the approach. Best known among the factor analytic theories are those developed by Spearman (1927), Burt (1949), Thomson (1951), Thurstone (1938), Vernon (1962, 1969), Guilford (1967), Cattell (1971), and Cattell and Horn (1978).

Spearman (1904) provided the first formal or mathematical statement of the common factor model, a model that was, however, limited to specification of a single common factor among a set of measures. The mathematical model developed by Spearman embodied a two-factor theory, as two classes of factors were hypothesized. The first class had a single member, the one general factor that was common to all tests in an analysis and, by extension, that represented the single element in common among all types of intellective activity. The second class of factors contained a theoretically infinite number of unique factors, each representing a combination of error variance as well as reliable variance specific to a given test, i.e., any particular form of intellective activity.

Rather later, Spearman (1923, 1927) provided something of comparable or greater value: a psychological theory of the cognitive bases of his two-factor theory of general intelligence. Spearman posited three processes that constituted the ways in which intelligence was exhibited: the apprehension of experience, the eduction of relations, and the eduction of correlates. The factor motivating an individual's cognitive activity was assumed to be *mental energy,* a force directed to certain "engines" or mental structures that were appropriate to the intellective task at hand. As the construct of nonspecific mental energy appeared to correspond well to the mathematically defined general factor, *g,* and the "mental engine" construct corresponded to the unique factors, the results of many analyses reported by Spearman (1927) lent credence to the hypothesis that there is a single, general factor of intelligence and that this factor perhaps has a biological and a genetic basis.

For many years, the major alternative to the two-factor theory of Spearman was the theory of primary mental abilities proposed by Thurstone and his associates (Thurstone, 1938). According to Thurstone's theory, there is a small number of functional unities or *primary factors* that reflect intellective performance in delimited domains. The several factors, while statistically correlated, were hypothesized to have functionally independent bases at both the cognitive and physiological levels.

Toward the end of their careers, Spearman and Thurstone were forced to accede to patterns of empirical data, Spearman admitting the existence of group factors and Thurstone recognizing the presence of a general factor obtained from analyzing correlations among obliquely rotated primary factors. The resulting portrait of ability structure was a hierarchy of factors, with more general factors toward the top of the hierarchy and more specific factors lower in the hierarchy. Such a hierarchy appears to fit well the models discussed by British theorists such as Burt (1949), Thomson (1951), and Vernon (1962). In the most complete presentation of the model, Vernon

(1962) had *g,* or general intelligence, at the apex of the hierarchy; two major subgeneral factors, verbal/educational (v:ed) and spatial/mechanical (k:m), immediately below *g;* and the array of narrower group factors at a lower level.

Given the general similarity of the hierarchical factor structures of human abilities presented by Vernon (1962) and others, it appears that all previous factor models of human abilities, except for the model developed by Guilford (1967), may be represented by a single hierarchy of factors. Indeed, Gustafsson (1984) claimed that a single hierarchial model well described previous research and theory on abilities and presented empirical evidence consistent with such a model. However, there are at least two considerations which are relevent before a single hierarchical model is accepted. First, Cattell (1971) predicted, on the basis of his theory of fluid and crystallized intelligence, that tests assessing types of knowledge that are explicitly taught should load on a crystallized intelligence factor regardless of the content included on the test. In line with Cattell's prediction, mechanical knowledge tests tend to load most highly on the crystallized intelligence factor, a finding replicated in many studies. This stands in contrast to the ability hierarchy presented by Vernon (1962), according to which tests of mechanical knowledge should load on the k:m subgeneral factor, a factor otherwise very similar to a fluid intelligence factor. Second, and more important for the present chapter, Cattell's theory of fluid and crystallized intelligence throws some doubt on the interpretability of a *g* factor. Since fluid and crystallized intelligence have different life span trends (Horn, 1980) as well as different heritabilities (Cattell, 1985), it is important that they be differentiated and not simply subsumed under one general rubric. Although evidence has been presented (Jenkinson, 1983) that performance for sixth grade subjects derived from several reaction time tasks correlates at about the same level of magnitude with both fluid and crystallized intelligence, it may be that different patterns of relationships would be found for subjects at different age levels.

Information Processing

There are several variants within the information processing approach to the study of intelligence, each focusing on different aspects of cognitive functioning. Two of the more general approaches are termed the cognitive correlates approach and the cognitive components approach (Pellegrino & Glaser, 1979). What they have in common is a shared paradigm of measuring rate or speed of reaction to stimuli with the aim of determining the type of mental representation or mental process central to a given type of intellectual activity. What separates the two approaches is the level of specificity of the processing models proposed. The cognitive correlates approach, on the one hand, focuses on relating performance on well-researched reaction time paradigms to performance on ability measures, such as traditional psychometric tests, without having explicit models specifying the elementary information processes involved in the reaction time tasks and the ability measures, thus failing to specify the bases of individual differences in either type of measure. The cognitive components approach, on the other hand, seeks explicitly to analyze the essential elements of complex reaction time tasks into the serial operation of a number of elementary information processes. Information processing strategies and regression weights for elementary processes are then correlated with performance on traditional individual difference measures of the same ability, to determine which parameters derived from the reaction time task account for observed individual differences on the traditional types of measures.

Since the focus of this chapter is on estimating the relationship between psychometric or Spearmanian measures of g and reaction time measures developed in the Galtonian tradition, we limit our discussion below to work done within the cognitive correlates approach. The so-called Galtonian measures we will discuss will be inspection time, evoked and event related potentials, and simple and choice reaction time. The former two approaches, inspection time and evoked and event related potentials, will be discussed only briefly. More detailed attention will be given to the simple and choice reaction time paradigm, as a great deal of attention has been given to this latter topic in current research literature.

MAJOR REACTION TIME PARADIGMS

Inspection Time

The inspection time (IT) paradigm is one in which the subject is asked to discriminate between the length of two lines of obviously different length that are presented side by side on a tachistoscope. The initial presentation duration is such that the subject is able to make the discrimination without difficulty. This is followed by decreasing the presentation duration, until the subject is brought to the level of exposure where he or she can make the discrimination with some predetermined level of accuracy (e.g., 85% or 95%). For nonretraded subjects, presentation durations ranging from 100 to 150 milliseconds (ms) are typically sufficient to allow discrimination of the length; for mildly retarded subjects, presentation durations approximately double those for the nonretarded are needed. These findings, using extreme group designs, suggest that mental age is a salient variable explaining difference in IT results. There is evidence, however, that this may not be the case, as differences in IT performance between mentally retarded and nonretarded individuals may be significantly related to differences in cognitive strategy

(Lally & Nettelbeck, 1977; Nettelbeck, 1982), and not simply differences in mental ability. Furthermore, evidence concerning the magnitude of correlation between IT and g-loaded measures is mixed. Some (e.g., Eysenck, 1983), claim very strong IT–IQ correlations, correlations of the magnitude of −.80 to −.90; others (e.g., Nettelbeck & Kirby, 1983) report correlations between IQ and IT around −.50; yet others (e.g., Vernon, 1983) have found correlations between IT and IQ to be essentially zero.

Results such as these indicate that a great deal of additional research is needed to establish (a) the magnitude of the relationship between IT and IQ, and (b) the functional nature of the IT–IQ relationship. Accordingly, caution should be used when generalizing about the usefulness of the inspection time paradigm as an index of general intellectual functioning.

Evoked and Event Related Potentials

One of the early empirical studies assessing the relationship between average evoked potential (AEP) waveform and psychometric intelligence was carried out by Ertl and Schafer (1969). Correlating latencies of the first four sequential components of the AEP with levels of performance on the Wechsler Intelligence Scale for Children and the Primary Mental Abilities Test, Ertl and Schaefer (p. 422) concluded that "evoked potentials, which reflect the time course of information processing by the brain, could be the key to understanding the biological substrate of individual differences in behavioural intelligence." The IQ–AEP correlations on which Ertl and Schafer based this conclusion ranged from .10 to .35, correlations that are surely interesting, but seemingly not of the magnitude to permit as bold a statement as was made.

An encompassing theoretical model, both positing and explaining a strong relationship between AEP and psychometric measures of g, has been put forth by A. E. and D. E. Hendrickson (Hendrickson & Hendrickson, 1980; Blinkhorn & Hendrickson, 1982; A. E. Hendrickson, 1982; D. E. Hendrickson, 1982). Assuming the common metaphor of the mind as computer, the Hendricksons suggested that differences in hardware, which can be assessed by waveforms evoked by auditory stimuli, reflect differences in biological constitution and may explain individual differences in psychometric measures of g. Central to the theorizing of the Hendricksons is what they term an R parameter, an estimate of the capacity of the brain's neuronal system for error-free synaptic transmission of impulses. The higher the value of the R parameter, the greater the efficiency of the nervous system, and the greater the probability of error-free signal transmission. These, in turn, are associated with higher levels of intelligence as well as more complex, longer AEPs.

The empirical support for the Hendrickson model comes primarily from their own work. In these studies, the AEPs were elicited by 85 decibel clicks, and the summary AEP waveform was obtained by averaging over the first 256 ms of a large number of individual evoked potentials. Using several measures of complexity of the AEP waveform, Blinkhorn and Hendrickson (1982) found a .54 correlation between AEP and IQ as assessed by the Raven Progressive Matrices, and D. E. Hendrickson found a .72 correlation between AEP and overall performance on the Wechsler Adult Intelligence Scale. Research replicating and extending the Hendrickson findings was recently reported by Haier, Robinson, Braden, and Williams (1983). In this study, Haier et al. provided evidence of correlation between AEPs and intelligence of the same general magnitude as those reported by the Hendricksons. Further, Haier et al. demonstrated that stimulus intensity affects AEP–intelligence correlations, and that that N140 and P200 portions of the AEP waveform were the primary components responsible for the AEP-IQ correlations.

Evidence consistent with these results has been recently summarized by Schafer (1985), who described previous work (Schafer; 1982, 1984) demonstrating substantial correlations between evoked potential amplitude and psychometric measures of g. In the 1982 study, Schafer presented three auditory stimulus conditions to mentally retarded and nonretarded adults. The three conditions involved presenting the stimuli (a) periodically, (b) randomly, and (c) contingent on the subject's own action. The findings indicated that the nonretarded subjects showed temporal expectancy effects; thus, when the auditory inputs were presented in the periodic or self-activation conditions, the AEPs were smaller than when the inputs were randomly presented. The data from the retarded subjects, on the other hand, indicated no such expectancy effects. Schafer concluded that the retarded individuals did not show the same level of inhibition as did the nonretarded subjects. Using data from 74 adult subjects, Schafer found a correlation of .66 (.82, corrected for attenuation) between IQ and a neural adaptibility score derived from the AEPs. These results were substantiated by a later study (Schafer, 1984) which, based on 52 subjects, revealed a correlation of .59 between level of AEP inhibition and WAIS IQ. Schafer (1985, p. 241) concluded that: "By identifying correlates of g factor intelligence outside the psychometric realm the evoked potential studies may help to elucidate the essential nature of g and hence of human intelligence."

Another approach using the evoked potential paradigm focuses more directly on individual differences in information processing elements or components. Here, problems whose solution requires specific cognitive processes are presented to the subject. Presentation of such problems elicits event-related potential waveforms that relate to specific information processing activities such as recognizing, encoding, classifying, selecting, memorizing, decision-making, etc. (Hillyard & Kutas, 1983; Kutas, McCarthy, & Donchin, 1977). The waveforms elicited are complex and represent both exogenous, stimulus-related factors, and endogenous, information-processing-related factors. The latter are usually assessed by the negative Nd wave and the positive P300 wave, both of which are observed 300 ms after stimulus presentation. The study of longer, event-related potentials stands in contrast to the study of early evoked potentials, such as used by the Hendricksons and Schafer; the latter appear to indicate level of anatomic development of the cortex and the fact that cortical pathways are functioning, while the former reflect the degree to which stimuli are processed (Parmellee & Sigman, 1983).

Related to this point, Donchin (1979) described some interesting research and theorizing concerning the relationship of speed–accuracy trade-offs in reaction time to the P300 waveform and biocybernetic systems. In one study, subjects were presented a series of male and female names on a cathode-ray tube. The subjects were asked to classify the names presented as either male or female. Two conditions were involved: (a) one in which the subjects were instructed to be certain that the classifications were correct, and (b) a second in which the subjects were asked to classify the names as quickly as possible. For the first condition, mean reaction times ranged from 536 ms for the correctly identified female names, to 632 ms for the correctly identified male names. For the second condition, the mean reaction times were 389 ms and 537 ms, respectively. The increased speeds of reaction were accompanied by increased numbers of classification errors. Of particular significance in evaluating the role of the P300 waveform as an index of cognitive functioning, gender classification errors were correlated with latency of the P300. When subjects reacted prior to the onset of the P300 wave, i.e., the reaction time for the male–female name classification was prior to the P300, the response was usually incorrect. When, on the other hand, the reaction time was slower than the onset of the P300, the subject was generally correct in the name–gender classification task. These results indicate that errors arise when speed of reaction outpaces the cognitive activity necessary for successful completion of a task and the manifestation of the P300 waveform indicates that appropriate task-related cognitive processes were engaged in by the subject.

In conclusion, it appears that interpretation of the meaning of the early waveforms observed by the Hendricksons, Schafer, and others is complicated by several factors: (a) that exogenous factors may be significantly involved in their manifestation, (b) that selective auditory attention may be an important factor in the results (Näätänen, 1982; Vanderhaeghen, 1982), and (c) that meaningful, correct results of cognition may have little to do with average evoked potentials. Nonetheless, and these caveats notwithstanding, the recent research on early evoked potentials is astounding in its implications. If the correlation between waveform and intelligence can be reliably shown to be of the magnitude reported by the Hendricksons, Schafer, and other researchers in the area, new conceptualizations of the bases of individual differences in intelligence will have to be developed.

Simple and Choice Reaction Time

The history of reaction time investigations can be traced back to the work of Donders (1969, originally published in 1868), who developed the subtractive method to estimate the time required for execution of elementary cognitive processes underlying choice reaction time. Prior to Donder's work, it was assumed that neural transmission and thinking were instantaneous. More recently, reaction time indices have been used for measuring speed of response for both simple and complex mental processes. The former is exemplified by the work of Hick (1952) and Hyman (1953), who investigated the relationship between reaction time and probabilistic uncertainties related to amount of information presented. The latter is represented by approaches that focus on separating fundamental aspects of the information processing system into component parts such as access to short-term and long-term memory. (For a detailed historical overview, the reader is referred to A. R. Jensen, 1982.)

The so-called Hick paradigm involves measuring simple and choice reaction time. Simple reaction time is assessed by measuring how long it takes a subject to lift his or her finger from a "home" button following the onset of a light located on a console directly in front of the subject. The time from onset of the light until the subject lifts his or her finger is termed the reaction time (RT). Movement time (MT) is measured by the time it takes the subject to move his or her finger from the "home" button to a button directly in front of the light that went on. Choice reaction time is measured in exactly the same way, except that the complexity of choice increases. That is, rather than one, known light that will go on, the subject is uncertain about whether one of two (one bit of information), one of four (two bits of information), or one of eight lights (three bits of information) will go on. For both simple and choice reaction time, the subject is given a variably timed warning signal, usually between 2 and 5 seconds, before the onset of one of the stimulus lights.

Carroll (1981) analyzed the simple and choice reaction time task in terms of the processing elements hypothesized to be involved in subject response. This is depicted in Figure 1. As may be noted from examination of the diagram, the task requires that respondents complete a series of independent information processing steps. These steps include attending to the warning signal and stimulus source, apprehending and encoding the stimulus, and converting the encoded stimulus into a plan to execute the action of lifting the finger from the "home" button and moving it to the appropriate button in front of the light that went on. Carroll used the term *decision time* to refer to the time the subject takes from the onset of the stimulus light to the execution of lifting the finger from the "home" button. Usually, decision time is simply

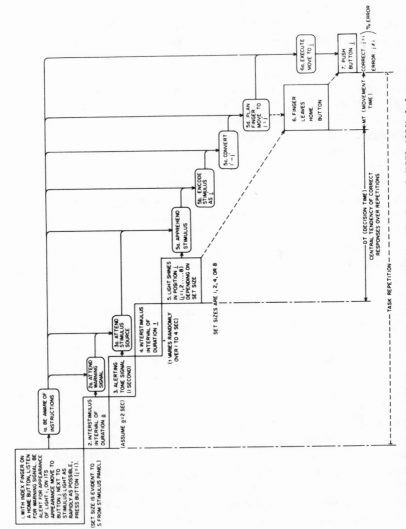

FIGURE 1. Dual time representation (DTR) chart for Jensen's (1979, 1980) choice reaction time task. (From Carroll, 1981).

referred to as reaction time. Although the diagram implies that the various attentional and information processing requirements are serially executed and independent, such may not be the case. In fact, there is strong evidence, to be discussed later, that individual differences as well as situational differences in the early part of the sequence may have pronounced effects on RT and MT performance.

A second type of choice reaction time task was developed by Sternberg (1966) to assess rate of search in short-term memory. The Sternberg paradigm involves presenting on a monitor a string of between one and seven digits, followed by a short delay, usually 2 to 5 seconds in duration, and then presentation of a digit that may or may not have been in the original display. The task for the subject is to indicate, as quickly as he or she can, whether or not the probe digit was in the original display. The time between presentation of the probe digit and the subject's response is the time taken to search the contents of short-term memory and make the requisite motoric response.

A third, classic paradigm, designed to assess speed of access to information stored in long-term memory, was developed by Posner, Boies, Eichelman, and Taylor (1969). In the so-called Posner paradigm, the subject is presented with letters that are physically the same or different (AA or AB) or semantically the same or different (Aa or Ab). The task of the subject is to indicate as quickly as possible whether subsequent paired letter presentations are physically and sematically the same or semantically the same but physically different. In order to make the response that a pair of letters is physically different but sematically the same, the subject must access semantic information stored in long-term memory; physically identical stimuli, on the other hand, require no such accessing of long-term memory, as simple perceptual comparison is all that is required to make a correct response.

The application of the general paradigms described above has, for the most part, involved study of specific information processing requirements of the tasks at the group level. More recently, there has been a significant amount of interest in research aimed at relating performance on a variety of reaction time measures, such as the Hick, Sternberg, and Posner paradigms, and variants of these, to psychometric intelligence, namely the general factor defined as Spearman's g. (Again the reader is referred to A. R. Jensen, 1982, for an historical overview.) As will be seen later in the chapter, most of this work has been directed at ascertaining the reliability and magnitude of correlations between reaction time parameters and intelligence. This is, undoubtedly, an important first step in the scientific investigation of an area. Nonetheless, it seems to us that the functional basis of the observed relationships needs to be demonstrated if the data are to be practically and theoretically meaningful. We will turn now to some of these considerations.

Different aspects of information processing, as assessed by reaction time measures, have been schematized in a general taxonomy of mental operations by Posner and McLeod (1982). The schematization, which is presented in Figure 2, has heuristic value for the purposes of this chapter, inasmuch as it may help to clarify potential theoretical and methodological issues concerning observed reaction time–psychometric *g* correlates, and, at the same time, give direction to the search for establishing the functional basis of these relationships.

Posner and McLeod posit two dimensions, specificity and dynamics, for classifying cognitive processes. Specificity refers to the degree of generality of application of a mental operation or structure; operations that are *specific* have applicability to only a rather delimited range of stimuli or problems, whereas operations that are more *general* have a much wider range of applicability. Dynamics, on the other hand, refers to distinctions that separate relatively *enduring* components, such as access to semantic knowledge, that change relatively slowly, from *temporary* components that change during execution of a task, potentially resulting in modification of performance. The four resultant types of process comprising the two-by-two classification are termed *structure, trait, strategy,* and *state.* The four types of processes are only partially independent, and may functionally interact to affect performance on a task; or, the types of processes may be impossible to separate conceptually or psychologically. For example, although strategies may be temporary and learned within a given situation, they may also be stable and enduring, constituting a fundamental, structural aspect of an individual's learned behavior repertoire. Hence, although the "strategy" and "structure" categorizations appear to be separate, they do not necessarily represent functionally or theoretically independent entities.

DYNAMICS

	ENDURING	TEMPORARY
SPECIFIC	STRUCTURE	STRATEGY
GENERAL	TRAIT	STATE

(SPECIFICITY)

FIGURE 2.   Taxonomy of Mental Operations. After Posner and McLeod, 1982.

Much of the research focused on exploring the relationships between reaction time measures derived from the Hick, Sternberg, or Posner paradigms and *g* appears to be guided by the assumption that the information processing components involved are both general and enduring, reflecting a fundamental, relatively static trait. It can be assumed that individual differences in the components assessed are substantially derived from individual differences in basic features of the neuro-anatomical system. Such a position is consistent with certain psychometrically based theories of intelligence, particularly Spearman's theory, according to which psychometric intelligence is assumed to be a trait that has its origins in neuro-anatomical structure and function. Therefore, based on Spearman's theory, individual differences in elementary information processing components and psychometric measures of *g* can be traced eventually to differences in biological make-up and function. Correlations observed between RT parameters and IQ are interpreted as evidential support for the centrality of the biological nature of intelligence.

The neurological or physiological models posited by the Hendricksons and by A. R. Jensen illustrate this point. In the Jensen model, which is shown in Figure 3, oscillations in excitatory potential are hypothesized to affect *both*

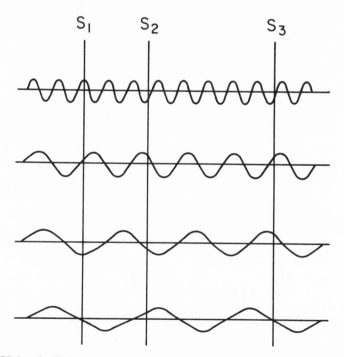

FIGURE 3.   Oscillation or waves of excitatory potential above and below threshold (horizontal lines) for excitation, showing faster and slower waves and stimuli (S_1, S_2, S_3) entering at different points in time. After Jensen (1980).

reaction time performance and general intelligence. The prime explanatory factor for individual differences in performance on RT tasks, as well as on measures of *g*, is that individual differences in frequency of oscillation naturally occur. Slow oscillations result in fewer waves above a necessary threshold level for stimulus reception and processing by the nervous system. More rapid oscillations, on the other hand, increase the probability of the individual being able to receive and respond to environmental stimuli. In short, persons who tend to have greater numbers of oscillations per unit time above the threshold level receive and can encode many more interpretable stimuli from the environment than individuals with fewer oscillations above the threshold. These individuals, on the average, should have higher levels of intelligence inasmuch as they have, over time, encoded significantly more information from their environments than those whose oscillations are slower. Individuals with faster oscillation rates, according to Jensen's theory, are also more likely to be both fast and consistent in their reaction time performance. This could occur because a person with a more rapid rate of oscillation would, on average, be more likely to have an oscillation above threshold coincident with a stimulus than would a person with a slower rate of oscillation.

Alternative models guiding both the search for and explanation of reaction time performance correlates of *g* can be drawn from the hierarchy proposed by Posner and McLeod. Such alternative models do not, in our opinion, necessarily deny the possibility that biological, neuroanatomical features may underlie and be common to both RT and IQ test performance. But, perspectives that posit an almost direct mapping of the dimensions assessed in information processing approaches onto the trait putatively assessed by *g*-loaded measures of intelligence seem to ignore the variety and complexity of factors that appear to be involved in RT performance as well as in the IQ measures themselves. For example, even though a single RT paradigm is used, it is possible that all four types of processes discussed by Posner and McLeod may be involved, affecting performance in varying ways and to varying degrees.

Using the categories of process proposed by Posner and McLeod, we will now turn to some issues involved in the search for explanations for observed relationships between Galtonian reaction time variables and parameters and Spearmanian, psychometric measures of *g*. We will rely primarily on recent data from our laboratory, focusing on data involving the Hick paradigm.

CORRELATES OF REACTION TIME PERFORMANCE

A number of investigations have been carried out using the Hick paradigm, correlating derived RT parameters, such as total median RT, median RT for 1, 2, and 3 bits of information, RT intercept and slope, and intraindividual variability in RT, with performance on g-loaded measures of intelligence. By way of a general summary of the results, the following points may be made. First, to the best of our knowledge, all of the studies have confirmed what is known as Hick's law, i.e., RT increases linearly as a function of bits of information. Of this, however, we will have more to say under Study III, which is discussed later in the chapter. Second, median RT at the various bit levels and RT intercept correlate consistently with psychometric measures of intelligence. These correlations tend to vary, but generally are only of moderate magnitude. Third, the most consistent and strongest correlate of g seems to be intraindividual variability of RT. The correlation is negative; thus, the greater the variability of RT, the lower the g performance. This correlation has been found for subnormal populations (Berkson & Baumeister, 1967), for normal populations (Jensen & Munro, 1979; Carlson & Jensen, 1982), and for gifted populations (Cohn, Carlson, & Jensen, 1985). Consistent with these findings are results which show that intraindividual variability seems to be a very salient RT variable separating IQ groups in extreme groups designs (Cohn, Carlson, & Jensen, 1985; Vernon, 1985.) Fourth, although the evidence is mixed on this point, several studies report nonsignificant correlations between RT slope and psychometric measures of g (Jensen & Munro, 1979; Carlson & Jensen, 1982; Carlson, Jensen, & Widaman, 1983).

Although correlations among Spearmanian measures of intelligence and reaction time performance on the Hick paradigm seem to be fairly consistent, the central question concerns the *meaning* of the correlations. It may be, if we once again consider the Posner and McLeod categories, that the theoretical assumption mapping a putative RT trait onto a putative psychometric g trait is essentially correct. If this were true, correlations between RT parameters and intelligence could be interpreted in a relatively straightforward manner, implicating central biological processes that affect the most general levels of information processing efficiency. On the other hand, if the theoretical assumption is incorrrect or incomplete, the contribution to individual differences made by structure, strategy, and state components will be disregarded. Further, important research aimed at understanding how these and other factors may contribute, either independently or conjointly, to RT performance itself and to the observed correlations among RT parameters and intelligence, will be ignored. In a slightly different vein, Borkowski and Maxwell (1985, p. 221) suggested that "the relationship of rate of processing to g takes on clear, unambiguous meaning only when it is contrasted with other potential correlates such as processing skills, metacognitive states, and domain-specific knowledge."

We will now turn to some of our recent data which address the role that individual differences in what Posner and McLeod term "state" play in the relationship between RT parameters and psychometric measures of g.

THE ROLE OF ATTENTION IN HICK RT PERFORMANCE

Study 1

The general hypotheses guiding the first investigation (see Carlson, Jensen, & Widaman, 1983), which we will summarize, were that factors such as arousal, orientation, and attention are involved in RT performance and explain a substantial amount of the variance in intraindividual variability in RT. We further hypothesized that variables such as attention significantly affect performance on measures such as the Raven Progressive Matrices test, perhaps the most widely used measure of Spearman's *g*, and account, to some extent, for the correlations among RT parameters, especially standard deviation of RT, and *g*. Several lines of evidence suggested the plausibility of the hypotheses. For example, work by Lansing, Schwartz, and Lindsley (1959) showed that warning signals given less than 100 ms before the test stimulus did not lead to alpha blocking, an index of cortical efficiency and arousal. Warning signals given around 400 ms prior to the test stimulus, on the other hand, did lead to alpha blocking and to faster reaction times. Accordingly, it appears that the level of arousal, affected by the elapsed time between a warning signal and presentation of the stimulus, affects RT performance in a significant way. (See Carroll's schematization in Figure 1.) Similarly implicating the role of arousal in RT performance, Sanders (1977) reported that both uncertainty of the interval between the warning signal and the task stimulus and intensity of the warning signal increase arousal and increase speed of response to a reaction time task.

Reference to Figure 1 also shows that attention deployment at the time of the stimulus may play a role in RT performance. This was empirically supported by Krupski and Boyle (1978), who showed that cardiac deceleration at the time of presentation of both the warning signal and the main stimulus correlated significantly with quicker reaction times. Kahneman (1973) reported similar results, although he used pupillary dilation as the index of attention or level of arousal.

In order to examine the relationship between attention, RT performance and *g*, data were collected on the following instruments for 105 seventh-grade children: The Hick reaction/movement time apparatus, the Raven Progressive Matrices, the California Test of Basic Skills (English and mathematics subsections), a rate of reading comprehension scale, and an attention measure. Since the attention measure is the only one probably not familiar to the reader, it will be described in some detail. The measure used was the random number generation task (RNG) developed by Evans (1978). This task was chosen because it provides an index of vigilance and attention deployment that assesses ability to concentrate on task requirements over a series of trials. After being informed what "randomness" means, the task of the subject was to generate 100 numbers randomly, using the digits 1 through 10. Each number was to follow the beat of a metronome, which occured every second. The numbers were recorded on a 10 × 10 matrix and analyzed for disproportion of sequence pairs within cells. The scores on the RNG task can range from 0.0 to 1.0, with the higher number reflecting less randomness and poorer attention deployment. Although the RNG is an unusual task, validity studies (Graham & Evans, 1977; Evans & Graham, 1980) have provided firm evidence that it is a sensitive and consistent index of attention deployment.

Table 1 reports the intercorrelations among the reaction time parameters, the ability and achievement measures, and the attention measure. The most consistent correlations among the reaction time parameters and the ability and achievement measures were for standard deviation of reaction time. Attention correlated significantly with standard deviation of reaction time and with total reaction time. RT slope did not correlate as highly with any of the ability measures or with the RNG.

In order to analyze further the relationships among the ability, achievement, and attention variables, a principal component factor analysis was performed. This resulted in two factors: "g" (Factor 1) and "attention" (Factor II). These results are displayed in Table 2.

Estimates of the strength of association among the derived factors and the information processing parameters were made by computing correlations among the "g" and "attention" factor scores and the reaction time parameter scores. The results can be seen in Table 3.

Examination of Table 3 will reveal that the standard deviation of reaction time was the only significant correlate of g, whereas both total reaction time and the standard deviation of reaction time correlated significantly with the "attention" factor. These relationships, though modest in magnitude, suggest that intraindividual variability in reaction time and speed of reaction time may be at least as closely related to attentional processes as to g. Within the context of the Posner and McLeod hierarchy, this implies that elements

TABLE 1
Intercorrelations Among RT Parameters and Correlations of RT Parameters
with Ability, Achievement, and Attention Measures

Parameter	Total RT	SD RT	Slope	Raven[1]	Reading[1]	CTBS[2]	Attention[3]
Total RT	1.00	.73**	.18	−.13	−.35**	−.16	−.17*
SD RT		1.00	.33**	−.21*	−.40**	−.20*	−.23**
Slope			1.00	−.02	−.23*	.01	.02

[1]N = 105, [2]N = 94, [3]N = 104.
*p < .05.
**p < .01.

TABLE 2
Loadings of Ability and Achievement
Variables on Factors Derived from
Principal Component Analysis

Variable	Factor I	Factor II
Raven	.68	.28
Reading	.53	−.43
Attention	−.07	.89
CTBS	.90	.01
Prof. Math	.86	−.01
Prof. English	.86	.11
Eigenvalue	3.05	1.06
Percent Variance	50.8	17.7

of what they term "state" components may be as involved in RT–g correlations as "trait" components. This was examined further in Study II.

Study II

The second study to be described is based on data gathered as part of a doctoral dissertation (Jensen, 1982). For several reasons, modifications in the design and implementation of Study I were made by (a) extending the sample to be studied to include subjects of various age groups (grade 5, N = 26; grade 9, N = 32; and a junior college group, N = 26), and (b) extending the range of tasks used to measure the variables of interest. Of the variety of measures used, those relevant to our present purposes were as follows: (a) the Hick reaction time/movement time apparatus, (b) the Raven Progressive Matrices test, (c) the Forward and Backward Digit span (FDS and BDS) subtests of the Wechsler, (d) the Random Number Generation Index (RNG), and (e) a measure of off-task glances observed between the warning signal of the reaction time measure and the presentation of the stimulus light. Since all the measures mentioned have already been described, or are likely to be fa-

TABLE 3
Correlations of RT and MT Parameters with "G"
and "Attention" Factor Scores

RT/MT Parameter	"G"	"Attention"
Total RT	−.08	.24*
SD RT	−.20*	.30**
Slope	.03	−.08

$*p < .05.$
$**p < .01.$

miliar to the reader, "glances" is the only index which will be elaborated on. In our effort to gain a fuller perspective of what we previously termed "attention," we included a measure which appears to be rather different from the RNG, yet still assesses an aspect of attentional processes. Our thinking was guided by research which showed that RT, as well as a number of other speeded measures, correlated significantly with the subjective estimates subjects gave of their susceptibility to distraction (Austin & Hemsley, 1978). Also, the number of off-task glances subjects made during the preparatory interval, i.e., the time between the warning signal and the onset of the main stimulus, correlated significantly with RT latency and variability of RT (Krupski, 1977; Krupski & Boyle, 1970).

The intercorrelations among the reaction time parameters and the ability and attention measures are shown in Table 4. Examination of the table reveals rather modest correlations, with the strongest relationships between RT and SDRT and among the ability measures (FDS, BDS, and Raven matrices). RT did not correlate significantly with any of the ability measures, although SDRT did. In addition, significant correlations were found between RNG and both RT and SDRT.

Unfortunately for the purposes of this discussion, the design of the study involved groups varying widely in age. Accordingly, chronological age (CA) was a confounding factor in the observed intercorrelations. In order to control for these confounding effects, CA was partialled out of the correlations among the ability, attention, and RT measures.

Consistent with the method of analysis used in Study I, principal component analysis with varimax rotation was performed on the ability and "attention" measures. The results, reported in Table 5, yielded two factors with eigenvalues greater than unity. Factor I, marked by the forward and backward digit span measures and the Raven matrices, was labeled g. Factor II, marked by the RNG and glances, was labeled "attention." The percentage of variance accounted for by factors I and II was 32% and 26%, respectively.

TABLE 4
Intercorrelations Among RT Parameters and Ability and
Attention Measures

	RT	SDRT	BDS	FDS	Raven	Glances	RNG
RT	—	.69	−.14	−.14	−.13	−.09	.27
SDRT		—	−.27	−.20	−.25	−.13	.25
BDS			—	.42	.33	.02	.16
FDS				—	.32	−.07	−.04
Raven					—	−.18	−.07
Glances						—	.31
RNG							—

R values > .19 significant, $p \leq .05$.

TABLE 5
Principal Component Analysis on Ability
and Attention Measures (Chronological Age
Partialled Out)

	Factor I	Factor II
BDS	.75	−.35
FDS	.76	.08
Raven	.62	−.06
Glances	.13	.72
RNG	.17	.78

The correlations of the CA-partialled RT parameters with the two factors are shown in Table 6. Inspection of this table reveals that RT does not correlate significantly with *g*, although SDRT does. Concerning the relationship between SDRT and *g*, the results are consistent with those reported in Study I. Consistency in performance on the RT task appears to be the best correlate of any of the Hick reaction time parameters with *g*, a finding that is in accord with the results of most investigations which have examined the relationship between intraindividual variability on the Hick reaction time task and performance on psychometric measures of *g*. Another result consistent with the data reported in Study I involves the positive correlation between the standard deviation of reaction time and "attention"; individuals who tend to be consistent in their RT performance tend to be higher on attention deployment (a high score on the RNG indicates poorer attention deployment) than less consistent individuals. The general conclusion stated earlier, that SDRT is as much related to attention deployment as to *g*, is given further support by these results.

Concerning total median RT, the results of Study II are again consistent with those of Study I insofar as RT correlated significantly with the "attention" factor. This implies that, in these studies, the significant zero order correlations between *g*-loaded measures of intelligence and RT may be due, at least partly, to the fact that both the RT tasks and intelligence measures require deployment of attention in order to attain high levels of performance.

TABLE 6
Correlations of Residual RT Parameters
with Factor Scores for "G" and "Attention"

	"G"	"Attention"
RT	.01	.16*
SDRT	−.17*	.20*

*Significant, $p < .01$.

Study III

The results of Studies I and II cast some doubt on the contention that the trait-like measures of psychometric g and measures derived from the Hick paradigm correlate consistently because both assess the same construct, intelligence. Rather, it appears that the most salient of the reaction time correlates of g, the standard deviation of reaction time, also is correlated with attention deployment. Recalling the discussion of Posner and McLeod (1982), it seems reasonable to suppose that the measures derived from the Hick paradigm reflect strategy or state variables as well as trait-like dimensions of individual differences.

Given the above speculation, we designed a study to determine the effect of procedural variations on Hick performance. Jensen (1985) referred to an unpublished study of practice effects on Hick performance, claiming that no significant effects had been found; this finding is consistent with the assumption that the Hick paradigm yields trait-like measures. However, the unpublished results are inconsistent with a large body of research on reaction time that documents rather predictable effects on RT as a function of practice. Research on RT has found that average RT tends to decrease as a function of practice, and that the RT effect of important structural variables tends to decrease with practice as well (Welford, 1980).

Translating these findings into the context of the Hick paradigm, we would expect to find results such as those portrayed in Figure 4. The topmost dashed line in the figure represents RT performance on the first session; the next lower line, performance on the second session; and so on. These hypothetical curves embody two major effects consistent with previous research on practice effects (Welford, 1980): (a) the intercept of the RT-bits function (i.e., performance at 0 bits) should decrease with increased practice, and (b) the slope of RT as a function of bits should decrease with increased practice.

In the vast majority of reaction time studies employing the Hick paradigm, subjects are typically presented with the 0-bit condition first, followed in order by the 1-, 2-, and 3-bit conditions. Because of this, practice and bit effects are perfectly confounded. Given this confounding, we would predict RT performance under the standard ordering of conditions to resemble that shown by the filled circles in Figure 4. Standard ordering should result in this pattern of results, because the 0-bit condition is administered to all subjects only under conditions of least practice on the task, and the 3-bit condition is administered to all subjects only when they are most practiced on the task. If, on the other hand, conditions were presented in the reversed order, starting with 3 bits and ending with 0 bits, RT performance should resemble the linear function defined by the boxes in the figure. Using the reversed order of presentation of conditions, practice and bit effects are again perfectly confounded. However, under the reversed order, practice and bit effects are perfectly in-

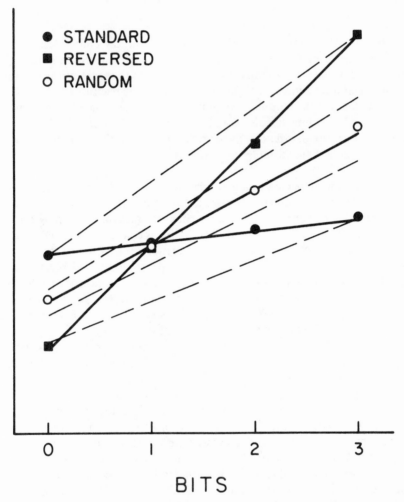

FIGURE 4. RT performance on the Hick paradigm as a function of bits, practice, and order of presentation.

versely correlated, whereas practice and bit effects are perfectly positively correlated under the standard order of presentation of conditions. Finally, a third ordering that is possible is a random ordering of conditions. Under random ordering, performance at each level of bits would be equally frequent during each session; practice and bit effects are, therefore, uncorrelated. Given random ordering of condition and estimating the relation between RT and bits across sessions would result in the linear function defined by the unfilled circles in Figure 4.

To summarize the patterns of predicted results portrayed in Figure 4, we predicted the highest RT intercept and lowest RT slope for the standard condition, the lowest RT intercept and steepest RT slope for the reversed condition, and middle range RT intercept and slope for the random condition. Similar predictions may be made regarding the effect of conditions on MT intercept and slope, except that the expected value of the MT slope is assumed to be zero, rather than some positive value as is the case for RT slope.

To test the preceding hypotheses, we randomly assigned 55 subjects to one of three orderings of conditions — standard, reversed, and random. The subjects were undergraduate students in an introductory psychology class. Each student was tested individually and received 60 trials using the Hick apparatus. Under the standard ordering, blocks of 15 trials were given in the 0-, 1-, 2-, and 3-bit conditions, respectively. Under reversed ordering, the blocks of 15 trials were presented in order, beginning with the 3-bit condition and ending with the 0-bit condition. Under random ordering, the 60 trials were broken up into 3 blocks of 20 trials; within each block of 20 trials, the subjects received five trials at each of the four levels of bits.

The results of the experiment were analyzed in two ways: as Condition × Bits repeated measures ANOVAs, using median RT and median MT at each bit as dependent variables; and as one-way ANOVAs, using Condition as the independent variable and intercept and slope for RT and MT computed for each subject as dependent variables. Because both methods of analysis provided identical patterns of findings, and because the latter analyses are easier to explain, only the results of the one-way ANOVAs will be presented here.

The results of the analysis of the RT intercept scores were clearly in line with our hypotheses. As shown in Table 7, the standard condition yielded the highest intercept, the reversed condition the lowest, and the intercept for the random condition fell between those for the other two conditions. Due to

TABLE 7
Results of ANOVAs on RT and MT Performance: Intercepts and Slopes

Dependent Variable	Condition		
	Standard (N = 19)	Random (N = 18)	Reversed (N = 18)
RT			
Intercept	420.8	408.0	403.0
	(47.4)	(29.4)	(39.7)
Slope	14.3	22.2	26.4
	(8.0)	(8.7)	(12.3)
MT			
Intercept	395.6	382.9	364.7
	(44.1)	(30.9)	(15.1)
Slope	− 4.3	− 0.1	8.3
	(9.2)	(5.2)	(9.2)

Note: Tabled values are means, with standard deviations in parentheses; all tabled values are reported in milliseconds.

rather high within-cell variability, the overall test of difference between conditions was nonsignificant, F(2,52) = 1.00. However, our a priori hypotheses were not only directional but specified a linear relation between RT intercept and condition, since the three levels of condition correspond to three equally spaced levels of practice. The linear trend of condition on RT intercept was of marginal significance, $t(52)$ = 1.40, p <. 09, one-tailed, and the quadratic trend was nonsignificant, $t(52)$ = .30, n.s. Thus, there was a distinct linear decrease in the intercept as a function of practice, a decrease that was of marginal significance.

The results of the ANOVA on the RT slope terms were also consistent with our hypotheses, as shown in Table 7. The overall effect of conditions was highly significant, $F(2,52)$ = 7.19, p < .002. Once again, there was a decided tendency for the RT slope to decrease linearly as a function of practice, $F(1,54)$ = 13.94, p < .001, and the quadratic effect of practice was nonsignificant, $F(1,54)$ = .44, n.s. As we had expected, practice effects led to a decrease in the RT slope values moving from the reversed to the random condition and, again, from the random to the standard condition.

The results of the ANOVAs on MT intercept and slope were also strongly supportive of our hypotheses. The main effect of condition on MT intercept was statistically significant, $F(1,52)$ = 8.27, p < .006, while the quadratic trend was nonsignificant, $F(1,52)$ = .09, n.s. The means for MT intercept, presented in Table 7, reveal the highest mean for the standard condition and the lowest mean for the reversed condition, as hypothesized.

Finally, with regard to MT slope, the means, presented in Table 7, again show the standard condition with the lowest slope and the reversed condition with the highest slope. The statistical significance of the difference among the three conditions was clear, $F(2,52)$ = 11.43, p < .0001. Furthermore, the linear trend of condition was very strong, $F(1,52)$ = 22.10, p < .0001, with no indication of significant deviation from linearity, $F(1,52)$ = .76, n.s.

The results of our analyses of order of administration, and therefore practice, on various indices derived from the Hick paradigm raise several issues for researchers using the paradigm to study RT—intelligence relations. A first, and most basic issue is the status of the indices of performance on the Hick paradigm. Given the effect of practice on intercept and slope estimates for both RT and MT, it is unclear whether such indices conform to the definition of trait-like measures. Perhaps after considerable practice on the Hick task, performance indexed by intercept and slope for RT and MT would be unaffected by further practice on the task. At such a point, the indices derivable from the Hick paradigm would appear to conform better to the notion of trait-like measures, but it is an open question whether such asymptotic indices would correlate higher or lower with psychometric measures of general intelligence.

A second issue that arises is that of bias in estimating parameters. Our results suggest that intercept and slope estimates for both RT and MT will be biased unless a random order of presentation is employed. As the vast majority of studies investigating RT–g relations used the standard order of presentation, the accumulated estimates from such studies regarding the correlation of Hick paradigm indices with psychometric measures of g may provide a rather biased, and possible very misleading, summary of RT–g relations.

A third, and final issue concerns the appropriateness of the indices derived from the Hick paradigm. The intercept and slope of RT and MT are obvious measures to estimate from data. However, our study demonstrated the effects of practice within a single session on such indices. Perhaps some rather different form of estimate of performance would be more predictive of psychometric g. For example, one could run subjects for one or two sessions per day across several days. From such an array of data, it would be possible to determine whether each subject had reached an asymptote in performance and, if so, how quickly the asymptote had been reached. Speed of reaching asymptote may be a better predictor of g than either initial or asymptotic intercept and slope of RT and MT. This is but one example of the attempt to specify indices of performance that may be theoretically more appropriate than the indices currently derived from the Hick paradigm.

SUMMARY AND SUGGESTIONS FOR FURTHER RESEARCH

In this chapter, we first presented several of the main approaches used in the study of intelligence. It was argued that several of the approaches have more in common than ordinarily thought. Criticisms which suggest that the psychometric tradition is devoid of ecological and adaptational significance seem to be rather one-sided. Secondly, we outlined the major Galtonian paradigms, specifically inspection time, evoked potentials, and reaction time. Several issues were discussed and caveats raised concerning relationships among parameters derived from Galtonian measures and those derived from Spearmanian measures. Thirdly, recent data were presented concerning Hick reaction time performance and the relationship between Hick parameters and g.

Several implications for research can be drawn from the considerations raised in the chapter. It appears to us that substantial research should be undertaken aimed at further exploration of the underlying dimensions involved in performance on reaction time measures. Data from several sources indicate that a variety of factors contribute to individual differences in performance. Concerning the Hick paradigm, the focus of our discussion, these involve mode of presentation, practice effects, attention, arousal, and vigilance, as well as general personality characteristics such as impulsivity and extroversion. It seems safe to surmise that similar factors are involved in performance on other reaction time paradigms. Work designed to investigate the cognitive and noncognitive dimensions involved in reaction time performance and the correlation of derived parameters with psychometric measures of intelligence should provide a most valuable information base and advance our theoretical conceptions in the area.

Another area of research which we feel important is in the area of evoked potentials. Though promising, the findings from research relating evoked potentials to general intelligence are inconclusive and should be extended. This would include exploration of the relationships among measures of psychometric intelligence, including both fluid and crystalized intelligence, and very early evoked potentials. Further, study should be undertaken to explore the relationships among later evoked potentials, i.e., beyond the 256-ms wave-form which Eysenck and others have used, and the information processing demands of several of the major reaction time tasks themselves. These would include the Hick, Sternberg, and Posner paradigms. Evidence (Buchsbaum, 1974) indicating that average evoked responses have fairly high heritabilities suggests that research along these lines would be most fruitful, potentially providing data which would help to clarify the source of individual differences in reaction time performance itself and the relationship among reaction time parameters and psychometric measures of intelligence.

REFERENCES

Arbitman-Smith, R., Haywood, H. C., & Bransford, J. D. (1984). Assessing cognitive change. In P. Brooks, R. Sperber, & C. McCauley (Eds.), *Learning and cognition in the mentally retarded.* Hillsdale, NJ: Erlbaum.

Austin, S. V., & Hemsley, D. R. (1978). Objective and subjective measures of distractibility. *Bulletin of the Psychonomic Society, 12,* 182–184.

Berkson, G., & Baumeister, A. (1967). Reaction time variability of mental defectives and normals. *American Journal of Mental Deficiency, 72,* 262–266.

Berry, J. W. (1980). Ecological analyses for cross-cultural psychology. In N. Warren (Ed.), *Studies in cross-cultural psychology, Vol. 2.* New York: Academic Press.

Berry, J. W. (1985). Towards a universal psychology of cognitive competence. In R. Diaz-Guerrero (Ed.), *Cross-cultural and national studies in social psychology.* Amsterdam, Netherlands: North Holland.

Blinkhorn, S., & Hendrickson, D. (1982). Averaged evoked responses and psychometric intelligence. *Nature, 295,* 596–597.

Borkowski, J. G. & Maxwell, S. E. (1985). Looking for Mr. Good-*g:* general intelligence and processing speed. *The Behavioral and Brain Sciences, 8,* 221–222.

Buchsbaum, M. S. (1974). Average evoked response and stimulus intensity in identical and fraternal twins. *Physiological Psychology, 2,* 265–274.

Burt, C. (1949). The structure of the mind: A review of the results of factor analysis. *British Journal of Educational Psychology, 19,* 100–111, 176–199.

Carlson, J. S., & Jensen, C. M. (1982). Reaction time, movement time, and intelligence: A replication and extension. *Intelligence, 6,* 265–274.

Carlson, J. S., Jensen, C. M., & Widaman, K. F. (1983). Reaction time, intelligence, and attention. *Intelligence, 7,* 329–344.

Carlson, J. S., & Wiedl, K. H. (1980). Applications of a dynamic testing approach in intelligence assessment: Empirical results and theoretical formulations. *Zeitschrift fuer Differentielle und Diagnostiche Psychologie, 1,* 303–318.

Carroll, J. (1981). Ability and task difficulty in cognitive psychology. *Educational Researcher, 10,* 11–21.

Cattell, R. B. (1971). *Abilities: Their structure, growth and action.* Boston: Houghton-Mifflin.

Cattell, R. B., & Horn, J. L. (1978). A check on the theory of fluid and crystallized intelligence with descriptions of new subtest designs. *Journal of Educational Measurement, 15,* 139–164.

Cattell, R. B. (1985). Intelligence and *g:* An imaginative treatment of unimaginative data. *The Behavioral and Brain Sciences, 8,* 227–228.

Charlesworth, W. R. (1979). Ethology: Understanding the other half of intelligence. In M. von Cranach, K. Foppa, W. Lepenies, & D. Ploog (Eds.), *Human ethology: Claims and limits of a new discipline.* Cambridge, England: Cambridge University Press.

Cohn, S. J., Carlson, J. S., & Jensen, A. R. (1985). Speed of information processing in academically gifted youths. *Personality and Individual Differences, 6,* 621–629.

Cole, M. & Scribner, S. (1974). *Culture and thought.* New York: Wiley.

Dasen, P. (1985). Social intelligence and technological intelligence: The divergence between two models. In R. Diaz-Guerrero (Ed.), *Cross-cultural and national studies in social psychology.* Amsterdam, Netherlands: North Holland.

Day, J. E., French, L., & Hall, L. K. (1985). Social interaction and cognitive development. In D. L. Forrest-Pressley, G. E. MacKinnon & T. G. Waller (Eds.), *Metacognition, cognition, and human performance.* New York: Academic Press.

Donchin, E. (1979). Event-related brain potentials: A tool in the study of human information processing. In H. Begleiter (Ed.), *Evoked Brain Potentials and Behavior.* New York: Plenum.

Donders, F. C. (1969). Over de snelheid van psychische processen. In W. G. Koster (Ed.), *Attention and Performance II, Acta Psychologica, 30,* 412–431.

Elkind, D. (1981). The form-trait fallacy. *Intelligence, 5,* 101–120.

Ertl, J. & Schafer, E. (1969). Brain response correlates of psychometric intelligence. *Nature, 223,* 421–422.

Evans, F. J. (1978). Monitoring attention deployment by random number generation: An index to measure subjective randomness. *Bulletin of the Psychonomic Society, 12,* 35–38.

Evans, F. J., & Graham, C. (1980). Subjective random number generation and attention deployment during acquisition and overlearning of a motor skill. *Bulletin of the Psychonomic Society, 15,* 391–394.

Eysenck, H. J. (1983). Revolution dans la theorie et la mesure de l'intelligence. *La Revue Canadienne de Psycho-Education, 12,* 3–17.

Galton, F. (1885). On the anthropometric laboratory at the late International Health Exhibition. *Journal of the Anthropological Institute, 14,* 205–219.

Galton, F. (1869). *Hereditary genius: An inquiry into its laws and consequences.* New York: Appleton.

Graham, C., & Evans, F. J. (1977). Hypnotizability and the deployment of waking attention. *Journal of Abnormal Psychology, 86,* 631–638.

Guilford, J. P. (1967). *The nature of human intelligence.* New York: McGraw-Hill.

Gustafsson, J.-E. (1984). A unifying model for the structure of human abilities. *Intelligence, 8,* 179–203.

Haier, R. J., Robinson, D. L., Braden, W. & Williams, D. (1983). Electrical potentials of the cerebral cortex and psychometric intelligence. *Personality and Individual Differences, 4,* 591–599.

Hendrickson, A. E. (1982). The biological basis of intelligence. Part I: Theory. In H. J. Eysenck (Ed.), *A model for intelligence.* New York: Springer.

Hendrickson, D. E. (1982). The biological basis of intelligence. Part II: Measurement. In H. J. Eysenck (Ed.), *A model for intelligence.* New York: Springer.

Hendrickson, D. E., & Hendrickson, A. E. (1980). The biological basis of individual differences. *Personality and Individual Differences, 1,* 3–33.

Hick, W. E. (1952). Rate of gain of information. *Quarterly Journal of Experimental Psychology, 4,* 11–26.

Hillyard, S., & Kutas, M. (1983). Electrophysiology of cognitive processing. *Annual Review of Psychology, 34,* 33–61.

Horn, J. L. (1980). Concepts of intellect in relation to learning and adult development. *Intelligence, 4,* 285–317.

Hyman, R. (1953). Stimulus information as a determinant of reaction time. *Journal of Experimental Psychology, 45,* 188–196.

Jensen, A. R. (1980). *Bias in mental testing.* New York: The Free Press.

Jensen, A. R. (1982). Reaction time and psychometric g. In H. J. Eysenck (Ed.), *A model for intelligence.* New York: Springer.

Jensen, A. R. (1985). The nature of the black-white difference on various psychometric tests: Spearman's hypothesis. *The Behavioral and Brain Sciences, 8,* 193–263.

Jensen, A. R. (1986). The g beyond factor analysis. In J. C. Conoley, J. A. Glover, & R. R. Ronning (Eds.), *The influence of cognitive psychology on testing and measurement.* Hillsdale, NJ: Erlbaum.

Jensen, A. R., & Munro, E. (1979). Reaction time, movement time, and intelligence. *Intelligence, 3,* 103–122.

Jensen, C. M. (1982). *Factors related to Hick reaction time and movement time and their effect on the relationship between reaction time or movement time and measures of cognitive ability.* Unpublished doctoral dissertation, University of California, Riverside.

Jenkinson, J. C. (1983). Is speed of information processing related to fluid or to crystallized intelligence. *Intelligence, 7,* 91–106.

Johnson, R. C. et al. (1985). Galton's data a century later. *American Psychologist, 40,* 875–982.

Kahneman, D. (1973). *Attention and effort.* Englewood Cliffs, NJ: Prentice-Hall.

Krupski, A. (1977). Attention processes: Research, theory and implications for special education. In B. Keough (Ed.), *Advances in special education I.* Greenwich, CN: JAI Press.

Krupski, A., & Boyle, P. R. (1978). An observational analysis of children's behavior during a simple reaction-time task: The role of attention. *Child Development, 49,* 340–347.

Kutas, M., McCarthy, G., & Donchin, E. (1977). Augmenting mental chronometry: The P300 as a measure of stimulus evaluation time. *Science, 197,* 792–795.

Lally, M., & Nettelbeck, T. (1977). Intelligence, reaction time and inspection time. *American Journal of Mental Deficiency, 82,* 273–281.

Lansing, R. W., Schwartz, E., & Lindsley, D. B. (1959). Reaction time and EEG activation under alerted and nonalerted conditions. *Journal of Experimental Psychology, 58,* 1–7.

Näätänen, R. (1982). Processing negativity: An evoked-potential inflection of selective attention. *Psychological Bulletin, 92,* 605–640.

Nettelbeck, T. & Kirby, J. (1983). Measures of timed performance and intelligence. *Intelligence, 7,* 39–52.

Nettelbeck, T. (1982). Inspection time: An index for Intelligence? *Quarterly Journal of Experimental Psychology, 34,* 299–312.

Overton, W. (1984). World views and their influence on psychological theory and research: Kuhn–Lakatos–Laudan. In H. Reese (Eds.), *Advances in child development and Behavior* (Vol. 18). New York: Academic Press.

Parmelee, A., & Sigman, M. (1983). Perinatal brain development and behavior. In M. M. Haith & J. J. Campos (Eds.), *Handbook of child psychology, Vol. 2. Infancy and developmental psychobiology.* New York: Wiley.

Pellegrino, J. W., & Glaser, R. (1979). Cognitive correlates and components in the analysis of individual differences. *Intelligence, 3,* 187–214.

Porteus, S. D. L. (1965). *Porteus maze test: Fifty years application.* Palo Alto, CA: Pacific Books.

Posner, M., Boies, S., Eichelman, W. & Taylor, R. (1969). Retention of visual and name codes of single letters. *Journal of Experimental Psychology, 81,* 10–15.

Posner, M., & McLeod, P. (1982). Information processing models — in search of elementary operations. *Annual Revue of Psychology, 33,* 477–514.

Raven, J. C. (1960). *Guide to the standard matrices.* Dumfries, Scotland: Grieve.

Reese, H., & Overton, W. (1970). Models of development and theories of development. In L. R. Goulet & P. Baltes (Eds.), *Life-span developmental psychology: Research and theory.* New York: Academic Press.

Sanders, A. F. (1977). Structural and functional aspects of the reaction process. In S. Dornic (Ed.), *Attention and performance VI.* Hillsdale, NJ: Erlbaum.

Schafer, E. W. P. (1982). Neural adaptability: A biological determinant of behavioral intelligence. *International Journal of Neuroscience, 17,* 183–191.

Schafer, E. W. P. (1984). Habituation of evoked cortical potential correlates with intelligence. *Psychophyisiology, 21,* 597.

Schafer, E. W. P. (1985). Neural adaptability: A biological determinant of g factor intelligence. *The Brain and Behavioral Sciences, 8,* 240–241.

Sharp, S. E. (1898–99). Individual psychology: A study of psychological method. *American Journal of Psychology, 10,* 329–391.

Spearman, C. (1904). "General intelligence" objectively determined and measured. *American Journal of Psychology, 15,* 201–293.

Spearman, C. (1923). *The nature of "intelligence" and the principles of cognition.* London: Macmillan.

Spearman, C. (1927). *The abilities of man.* New York: Macmillan.

Sternberg, S. (1966). High speed scanning in human memory. *Science, 153,* 652–654.

Thomson, G. H. (1951). *The factorial analysis of human ability* (5th edition). Boston: Houghton Mifflin.

Thurstone, L. L. (1938). Primary mental abilities. *Psychometric Monographs,* No. 1.

Vanderhaeghen, C. N. (1982). Psychobiologie de l'attention temps de reaction et potentiels evoqués. *L'Année Psychologie, 82,* 473–495.

Vernon, P. A. (1983). Speed of information processing and intelligence. *Intelligence, 7,* 53–70.

Vernon, P. A. (1985). Individual differences in general cognitive ability. In L. C. Hartlage & C. F. Telzrow (Eds.), *The neuropsychology of individual differences: A developmental perspective.* New York: Plenum.

Vernon, P. E. (1962). *The structure of human abilities.* London: Methuen.

Vernon, P. E. (1969). *Intelligence and cultural environment.* London: Methuen.

Wechsler, D. (1939). *The measurement of adult intelligence.* Baltimore, MD: Williams & Wilkins.

Wechsler, D. (1975). Intelligence defined and undefined: A realistic appraisal. *American Psychologist, 30,* 135–139.

Welford, A. T. (1980). *Reaction times.* New York: Academic Press.

Wissler, C. (1901). The correlation of mental and physical tests. *Psychological Review Monographs,* Supplement 3, No. 6.

CHAPTER 4

Individual Differences in the Hick Paradigm

Arthur R. Jensen
University of California, Berkeley

The theorem of "the indifference of the indicator," put forth by Spearman (1927, p. 197), is one of the most important and most surprising principles in differential psychology. As noted by Spearman, this principle (call it "hypothesis" if you prefer) also has practical implications for psychometric tests of general ability, or intelligence. Our working definition of intelligence is g, the most general factor (in a hierarchical factor analysis) of any large and diverse collection of cognitive tasks, or mental tests. Among persons of reasonably similar linguistic, cultural, and educational background, current standardized IQ tests afford a good, but not perfect, estimate of g. Spearman's so-called theorem of "the indifference of the indicator" of g refers to the proposition that the formal characteristics and specific information content of a task are irrelevant to the measurement of intelligence, provided only that the task is g loaded (i.e., correlated with the g factor) and that the formal characteristics and information demands of the task (referred to by Spearman as the task's "fundaments") are appropriate for the individuals tested. Spearman (1927) stated his theorem as follows:

> For the purpose of indicating the amount of g possessed by a person, any test will do just as well as any other, provided only that its correlation with g is equally high. With this proviso, the most ridiculous "stunts" will measure the self-same g as will the highest exploits of logic or flights of imagination.
>
> Another consequence of the indifference of the indicator consists in the significance that should be attached to personal estimates of "intelligence" made by teachers and others. However unlike may be the kinds of observation from

which these estimates may have been derived, still in so far as they have a sufficiently broad basis to make the influence of g dominate over that of the s's [spe-
cific factors], they will tend to measure precisely the same thing.

And here, it should be noticed, we come at last upon the secret why all the
current tests of "general intelligence" show high correlation with one another,
as also with g itself. The reason lies, not in the theories inspiring these tests
(which theories have been most confused), nor in any uniformity of construction (for this has often been wildly heterogeneous), but wholly and solely in the
above shown "indifference of the indicator." Indeed, were it worth while, tests
could be constructed which had the most grotesque appearance, and yet after
all would correlate quite well with all the others. (pp. 197–198)

A test that might be thought to have a "grotesque" apperance, as an indicator
of g, is one which measures a person's reaction time (RT) to quite simple
stimuli. The RT test is "simple" in the sense that every individual in the
sample of persons selected to be tested is fully capable of understanding the
task requirements and of performing the task correctly, after little or no practice. The only reliable individual differences in performance must derive
from the RT, or response latency, itself.

A test of the hypothesis that individual differences on such a simple test of
RT are correlated with individual differences in raw scores (number of correct answers) on conventional complex tests of intelligence, such as the
Wechsler Intelligence Scale or the Raven Progressive Matrices, which are
highly g-loaded tests, would constitute a stringent and striking test of "the indifference of the indicator." A significant correlation between RT and IQ, especially where the IQ is obtained from unspeeded tests without time pressure,
would prove that tasks requiring reasoning, "higher mental processes," or, in
Spearman's words, "the eduction of relations and correlates," although they
are good indicators of g, are not *essential* conditions for the manifestation of
individual differences in g. Reliable correlations between RT and IQ would
suggest that g is a perfectly continuous variable with respect to its loading in
various cognitive tasks. That is, there is probably no point on the whole continuum of task complexity that marks the appearance or disappearance of g.
It would seem a reasonable hypothesis that the true (i.e., disattenuated) loadings of g on *all* cognitive tasks, of whatever complexity, range continuously
from some low but nonzero value to some value approaching 1. This would
mean that some part of the variance in the g of conventional psychometric
tests of intelligence does not depend on reasoning, or problem solving, or the
other types of specific items of knowledge and skills that typically lend IQ
tests their "face validity" as assessments of intelligence. A comprehensive
theory of intelligence should account for the correlation between cognitive
tasks that are highly dissimilar in their superficial characteristics, such as vocabulary, block designs, backward digit span, and Raven's Matrices. Corre-

lations between RT and unspeeded psychometric tests pose an even greater challenge to theories of intelligence.

The hypothesis of a mental speed factor that is conceptually independent of any particular type of cognitive task, as psychometric *g* is independent of any particular kind of mental test (i.e., "the indifference of the indicator"), was first suggested by Galton. It is finally being recognized as one of the key theoretical issues in the study of intelligence. It may even be hypothesized, although it is by no means yet demonstrated, that the presumed mental speed factor and psychometric *g* both reflect one and the same basic phenomenon or theoretical construct, whatever its nature. No one could reasonably deny its virtually infinite variety of specific behavioral manifestations. Individual differences in all these various manifestations of *g* are correlated to some degree as a result of their common link to the hypothesized basic phenomenon responsible for *g*, which is presumably some as yet unknown aspect of brain function.

The terms *mental* and *cognitive* can be used interchangeably in this context. All that I intend to mean by them here is that tests or tasks described as "mental" or "cognitive" are those in which, for the population tested, a negligible part of the variance in performance is attributable to individual differences in sensory acuity or motor strength or dexterity per se.

The Hick Reaction-Time Paradigm

Simple RT is the person's response latency to the onset of a single stimulus, or signal. *Choice* RT is the response latency to any one of two or more distinct signals that may occur, each calling for a different response. It has been well established, since at least as far back as the early reaction time studies of Donders (1969), that choice RT is greater than simple RT. In proposing his "subtraction method," Donders argued that the time difference between simple and choice RT (i.e., mean choice RT *minus* mean simple RT) was a measure of the time required for the mental processes of *discrimination* and *choice decision*.

Merkel (1885) was the first RT investigator to use a fairly large number (n) of choice alternatives — 10, in fact. He measured the mean RT when the reaction stimulus was one of n alternative stimuli calling for different responses, with n (also referred to as *set size*) varying from 1 to 10. He discovered that the mean RT was a smooth, negatively accelerated increasing function of n.

A precise mathematical relationship between RT and n was first formulated by a German psychologist Blank (1934), who noted that RT increases as a linear function of the logarithm of n. (The base of the logarithm is irrelevant to this relationship, since all logarithms, to whatever base, are just linear transformations of one another.) Thus, Blank discovered the simple linear relationship

$$\triangle RT = K \log n,$$

where $\triangle RT$ is the increment in choice RT over simple RT, K is the slope constant, and n is the degrees of choice. Peculiarly, Blank has been almost completely forgotten (e.g., there is not even a single reference to him in the most comprehensive book on reaction time [Welford, 1980]), and Equation 1 has become known as *Hick's Law*.

Hick's (1952) real contribution, however, was not the discovery of a logarithmic relationship between RT and n, but the description of this relationship in terms of information theory, following the original formulations of Shannon and Weaver (1949). In information theory, the unit measure of *information,* as technically defined, is termed a *bit* (a contraction of *binary digit*). One *bit* of information is the amount of information which, when provided, reduces uncertainty by one half. In other words, a bit is a unit of information equivalent to the result of a choice between two equally probable alternatives (n). Here again is the same parameter, n, or degrees of choice. A bit, then, is the binary logarithm (i.e., the logarithm to the base 2, or $\log_2$) of n. Hick (1952) refers to the "rate of gain of information" with increasing degrees of choice in this technical sense of "information" borrowed from information theory. Hence Hick's Law is actually just a special expression of the general logarithmic relationship noted by Blank (Equation 1). Hick's Law is best thought of as follows:

$$\triangle RT = K \log_2 n.$$

This does not differ from Equation 1, except for specifying the base of the logarithm, which, in effect, scales the values of n in terms of bits of information. This formulation of a binary aspect in choice RT has certain implications for a model of the process by which RT increases as a function of degrees of choice, which is discussed in Hick's now famous paper.

A minor modification of Equation 2 was also proposed by Hick to take account of the subject's additional uncertainty about just *when* any one of the n reaction stimuli would occur. He assumed simply that this degree of uncertainty as to the exact moment of stimulus onset was equivalent to the degree of uncertainty of adding one more choice alternative, and hence modified Equation 2 as follows:

$$\triangle RT = K \log_2 (n + 1).$$

Hick reported that this formula fit the then available data slightly better than the simpler formula of Equation 2.

Hick's Law is also referred to occasionally as the Hick-Hyman Law, because of the further investigation of it by Hyman (1953), who measured the effects of differing probabilities of each of the n signals. Hyman found no need for the $+1$ added to n in Hick's modified formula (Equation 3), and, for the condition of equal probability of occurrence of each of the n signals and error-free performance, proposed the following formula:

$$CRT = SRT + K \log n,$$

where CRT is choice reaction time, SRT is simple RT (i.e., $n = 1$), and K and n are as previously defined. K, therefore, represents the constant increment in RT as a logarithmic function of n. This formulation fits existing data quite well. (The particular base of the logarithm, of course, does not affect the fit in the least, but there are other advantages to using $\log_2$, in terms of information theory models of neural models based on the binary all-or-none law of nerve cell discharge.) Because the measurement of RT for any value of n is liable to some degree of error, as are any physical measurements, and simple RT (i.e., $n = 1$) is no exception, a more accurate fit to the data is provided by the following:

$$RT = a + b \log_2 n,$$

where a is the *intercept* and b is the *slope* of the regression of RT on $\log_2 n$. The regression equation, of course, provides the best possible fit of the RT data points to a straight line increasing function of $\log_2 n$. The *intercept, a,* is usually interpreted a representing the best estimate of the total time required for the processes of attention and sensory registration of the reaction stimulus (RS), transmission of the signal to the brain via the afferent nerves, central reception or encoding of the RS, transmission via the efferent nerves of the impulse to respond, and muscle lag in response execution. The *slope, b,* is interpreted as the amount of time required for the central processes of discrimination and choice. Because the length of time increases at a constant rate as a function of $\log_2 n$, the slope parameter b can be termed the *binary processing time.* Figure 1 shows the fit of Equation 5 to the mean RTs obtained by Merkel (1885) for 1, 2 . . . 10 values of n. Although Merkel obtained his RT data 50 years before anyone had discovered the linear relationship to the logarithm of n, his data, as can be clearly seen in Figure 1, fit the linear function to a remarkable degree. The goodness of fit for Merkel's data is indicated by the linear correlation (Pearson r) of $+.995$ between RT and the logarithm of n. This generic phenomenon of the fit of choice RTs to a linear function of the logarithm of the number of equally probable choice alternatives has come to be more generally referred to as Hick's Law.

Hick's Law and intelligence. This phenomenon has become of interest to differential psychologists mainly as the result of an experiment by Roth (1964) published in an obscure German psychological journal and first brought to the attention of British and American psychologists by Eysenck (1967). Roth reported a correlation of -0.39 between the *slope* of the regres-

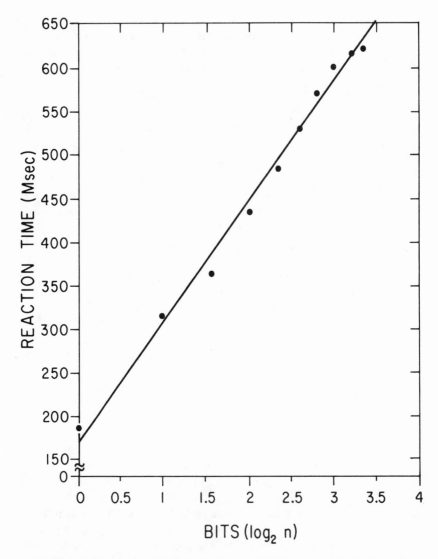

FIGURE 1. Mean RTs to stimulus arrays conveying various amounts of information scaled in bits; *n* is the number of choice alternatives. (Data from Merkel, 1885, as reported by Woodworth & Schlosberg, 1956, p. 33.).

sion of RT on $\log_2 n$, or bits, and a psychometric measure of general intelligence. That is, the more intelligent subjects showed a lower rate of increase in RT with increasing bits of information than the less intelligent subjects. Moreover, Roth found no significant correlation between the RT *intercept* and intelligence. These findings suggested that individual differences in intelliligence might be conceived of essentially in terms of differences in the *rate* of information processing. An individual's *rate* of information processing could be simply quantified as $1/b$, that is, the reciprocal of the slope, b, in Equation 5, expressed as bits per unit of time. Individual differences in rate of information processing, even amounting to only a few milliseconds per bit of information, as measured in the multiple-choice RT procedure, could presumably have considerable consequences when multiplied by months or years of individuals' exposure to all the information offered by the environment. The resulting differences could account, at least in part, for the relatively large differences observed between individuals in general knowledge, vocabulary, and the many other developed cognitive skills assessed by IQ tests. Such far-reaching implications of the RT–IQ correlation were presaged by Peak and Boring (1926) on the basis of much earlier investigations of the relation of RT to psychometric intelligence:

> If the relation of intelligence (as the tests have tested it) to reaction time of any sort can finally be established, great consequences, both practical and scientific, would follow. (p. 93)

Hence, Roth's findings with the Hick paradigm clearly merited further investigation. This was where my own research on RT began. The purpose of the present chapter is to summarize the main results of the many studies of the Hick paradigm conducted in my laboratory, in addition to the most directly comparable studies by other researchers who have used apparatus and procedures that are highly similar to mine. Only studies expressly concerned with individual differences in RT and their relation to psychometric g are considered here. The experimental psychology of the Hick phenomenon per se is not of primary interest in the present treatment. That topic has been quite thoroughly surveyed elsewhere (e.g., Kirby, 1980; Smith, 1980; Teichner & Krebs, 1974; Welford, 1980).

Measurement of Parameters of the Hick Paradigm

The linear relationship of RT to log n has been demonstrated with a variety of apparatuses and procedures that differ in almost every imaginable way except that they all yield measurements of RT under varying degrees of choice. For the studies conducted in my laboratory, I have devised a quite simple apparatus. By now, to my knowledge, it has been replicated in its essential features in at least ten other laboratories, in America, Britain, and Australia.

An important feature of this apparatus, a feature seldom found in earlier studies of choice RT, is the separation of RT and *movement time* (MT). This is made possible by the use of a "home" button, which the subject holds down with the index finger of his preferred hand until the onset of the *reaction stim-*

ulus (RS), whereupon the subject releases the home button and moves his or her finger to press the button closest to the RS. RT is defined as the time interval between onset of the RS and the subject's releasing the home button. MT is the interval between the release of the home button and depressing the button which terminates the RS.

The subject's response console of the apparatus for measuring RT and MT is shown in Figure 2. It consists of a panel, 13 in × 17 in, painted flat black, and tilted at a 30° angle. At the lower center of the panel is a red pushbutton, 1/2 in in diameter — the "home" button. Arranged in a semicircle about the "home" button are eight red pushbuttons, all equidistant (6 in) from the home button. Half an inch above each button (except the home button) is a 1/2 in faceted green light. Different flat black overlays can be fastened over the console so as to expose arrays having different numbers of light/button alternatives (i.e., the *n* of the Hick paradigm). Typically, we have used set

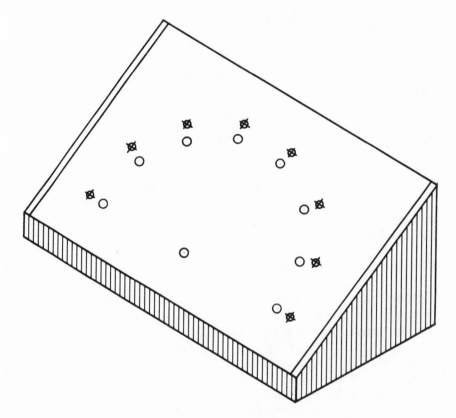

FIGURE 2. Subject's response console of the RT-MT apparatus. Pushbuttons indicated by circles, green jeweled lights by crossed circles. The "home" button is in the lower center, 6 in. from each response button.

sizes of 1, 2, 4, and 8 light/buttons, corresponding to 0, 1, 2, and 3 bits of information in the technical sense.

The preliminary instructions to the subject in most studies begins with all eight buttons exposed and the experimenter explaining the aim and procedure of the study. Subjects are told that the apparatus measures their speed of reaction and that we are investigating the theory that RT is related to IQ, or general intelligence. Subjects are told to respond as quickly as possible without making errors, the aim being to turn out the light as quickly as they can. There is no mention of the distinction between RT and MT. Subjects are given several practice trials on the 8-button condition to familiarize them with the task. Then the first overlay is put on the console, exposing only one light/button, and routinely five practice trials are given, or, if necessary, as many more trials as seem needed for the subject to fully understand the task. Before beginning the test trials, subjects are routinely asked if they feel confident with the task and are ready to do their best. So far in our experience, only severely retarded subjects, with IQs below 50, have required anything more than these standard preliminaries. With retarded persons, and probably with young children, it is often necessary for the experimenter to demonstrate the required performance until the subject "catches on."

The number of trials at each set size has been 15 in most studies, but 20 and 30 trials have also been used. In some studies, the whole test has been repeated on two or more different days. A single trial consists of the subject's placing his or her index finger on the home button. Within 1 to 2 seconds, an auditory warning signal is sounded (a "beep" of 1 sec duration), followed, after a random interval of from 1 to 4 sec, by one of the green lights going "on." As quickly thereafter as he or she can, the subject lifts his finger from the home button and moves 6 in to touch the microswitch pushbutton directly below the light, which thereupon goes "off." RT and MT are registered in milliseconds by two electronic timers with an accuracy of within ± 1 msec. In more recent studies, the response console has been interfaced with a computer (IBM-PC), and all RTs and MTs are automaticaly recorded on diskettes. The entire sequence of test trials is programmed and controlled by the computer.

In all studies so far, set sizes have been presented in ascending order, i.e., 1, 2, 4, and 8. Imagine the light/button pairs in Figure 2 numbered 1 to 8, going from left to right. Then the light/button pairs exposed by the overlays for each set size are as follows:

Set Size (n)	Light/Button Position
1	5
2	4, 5
4	3, 4, 5, 6
6	2, 3, 4, 5, 6, 7
8	All positions

The position of the light that goes "on" in any given trial is random, with the constraint that each light goes "on" an approximately equal number of trials within the limits of ± 1 trial. In a given study, every subject receives the same "random" order of light positions. Our aim has not been to study the effects of experimentally manipulating task conditions, but to measure individual differences under uniform conditions for all subjects.

The apparatus is so constructed as to make anticipatory responses impossible. That is, if the subject's finger leaves the home button before the onset of the light, the light does not go "on," nothing is recorded, and the trial cycle must begin again. Since RTs of less than 150 msec are virtually impossible, due to a physiological limit, RTs of less than 150 msec are discarded as "outliers." Outliers at the other extreme have been eliminated by one of two criteria in various studies. RTs or MTs greater than 999 msec are discarded and that particular trial is repeated, but not until all the remaining trials have been completed. The other criterion for outliers is RTs (or MTs) that fall more than 3 SDs above the subject's own mean RT. We have found that these methods for Winsorizing the distribution of each subject's RTs make a negligible difference when the *median* of RT over trials is used to represent the subjects average RT for a given set size. Because the distribution of single-trial RTs for a given subject is always skewed to the right (i.e., toward longer RTs), its arithmetic mean is not as good a measure of central tendency as the median, which is relatively insensitive to extreme values or outliers. For this reason, too, the median has generally been found to have higher split-half and retest reliabilities than the mean. Another advantage of the median over the mean is that the mean RT over trials tends to reflect the standard deviation of RT over trials (symbolized $RT\sigma_i$), which is another parameter of theoretical interest. Because there is a physiological limit to the speed of reaction, RTs for a given subject vary more *above* the subject's median RT than below it. Variations of RT in the upward direction, that is, *above* the median, increase both the standard deviation and the mean, causing these variables to be correlated to some degree through confounding. The median, however, is not nearly so confounded with the trial-to-trial variation in RT as is the mean. The same conditions also pertain to MT. A more comprehensive exposition of chronometric techniques for the study of individual differences has been presented elsewhere (Jensen, 1985).

Variables Derived from the Hick Paradigm

The main variables that we have derived from the Hick paradigm, as represented by the RT-MT apparatus described previously, are listed in Table 1. Each of the variables listed in Table 1 is derived from the RT or MT data obtained on an individual subject. Some, but not all, of these variables have been extracted from the raw RT and MT data in any given study. At present,

TABLE 1
Parameters of the Hick Paradigm for Individuals

Variable	Description	Symbol
Reaction Time Variables		
Median RT	Median RT over all trials for a given number of bits, indicated by the subscript.	RT_0, RT_1, RT_2, RT_3
Mean Median RT	Mean of all the median RTs obtained at each number of bits.	$RT\bar{X}$
Intraindividual Variability	The average standard deviation (*SD*) of RTs over trials at each number of bits.[a]	$RT\sigma_i$
Intercept of RT	Intercept of the regression of median RTs on bits.	RT Int. or RTa
Slope of RT	Slope of the regression of median RT on bits.	RT Slope or RTb
Movement Time Variables[b]		
Median MT	Median MT over all trials for a given number of bits, indicated by the subscript.	MT_0, MT_1, MT_2, MT_3
Mean Median MT	Mean of all the median MTs obtained at each number of bits.	$MT\bar{X}$
Intraindividual Variability	The average *SD* of the MTs at each number of bits.[a]	$MT\sigma_i$

[a]The proper average of the *SD*s is the square root of the mean squared *SD*s at each number of bits. In most studies the distribution of an individual's RTs and MTs are Winsorized to eliminate outliers before calculating medians, means, or standard deviations. For normal subjects, RTs and MTs falling outside the range of 170 to 999 msec, or falling outside the range of $\pm 3\sigma$ of the individual's mean RT (or MT) are discarded.

[b]The *intercept* and *slope* are not ordinarily computed for MT, as it has been found that the MT intercept does not differ reliably from the mean median MT, and the slope does not differ reliably from 0, either for individuals or for groups.

it would be much too costly in time and effort to justify the slight gain in information that might result from a reanalysis of all of the original raw data from past studies, just for the sake of being able to include the computation of every variable we have ever looked at from every set of data that we have ever obtained. Instead, I will survey the available evidence in the manner that has become known as meta-analysis, which uses as its data base only the particular statistics that have already been computed in any past study.

Descriptions and Identifying Sample Identification Numbers (SID) of 33 Study Samples

To facilitate the presentation of statistics on various Hick parameters derived from a pool of 33 studies, each study will henceforth be identified by a sample identification number (SID). The SID numbers are used henceforth in all tables and the text to identify each of the 33 samples for which Hick data were available.

Only three criteria jointly determined the selection of the studies in this review: (a) the study involves parameters of the Hick paradigm; (b) the apparatus and procedures for measuring the Hick variables do not differ essentially from the RT-MT apparatus described previously, in which RT and MT are always measured separately; and (c) the study's primary focus is individual or group differences in the Hick parameters and their relationship to conventional psychometric assessments of ability. Some of the studies have not appeared previously in the literature and some of the statistics from studies that have been referenced in the literature are presented here for the first time. Not every possible type of analysis of the RT-MT data and not every Hick parameter was relevant to the particular hypotheses under consideration in any given past study, and therefore they have not previously had an appropriate occasion for presentation, which is provided by the present comprehensive review and meta-analysis. The 33 independent study samples, comprising a total of 2317 subjects, are identified in Table 2. Unless specified otherwise, subjects were given 15 trials on each set size.

TABLE 2
Description of 33 Study Samples (Identified by SID Numbers) Used in RT-MT
Studies of the Hick Paradigm

SID No.	N	Study Sample	Reference
1*	50	Univ. undergrads.	Jensen (1979)[a]
2*	25	Univ. undergrads.	Jensen (1982a,b)
3*	100	Univ. undergrads. Test-retest on different days. Results based on composite of Day 1 + Day 2 data	Jensen lab.[b]
4*	50	Univ. undergrads. — Males	Jensen lab.
5*	50	Univ. undergrads. — Females	Jensen lab.
6*	57	Univ. undergrads. — Males	Jensen (1982a)
7*	48	Univ. undergrads. — Females	Jensen (1982a)
8*	10	Univ. undergrads. tested 15 trials on set sizes 1, 2, 4, 8 on each of 9 days, 1 or 2 days apart	Jensen (1979)
9	48	Univ. undergrads. tested on *new* RT-MT apparatus	Jensen lab.[c]
10*	100	Univ. students (35 male, 65 female)	Vernon (1981a, 1983)
11*	50	Univ. students	Paul (1984)
12*	119	Vocational college freshmen — white males	Jensen (in press)[d]
13*	99	Vocational college freshmen — black males	Jensen (in press)
14*	56	Vocational college — white males	Vernon & Jensen[d] (1984)
15*	50	Vocational college — black males	Vernon & Jensen (1984)
16*	39	9th grade girls (mean age 14.7 yrs.) in upper-middle SES school. 30 trials at each set size: 1, 2, 4, 6, 8	Jensen & Munro (1979)
17*	162	4th, 5th, & 6th graders (mean age 10.75 yrs., $SD = 0.93$), 76 boys, 86 girls, in upper-middle SES	Jensen (1982a)

TABLE 2 *(Continued)*

SID No.	N	Study Sample	Reference
		school. Mean IQ = 112, SD = 14. 30 trials on each set size: 1, 2, 4, 6, 8	
18*	99	High school students (mean age 16.7 yrs., SD = 1.62). Normal hearing (HC) = 37; deaf children of hearing parents (HP) = 31; deaf children of deaf parents (DP) = 31. 59 males, 40 females. 20 trials on each set size: 1, 2, 4, 8	Braden (1985)[e]
19*	60	Gifted 7th graders (mean age 13.5 yrs., SD = 1.25) enrolled in college courses in math & science; top 2 to 3% in scholastic aptitude	Cohn, Carlson, & Jensen (1985)
20*	72	Average and superior 7th graders (mean age 13.2 yrs., SD = 0.42), mean at 85th percentile in scholastic achievement on California norms	Cohn, Carlson, & Jensen (1985)
21	76	Gifted high school students (mean age 14.9 yrs., SD = 1.33). SAT and Raven Matrices scores on a par with university students who are 5 to 6 yrs. older. 15 trials on set sizes 1, 2, 4	Wade (1984)
22	20	Average 9th grade girls (mean age 14.4 yrs., SD = 0.62), middle-class school. 20 trials at set sizes 1, 2, 4, 8	Carlson & Jensen (1982)
23	105	Average 7th grade pupils (mean age 13.1 yrs., SD = 0.48), middle-class school. 25 trials at set sizes 1, 2, 4, 8	Carlson, Jensen, & Widaman (1983)
24	59	Elementary school children – white (mean age 8.3 yrs., SD = 1.45). Mean WISC-R Full Scale IQ = 123.5, SD = 11.2	Hemmelgarn & Kehle (1984)
25*	46	Mildly retarded young adults – 30 males, 16 females (mean age 20.9 yrs., SD = 2.97). Mean IQ Approximately 70	Vernon (1981b)
26*	58	Sheltered workshop unskilled manual workers (American) – 37 white, 21 nonwhite (mean age 33.6 yrs., SD = 12.8, range 18 to 72 yrs.). Mean IQ approximately 80. 20 trials on set sizes 1, 2, 4, 8	Sen, Jensen, Sen, & Arora (1983)
27*	60	Severely retarded adults, institutionalized (mean age 31.3 yrs., SD = 11.7). Stanford-Binet mean IQ = 38.53, SD = 14.41, range = 14 to 62	Jensen, Schafer, & Crinella (1981)
28*	76	Elderly volunteers – 26 males, 50 females (mean age 67.84 yrs., SD = 8.65, range 51 to 87). Physically active, no sensory-motor impairments. Mean years of education = 15.25.	Ananda (1985)
29	182	Adults – 127 males, 55 females. 41 handicapped workers (mean age 20.5 yrs., SD = 2.6; IQ = 68, SD = 10); 82 vocational college trade apprentices (mean age 17.92 yrs., SD = 1.58; IQ = 109, SD = 10); 59 univ. undergrads. (mean age 23.5 yrs., SD = 6.75; IQ = 124, SD = 7). 64 trials on set sizes 2, 4, 8	Nettelbeck & Kirby (1983)

TABLE 2 *(Continued)*

SID No.	N	Study Sample	Reference
30	40	Adults—26 males, 14 females (mean age [males] 23.92 yrs., *SD* = 4.15; [females] 26.29 yrs., *SD* = 8.30). WAIS Full Scale IQ = 105.23, *SD* = 18.99. 20 trials on set sizes 1, 2, 4, 8	Barrett, Eysenck, & Lucking (1986)
31	46	Adults—22 males, 24 females (mean age [males] 27.52 yrs., *SD* = 6.77; [females] 28.21 yrs., *SD* = 7.16). WAIS Full Scale IQ = 106.57, *SD* = 13.18. 20 trials on set sizes 1, 2, 4, 8	Barrett, Eysenck, & Lucking (1986)
32	112	Young adult male U.S. Navy trainees in electronics course. 11 trials on set sizes 1, 3, 5	Larson & Rimland (1984)[f]
33	93	College undergrads.—52 males, 41 females (18 to 22 yrs.). 11 trials on set sizes 1, 3, 5	Larson & Saccuzzo (1985)[f]

*Indicates studies performed in Jensen's laboratory with the original RT-MT apparatus first described in Jensen & Munro (1979).

[a]The university students in every study sample from No. 1 to No. 11, whose ages fall mostly between 18 and 22 years, have been found to have scores on standard norm-referenced tests that fall almost entirely above the 75th percentile of the general population. Typical samples of these university students have mean Full Scale IQs of between 120 and 125 on the Wechsler Adult Intelligence Scale (WAIS), with *SDs* of about 8; thus the IQ variance in this population is only slightly greater than one fourth of the IQ variance in the general population.

[b]Studies from Jensen's laboratory, not previously published.

[c]The *new* RT-MT console is essentialy the same as the old one (described in the text), except for one feature: the 8 stimulus lights and response buttons are one and the same, i.e., they are pushbuttons that can light up; touching the lighted button turns the light off. (Used only for SID #9). This arrangement maximizes *stimulus-response compatibility,* that is, the degree of proximity, correspondence, or similarity between the reaction stimulus and the required response to the stimulus.

[d]The vocational college students are mostly 18 to 20 years of age. Nearly all score above the 25th percentile on scholastic aptitude and intelligence tests, with an estimated average IQ of 107. Due to self-selection of students, the black-white difference is generally less than half the difference found in the general population.

[e]These three groups differ so slightly on all of the Hick parameters as to justify treating them as a single group for most analyses. Where they are treated separately, the normal group is labeled HC, the others HP and DP.

[f]This apparatus differs from Jensen's RT-MT apparatus by presenting the array of stimulus "lights" of varying set sizes on a computer monitor; response keys directly below the stimulus "lights" are located on the top row of the computer keyboard; the keyboard space bar serves as the home button. The apparatus measures RT and MT (in msec) for set sizes 1, 3, and 5.

Conformity of RT Data to Hick's Law

Does the RT-MT apparatus and procedure used in the studies under review yield data that conform to Hick's Law? This question is addressed here both in terms of the conformity of group means of RT data and the conformity of individuals' RTs to Hick's Law.

Group data. The 27 studies that present RT means for various set sizes are summarized in Table 3. The degree of fit to the linear regression of RT on bits (i.e., $\log_2 n$), or the conformity to Hick's Law, is indicated by the size of the Pearson r in the last column of Table 3. The unweighted and N-weighted means of r were obtained via Fisher's Z transformation. (The untransformed rs average .992 and .993 for the unweighted and N-weighted means, respectively.) The corresponding standard deviations are .006 and .003, for the unweighted and N-weighted mean r. The rs for the 27 data sets range between .971 and .999, with a median r of .994. The lowest r (.971) is for SID #9,

TABLE 3
Mean Median[a] RT (in msec) as a Function of Bits and Regression of RT on Bits in 27 Independent Samples (N = 1850)

SID No.	Group	N	0	1	2	3	r
1	University Students	50	278	317	335	359	.985
2	University Students	25	300	335	357	380	.993
3	University Students	100	295	326	350	374	.998
4	University Males	50	291	325	351	370	.991
5	University Females	50	300	325	350	380	.999
6	University Males	57	283	316	341	371	.999
7	University Females	48	318	358	381	406	.991
8	University Students	10	257	286	298	321	.989
9	University Students	48	282	299	315	319	.971
10	University Students	100	312	345	363	387	.993
11	University Students	50	299	333	359	379	.994
12	Vocational College Whites	119	339	—	397	430	.999
13	Vocational College Blacks	99	343	—	411	461	.995
14 + 15	Vocational College Males	106	309	347	375	399	.994
16	9th Grade Girls	39	291	333	356	390	.995
17	4th, 5th, 6th Graders	162	303	351	380	424	.996
18	High School Students	99	301	334	356	383	.997
19	Gifted 7th Graders	60	319	355	383	412	.998
20	Average 7th Graders	72	373	442	480	523	.990
21	Gifted 9th Graders	76	322	341	364	—	.999
23	Average 7th Graders	105	450	480	497	525	.995
24	Elem. Sch. Ages 6–11	59	449	494	520	545	.988
25	Retarded Adults	46	480	554	599	707	.987
26	Retarded & Borderline Adults	58	513	590	689	878	.977
28	Elderly	76	337	392	426	452	.986
30	Average Adults	40	298	317	347	380	.993
31	Average Adults	46	316	332	353	375	.997
	Unweighted Mean		332	369	397	436	.995
	N-Weighted Mean		335	373	401	439	.995

[a]This is the mean (over N individuals) of the N individuals' median RT (over t trials) at each number of bits.

which is the only one not tested with the usual apparatus. This one sample was tested with a new version of the RT-MT apparatus in which the 8 stimulus lights and pushbuttons are one and the same; that is, they are lighted pushbuttons. The maximization of S-R compatibility (defined in Table 2, footnote c) apparently causes slightly lesser conformity to Hick's Law as well as a considerably smaller slope. The slope for SID #9 is strikingly out of line from that of the other groups of university students (SID #1-8) drawn from essentially the same pool. But the intercept for SID #9 is not at all atypical.

An analysis of variance and trend analysis can be performed on the data of Table 3, in which the rows are Studies and the columns are Set Size scaled as bits. This analysis is shown in Table 4. The only two significant main effects are differences between studies in overall mean RT and the linear trend of RT on bits. The eta squared (η^2) indicates the percentage of the total variance represented in Table 3 that is attributable to each source. (Note: Individual differences are not represented in this analysis, in which the units of analysis are group means.) It is clear from the correlations in Table 3 and from the analysis of variance testing goodness of fit of RT to a linear regression on bits that there is indeed an extremely high degree of conformity of group means to Hick's Law.

Only one group on which means were available for 0, 1, 2, and 3 bits has been intentionally omitted from Table 3. This is SID #27, which consists of severely retarded institutionalized adults, whose performance was in so many ways highly atypical of all other subjects who have ever been tested (including the mildly retarded) as to warrant not averaging this atypical group with all the others. The mean median RT and MT for the severely retarded subjects are shown in Figure 3. This is also the only group ever tested that shows longer MT than RT.

In contrast, Figure 4 shows the overall unweighted and N-weighted mean RT based on the 27 samples in Table 3. The fit of the data points to the straight line is $r = .998$ for both the unweighted and N-weighted means.

TABLE 4
Analysis of Variance and Trend Analysis of RT Means in Table 3[a]

Source	df	Mean Squares	F	n^2 (× 100)
Studies (S)	23	33641.9	40.04*	79.81
Bits (B)				
Linear Component[b]	1	137246.8	163.36*	14.16
Nonlinear Component	2	233.2	.28	.05
Residual (S × B)	69	840.1		5.98

[a]SID #12, #13, and #21 were omitted to avoid empty cells in the ANOVA.
[b]The trend analysis is based on the linear regression of RT on bits.
*$p < .001$.

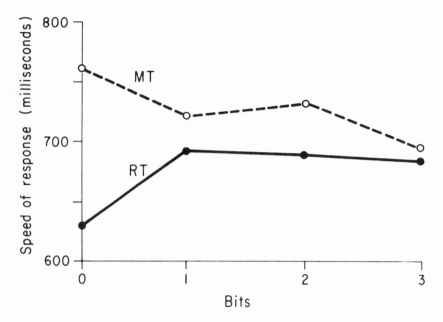

FIGURE 3. Mean median RT and MT as a function of bits, in 60 severely retarded adults (mean Stanford-Binet IQ = 39). (Data not included in Table 3.) (From Jensen, Schafer, & Crinella, 1981.)

The data of Table 3 can be used to examine the question of whether Hick's alternative formulation, RT = a + $\log_2 (n + 1)$, fits the data better than RT = a + $\log_2 n$. The regression of RT on $\log_2 (n + 1)$ was calculated for each of the 27 studies. The weighted mean index of fit, r = .993 (SD = .018), scarcely differs from the corresponding r = .995 (SD = .003) for the regression of RT on $\log_2 n$. However, the fit of the formula with n was better than that of the formula with $(n + 1)$ in 19 of the 27 studies, as compared with only six studies for which the formula with $(n + 1)$ showed the better fit. (There was equal fit [to 4 decimal places] in two studies.) The difference between 19 and 6 is significant (χ^2 = 6.76, 1 df, p < .01). Thus, the difference in fit favors the simpler formula; at least, there is no evidence of an advantage of $(n + 1)$ instead of n in the formulation of Hick's Law.

Another question we can ask of these data is whether the mean RT for set size 1 (i.e., simple RT or 0 bits, signified as RT_0) is at all out of line with the mean choice RTs at set sizes 2, 4, and 8 (i.e., 1, 2, and 3, bits). Some investigators (e.g., Nettelbeck & Kirby, 1983) have omitted a set size of 1 in their studies on the ground that there is some essential difference between simple and choice RT. Of course, the processes of discrimination and choice are not present in RT_0. But does this affect the degree of fit to Hick's Law? To find out, the regression of RT on bits was calculated in each study for 1, 2, and 3

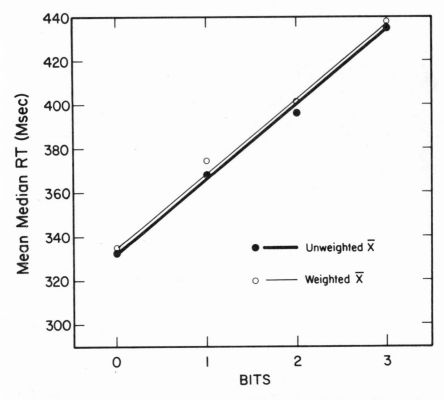

FIGURE 4. Observed conformity of RT data to Hick's law shown by the unweighted and N-weighted means of the median RT as a function of bits, based on 27 of the independent samples of Table 3 comprising a total of 1850 subjects.

bits, that is, omitting RT_0. Only 24 of the 27 studies in Table 3 are suitable for this analysis, because only three set sizes were used in three studies. Table 5 shows the effects of including or excluding RT_0 on the intercept, slope, and fit to Hick's Law (using $\log_2 n$). *It can be seen that the differences are very slight. If RT_0 were significantly out of line with Hick's Law for choice* RT, we should expect RT_0 to differ significantly from the *intercept* of the regression of RT on 1, 2, and 3 bits. This intercept should closely predict RT_0. A correlated *t* test based on these 24 studies was performed to test the significance of the difference between the *actual* mean RT_0 and the *intercept* (or *predicted* mean RT_0) based on only 1, 2, and 3 bits. The difference (of 5.3 msec) does not even approach significance ($t = 1.21$, $df = 23$). Thus, it appears that Hick's Law holds about equally for set sizes involving both simple and choice RTs as for exclusively choice RTs. For obtaining measures of the intercept and slope of RT in the Hick paradigm, there seems to be no justification for excluding RT_0.

It has also been found that Hick's Law holds even when the subject is *not*

TABLE 5
Unweighted and N-Weighted Means and Standard Deviations
(Over 24 Samples[a]) of Intercept, Slope, and Index of Fit *(r)* to
Hick's Law When RT_0 (in msec) Is Included or Excluded

Parameter	Condition RT_0	Unweighted $\bar{X}$	SD	N-Weighted $\bar{X}$	SD
Intercept	Included	333.40	65.90	336.55	62.38
	Excluded	336.75	60.82	341.10	57.94
Slope	Included	33.82	21.47	34.11	19.58
	Excluded	32.27	26.64	32.22	24.31
Fit *(r)*	Included	.994	.007	.994	.006
	Excluded	.998	.012	.998	.010

[a]SID #12, #13, and #21 are necessarily excluded because these studies
used only 3 levels of bits, which makes it meaningless to calculate the
regression parameters on only two points when RT_0 is excluded.

required to turn out the stimulus light (referred to as *single response,* as contrasted with *double response,* where the subject has to turn off the reaction stimulus after releasing the home button). All the subject has to do is lift his or her finger off the home button when one of the lights goes on. The results are shown in Figure 5. Not having to "program" the hand movement to turn out the stimulus light cuts about 30 msec off the RT, that is, the time to release the home button after onset of the reaction stimulus. The Hick phenomenon apparently reflects the degree of prior uncertainty of which signal will occur rather than the processes that determine the choice response *after* the signal has occurred.

Conformity of individuals' RT to Hick's Law. An individual's median RT (over trials for any given set size) is less erratic than the mean RT, and therefore shows greater conformity to Hick's Law. Hence, the median RT is used in all the analyses discussed here.

Hick's Law applies to individuals as well as to groups. However, there are individual differences in the degree of conformity, but whether they are reliable individual differences is not yet established.

In one set of data from my lab (SID #3), in which 100 university students were given 15 trials on 0, 1, 2, and 3 bits on each of two days, the test-retest reliability of conformity to Hick's Law was close to zero and completely nonsignificant. It is as if nonconformity on any given test occasion were merely due to momentary erracticness or flukes in the course of the subject's performance, but at present this is sheer conjecture. In the above-mentioned study, only one subject on one day showed a *negative* fit to Hick's Law, that is, a *negative* slope of RT on bits.

The greater the number of trials, in general, the closer do individuals' data fit Hick's Law. Ten subjects given 15 trials on 9 different days showed a better fit to Hick's Law for the mean RT over all days than for any single day. The flukes of nonconformity tend to average out with a larger number of

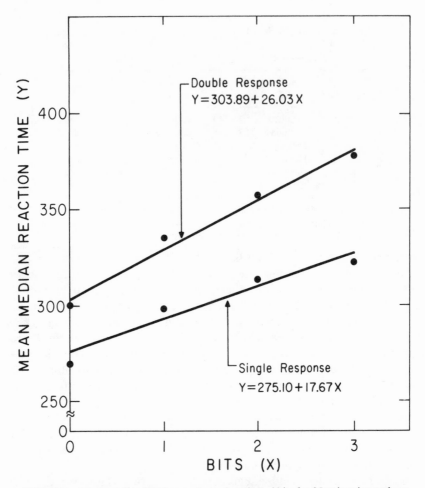

FIGURE 5.   Mean median RT (in msec) as a function of bits for 25 university students (SID #2) on RT-MT apparatus under conditions requiring (a) a differential ballistic response to the reaction stimulus (double response) and (b) simply removing index finger from the "home" button when the reaction stimulus occurs but not being required to make any movement to turn off the reaction stimulus (single response).

trials or test sessions. The present evidence does not rule out the possibility that there are no true individual differences in degree of conformity to Hick's Law, and that all individuals will increasingly conform as a function of the number of trials. Hence, varying degrees of nonconformity, rather than representing a true or lawful individual differences phenomenon, may be just a matter of the unreliability of the median RTs, which is a function of the number of measurements, or trials. Every one of the 10 subjects tested on 9 days showed a better fit to Hick's Law for the composite data over all days than for the average fit for each day. The mean fit (*r*) for single days was .934, *SD* = .036; for the composite, it was .976, *SD* = .018. A correlated *t* test shows the difference to be highly significant ($t = 5.93, df = 9, p < .001$). Since the reliability of each subject's RT at each set size is greater for the composite data than for the data on any one day, if some subjects truly were nonconformists while others were conformists to Hick's Law, we should expect a *lower* index of fit for some subjects in the most reliable composite data than in the single-day data, and we should also expect greater variance among the subjects' rs for the composite RT data than for the subjects' means of the rs on single days. However, the data show just the opposite of both of these outcomes than would be expected if there were reliable individual differences in degree of conformity to Hick's Law that are not merely attributable to unreliability of the RT measurements on any particular set size in any one test session with a limited number of trials. The variance of the index of fit (r) is significantly greater ($F[9,9] = 4.33, p < .01$) for the mean of the subjects' rs over single days than their rs based on the composite data over all days. Because there were only 10 subjects (all of them university students) in this particular study, however, the results should be viewed as only suggestive rather than conclusive. The hypothesis regarding true conformity to Hick's Law by certain individuals still remains to be rejected, if indeed it is false.

In any case, individual conformity to Hick's Law is remarkably high, in general, as indicated by the Pearson correlation of a person's median RTs with bits over set sizes. This index of fit was obtained for individuals in several studies, with the results shown in Table 6. The mean values of r are all quite high, averaging about .93. The squares of these rs, of course, represent the proportions of variance in median RTs accounted for by their linear regression on bits, which, for individuals, is about .86.

To get some idea of the "types" of nonconformity to Hick's Law that turn up in a large sample, the RT data of 225 vocational college males (SID #12 & 13, in addition to 7 other Ss whose psychometric data were incomplete in #12 & 13 and were therefore omitted in certain other analyses) have been examined in terms of the rank order of the median RTs (based on 15 trials) at 0, 2, and 3 bits. The predicted rank order of the median RTs would be 1-2-3, in accord with Hick's Law. The percentage of individuals having different rank orders of their median RTS for 0, 2, and 3 bits is as follows:

Rank Order				Percent
1	*2*	*3*	(*Predicted*)	*77.78*
1	3	2		13.33
2	1	3		4.00
2	3	1		0.89
3	1	2		0.89
3	2	1		0.89
1	2.5	2.5		2.22
1.5	1.5	3		0
				100.00

TABLE 6
Conformity of Individuals' Median RTs to Hick's Law as
Indexed by Correlation Between Median RT and Bits in
Five Independent Samples (N = 581)

			Fit (r)	
SID No.	Group	N	Mean	SD
1	Univ. students	50	.930	.099
6 + 7	Univ. students	105	.931	.112
12 + 13	Vocational college students	225	.928	.115
16	9th grade girls	39	.944	.076
17	4th, 5th, 6th graders	162	.919	.161
	Unweighted Mean		.930	.113
	N-Weighted Mean		.927	.123

The mean fit of individuals's RTs to Hick's Law for this sample is $\bar{r} = .928$, $SD = .115$.

Movement Time (MT) and Its Relation to RT

MT displays very little, if any, resemblance to RT. It would seem safe to say that Hick's Law applies exclusively to RT. This is one argument for measuring RT and MT separately rather than as a single amalgam, as has been done in many studies. Table 7 presents the mean median MTs as a function of bits in 21 studies. The *slope* of the regression of MT on bits averages only slightly more than 2 msec/bit, as compared with about 34 msec/bit for RT. There is no appreciable conformity to Hick's Law for MT, with the index of fit averaging $r = .35$ and six of the 21 studies even going counter to Hick's Law by *negative* slopes. The linear component in the trend of MT on bits, although small, is nevertheless fully significant in these data, as seen in the analysis of variance and trend analysis presented in Table 8. The eta squared (η^2), or the percentage of the total variance, shows that the linear trend of MT on bits accounts for only 0.3% of the total variance. The η^2 of Table 8 may be compared with the corresponding values for RT in Table 4 as striking evidence of the great dissimilarity between MT and RT. Figure 6 shows the N-weighted means of the MTs in 21 independent samples totalling 1573 subjects. The regression equation for the straight line in Figure 6 for MT can be compared with the corresponding equation for RT:

$$MT = 246 + 3(bits)$$
$$RT = 336 + 34(bits)$$

The fact that the RT intercept averages 90 msec greater than the MT intercept comes as a surprise to most people. In our early studies, we routinely asked

TABLE 7
Mean Median MT as a Function of Bits and Regression of MT on Bits in 21 Independent
Samples (N = 1573)

SID No.	Group	N	0	1	2	3	Int.	Slope	r
			Bits				*Regression*		
1	University Students	50	215	203	209	223	208	3.00	.453
2	University Students	25	252	234	245	258	243	2.90	.363
3	University Students	100	243	227	239	256	234	5.10	.551
4	University Males	50	233	216	226	247	223	5.20	.515
5	University Females	50	254	239	252	264	246	4.30	.540
6	University Males	57	222	203	219	218	215	0.40	.061
7	University Females	48	275	269	284	276	273	1.90	.371
9	University Students	48	207	209	213	226	205	6.10	.922
10	University Students	100	211	203	215	223	206	4.80	.744
11	University Students	50	227	214	224	243	250	−7.70	−.390
12	Vocational College Whites	119	249	—	247	250	249	−.01	−.005
13	Vocational College Blacks	99	291	—	297	295	292	1.44	.819
14 + 15	Vocational College Males	106	213	209	217	217	211	1.97	.663
16	9th Grade Girls	39	187	190	198	206	185	6.50	.983
17	4th, 5th, 6th Graders	162	203	191	196	198	195	−1.00	−.260
18	High School Students	99	178	180	190	190	178	4.60	.927
19	Gifted 7th Graders	60	245	233	243	238	241	−1.10	−.264
20	Average 7th Graders	72	328	327	350	353	325	9.80	.909
23	Average 7th Graders	105	325	323	321	325	324	−0.20	−.135
26	Retarded & Borderline Adults	58	444	426	451	447	437	3.40	.397
28	Elderly	76	321	311	318	318	317	−2.00	−.061
	Unweighted Mean		253	242	255	261	251	2.44	.386
	N-Weighted Mean		251	240	253	257	249	2.17	.351

TABLE 8
Analysis of Variance and Trend Analysis of MT Data in Table 7[a]

Source	df	Mean Squares	F	n^2 (×100)
Studies (S)	18	16254.6	486.4*	98.5
Bits (B)				
Linear Component	1	1060.8	31.7*	0.3
Nonlinear Component	2	849.4	25.4*	0.6
Residual (S × B)	54	33.4		0.6

[a]Two samples (SID #12, #13) from Table 7 did not have MTs at 4 levels of
bits, and were therefore omitted to avoid empty cells in the ANOVA.
*$p < .001$.

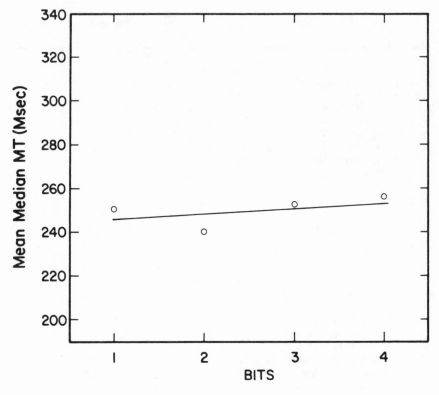

FIGURE 6. *N*-weighted mean median MT as a function of bits, based on 21 independent samples comprising a total of 1573 subjects.

subjects, after they were tested, whether they felt it took longer to get their finger off the home button (i.e., RT) or, once they released the home button, to move it 6 inches to touch the button that turns off the light (i.e., MT). Their subjective impression was that their MT was considerably greater than their RT; many, in fact, felt the RT was virtually instantaneous with the onset of the light, and they did not subjectively experience any lengthening of RT with increasing set size. Obviously, Hick's Law is not generally a consciously or subjectively experienced phenomenon.

Correlation between RT and MT within subjects. Some experimental psychologists have conjectured that some subjects may try to improve their RT and "defeat" Hick's Law to some extent by adopting the strategy of getting off the home button as soon as possible after the onset of the RS light and "hovering" briefly to make their choice decision while moving toward the button that turns out the light, thereby shifting some of the time for the decision process from RT to MT, which would have the effect of decreasing RT and increasing MT on any given trial. If this were a general strategy for any given subject, although not applied exactly equally on every trial, one should predict that the correlation (over trials) between the subject's RT and MT would become increasingly negative with increasing bits of information, that is, with increasing demands on the process of decision or choice.

To examine this strategy hypothesis, the RT and MT data of three samples (SID #6, #7, and #17), totalling 267 subjects, were correlated over trials *within* subjects for each set size. That is, for each subject on each set size a correlation (Pearson r) was obtained between the paired RTs and MTs over trials. SID #6 and #7 (57 male and 48 female university students) had 15 trials on set sizes 1, 2, 4, and 8. SID #17 (162 elementary school children in grades 4 to 6) had 30 trials on set sizes 1, 2, 4, 6, and 8. The means of the within-subject correlations between RT and MT at each set size and their *SD*s are shown in Table 9. The absence of a single correlation in the whole table that even approaches significance means that we cannot reject the hypothesis that the within-subjects correlation between RT and MT is zero.

One might argue, however, that only certain subjects adopt the strategy of shifting some part of the time for the decision process from RT to MT, and that their negative correlations between RT and MT are simply swamped and obscured by the more or less random correlations produced by the many subjects who do not adopt the strategy. If this were the case, we should expect that the subjects who have adopted the strategy and produce negative RT × MT correlations would do so with some consistency across different set sizes. That is, for a given subject, if the strategy effect showed up as a negative RT × MT correlation at one set size, there should be a greater-than-chance probability that a negative correlation would also show up at other set sizes. The consistency of negative or positive RT × MT correlations for subjects across set sizes was tested in SID #6 ($N = 57$) by means of a chi squared test on each

TABLE 9

Mean Correlation for Three Independent Samples Between RT and MT Over Trials[a] *Within* Subjects ($N = 267$)

Set Size	SID #6 (N = 57)		SID #7 (N = 48)		SID #17 (N = 162)		Grand Mean	
	Mean r	SD r	Mean r	SD r	Mean r	SD r	Mean r	SD r
1	+ .057	.330	− .033	.338	+ .008	.180	+ .011	.283
2	− .007	.330	− .015	.277	.000	.195	− .007	.267
4	− .087	.308	+ .032	.326	+ .024	.208	− .010	.281
6	−	−	−	−	− .007	.198	− .007	.198
8	− .009	.307	− .094	.269	− .037	.184	− .047	.253
Grand Mean	− .012	.319	− .027	.302	− .002	.193	− .012	.256

[a]Number of trials at each level of bits: SID #6 = 15 trials, SID #7 = 15 trials, SID #17 = 30 trials.

2×2 contingency table for the consistency of positive and negative correlations across different adjacent set sizes (n), as follows:

	$n = 2$			$n = 4$			$n = 8$	
	$-r$	$+r$		$-r$	$+r$		$-r$	$+r$
$n = 1$ $+r$	18	12	$n = 2$ $+r$	16	8	$n = 4$ $+r$	15	6
$-r$	15	12	$-r$	20	13	$-r$	20	16

$\chi^2 = 0.11$	$\chi^2 = 0.22$	$\chi^2 = 1.41$
$\phi = -.04$	$\phi = -.06$	$\phi = -.16$

None of the χ^2 (1 df) values even approaches significance at the .05 level. The phi coefficients (ϕ) may be interpreted like a correlation coefficient, showing the consistency or reliability of subjects' tendency to produce positive or negative RT × MT correlations. The average value of ϕ is a nonsignificant $-.087$. There is simply no evidence that individuals' positive and negative correlations between RT and MT at different set sizes are anything other than random fluctuation of the rs about the true correlation of zero.

The meaning of the significant and substantial *positive* correlation between *individual differences* in RT and MT (i.e., the *between*-subjects r) is discussed in a later section.

Effects of Practice on Hick Parameters and S-R Compatibility

The literature on choice RT shows that practice reduces choice RT and that the practice effect may even extend over as many as 45,000 trials (Teichner & Krebs, 1974). The degree of practice effect seems to be most affected by the degree of *stimulus–response compatibility* of the RT task. S-R compatibility varies according to the degree of spatial proximity, correspondence of order, or other physical or relational similarity between the various choice reaction stimuli and the differential responses that the subject must make to the stimuli. When the S-R compatibility is low, there is an increased effect of practice. What apparently is influenced by practice is the translation mechanism between stimulus and response, and the extent of improvability of the "translation" process is lessened as S-R compatibility is increased. As noted previously, the RT-MT apparatus used in our studies comes near to maximizing S-R compatability by (a) the use of a home button, permitting the RT response to be made for different degrees of choice without the need for response selection; and (b) the close proximity of the RS lights to the corresponding pushbuttons, which minimizes confusion as to the movement response the subject must make to turn out the light. It is probably because of these factors that the practice effects we are able to detect in our RT data are of almost negligible magnitude, at least within the typical time frame of the RT-MT test — 15 to 30 trials.

The question of practice effect, or learning, is of theoretical importance for the interpretation of the negative correlation between RT and IQ (or psychometric *g*) and the negative correlation between the slope of RT (on bits) and IQ. If IQ reflects learning ability, and subjects are improving their RT with practice at differential rates according to their learning ability, then it would be learning ability rather than mental speed per se that is mainly the basis for the RT-IQ correlation. If, on the other hand, practice effects on RT appear to be minimal, an interpretation of the RT-IQ relationship in terms of individual differences in learning ability is less tenable. Put most simply, if practice effects, dependent on learning, were prominent, the path diagram (below) on the left would seem a likely interpretation of the RT-IQ correlation, whereas, if practice effects are negligible, the diagram on the right would seem more warranted. (Arrows indicate causal relationship, curved dashed lines indicate correlation without causation.)

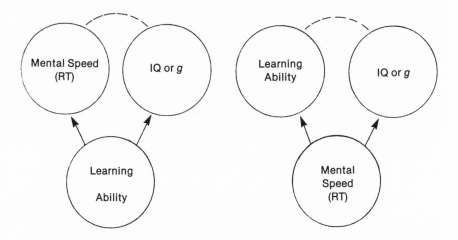

Hence, we must examine the effects of practice on the key Hick parameters derived from the same kind of RT data obtained under conditions typical of those that have been found to show a relationship between the RT parameters and IQ.

Table 10 shows the mean of the median RTs to the first three and last three of 15 trials in two studies. Also shown are the intercepts, slopes, and the *r* index of fit to Hick's Law. In both samples, the mean RTs for the first and last three trials differ only slightly and nonsignificantly, and what little difference there is actually is the opposite to what would be expected in terms of learning, or improvement with practice. The intercept and slope parameters also

TABLE 10
Means for Two Samples of Median RTs (in Msec) on the First 3 Trials Compared to the Same of the Last 3 Trials

	Bits				Intercept	Slope	r
	0	1	2	3			
SID #10 (N = 100)							
First 3 Trials	312.8 ± 8.6[a]	342.5 ± 10.3	360.4 ± 11.0	389.3 ± 10.5	314.1	24.7	.996
Last 3 Trials	315.2 ± 9.4	349.3 ± 11.8	368.3 ± 11.1	388.0 ± 10.6	319.6	23.7	.989
SID #14 + #15 (N = 106)							
First 3 Trials	309.0 ± 8.2	348.3 ± 9.1	368.3 ± 11.2	393.8 ± 9.7	313.7	27.5	.990
Last 3 Trials	313.1 ± 10.4	351.2 ± 9.8	375.4 ± 11.3	406.0 ± 12.9	316.0	30.3	.996

[a]Indicates the 95% confidence interval, i.e., $\bar{X} \pm 1.984 SE_{\bar{X}}$.

show no practice effects, and there is no appreciable effect on the degree of fit to Hick's Law.

Figure 7 (based on SID #12) shows the effects of practice on RT and MT over 30 trials. Practice effects should be approximately equal for odd- and even-numbered trials. These are shown in the left-hand panel of Figure 7. As expected, the results for odd and even trials barely differ. On the other hand, whatever practice effects occur in the course of 30 trials should be expected to show up as a difference between the means of the first set of 15 trials (i.e., trials 1–15) and the second set of 15 trials (i.e., trials 16–30). This comparison is shown in the right-hand panel of Figure 7. The results are statistically indis-

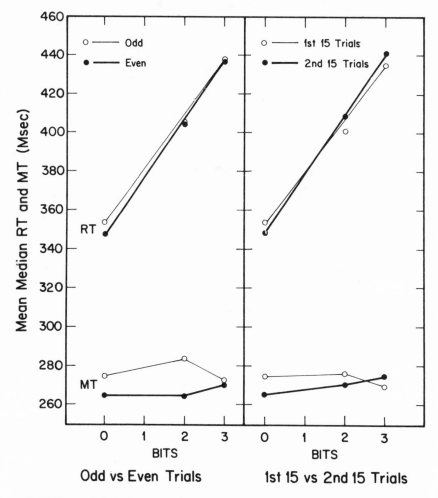

FIGURE 7.   RT and MT on odd and even trials of 30 trials (left panel) and on the first set of 15 and second set of 15 trials (right panel), based on Sample #12 ($N = 103$).

tinguishable from those in the comparison of odd and even trials. Hence, there is no evidence of a practice effect. The main Hick parameters of the RT data in Figure 7 are seen in Table 11; they also show no practice effects.

Does practice on two different days one or two days apart have an effect on RT intercept, slope, and fit? Table 12 shows the results in combined SIDs #3, #4, and #5. The RT intercept, although less by only about 6 msec on the second set of 15 trials, differs significantly at the .05 level. The difference in slope is in the theoretically unexpected direction, and is statistically negligible. Note that the Day 1 × Day 2 correlation is much higher for the intercept than for the slope; the r_{12} is an estimate of the retest reliability of these parameters. One can hardly make much of the significant 6-msec Day 1–Day 2 difference in intercepts. Another study SID #11, $N = 50$), in which subjects were also tested with 15 trials in each of two sessions on different days less than a week apart, showed nonsignificant ($t < 1$) differences on both intercept and slope. The regressions of RT on bits were as follows:

Day 1: 306.47 + 26.96(bits), $n = .989$
Day 2: 303.23 + 23.89(bits), $r = .996$

Does prolonged practice beyond two sessions on separate days produce larger effects? To find out, 10 university students (SID #8) were given 15 trials in each of nine test sessions on alternate weekdays; the testing was spread over 3 to 4 weeks. The mean intercept of the median RT on bits is plotted across days of practice in Figure 8. There is evidence of a slight but significant practice effect. An ANOVA performed on these data showed the *Days* main effect to be significant, $F(8,72) = 3.53, p < .01$. (For Subjects, $F[9,72] = 16.55, p < .001$. Eta squared [× 100] for Days is 11.33%; for Subjects, 59.77%. The average single-session reliability of individual differences in the intercept in this sample is .63; the composite data over all 9 days has an intercept reliability of .94.) The largest difference is Day 1–Day 8 ($t = 2.74, p < .05$), amounting to 29 msec. But this effect lies far outside the typical time frame of the RT data of most of the studies that have reported correlations between RT parameters and IQ. Even the difference of 12 msec between

TABLE 11
Regressions of RT on Bits and Index of Fit (r)
to Hick's Law for Conditions in Figure 7

Condition	Intercept	Slope	Fit (r)
Odd Trials	353.5	27.9	.997
Even Trials	347.5	30.1	.999
First 15 Trials	352.5	26.8	.994
Second 15 Trials	348.4	31.1	1.000
Mean	350.5	29.0	.998

TABLE 12
Mean Intercept and Slope of Regression of RT on
Bits (0, 1, 2, 3) in Sessions of 15 Trials Each on
Two Days (N = 200)

Occasion	Intercept	Slope	Fit (r)
Day 1	300.2 ± 4.7[a]	25.6 ± 1.5	.998
Day 2	294.3 ± 4.3	26.6 ± 1.4	.980
Correlation, r_{12}	+.721	+.341	

[a]Indicates 95% confidence interval, i.e., $\bar{X} \pm 1.96 SE_{\bar{X}}$.

Days 1 and 2 is nonsignificant at the .05 level by a 1-tailed test (correlated t = 1.55). The significance of the Days effect shown by the ANOVA is attributable entirely to the difference between the means of the first 2 days and the mean of the last 7 days; there are no significant differences within each of these two sets. The average linear decrement in RT intercept over all 9 days of practice is only 2 msec per day.

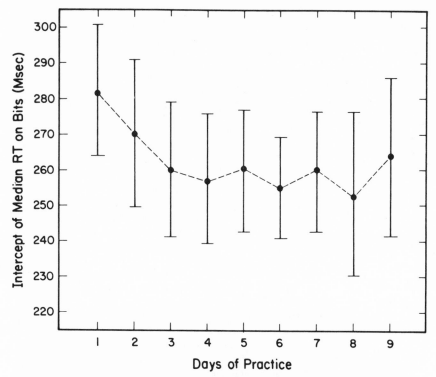

FIGURE 8.   Intercept of the regression of median RT on bits over 9 days of practice by 10 subjects. The vertical lines indicate the 95% confidence intervals, with 9 df (i.e., X ± 2.262$SE_{\bar{X}}$).

Figure 9 shows the mean slope of the regression of RT on bits across 9 days of practice. Again, the difference between the first 2 days is nonsignificant (correlated $t = 1.45$), but the overall differences across all 9 days are significant, $F(8,72) = 2.21, p < .05$. The average linear decrement in slope across all 9 days of practice amounts to only 0.45 msec per day. (Eta squared [×100] for Days is 13.87%; for Subjects, 29.63%. The average single-session reliability of individual differences in the slope measure in this sample is only .26; the composite data over all 9 days has a slope reliability of .76.)

All of these data point to the conclusion that practice effects on RT are nil with the present apparatus and procedure, at least within the number of trials used in the studies of the relation of RT parameters to IQ. Since practice effects across trials within each set size are nil, it is so highly improbable that practice effects would transfer across set sizes that, so far, we have not per-

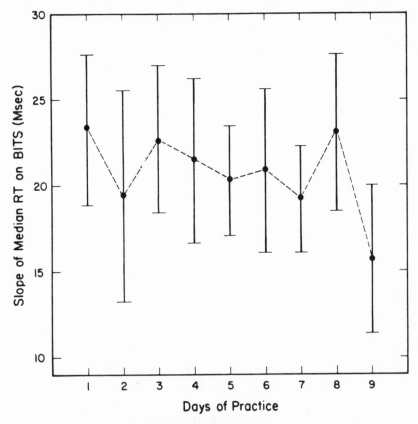

FIGURE 9.   Slope of the regression of median RT on bits over 9 days of practice by 10 subjects. The vertical lines indicate the 95% confidence intervals.

formed a direct experimental test for such an effect by varying the order of administering the different set sizes. It is desirable in any one study of individual differences to maintain uniform conditions of testing for all subjects, and it has not seemed worth sacrificing this advantage to test the exceedingly small probability that there is greater positive transfer of practice *between* sets than *within* sets. There is no theory or rationale that would predict this unlikely possibility. Moreover, positive transfer between sets would have the effect of distorting the fit of the RT data to Hick's Law, making the increase in RT as a function of bits a negatively accelerated function rather than the perfectly linear function that is actually found.

Effects of Position-Response Preferences on RT

Some relatively small part (averaging about 30 msec for university students) of a person's total RT on any given trial appears to be attributable to the time required to program the ballistic movement response prior to the subject's removing his or her finger from the home button. If there are differential preferences or response tendencies for different light/button positions, this variable increment in RT attributable to programming the movement response would constitute a part of the subject's error variance. However, since there are 15 or more trials at each set size and every light/button position is targeted an equal number of trials (± 1), these variable increments in RT would tend to average out with an increasing number of trials. Therefore, they should constitute no real problem for the measurement of individual differences in RT. Any such response biases, if they in fact exist and affect RT, would most likely attenuate correlations between RT and IQ.

To determine if there are any general or average position biases, the mean RT has been determined for each of the eight light/button positions for a total of 309 vocational college men (combined Samples #12, #14, #15). The results are shown in Figure 10. Although there is no clearly discernible pattern, and the largest difference is only 20 msec, the differences overall are significant with such a large sample. The percentage of the total variance (eta squared) accounted for by the main effect of Positions is only 1%. Eta squared for Subjects (i.e., individual differences in overall mean RT on set size 8) is 80%. The eta squared for the Subjects $\times$ Positions interaction is 19%. This variance due to individual position biases is largely averaged out in the mean, since the various positions of the RS occur with nearly equal frequency. Whatever small proportion of this variance that would get into the individual difference between subjects' mean RTs at a given set size would constitute part of the measurement error, and could only attenuate correlations between RT and psychometric test scores.

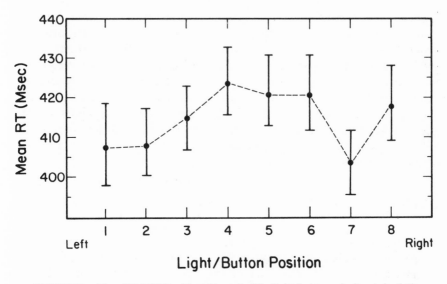

FIGURE 10.   Mean RT (of 309 subjects) to each of the light/button pairs in set-size 8; the light/button pairs, as described in Figure 2, were arranged in a semicircle of 6-inch radius, and are numbered here 1 to 8, from left to right. The vertical lines are the 95% confidence intervals (i.e., $\overline{X} \pm 1.96SE_{\overline{X}}$).

$RT\sigma_i$: Intraindividual Variability in RT

Intraindividual variability in RT, henceforth symbolized as $RT\sigma_i$, is quantified as the average of the standard deviations of an individual's RTs over a given number of trials at each set size. Experimental psychologists studying RT have paid peculiarly little attention to intraindividual variability in RT. This variable became of interest early in our RT research, when it was discovered that there are reliable individual differences in $RT\sigma_i$ and that these often showed a higher correlation with IQ than the RT itself. It also seemed a reasonable hypothesis that $RT\sigma_i$ is a more fundamental variable than the mean or median RT. That is, one can explain how individual differences in the mean RT could be the result of individual differences in $RT\sigma_i$ more easily than one can explain the reverse. If there is a lower limit (the so-called "physiological limit") to the shortest RT that a person can perform, and if persons differ relatively little in their shortest possible RTs, then individual differences in the spread of RTs above this lower limit will create individual differences in the measures of the central tendency of the RTs. Hence, the main source of individual differences in RT could arise, not from any basic neural processes that differ in speed of execution, but from differences in the moment-to-moment probability of occurrence of certain processes — an intermittency or oscillation of response potential that would make for trial-to-trial variation in RT.

The average correlation between median RT and $RT\sigma_i$ in most studies is about $+.6$, but the true correlation is greatly attenuated by the rather low reliability of $RT\sigma_i$. We have not obtained retest reliability coefficients of $RT\sigma_i$ higher than .6. (In one large study [SID #3, 100 university students], the retest reliability of $RT\sigma_i$ was only $+.422$.) Hence, if the correlation between median RT and $RT\sigma_i$ were corrected for attenuation, it could conceivably even be close to 1. The two measures thus would be redundant, at least when based on the same set of RT data. However, in order to find out whether median RT and $RT\sigma_i$ actually reflect the same or different individual differences, it is necessary to determine the correlation between them on experimentally independent sets of data. This was done by Paul (1984, pp. 60–61), with SID #11 (50 university students). The individuals' median RTs obtained in one test session (Day 1) were correlated with $RT\sigma_i$ obtained in another test session (Day 2), and vice versa. The two correlations between the experimentally independent measures of median RT and $RT\sigma_i$ were averaged and then corrected for attenuation of each variable. The raw correlation was only $+.33$; corrected for attenuation it was $+.67$. Exactly the same kind of analysis was done on SID #9 (48 university students); the disattenuated correlation between median RT and $RT\sigma_i$ was $+.61$. These studies suggest that, in the Hick paradigm, median RT and $RT\sigma_i$ share only about two thirds of their variance in common.

In any case, what we now know with considerable certainty about $RT\sigma_i$ with respect to Hick's Law is that it behaves very differently from the median RT. $RT\sigma_i$ is a linear function, not of log n, but of n itself. Table 13 shows $RT\sigma_i$ as a function of set size (n) in 18 independent samples totalling 1402 subjects. The average fit of $RT\sigma_i$ to a linear function of n is .94. (The fit to the composite data of all 18 studies is .99.) When $RT\sigma_i$ is regressed on bits, however, the average fit is only .86 (.91 for the composite data). Thus $RT\sigma_i$ shows almost as good a linear fit to n as median RT shows to log n. The linear relationship can be seen more clearly in Figure 11. As far as I can determine, this empirical relationship has not been mentioned elsewhere in the RT literature, except in Jensen (1982a, p. 104). An ANOVA trend analysis of the data in Table 13 shows a highly significant ($F[1,42] = 15.93$, $p < .001$) linear trend of the mean $RT\sigma_i$ on n; the nonlinear component of the variance is nonsignificant ($F[2,42] = 0.12$). Eta squared ($\times$ 100) for the different sources of variance are: Between Studies, 59.4%; Linear component of the regression of $RT\sigma_i$ on n, 11.1%; Nonlinear component, 0.6%; Residual, 29.3%.

The mean values of $RT\sigma_i$ (averaged over set sizes) and their standard deviations in 29 independent samples ($N = 1812$) are shown in Table 14.

The outstandingly puzzling feature in Table 14. is that the values of $RT\sigma_i$ in two of the three groups in SID #29 (Nettelbeck & Kirby, 1983) appear surprisingly large for SID #29A and #29U, in comparison to $RT\sigma_i$ in other similar groups. One may wonder if Nettelbeck and Kirby calculated $RT\sigma_i$ differently, but, according to their article (p. 43), it was calculated by the same

TABLE 13

Mean Intraindividual Variability ($RT\sigma_i$) in RT as a Function of Set Size (n) and Regression of $RT\sigma_i$ on n in 18 Independent Samples ($N = 1402$)

SID No.	Group	N	Set Size (n) 1	2	4	8	Regression of $RT\sigma_i$ (in Msec.) on n Int.	Slope	r
1	University Students	50	29	34	33	44	28.2	1.88	.953
2	University Students	25	32	33	40	57	26.9	3.62	.990
3	University Students	100	37	37	67	66	34.7	4.61	.831
6 + 7	University Students	105	32	32	41	52	28.0	2.98	.991
9	University Students	48	35	42	47	61	33.0	3.52	.991
10	University Students	100	35	36	40	53	31.1	2.69	.983
11	University Students	50	37	35	38	48	33.1	1.71	.954
12	Vocational College Whites	119	45	—	48	64	40.8	2.73	.958
13	Vocational College Blacks	99	54	—	61	83	47.9	4.17	.973
17	4th, 5th, 6th Graders	162	43	52	60	87	37.1	6.25	.995
18	High School Students	99	33	36	40	61	27.2	4.11	.984
19	Gifted 7th Graders	60	34	36	48	78	24.8	6.48	.993
20	Average 7th Graders	72	82	71	83	118	65.8	6.03	.914
21	Gifted 9th Graders	76	35	35	43	—	31.0	2.73	.930
23	Average 7th Graders	105	80	73	76	96	70.9	2.76	.833
25	Retarded Adults	46	93	120	227	400	41.7	44.87	.998
30	Average Adults	40	47	43	42	85	32.5	5.76	.866
31	Average Adults	46	54	47	46	71	43.2	2.98	.778
	Unweighted Mean		46.5	47.6	60.0	89.7	37.7	6.10	.940
	N-Weighted Mean		46.3	47.3	58.2	83.5	38.8	5.27	.943

method used in Jensen's studies. This striking discrepancy remains unexplained.[1]

---

[1]Nettelback (personal communication, May 29, 1986) has informed me that the values of RT and MT in SID #29 were in fact calculated differently from the calculation used in the other studies listed in Table 14, due to a misconception of Jensen's method, which was misleadingly described in Jensen (1983) as the "root mean square of the variances among trials within bits" (p. 111), whereas Jensen's method is properly described as the square root of the mean of the variances over trials within bits. The results in SID #29 as calculated by Jensen's method, however, differ only slightly from the method used by Nettelbeck and Kirby (1983). Nettelbeck has provided the values obtained by Jensen's method of calculation, as follows:

	$RT\sigma_i$ Mean	SD	$MT\sigma_i$ Mean	SD
Handicapped workers	297	94	115	59
Apprentices	91	20	77	25
University Students	121	61	87	52

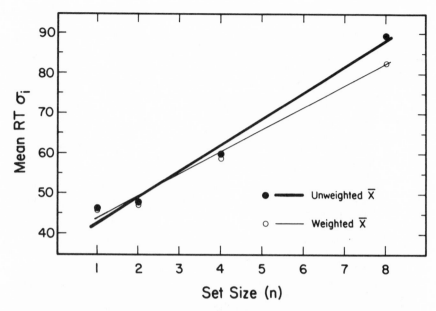

FIGURE 11.   Unweighted and N-weighted mean RTσ_i as a function of set size (n), based on 18 independent samples comprising a total of 1402 subjects. The fit of the data points to the linear function is $r = .990$ for the unweighted and $.991$ for the N-weighted means.

Random Nature of Intraindividual Variability in RT Across Trials

If, for a given set size (n) there are (a) reliable individual differences in the central tendency (mean or median) and intraindividual variability of RTs over trials, and if there were (b) no learning or other systematic changes in RT across trials, and if (c) any given subject's RT on any single trial were purely random deviation (with a standard deviation σ_i over trials for the given subject) from the subject's own mean RT across all trials, then the coexistence of only these three conditions would be sufficient to result in a matrix of covariances of RTs between trials over N number of subjects that would necessarily show the following two features: (a) it would be a significant matrix — that is, the average covariance would be greater than zero (because there are reliable individual differences in RT); and (b) the *true* covariances would be *homogenous,* and the variation between all of the obtained covariances in the matrix would constitute merely chance deviations from the constant true covariance, due to the randomness of every subject's RT on ev-

---

The remaining discrepancy from other studies may be at least partially explained by the fact that individuals' distributions of RTs and MTs were not Winsorized to eliminate outliers, as was done in most of the other studies. Nettelbeck remarks that there were "occasional very long and very short responses."

TABLE 14
Mean and Standard Deviation of Intraindividual Variability (in Msec.) in RT
in 29 Independent Samples (N = 1812)

SID No.	Group	N	Mean	SD
1	University Students	50	35.23	8.91
2	University Students	25	40.46	10.74
3	University Students	100	26.84	7.88
4	University Males	50	25.77	7.51
5	University Females	50	27.90	8.16
6	University Males	57	35.30	16.07
7	University Females	48	43.69	20.21
10	University Students	100	41.20	13.61
11	University Students	50	39.45	15.45
12	Vocational College Whites	119	52.62	26.67
13	Vocational College Blacks	99	65.99	34.11
14	Vocational College Whites	56	47.45	16.15
15	Vocational College Blacks	50	41.85	13.05
16	9th grade girls	39	35.32	11.80
17	4th, 5th, 6th graders	162	63.35	27.07
18HC	High School Hearing Children	37	59.23	21.95
18HP	High School Deaf Children of Hearing Parents	31	62.47	25.47
18DP	High School Deaf Children of Deaf Parents	31	52.73	12.57
19	Gifted 7th Graders	60	26.47	12.80
20	Average 7th Graders	72	88.71	27.64
21	Gifted 9th Graders	76	37.36	14.52
25	Retarded Adults	46	219.80	102.10
27	Severely Retarded Adults	60	235.16	220.09
28	Elderly	76	59.19	28.27
29H	Handicapped Workers	41	337.00	−
29A	Apprentices	82	102.00	−
29U	University Students	59	122.00	−
30	Average Adults	40	54.10	15.80
31	Average Adults	46	54.35	15.61

ery trial. A test of this set of conditions is provided by a statistical test of the hypothesis that all of the observed covariances are merely chance sampling deviations from a single true covariance. A statistical test of this null hypothesis is provided by Lawley (1963) in the form of a likelihood ratio statistic, l; the value $-2 \log l$ closely approximates a chi square distribution with $[n(n + 1)/2] - 2$ degrees of freedom, where n is the number of variables (in this case, number of trials). This statistical test was applied to the 10 × 10 variance-covariance matrix of trials 6 through 15 (out of a total of 15 trials) on the RT data of set sizes 1 and 8 for 100 university students (SID #3) tested on two occasions separated by 1 or 2 days. For neither set size 1 nor 8, on neither day, could the null hypothesis be rejected; the overall differences between the covariances among the RTs on every trial are far from significant. This finding is consistent with the hypothesis that, for a given subject, at a given set size, the RT on each trial is a random selection from the subject's total "population" of potential RTs, with the mean and standard deviation of RT as parameters of the given subject. The fact that the average correlation of RTs between trials is about 0.4 only indicates that there are reliable individual differences between subjects' mean RTs. When learning or other systematic change in performance takes place over a number of trials, as in laboratory learning experiments, the pattern of trial-to-trial correlations or covariances between the performance measures generally produces what is termed a *simplex* pattern, that is, the covariances between the performance measures on different trials decrease regularly the further apart the trials are. RT data, however, do not show even the slightest resemblance to the simplex pattern.

Correlations Between RTs Across Set Sizes

Another phenomenon, perhaps as lawful as Hick's law itself, is the simplex pattern of correlations between median RTs at every set size. Since SID #17 (162 elementary school children) is large and was given a larger number of different set sizes ($n = 1, 2, 4, 6, 8$) than other samples, with 30 trials at each set size, thereby making for somewhat higher reliability of individuals' median RTs at each set size, it can serve well to illustrate this "corollary" of Hick's Law. Table 15 shows the intercorrelations between median RTs of different set sizes; the correlation coefficients above the diagonal are corrected for attenuation, using the Spearman-Brown boosted split-half (odd-even trials) internal consistency reliability coefficient. It can be seen that the hierarchical pattern of correlations comes strikingly close to a perfect simplex. This is more especially true of the disattenuated correlations shown above the diagonal.

A perfect simplex pattern of correlations can be generated by what is termed an *overlap model,* which is based on the idea of overlapping or com-

TABLE 15
Correlations[a] Between Median RTs for Different Set
Sizes Based on Sample #17($N = 162$)

Set Size	1	2	4	6	8
1		.90	.80	.76	.72
2	.86		.80	.80	.77
4	.76	.86		.96	.90
6	.70	.74	.89		.99
8	.67	.72	.84	.90	

[a]Correlations above diagonal are corrected for attenuation.

mon elements between variables. It is best to think of this, not in terms of common *elements* in any real sense, but simply in terms of overlapping or shared variance, whatever the source of variance may be. The overlap model predicts the relative magnitudes of the correlations between different set sizes as follows. Designate any two set sizes as n_x and n_y, where $n_x < n_y$; that is, n_x is a subset of n_y. Then n_x/n_y is the proportion of the set n_y that is shared with the set n_x. Thought of in correlational terms, n_x/n_y is the proportion of variance in n_y that is predicted by n_x, and the correlation between n_x and n_y, therefore, is the square root of their ratio, that is, $\sqrt{n_x/n_y}$. For example, the correlation between set size 1 and set size 2 is $r_{1,2} = \sqrt{1/2} = .71$; between 1 and 4 is $r_{1,4} = \sqrt{1/4} = .50$; $r_{1,6} = \sqrt{1/6} = .41$, and so on. The matrix of correlations generated by this model is shown in Table 16, below the diagonal. This matrix is a perfect simplex. How closely do the actual correlations in Table 15 fit the simplex correlations in Table 16? An index of fit (r) is the correlation between the 10 actual rs and their corresponding theoretical rs. For the raw correlations, the fit (r) is .974; for the disattenuated correlations, the fit is .997. This is a remarkably high degree of fit between the pattern of the actual correlations and the simplex pattern generated by the overlap model. The two sets of correlations differ in absolute size, but this feature is unessential to the model. A linear transformation can be used on the theoretical rs to give them the same mean and variance as the disattenuated obtained rs, and such transformed theoretical rs are shown above the diagonal in Table 16, for comparison with the actual disattenuated rs above the diagonal in Table 15.

The close fit of the correlations to the simplex model is a natural consequence of two features of the RT data: (a) the increase in RT as a function of set size, and (b) a considerable degree of independence of individual differ-

TABLE 16
Theoretical Correlations[a] Between Set Sizes
Derived from the Overlap Model

Set Size	1	2	4	6	8
1		.90	.79	.74	.71
2	.71		.90	.83	.79
4	.50	.71		.96	.90
6	.41	.58	.82		.98
8	.35	.50	.71	.87	

[a]Correlations *below* the diagonal are directly derived from overlap model. Correlations *above* the diagonal are a linear transformation of these, to give them the same mean and variance as the disattenuated correlations for the actual data shown in Table 15.

ences in the intercept and slope of this function. These two conditions alone are sufficient to create the observed simplex. Table 17 shows the correlations between RTs at set sizes 1, 2, 4, and 8 for all the samples for which these correlations are available, along with the index of fit (r) to the correlations predicted by the overlap model. The average fit over the separate samples is .893 (unweighted rs) and .898 (N-weighted rs), but the fit to the composite mean correlations (i.e., the bottom two rows in Table 17) is .962 (unweighted means) and .958 (N-weighted means). The fact that the degree of fit to the overall means is higher than the mean fit of the separate samples suggests that the patterns of correlations in the various samples are all approximations to the simplex model, but are attenuated by measurement error and sampling error.

Correlations Between Hick Parameters

The correlations between various Hick parameters are of concern when one considers the selection of two or more parameters to be entered into a multiple regression equation for the prediction of IQ or other psychometric scores. The optimal equation, of course, is one in which each of the predictor variables is significantly correlated with the criterion variable (e.g., IQ) and in

TABLE 17
Correlation Coefficient (Decimal Omitted) Between RTs at Each Set Size (n = 1, 2, 3, 4, 8) in 11 Independent Samples (N = 941)

SID No.	Group	N	RT1 × RT2	RT1 × RT4	RT1 × RT8	RT2 × RT4	RT2 × RT8	RT4 × RT8	Fit to Model r
1	University Students	50	829	718	558	788	553	675	.775
6	University Students	57	869	761	644	842	786	818	.934
7	University Females	48	788	741	689	897	783	869	.870
10	University Students	100	812	779	693	924	845	891	.943
11	University Students	50	863	733	735	901	853	911	.854
12	Vocational College Whites	119		804	732			869	.992
13	Vocational College Blacks	99		646	507			745	.981
16	9th Grade Girls	39	874	779	693	930	814	877	.956
17	4th, 5th, 6th Graders	162	861	758	675	857	716	843	.981
18	High School Students	99	837	768	651	901	737	853	.964
19 + 20	Gifted & Average 7th Graders	118	769	850	641	886	762	757	.570
	N		723	941	941	723	723	941	
	Unweighted Mean		833	758	656	881	761	828	.962
	N-Weighted Mean		830	763	656	881	758	827	.958

which the correlations between the predictor variables are low, thereby minimizing their redundancy. The correlations between the Hick parameters that have been most frequently calculated in previous studies are collected in Table 18. All of the N-weighted mean correlations larger than .07 are significant beyond the .01 level (2-tailed). The correlations are also shown corrected for restriction of range and attenuation, in the last two rows of Table 18. These corrected values give a somewhat better idea of the degree of redundancy between pairs of variables. The corrections are probably overly conservative and, if anything, underestimate the true correlations in the general population. All of the samples in Table 18 are restricted in range of IQ. In nearly every sample, the degree of restriction amounts to more than 50% of the variance in the general population. Correction of the RT correlations for range assumes that the variance of the RT variables is reduced by 5%, due to incidental restriction of the samples on IQ, assuming the IQ variance is reduced 50% and that IQ accounts for 10% of the variance in the RT variable. Based on these reasonable and empirically based average estimates, the correlation corrected for restriction of range can be calculated from Formula 8 in Gulliksen (1950, p. 133). Correction for attenuation is conservatively based on assuming an internal consistency reliability of .90 for all variables.

Intercept × slope correlation. One correlation between Hick parameters, the correlation between RT intercept and slope (RTa × RTb), calls for special comment, in view of the fact that some theoretical importance has been claimed for this particular correlation, which, as can be seen in Table 18, is the only *negative* correlation between any of the Hick parameters. The observed negative correlation between intercept and slope has been interpreted as evidence that something other than a general speed factor is involved in Hick performance, and that a different *strategy* for minimizing RT is adopted in responding to a small number of alternatives (or bits of information) from that used in responding to a larger number of alternatives. For example, Nettelbeck and Kirby (1983) make quite an important point of the negative intercept × slope correlation, as follows:

> There are aspects to these data which are concordant with the possibility that certain strategies for responding have influenced outcome. In the first place, the strong negative correlations between the slope and intercept of regression functions for DT [i.e., RT] and MT within all three groups raise doubts about whether the regression of RT on bits can reliably distinguish rate of processing from fundamental delays in the subject's response system, as Hick's Law proposes. *If it were the case that both variables were interacting with a third, like intelligence, then one would expect a positive correlation between slope and intercept.* The negative relationship suggests instead that some subjects have applied different criteria for responding at different levels of choice. One plausible possibility is that some responses have been disproportionately more carefully made when eight stimulus alternatives were involved, although other

TABLE 18

Correlation Coefficients (Decimals Omitted) Between Various Parameters[a] of the Hick Paradigm
in 16 Independent Samples ($N = 1199$)

SID No.	Group	N	RT × RTa	RT × RTb	RT × $RT\sigma_i$	RT × MT	RTa × RTb	RTa × $RT\sigma_i$	RTa × MT	RTb × $RT\sigma_i$	RTb × MT	$RT\sigma_i$ × MT
1	University Students	50			39		−29	18	25	42	31	12
2	University Students	25	83	−23		53	−72	21	54	25	−25	53
3	University Students	100					01	47	35	41	−08	33
4	University Males	50					09	50	34	36	−23	33
5	University Females	50				42	−11	43	35	50	11	29
6	University Males	57		−00		56					−01	
7	University Females	48		30		55					02	
10	University Students	100	92	33	55	57	−07	43	57	36	03	24
12	Vocational College Whites	119		61		57						
13	Vocational College Blacks	99		53		53						
12 + 13	Vocational College Students	218		50	70	37				43	18	44
16	9th Grade Girls	39			48							
17	4th, 5th, 6th Graders	162				49	03				32	
18	High School Students	99			47	61						41
22	Average 9th Graders	20			83							
23	Average 7th Graders	105		18	73	35				33	−06	32
28	Elderly	76				64						
	Unweighted Mean		877	277	593	516	−151	371	401	382	032	335
	N-Weighted Mean		902	321	619	507	−064	403	407	394	087	349
	Total N	125		553	606	787	537	375	375	698	965	797
Corrected for Range and Attenuation												
	Unweighted Mean		976	374	679	601	−277	460	488	470	226	426
	N-Weighted Mean		1000	413	707	593	−234	491	494	482	243	439

[a] RT – Mean median RT.
RTa – Intercept of regression of RT on bits.
RTb – Slope of regression of RT on bits.
$RT\sigma_i$ – Intraindividual variability in RT over trials.
MT – Mean MT.

143

explanations are equally viable. The important consideration here is that strategies of this kind could increase the slope while decreasing the intercept of the regression function. (pp. 49–50, emphasis added)

And elsewhere, Nettlebeck (1985) states:

Roth (1964) also reports a significant correlation of − .41 between the slope and the intercept of the regression function. This outcome, which is inconsistent with a speed model of intelligence, has been confirmed by Nettelbeck and Kirby (1983). It suggests that subjects apply different criteria for responding at different levels of choice. (p. 235)

The observed negative correlation between intercept and slope, however, is an unsound basis for any such theorizing as is displayed in the above quotes, because the negative correlation is merely a mathematical artifact arising necessarily from the fact that, when intercept and slope are calculated on the same set of data, they both share the same measurement errors, which are negatively correlated in the two parameters. That is, the very same errors that increase the slope also necessarily decrease the intercept, and vice versa. The correlation between intercept (a) and slope (b) due solely to their shared errors of measurement is provided by the following formula (from Marascuilo & Levin, 1983, p. 161):

$$r_{ab} = \frac{-\overline{X}}{\sqrt{\frac{\Sigma X^2}{N}}} ,$$

where X is the values on the abscissa (in this case, bits) and N is the number of bivariate data points that enter into the computation of the regression of the ordinate values on the abscissa values (in this case, the regression of median RT on bits). With 0, 1, 2, 3 bits, as typically used in most studies, $r_{ab} = -.80$. Hence the true, or error-free, correlation between intercept and slope is bound to be obscured or even reversed in sign by this large negative correlation between their errors of measurement.

Since errors of measurement tend to be averaged out in the group mean when the number of subjects is large, it should be instructive to look at the correlation between intercept and slope based on group means. The mean intercepts and mean slopes of the 27 independent samples in Table 3 are *positively* correlated, Pearson $r = +.71$, Spearman rank-order correlation = + .55. The correlation between the mean intercepts and mean slopes of Table 22 is + .42. Hence, it appears that the true correlation between intercept and slope is a *positive* correlation, probably of substantial magnitude.

The true correlation between intercept and slope based on individuals *within* a given sample can be properly determined only by obtaining the two parameters from two experimentally independent sets of data (so that errors will be uncorrelated), and then correcting the correlation for attenuation based on the reliability of each parameter. This has been done in two large samples, each given 30 trials, divided into sets of 15 odd- or even-numbered trials. The odd and even trials, being experimentally independent, have uncorrelated errors of measurement. SID #17 ($N = 162$) gives the following correlations:

Even

		Intercept	Slope
Odd	Intercept	.910	−.037
	Slope	−.027	.724

Odd intercept × odd slope, $r = -.210$

Even intercept × even slope, $r = -.109$

The mean correlation between odd and even intercepts × slopes is ($-.027 + -.037)/2 = -.032$. The correction for attenuation term based on the reliabilities (for 15 trials) is $\sqrt{(.910)\,(.724)} = .812$. So the correlation of $-.032$ corrected for attenuation is $-.039$, which is the best estimate of the true correlation between individual measures of intercept and slope in this sample. This correlation, with 160 *df*, does not differ significantly from zero ($t < 1$).

Combined SID #12 and #13 (total $N = 218$) give the following correlations:

Even

		Intercept	Slope
Odd	Intercept	.866	−.078
	Slope	−.139	.721

Odd intercept × odd slope, $r = -.255$

Even intercept × even slope, $r = -.248$

The mean correlation between odd and even intercepts × slopes is ($-.139 + -.078)/2 = -.109$, which is not significantly different from zero ($t = 1.62$, $p < .10$). The correction for attenuation term based on the reliabilities (for 15 trials) is $\sqrt{(.866)\,(.721)} = .790$. So the correlation of $-.109$ corrected for attenuation is $-.138$. This disattenuated correlation, with 216 df, is also nonsignificant ($t = 1.62, p < .10$). (Significance tests of disattenuated correlations are explicated by Forsyth & Feldt, 1969.) These two studies raise the question of whether there is a zero correlation or a positive correlation between slope, as was found when *mean* intercepts and slopes were correlated. The two types of correlations seem to yield different answers to the question. In any case, it is important to note that the correlations between intercept and slope based on experimentally independent sets of data are considerably smaller than the correlations based on one and the same set of data. Clearly, a large part of the negative correlation generally found between intercept and slope is attributable to the artifact resulting from their correlated errors of measurement. To date, there is no evidence of a significant *negative* correlation between true-score measurements of intercept and slope.

Reliability of Hick Parameters

Internal consistency reliability coefficients based on split-half (odd-even trials) within single test sessions have been determined in five independent studies (total $N = 550$). (One of these is Cronbach's coefficient alpha, which is the same as the mean of all possible split-half reliabilities.) Test-retest reliability coefficients based on test sessions on separate occasions two or three days apart have been determined in six independent studies (total $N = 290$). (The reliability of every Hick parameter was not determined in every study.) The reliability coefficients are shown in Table 19. The internal consistency (split-half) reliability is always higher than the retest reliability, and both types of reliability coefficients are generally higher for MT than for RT. RT slope has the lowest retest reliability of any parameter, and $RT\sigma_i$ is hardly better. Yet the split-half reliability of these parameters is generally satisfactory. But individual differences in RT slope and $RT\sigma_i$ are very unstable from one day to the next. This fact, of course, greatly attenuates the correlations of these parameters with any other variables. Their reliability can be raised by averaging the data from repeated tests given on as many days as required to achieve a satisfactory level of reliability, but this is usually unfeasible for any practical purposes. Considering the relatively low reliability of $RT\sigma_i$, its correlations with psychometric g are higher, on average, than the correlations for any other of the Hick parameters. This fact would seem to suggest a certain primacy to the $RT\sigma_i$ variable, as if intraindividual variability in RT were the basic source of the correlations of all other Hick parameters with g. Individual differences in all the other Hick RT parameters might be interpretable as merely derivatives of individual differences in intraindividual variability.

The odd-even split-half reliability (Spearman-Brown boosted) of RT and

TABLE 19
Reliability Coefficients (Decimals Omitted) of RT and MT Variables

				Reaction Time			Movement Time	
SID No.	N	Reliability	Mean[a]	Intercept	Slope	$RT\sigma_i$	Mean	$MT\sigma_i$
3	100	Split-half[b]		97	75	65	96	81
3	100	Retest[c]		72	35	42	84	56
4	50	Retest[c]		73	50	48	89	56
5	50	Retest[c]		71	16	35	87	52
8	10	Split-half	97	96	89	72	99	64
8	10	Retest[d]	82	72	16	07	94	37
11	50	Retest[c]		49				
12 + 13	218	Split-half[b]		93	84		91	
17	162	Split-half[b]		95	84		76	
21	60	Cronbach's Alpha[f]	93		68[e]			
21	30	Retest[c]	84		59			
N-Weighted X̄ Split-half			94	95	81	66	87	79
N-Weighted X̄ Retest			84	72	39	40	86	54

[a]Mean of median RTs at each set size.
[b]Split-half reliability is always odd-even trials, and boosted by the Spearman-Brown formula.
[c]Test-retest reliability based on correlation between test sessions 2 or 3 days apart (*not* boosted by Spearman-Brown formula).
[d]Based on average correlation between test sessions 2 or 3 days apart.
[e]Split-half reliability.
[f]This is the same as the mean of all possible split-half reliability coefficients, boosted by Spearman-Brown formula.

MT for 30 trials was determined for means and medians at each set size in SID #16 (39 ninth grade girls), with the following results:

	Reaction Time		Movement Time	
Set Size	Mean	Median	Mean	Median
1	.884	.830	.746	.967
2	.929	.912	.866	.963
4	.909	.912	.734	.934
6	.885	.899	.752	.927
8	.878	.884	.855	.933
Mean	.897	.887	.791	.945

The boosted split-half reliability of RT slope in this study was .76.

Reliability in the form of Cronbach's (1951) alpha coefficient for the mean of 30 trials was obtained in SID #17 (162 elementary school children, grades 4–6):

Set Size	RT	MT
1	.954	.701
2	.955	.758
4	.951	.728
6	.933	.781
8	.917	.771
Mean	.942	.748

Boosted split-half reliabilities for 30 trials for mean RT and MT in combined SID #12 and 13 (218 vocational college males) are as follows:

Set Size	RT	MT
1	.925	.897
4	.922	.909
8	.914	.893
Mean	.920	.900

Combined SID #6 and 7 (105 university students) have the boosted split-half reliabilities for 15 trials for median RT and MT:

Set Size	RT	MT
1	.962	.942
2	.955	.953
4	.948	.930
8	.863	.921
Mean	.932	.937

Median RT and MT have the following boosted split-half reliabilities for 15 trials in SID #1 (50 university students):

Set Size	RT	MT
1	.947	.931
2	.872	.961
4	.836	.977
8	.949	.961
Mean	.901	.957

In none of these samples is there a tendency for the reliability of either RT or MT to increase with increasing set size. The increase in correlation between

RT and psychometric *g* with increasing set size, therefore, cannot be attributed to increasing reliability of RT with increasing set size. The same holds true for test-retest reliability, as shown for median RT and MT (15 trials on each of 2 days) in SID #11 (50 university students):

Set Size	RT	MT
1	.681	.802
2	.818	.835
4	.770	.887
8	.770	.770
Mean	.760	.823

Relationship of Hick Variables to Age

There has been no systematic study as yet using the RT-MT apparatus that focuses specifically on the relationship of Hick variables to age from early childhood to maturity and beyond. Fairweather and Hutt (1978) investigated age effects on Hick parameters in groups of children at each year of age from 5 through 11, with set sizes of 2, 4, and 8, but their apparatus was quite different from that used in the studies included in this review. RT and MT were not measured separately; responses were made with the fingers of each hand placed over pushbuttons; the reaction stimuli were numerals. Because of these differences, the results are not comparable in absolute magnitudes to those found with the RT-MT apparatus, but the relationships of the Hick parameters to age were fairly similar to those found with the RT-MT apparatus reviewed below. The most striking finding was the age differences in the slope of RT on bits, the slope decreasing with increasing age.

Telzrow (1983), using the Jensen RT-MT apparatus, found that RT and MT can be reliably measured in children as young as 2 years. She measured RT and MT for set size of 8 (3 bits) only, in three groups of white middle-class children, ages 26–34 months ($N = 15$), 42–50 months ($N = 17$), and 65–77 months ($N = 17$). In this age range, mean RT and MT decrease markedly and significantly ($p < .001$) as a function of age:

Age (mos.)		RT		MT	
Range	$\overline{X}$	$\overline{X}$	SD	$\overline{X}$	SD
26–34	30.8	967	351	1256	518
42–50	46.2	840	196	652	218
63–77	69.5	583	137	410	108

Hemmelgarn and Kehle (1984) report RT as a function of bits in 59 intellectually superior children (WISC-R Full Scale IQ, $\overline{X} = 123.5$, $SD = 11.2$), ranging in age from 6 to 11 years. The data are shown in Table 20. It can be seen that RT intercept and slope parameters decrease with age in a nearly linear fashion. The last three rows of Table 20 show the regression of RT on age at each level of bits.

The RT data (mean and σ_i) of SID #17 (160 school children, ages 9 to 14) were regressed on age (in months), with the results shown in Figure 12, which indicates that the negative slope of the regression of both mean RT and RTσ_i on age increases monotonically as a function of set size scaled in bits. Clearly, there is a systematic relationship between RT and age which is also related to the information load of the reaction stimulus. At some point in later maturity, the relationship between age and both RT and MT reverses course, and RT and MT increase with increasing age. Ananda's (1985) study of 76 elderly adults of ages 51 to 87 years (SID #28), whose educational level is comparable to that of university students, shows that RT and MT are about 50 to 100 msec greater in the elderly, and the mean slope of RT on bits is about 10 msec greater. In fact, the elderly adults (mean age 67.8 years, $SD = 8.65$) are even outperformed by school children in the 4th, 5th, and 6th grades (SID #17). These comparisons can be seen in Tables 3 and 7.

There are eight samples in which correlations have been computed between age and various Hick parameters, as shown in Table 21. Most of these samples have a restricted age range and therefore are far from ideal for the study of age effects on RT and MT, showing quite small correlations. Their value lies in showing that controlling for age in RT studies based on relatively homogeneous age groups would scarcely make any difference.

TABLE 20
RT as a Function of Age in 59 Intellectually Superior Children of Ages 6 to 11 Years (Data from Hemmelgarn & Kehle, 1984)

Age (Yrs.)	Bits				RT Parameters		
	0	1	2	3	Intercept	Slope	Fit (r)
6–7	492.4	558.3	618.0	630.1	503.8	47.28	.966
7–8	464.1	513.5	535.8	559.0	472.1	30.70	.978
8–9	452.8	498.3	506.2	535.1	459.9	25.48	.965
10–11	386.9	407.0	420.0	454.4	379.7	23.70	.968
Mean	449.1	494.3	520.0	544.65	455.1	31.25	.988
Regression on Age							
Intercept	662.2	797.7	908.3	889.5			
Slope	−25.83	−36.78	−47.06	−41.80			
Correlation (r)	−.988	−.989	−.983	−.985			

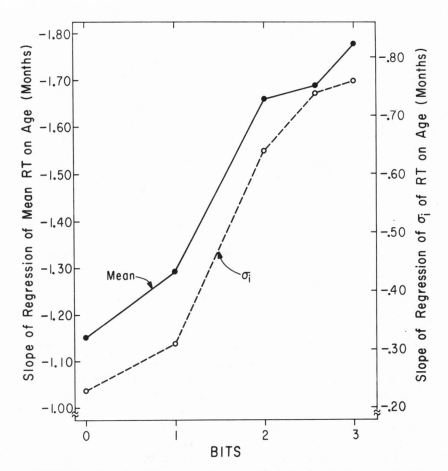

FIGURE 12.   Slope (i.e., RT decrement in msec per 1 month of age) of the regression of mean RT and intraindividual variability (σ_i) of RT on age, as a function of bits of information, for 160 children of ages 9 to 14 years (SID #17).

Relationship of Hick Variables to Intelligence

The relationship of Hick variables to intelligence can be expressed in either one of two ways: (a) by comparison of the means of Hick variables in criterion groups that differ in their average level of intelligence, and (b) by the correlation coefficient between Hick variables and scores on intelligence tests within a given sample. The size of the obtained correlation coefficient is partly a function of the restriction of range of ability in the particular sample and the reliability of the correlated variables. The samples in nearly all of the studies under review have a restricted range of intelligence compared with the

152 JENSEN

TABLE 21
Correlation Coefficient (Decimal Omitted) Between Age and Hick Variables in 8 Independent Samples ($N = 606$)

SID No.	Group	N	Age (Yrs.)		Hick Variable[a]				
			Mean	SD	$RT\bar{X}$	RTa	RTb	$RT\sigma_i$	$MT\bar{X}$
2	University Students	25	20.14	2.46	−192	−003	−226	−149	−213
6	University Males	57	19.17	1.39	−035		−121		−217
7	University Females	48	19.04	1.56	+043		+037		−023
10	University Students	100	21.43	2.63	−092	−068	−071	−071	+108
16	9th Grade Girls	39	14.65	0.76	−108				−165
17	4th, 5th, 6th Graders	162	10.75	0.93			−291	−192	
18	High School Students	99	16.72	1.62	+130			+120	+060
28	Elderly	76	67.84	8.65	+258			+150	+403

[a]$RT\bar{X}$ — Mean median RT.
RTa — Intercept of regression of RT on bits.
RTb — Slope of regression of RT on bits.
$RT\sigma_i$ — Intraindividual variability of RT over trials.
$MT\bar{X}$ — Mean MT.

general population. The IQ variance of the university samples, for example, is only about one fourth of the IQ variance in the general population. Measurement error is averaged out in groups when N is large, although it is reflected in the standard deviation and the standard error of measurement, thereby attenuating any statistical test of the significance of the mean difference. A mean difference expressed in standard deviation, or σ, units is also attenuated by measurement error, or imperfect reliability.

Group means and differences on Hick variables. Table 22 shows the mean intercept and slope of the regression of median RT on bits in the 33 samples in which these parameters were computed. The standard deviation (*SD*) was not computed in all studies. For both intercept and slope, the *SD* of the sample means is much larger than the *SD* of individuals *within* samples, which is evidence of the restricted range of ability within samples.

Not all of the samples can be meaningfully compared with respect to general intelligence, because they differ markedly in chronological age. Also, statistical tests of significance of the differences can be performed only between samples for which *SD*s are available. The groups of comparable age but differing in mean IQ (the second group in each pair having the higher mean IQ) that can be compared on RT slope are shown in Table 23. In every comparison, the slope differs significantly in the predicted direction. This is quite compelling evidence that, as Roth (1964) originally discovered, RT slope is inversely related to intelligence. The mean differences, in standard deviation units (σ Diff.), range from $.30\sigma$ to $.70\sigma$ in the various comparisons.

TABLE 22
Mean and Standard Deviation of Intercept and Slope of Regression of Median RT (in Msec) on Bits in 33 Independent Samples (Total N = 2067)

SID No.	Group	N	Intercept Mean	Intercept SD	Slope Mean	Slope SD
1	University Students	50	283.19	25.40	26.02	10.23
2	University Students	25	306.36	36.44	28.38	14.67
3	University Students	100	297.24	29.98	26.11	8.71
4	University Males	50	294.77	31.63	26.21	9.79
5	University Females	50	299.70	28.33	26.01	7.58
6	University Males	57	284.47		28.81	10.70
7	University Females	48	322.47		28.86	11.65
10	University Students	100	314.93		24.54	11.23
11	University Students	50	302.55		26.41	11.77
12	Vocational College Whites	119	338.29		30.13	16.86
13	Vocational College Blacks	99	340.44		38.74	20.06
12 + 13	Vocational College Total	218	339.35		34.04	18.38
14	Vocational College Whites	56	313.09	39.84	29.86	12.66
15	Vocational College Blacks	50	312.01	32.63	29.77	13.22
14 + 15	Vocational College Total	106	312.58	36.45	29.82	12.86
16	9th grade girls	39	295.00		30.98	10.79
17	4th, 5th, 6th graders	162	305.90	40.40	39.20	14.32
18	High School Students	99	303.13		26.70	
19	Gifted 7th Graders	60	320.44		32.73	15.84
20	Average 7th Graders	72	382.63		46.32	21.99
21	Gifted 9th Graders	76	324.11		23.59	15.33
23	Average 7th Graders	105	451.70		24.20	
24	Ages 6–7	15	503.78		47.28	
24	Ages 7–8	15	472.05		30.70	
24	Ages 8–9	15	459.88		25.48	
25	Retarded Adults	46	476.20		72.50	61.60
26	Retarded & Borderline Adults	58	488.75		119.33	78.13
28	Elderly	76	345.02		37.86	
29	Handicapped Workers	41	374.00		112.00	
29	Apprentices	82	300.00		52.00	
29	University Students	59	278.00		44.00	
30	Average Adults	40	294.38	33.51	27.48	12.90
31	Average Adults	46	313.99	39.85	20.00	12.73
33	State College Students	93	278.57		57.02	
	Mean (Unweighted)		343.11	34.04	37.91	18.31
	Mean (N-Weighted)		333.02	34.59	37.85	17.73
	SD (Unweighted)		66.58	5.01	22.30	17.22
	SD (N-Weighted)		56.74	5.26	20.69	15.33

TABLE 23
RT Slope Comparisons (in Msec) Between Samples of Comparable Age That Differ
in Mean IQ

SID No.	Comparison Groups	N	Mean Slope	SD	σ Diff.[a]	t	r^b_{pbs}
20	Above-Average 7th Graders	72	46.32	21.99			
19	Gifted 7th Graders	60	32.73	15.84			
	Difference		13.59		0.70	4.12**	−.305
16	Above-Average 9th Graders	39	30.98	10.79			
21	Gifted 9th Graders	76	23.59	15.33			
	Difference		7.39		0.53	3.00*	−.243
12, 13, 14, 15	Vocational College Students	324	32.66	16.55			
1–7, 10, 11	University Students	530	26.48	10.37			
	Difference		6.18		0.47	6.03**	−.224
13, 15	Vocational College Blacks	149	35.73	17.76			
12, 14	Vocational College Whites	175	30.04	15.52			
	Difference		5.69		0.34	3.04	−.167

[a]The difference expressed in average standard deviation units:

$$\sigma \, \text{Diff} = (\overline{X}_1 - \overline{X}_2)/\sigma, \text{ where}$$
$$\sigma = \sqrt{(N_1 s_1^2 + N_2 s_2^2)/(N_1 + N_2)}$$

[b]Point-biserial correlation between group dichotomy and slope, which is negatively correlated with the groups' mean IQs.
*$p < .01$ (two-tailed).
**$p < .001$ (two-tailed).

These are not only significant but also quite substantial differences. Corrected for attenuation, these σ differences and the point-biserial correlations (r_{pb}) would be considerably enlarged, in view of the quite low reliability of the slope measure for individuals.

Another Hick variable which has generaly shown a more marked relationship to IQ than RT slope is trial-to-trial intraindividual variability ($RT\sigma_i$). Table 24 compares the samples of comparable age but differing mean IQ for which the mean and *SD* of $RT\sigma_i$ are available. There is one anomalous finding in Table 24; the gifted 9th graders (SID #21) do not differ significantly from the 9th grade girls, who, although a superior group, do not match the

TABLE 24
Mean and Standard Deviation of Intraindividual Variability in RT (in Msec), the Standardized Group Mean Difference (σ Diff.), and *t* Test of the Significance of the Difference

SID No.	Groups	N	Mean	SD	σ Diff.	t
20	Average 7th Graders	72	88.71	27.64		
19	Gifted 7th Graders	60	26.47	12.80		
	Difference		62.24		2.81	17.54**
12, 13, 14, 15	Vocational College Students	324	54.15	26.27		
1–7, 10, 11	University Students	530	34.61	12.59		
	Difference		19.54		1.03	12.54**
13 + 15	Vocational College Blacks	149	57.89	28.81		
12 + 14	Vocational College Whites	175	50.97	23.81		
	Difference		6.92		0.26	2.33*
4 + 6	University Males	107	30.85	12.81		
5 + 7	University Females	98	35.63	15.30		
	Difference		− 4.78		− 0.34	− 2.41*
16	9th Grade Girls	39	35.32	11.80		
21	Gifted 9th Graders	76	37.36	14.52		
	Difference		− 2.04		− 0.15	− 0.81
18	High School Pupils	99	58.21	20.80		
21	Gifted 9th Graders	76	37.36	14.52		
	Difference		20.85		1.14	7.80**

*$p < .02$ (two-tailed).
**$p < .001$ (two-tailed).

gifted group in ability. The gifted 9th graders, however, differ very significantly in the predicted direction from the slightly-above-average high school group (SID #18) who are more than two years older. Mentally retarded groups have not been entered into any of the comparisons in Tables 23 and 24. They differ extremely (in the expected direction) from the nonretarded samples of comparable age.

Discrimination in terms of Hick parameters between groups that differ in psychometric *g*, or the correlation of these parameters with *g*, clearly does not depend on the presence of retarded or borderline subjects in the sample. Differences in any part of the IQ continuum are reflected by certain Hick parameters. The comparison of SID #19 and #20 (gifted and nongifted but above-average 7th graders, from Cohn et al., 1985) illustrates this point. Figure 13 shows the RT and MT of the gifted (G) and nongifted (NG) groups (*N*

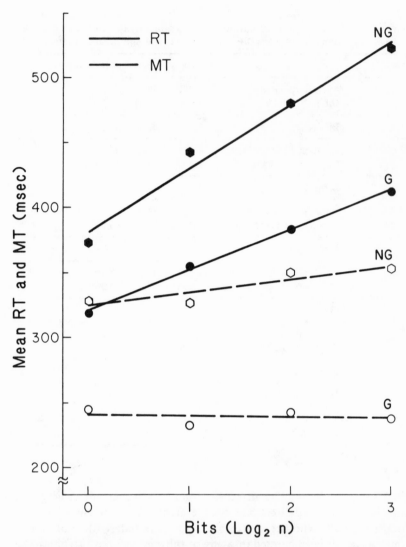

FIGURE 13. Reaction time (RT) and movement time (MT) in nongifted (NG, SID #20) and gifted (G, SID #19) groups as a function of bits of information.

= 60 and 72, respectively). The groups differ significantly (< .001) at every set size on both RT and MT and on RT slope and RTσ_i. A discriminant analysis based on 16 variables (median RT, RTσ_i, mean MT and MTσ_i at each set size) correctly classified 87.1% of all the subjects as gifted or nongifted; the corresponding shrunken multiple correlation is .64. Approximately 92% of the gifted group and 83% of the nongifted group were correctly classified solely on the basis of these Hick variables. (See Cohn et al., 1985, for details on other RT paradigms in these groups.)

Correlations between Hick parameters and intelligence.   Table 25 shows the correlations between various Hick parameters and intelligence measures in 26 independent samples. SID #29, #30, and #31 in Table 25 are of particular interest, because they have the least restriction of variance in IQ and therefore the correlations between IQ and the Hick parameters are probably better estimates of what would be obtained in the general population. In fact, SID #21 was composed of 91 young adults selected from three different samples of differing IQ levels in such a way as to approximate the normal distribution of IQ in the general population (Nettelbeck & Kirby, 1983). This normally distributed sample yields larger correlations between IQ and RT intercept, RT slope, and $RT\sigma_i$ ($rs = -.36, -.41,$ and $-.71,$ respectively) than any other samples. SID #30 and #31 (Barrett et al., 1986) have WAIS IQ standard deviations of 18.99 and 13.18, respectively, as compared with $\sigma = 15$ in the standardization population. Most of the other samples in Table 25 are rather restricted in IQ variance. All of the overall N-weighted mean correlations are highly significant ($p < .001$) except for $MT\sigma_i$, for which $t < 1$. Of the four RT variables, RT slope yields the weakest, albeit significant, correlation, in part because of its low reliability. Our best estimate of its test-retest reliability is .39, and assuming a reliability of .90 for the intelligence measurements, the N-weighted mean r corrected for attenuation would be $-.20,$ which is about the same as the *un*corrected correlation between $RT\sigma_i$ and intelligence despite the fact that $RT\sigma_i$ has about the same low reliability as RT slope. If we conservatively estimate the overall restriction of IQ variance within these samples as one half the population variance, and assume a reliability of .90 for IQ, and the average estimates of the test-retest reliability of the Hick parameters (from Table 19), and use these estimates in the appropriate formulas (Gulliksen, 1950, pp. 101, 137) to correct the N-weighted mean correlations for restriction of variance and for attenuation due to measurement error, the corrected correlations (r_c) of the various parameters with IQ are as follows:

	r_c
Mean RT	$-.32$
RT Intercept	$-.25$
RT Slope	$-.28$
$RT\sigma_i$	$-.48$
Mean MT	$-.30$
$MT\sigma_i$	$-.02$

These corrected coefficients may be viewed as rather conservative estimates of the true population correlations of the Hick parameters with psychometric

TABLE 25

Correlation Coefficient (Decimal Omitted) Between Intelligence Measures and RT and MT Parameters in 26 Independent Samples ($N = 1961$)

SID No.	Group	N	$RT\bar{X}$	RT Int.	RT Slope	$RT\sigma_i$	$MT\bar{X}$	$MT\sigma_i$	Intelligence Test
1	University Students	50		+10	-41	-35	-25	+10	Advanced Raven
1	University Students	50		+22	-00	-08	-16	+02	CMT[a]
2	University Students	25	-13	-17	+02	-43	-25	+23	Advanced Raven
3	University Students	100		-08	+03	-14	-21	-28	Advanced Raven
4	University Males	50		-08	+08	-14	-27	+09	Raven
4	University Males	50		-07	00	+01	-18	-06	CMT[a]
5	University Females	50		-16	-04	-12	-34	+01	Advanced Raven
5	University Females	50		+10	-23	+00	-17		CMT[a]
6 + 7	University Males + Females	51	+07		-25		-22		SAT–Verbal[b]
6 + 7	University Males + Females	51	+11		-21		-32		SAT–Math[b]
10	University Students	100	-17	-14	-09	-15	-26	+23	WAIS–VIQ[c]
10	University Students	100	-26	-15	-30	-42	-25	+01	WAIS–PIQ[c]
10	University Students	100	-25	-17	-22	-32	-30	+14	WAIS–FSIQ[c]
11	University Students	50	-05	-17	-15	-36	-29	-09	Advanced Raven
12 + 13	Vocational College Students	218	-22	-01	-06	-24	-13	-03	Advanced Raven
14 + 15	Vocational College Students	106	-06		-09	-14	-09	+13	Advanced Raven
16	9th Grade Girls	39	-39		-30	+07	-07	-11	SCAT[d]
17	4th, 5th, 6th Graders	162	-19	-03	-05	-31	-43	+07	Standard Raven
17	4th, 5th, 6th Graders	162	-15	-20	-05				Verbal IQ[f]
17	4th, 5th, 6th Graders	162	-30	-11	-02	-10	-20	-01	Nonverbal IQ[f]
18	High School Students	99	-07						Standard Raven
19	Gifted 7th Graders	60							Standard Raven
20	Average 7th Graders	72			-15				Standard Raven
21	Gifted 9th Graders	76			-20	+12			Standard Raven
22	Average 7th Graders	20	-54		+17	-71	-43	-64	Standard Raven
22	Average 7th Graders	20	-54		+36	-71	-40	-68	Read. Comp.
22	Average 7th Graders	11	-66			-80	-55	-83	CTBS[g]
23	Average 7th Graders	105	-13		-09	-21	-02	-33	Standard Raven

No.	Sample	N	1	2	3	4	5	6	Criterion Test
23	Average 7th Graders	94	−35		−03	−40	−23	−24	Read Comp.
23	Average 7th Graders	104	−16		00	−20	+01	−19	CTBS[g]
24	Elem. Sch. Ages 6–11	59			−32	−22	+05		WISC–FSIQ[c]
25	Retarded Adults	46			+09		−25		Standard Raven
26	Ret. & Borderline Adults	58	−34		−21		−32		Standard Raven
28	Elderly	76	−45			−23	−49	−16	Standard Raven
28	Elderly	76	−09			−27	−26	+10	Mill Hill Voc.
28	Elderly	76	−29			−29	−43	−02	Total IQ[h]
29	Normally Distributed Adults	91		−36	−41	−74		−13	IQ[i]
30	Average Adults	40	−37	−30	−08	−23			WAIS–FSIQ[c]
30	Average Adults	40	−49	−33	−21	−30			WAIS–VIQ[c]
30	Average Adults	40	−46	−34	−15	−29			WAIS–PIQ[c]
31	Average Adults	46				−40			WAIS–FSIQ[c]
32	Navy Recruits	112			−13				Comp. Exam.
	Total N		1195	774	1558	1397	1302	1154	
	Unweighted Mean		−255	−123	−106	−275	−249	−103	
	N-Weighted Mean		−201	−117	−117	−208	−189	−011	
	t test of N-Weighted Mean		7.08*	3.29*	4.65*	7.94*	6.94*	0.37	
	Corrected for Range, Unweighted Mean		−350	−172	−149	−375	−341	−145	
	Corrected for Range, N-Weighted Mean		−279	−165	−165	−288	−263	−016	
	Disattenuated Unweighted Mean		−389	−191	−165	−417	−379	−161	
	Disattenuated N-Weighted Mean		−309	−183	−183	−320	−292	−017	

[a]Terman Concept Mastery Test.
[b]SAT – Scholastic Aptitude Test.
[c]Wechsler Adult Intelligence Scale (VIQ = Verbal IQ; PIQ = Performance IQ; FSIQ = Full Scale IQ).
[d]School and College Aptitude Test.
[e]Armed Services Vocational Aptitude Battery.
[f]Lorge-Thorndike Intelligence Test.
[g]Comprehensive Test of Basic Skills.
[h]Total IQ based on composite of Mill Hill Vocabulary and Standard Raven scores.
[i]Total IQ for each of the three subgroups composing this sample is based on three different tests: Advanced Raven, Standard Raven, and WAIS Full Scale IQ.
*$p < .001$, two-tailed.

g. Two correlations not included in the above were obtained on 49 preschool children, ages 26 to 77 months (Telzrow, 1983). Mean RT and mean MT (for set size 8) correlated − .30 and − .46, respectively, with age-standardized IQ scores on the Peabody Picture Vocabulary Test. Corrected for attenuation (based on split-half reliability), these correlations become − .34 and − .57. It is noteworthy that MT yielded the higher correlation in this very young group.

Hemmelgarn and Kehle (1984) made an interesting discovery concerning the correlation of RT slope with WISC-R subtest scores. In a group of 59 intellectually superior elementary school children, it was found that the 12 subtests of the WISC-R were correlated (negatively) with RT slope to the degree that the subtests were loaded on the *g* factor of the WISC-R battery. Hemmelgarn and Kehle correlated individual differences in RT slope with scores on each of the 12 WISC-R subtests, partialling out chronological age. The profile of these 12 correlations shows a rank-order correlation of − .83 (*p* < .01) with the profile of the 12 subtests' *g* loadings. (The overall correlation between RT slope and Full Scale IQ was − .32.) This finding, which may help to elucidate the nature of *g,* warrants attempts at replication.

Multiple correlation of Hick parameters with IQ. The unweighted and *N*-weighted intercorrelations among the Hick variables and their correlations with IQ can be used to obtain an estimate of the overall multiple correlation (*R*) between the several Hick variables and IQ. This has been done for the correlations corrected for attenuation and restriction of range. The correlation matrices for the unweighted and *N*-weighted values are shown in Table 26. The multiple *R* between the Hick variables and IQ is .50, using unweighted correlations, and .36, using the *N*-weighted correlations. Both *R*s are significant beyond the .001 level. (Using the mean correlations not corrected for range or attenuation, the corresponding *R*s are .322 and .242.) Hence, it would seem safe to say that the best estimate of true multiple correlation in the population between Hick parameters and IQ, or psychometric *g,* falls somewhere between about .35 and .50.

RT and MT Correlation with IQ as a Function of Set Size

A theoretically important aspect of psychometric *g* is its apparent relationship to task complexity (Jensen, 1987a). This phenomenon has been in the foreground of *g* theory since the early days of factor analysis. A special case of this phenomenon would seem to be the finding in early RT research that choice RT is more highly correlated with IQ than is simple RT. Lemmon (1927), for example, found correlations of − .08 and − .25 of IQ with simple RT and choice RT in 100 university students. If speed or efficiency of information processing is hypothesized to be an essential aspect of *g,* one should predict an increasing correlation between *g* (or IQ) and RT as the informa-

TABLE 26
Mean Correlations (Decimals Omitted),[a] Corrected for
Restriction of Range and Attenuation, Between Hick Variables and IQ

Variable	IQ	$RT\bar{X}$	RTa	RTb	$RT\sigma_i$	$MT\bar{X}$
IQ		− 389	− 191	− 165	− 417	− 379
Mean RT (RT $\bar{X}$)	− 309		979	374	679	601
RT Intercept (RTa)	− 183			− 277	460	488
RT Slope (RTb)	− 183	413	− 234		470	226
$RT\sigma_i$	− 320	707	491	482		426
Mean MT (MT $\bar{X}$)	− 292	593	494	243	439	

[a]Above diagonal: unweighted correlations.
Below diagonal: N-weighted correlations.

tion processing demands of the reaction stimulus increase, at least up to some critical point on the complexity continuum beyond which response latency is influenced by specific acquired strategies or by certain noncognitive factors that are not themselves correlated with g. RT in the Hick paradigm lends itself to a test of this hypothesis. Because of its central place in g theory, it merits quite thorough examination in terms of all the available data.

Table 27 shows the correlations of RT and MT with intelligence measures at each set size (scaled in bits). All of the N-weighted mean rs are significant ($p < .001$), and are shown graphically in Figures 14 and 15. The increase in r as a function of bits is almost perfectly linear; the correlation between r and bits is − .987 for the unweighted means and − .979 for the N-weighted means. The increasing (negative) correlation for RT is what one would predict for an index of information processing capacity related to g. MT shows a slightly opposite trend.

A trend analysis performed on the RT correlations of Table 27 (and graphed in Figure 14) shows a highly significant linear trend ($F[1,84] = 12.12$, $p < .001$), while the mean deviations from linearity are quite nonsignificant ($F < 1$). Eta squared ($\times 100$) for the linear component is 13.51%. A parallel analysis of the MT correlations in Table 26 (graphed in Figure 15) shows a nonsignificant ($F[1,57] = 1.34$) linear component and nonsignificant ($F < 1$) nonlinear component.

Since there are substantial differences between studies in the average size of the correlations between RT and IQ, we must perform an analysis of the Table 27 data that examines whether the linear trend of RT × IQ correlation on bits remains when all studies have been equated for the average value of their correlations over bits. This can be done by converting the four correlations in each study to percentages, by dividing each r by the sum of all four rs

TABLE 27

Correlation Coefficient (Decimal Omitted) Between Intelligence Measures and RT and MT as a Function of Bits in 15 Independent Groups (N = 1129)

SID No.	Group	N	RT (Bits)				MT (Bits)				Intelligence Measure
			0	1	2	3	0	1	2	3	
1	University Students	50	+09	−02	−06	−32	−21	−29	−23	−14	Advanced Raven
1	University Students	50	+24	+10	+25	+12	−41	−31	−36	−33	CMT[a]
2	University Students	25	−12	−06	−12	−11	−21	−15	−17	−11	Advanced Raven
6	University Males	40	−03	−06	−11	−18					SAT−Verbal[b]
6	University Males	40	+37	+34	+37	+18					SAT−Math
10	University Students	100	−11	−19	−17	−16	−31	−24	−24	−23	WAIS−VIQ[c]
10	University Students	100	−11	−25	−29	−30	−23	−26	−24	−25	WAIS−PIQ[c]
10	University Students	100	−13	−25	−26	−27	−31	−29	−28	−28	WAIS−FSIQ[c]
10	University Students	100	−14	−22	−24	−21	−28	−30	−29	−27	Advanced Raven
11	University Students	50	+03	−04	−09	−08	−11	−11	−15	−14	Advanced Raven
12 + 13	Vocational College Students	218	−20	—	−19	−19	−17	—	−11	−10	SCAT[d]
12 + 13	Vocational College Students	218	−15	—	−15	−11	−08	—	−03	−03	ASVAB[e]
16	9th Grade Girls	39	−26	−33	−41	−35	−38	−43	−36	−36	Standard Raven
17	4th, 5th, 6th Graders	162	−08	−02	−04	−12	−05	−06	−12	−10	Standard Raven
17	4th, 5th, 6th Graders	162	−25	−16	−17	−21	−13	−14	−13	−13	Verbal IQ[f]
17	4th, 5th, 6th Graders	162	−18	−11	−11	−14	−16	−08	−17	−11	Nonverbal IQ[f]
19 + 20	Gifted vs. Avg. 7th Graders	130	−41	−53	−54	−54					r_{pbs} G/NG[g]
22	Average 7th Graders	20	−66	−69	−89	−89	−64	−60	−70	−49	Standard Raven
22	Average 7th Graders	20	−50	−36	−58	−60	−41	−37	−42	−34	Read. Comp.
22	Average 7th Graders	11	−69	−54	−71	−60	−60	−51	−53	−48	CTBS[h]

N	Group									Criterion
22	Average 7th Graders	-25	-14	-13	-18	-36	-27	-24	-33	English GPA[i]
22	Average 7th Graders	-24	-15	-22	-29	-07	+15	00	-13	Math GPA[i]
23	Average 7th Graders	-12	-07	-07	-19	+01	00	-03	-07	Standard Raven
23	Average 7th Graders	-33	-29	-32	-33	-22	-21	-21	-26	Read. Comp.
23	Average 7th Graders	-20	-09	-11	-17	+02	+05	+01	+02	CTBS[h]
25	Retarded Adults	-25	-27	-31	-06					Standard Raven
26	Ret. & Borderline Adults	-34	-31	-33	-36					Standard Raven
29	Normally Distributed Adults	—	-63	-65	-67	—	-56	-53	-45	IQ[j]
30	Average Adults	-27	-35	-39	-29					WAIS–VIQ[c]
30	Average Adults	-32	-42	-47	-46					WAIS–PIQ[c]
30	Average Adults	-32	-41	-45	-40					WAIS–FSIQ[c]
31	Average Adults	-14	-21	-19	-15					WAIS–FSIQ[c]
	Unweighted Mean	-19	-21	-24	-26	-24	-22	-23	-21	
	N-Weighted Mean	-18	-19	-22	-23	-17	-17	-15	-14	
	t test of N-Weighted Mean	6.1*	5.9*	7.6*	7.9*	4.7*	4.1*	4.3*	4.0*	

[a] Terman Concept Mastery Test.
[b] SAT – Scholastic Aptitude Test.
[c] Wechsler Adult Intelligence Scale (VIQ = Verbal IQ; PIQ = Performance IQ; FSIQ = Full Scale IQ).
[d] School and College Aptitude Test.
[e] Armed Services Vocational Aptitude Battery.
[f] Lorge-Thorndike Intellligence Test.
[g] Point-biserial correllation based on gifted and nongifted 7th graders.
[h] Comprehensive Test of Basic Skills.
[i] GPA – Grade Point Average.
[j] See Nettelbeck and Kirby (1983, p. 44) for description of IQ tests.
*p < .001 (two-tailed).

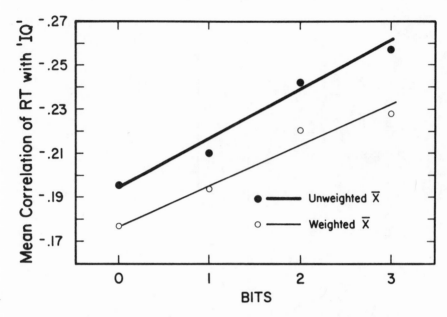

FIGURE 14. Mean unweighted and *N*-weighted correlations between RT and IQ based on 15 independent samples comprising a total of 1129 subjects.

and multiplying by 100. The unweighted mean percentages at each level of bits, then, are:

Bits:	0	1	2	3
Mean %:	21.6	23.2	26.7	28.4

The linear correlation, *r*, between *bits* and *mean %* is .987, indicating a strong degree of linear relationship between the RT × IQ correlations and bits of information. This relationship indeed appears to be real. However, it is not a very reliable or constant phenomenon in many single studies. A number of methodologically sound studies have failed to find the consistently increasing correlation between RT and IQ as a function of bits (e.g., Barrett et al., in press). To get some idea of the degree of agreement of individual studies with the monotonically increasing trend line obtained from the average of all studies, the four correlations in each study were ranked from lowest to highest and the ranks were correlated with the rank order expected on the hypothesis of a monotonically increasing trend, i.e., 1, 2, 3, 4. The rank-order correlation, averaged over all studies, is ρ = .394, *SD* = .457. (The corresponding Pearson *r* = .404, *SD* = .477.) This quite low average correlation reflects the fact that there is not a very high degree of agreement of single studies with the model of monotonically increasing correlation of RT with IQ

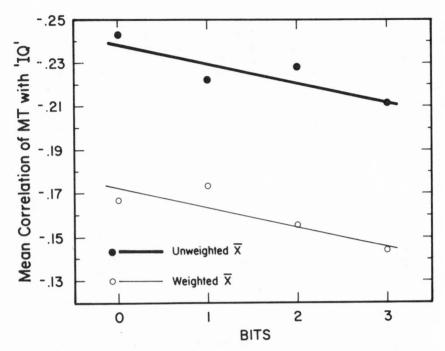

FIGURE 15.   Mean unweighted and N-weighted correlations between MT and IQ, based on 8 independent studies comprising a total of 759 subjects.

as a function of set size. The mean rank correlation between all possible pairs of studies as calculated by Kendall's coefficient of concordance is $W = .167$, which, though small, is significant ($F[2.93/82.17] = 5.60, p < .01$). Another way of looking at the degree of agreement of the 29 studies that used set sizes corresponding to 0, 1, 2, 3 bits is to tabulate the frequency of the rank order of the size of the RT × IQ correlation at each level of bits, as shown in Table 28. The frequent departures of the RT × IQ correlation from a perfect monotonically increasing function of bits is most probably attributable to sampling error. Correlation coefficients in the lower range that we are viewing here have quite large standard errors for sample sizes of less than 50 subjects, which is typical in these studies. (Among these 29 data sets, however, degree of conformity to a monotonic increase in correlations is not significantly related to sample size.) Although the increase in the RT × IQ correlation with bits is a rather weak and erratic phenomenon in the Hick paradigm, it is consistent with the findings of RT × IQ correlations increasing as a function of task complexity in a number of other RT tasks that differ in complexity (e.g., Vernon & Jensen, 1984).

Correlation between $RT\sigma_i$ and IQ as a function of set size. Of all the Hick parameters we have examined, intraindividual variability of RT, $RT\sigma_i$,

TABLE 28
Frequencies of Rank Order of the Size of the
RT × IQ Correlation at Each Level of
Bits in 29 Data Sets[a] (N = 911)

Rank of r	0	1	2	3
			Bits	
1	14	9	2	1
1.5	1	2	3	0
2	3	10	7	7
2.5	0	0	0	0
3	5	5	7	8
3.5	2	0	3	3
4	4	3	8	10
$\bar{X}$[b]	2.05	2.03	2.80	3.08
SD	1.19	0.97	1.00	0.87

[a]All the 29 sets in Table 27 that give RT × IQ correlations for 0, 1, 2, 3, bits.
[b]$\bar{X}$ is the mean rank order of the RT × IQ correlation over the 29 data sets.

is generally a better correlate of IQ, even despite its lower reliability, than all of the other parameters except RT slope, which has about the same reliability as $RT\sigma_i$. Yet the correlation between $RT\sigma_i$ and IQ shows no significant relation to set size, as can be seen in Table 29. This finding is strikingly inconsistent with the oscillation model originally proposed by Jensen (1982a, pp. 127–131) in that individual differences in an oscillatory mechanism were hypothesized to underlie individual differences both in $RT\sigma_i$ and in g. Since $RT\sigma_i$ increases linearly as a function of set size (see Figure 11), with increasing set size one should predict a greater opportunity for individual differences in the oscillation process hypothesized to underlie both $RT\sigma_i$ and g to be increasingly manifested, thereby making for a monotonically increasing (negative) correlation between $RT\sigma_i$ and g as a function of set size. This prediction was not borne out in the least, judging from the 16 data sets based on eight independent samples comprising 603 subjects shown in Table 29. This is the only really substantial anomaly for the oscillation model. It seems no less anomalous in terms of the model of different error rates in synaptic transmission of information proposed by A. E. Hendrickson (1982), as explicated in Eysenck's chapter in the present volume. It also seems inconsistent with the general finding in other studies that the size of the correlation between psychometric g and $RT\sigma_i$ in various RT tasks is directly related to task complexity, and that both RT and $RT\sigma_i$ increase as a function of task complexity (e.g., Vernon & Jensen, 1984). Therefore, it is puzzling that the $RT\sigma_i$ × IQ correlation does not increase with increasing set size in the Hick paradigm.

TABLE 29

Correlation Coefficient (Decimal Omitted) Between Intelligence and Intraindividual Variability (RTσ_i) As a Function of Set Size (n) in 8 Independent Samples ($N = 603$)

SID No.	Group	N	Set Size (n)				Intelligence Measure
			1	2	4	8	
1	University Students	50	−07	−03	−18	−38	Advanced Raven
1	University Students	50	−01	+20	+14	−27	Concept Mastery Test
2	University Students	25	−32	−41	−33	−21	Advanced Raven
10	University Students	100	−12	−05	−12	−10	WAIS Verbal IQ
10	University Students	100	−34	−25	−21	−33	WAIS Performance IQ
10	University Students	100	−26	−17	−19	−24	WAIS Full Scale IQ
10	University Students	100	−33	−10	−16	−33	Advanced Raven
11	University Students	50	−16	−10	−28	−18	Advanced Raven
17	4th, 5th, 6th Graders	162	+01	−11	−24	−26	Standard Raven
17	4th, 5th, 6th Graders	162	−11	−15	−21	−18	Lorge-Thorndike Verbal IQ
17	4th, 5th, 6th Graders	162	−09	−17	−27	−17	Lorge-Thorndike Nonverbal IQ
19 & 20	Gifted vs. Avg. 7th Graders	130	−60	−54	−45	−37	Point biserial r, Gifted/Avg.
30	Average Adults	40	−23	−07	−33	−16	WAIS Full Scale IQ
30	Average Adults	40	−25	−01	−26	−10	WAIS Verbal IQ
30	Average Adults	40	−19	−14	−37	−15	WAIS Performance IQ
31	Average Adults	46	−40	−17	−28	−20	WAIS Full Scale IQ
	Unweighted Mean		−22	−14	−25	−23	
	N-Weighted Mean		−26	−21	−28	−25	
	t test		6.72*	5.36*	7.24*	6.32*	
	Corrected for Range, Weighted Mean		−36	−29	−39	−34	
	Disattenuated, Weighted Mean		−40	−33	−43	−38	

*$p < .001$, two-tailed.

Explanations of the RT × IQ Correlation

The aim of this chapter has been simply to review the empirical evidence on individual differences in the parameters of the Hick RT paradigm. Theoretical speculations about these findings must be the subject for another article. Some of the main theoretical issues put forth in the recent past on the RT–IQ relationship are reviewed in Eysenck's chapter in this volume. In view of all the evidence I have presented in the present chapter, I doubt that, at present, we have an adequate theory to explain all of the now quite well established facts of individual differences in Hick variables and their relation to psychometric g. The substantial correlations between all of the various Hick parameters, and the fact that they are all correlated to much the same degree with IQ, allowing for differences in reliability, suggests that some quite general factor in the speed or efficiency of performance is reflected in all aspects of the Hick paradigm. Individual differences in the Hick RT intercept are also substantially correlated with the RT intercepts of both the Sternberg memory search and the Neisser visual search paradigms (Jensen, 1987b). The early expectation that the various parameters, presumably reflecting different cognitive processes, would clearly differentiate among individuals, is not borne out by the present evidence. Theoretically, RT slope should be a purer index of rate of information processing than RT intercept, yet they are correlated with IQ about equally. And MT, which supposedly reflects a motor skill component rather than an information processing component, is about as highly correlated with IQ as is RT. In a study using a variety of different RT tasks, Ananda (1985) found that scores on verbal and nonverbal intelligence tests (Raven Matrices and Mill Hill Vocabulary) had their largest loadings (−.648 and −.480) on the general factor (first principal component) common to both RT and MT, both variables showing large positive loadings on the same general factor. The intelligence measures have near-zero loadings (−.03 and −.13) on the bipolar factor which distinguishes RT from MT (with positive and negative loadings respectively). Although it is not yet unarguable, the evidence on the Hick parameters seems to indicate that g is more highly correlated with a general factor common to all of the Hick RT and MT variables than with any particular cognitive processing components that can be inferred from certain parameters of the Hick paradigm. One might even go so far as to hypothesize that the general factor of a large and diverse battery of RT tasks (that is, all the RT and MT parameters derived from them) is one and the same general factor as found in the factor analysis of any large and diverse battery of conventional psychometric tests of mental ability.

Although there is presently no truly detailed and comprehensive theory of all the individual differences phenomena observed in the Hick paradigm, there are several theoretical speculations abroad which I think are either flatly contradicted by the evidence or are the least likely to prove correct. It would seem worthwhile to mention these unpromising notions briefly.

Common speed factor in test taking. This is the notion that since some psychometric tests are speeded or timed, and individuals presumably differ in response to time pressure and in speed of work, such tests will be correlated with RT, which is also a measure of speed. This conjecture is contradicted by various lines of evidence. In the first place in nearly all of our RT studies, we have used tests that were not only unspeeded and untimed but in which subjects were explicitly urged to take all the time they needed, to attempt every item, and to check their answers. In most studies, subjects were tested individually on the psychometric tests as well as on the RT tests, so as not to feel they were in competition or to have any clues about how fast others completed the tests. Secondly, in specific investigations in which some tests were speeded and others given without time limit, there was no significant difference in the tests' correlations with RT measures. If anything, there is even a tendency for unspeeded tests to show slightly higher correlations with RT than speeded tests. (See Vernon, Nador, & Kantor, 1985, and Vernon and Kantor, 1986, for a detailed discussion of studies specially directed at this point.) Thirdly, individual response latencies on items of complex tests, such as the Raven, are not significantly correlated with psychometric *g*. Also, highly speeded tasks in which the task requirements per se are quite simple, such as clerical checking, letter cancellation, and the like, are among the poorest psychometric correlates of IQ or *g*, and they also show the weakest correlations with RT (Vernon & Jensen, 1984, p. 417).

Strategies and speed-accuracy trade-off. So far no one has made a serious case for the idea that the individual differences in certain performance strategies account for the RT × IQ correlation. As pointed out previously, the conjecture that different strategies are involved in the RT slope was suggested by Nettlebeck and Kirby (1983) on the basis of their observation of a negative correlation between RT intercept and RT slope. But the negative correlation is shown to be an artifact due to negatively correlated measurement errors. Nettlebeck and Kirby (1983) also suggest that a negative correlation between RT slope and MT intercept observed in one of their samples indicates a strategy of "making a movement after detecting only the presence of a signal, but then delaying movement so as to permit a further decision during movement about which alternative was involved" (p. 50). Although something like this may occur in the mentally retarded and in very young children, we have found not the slightest suggestion of it in normal samples of school age and above. This strategy, if adopted by some subjects and not by others, would be expected to cause a negative correlation between RT and MT, which is not found. Also, as seen in Table 16, the 18 studies (total *N* = 375) in which a correlation was obtained between RT slope and mean MT (which is almost perfectly correlated with MT intercept) do not show a negative correlation between these variables; the N-weighted mean correlation (over 18 studies) is $+.087$ ($+.243$ corrected for restriction of range and attenuation).

The most commonly offered explanation of RT $\times$ IQ correlation is in terms of a speed–accuracy trade-off, or the conjecture that brighter subjects try to improve their RT performance by sacrificing response *accuracy* for an increased *speed* of response. This hypothesis is unconvincing for two main reasons. First, with the use of a home button, which the subject merely has to release, response accuracy with respect to RT is virtually assured; inaccuracy of response would show up as a failure to touch the button that turns off the reaction stimulus light, thereby affecting movement time, not RT. So simple is the RT task that such response errors are extremely rare in this procedure and are completely absent in the vast majority of subjects. Second, and more important, is the fact that if a speed–accuracy trade-off accounted for any part of the individual differences in either RT or MT, there should be a *negative* correlation between response error rate and RT (or MT). Yet all RT studies in which both RTs and error rates have been measured show a *positive* correlation between RT and errors. The faster responders are also the more accurate responders. There is no evidence in our various RT studies or in anyone else's for a *between*-subjects speed-accuracy trade-off. Speed-accuracy trade-off is a *within*-subjects phenomenon, accounting for *negative* correlations (*within* subjects) between RTs and error rates under different levels of task difficulty. It presents no problem for interpreting the correlation between individual differences in RT and IQ, because the *between*-subjects correlation of RT and error rate is a *positive* correlation, and both RT and error rate are *negatively* correlated with IQ. These relationships can be explained more easily with reference to Figure 16. On the *simple task,* hypothetical persons A, B, and C are shown to have the same short RT and low error rate. On the *complex task,* the latest ability differences between A, B, and C are manifested as variation in their RTs and error rates. Their performances, as reflected jointly by RT and errors, will tend to fall somewhere on each of the arcs that describe the speed–accuracy trade-off and are different for each person. If the same low error rate of the simple task is to be maintained for the complex task, the RT is greatly increased for all persons (vertical line = zero speed–accuracy trade-off). If the RT in the simple task is to be maintained in the complex task, the error rate is greatly increased for all persons (horizontal line = 100% speed–accuracy trade-off). So the arc for each person describes an *inverse* relationship (or *negative* correlation) between RT and error rate. But *between* persons, RT and error rate show a *direct* relationship (or *positive* correlation). The line marked X in Figure 16 indicates a fairly high speed–accurracy trade-off for a typical RT study, if the error rate (on the abscissa) is assumed to range between *zero* and *chance.* Thus the shaded area represents the most desirable region for performance when

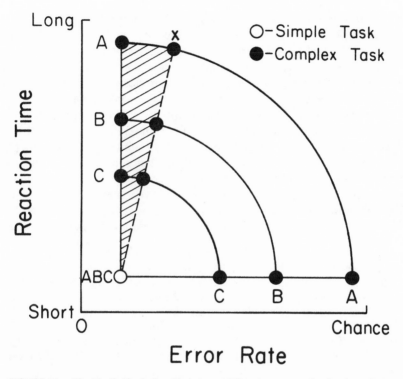

Error Rate

FIGURE 16.   The idealized relationship between RT and error rate for simple and complex tasks. The arcs describe the speed–accuracy trade-off for hypothetical persons, A, B, and C, who are shown here as performing equally on the simple task. Shaded area represents most desirable region of speed–accuracy trade-off for RT studies.

studying individual differences in RT in that it spreads out individual differences in RT much more than in error rate, a feature observed in all of our RT studies. Hence the observed correlation between RT variables and IQ can in no way be accounted for in terms of speed–accuracy trade-off.

Motivation or Arousal.   Could it be simply that the more highly motivated subjects, because of their greater motivation, perform better on both the RT tasks and the IQ tests, thereby causing them to be correlated through the common factor of motivation? This possibility has not been conclusively ruled out, but it seems an improbable hypothesis. The fact that an increase in the complexity of RT tasks causes RT to be more highly correlated with *g* runs counter to what is known about the relationship of motivation or drive to efficiency of performance as a function of task complexity. The well-established empirical generalization known as the Yerkes-Dodson Law (Yerkes & Dodson, 1908) states that the optimal level of drive (D) for learning or performance of a task is inversely related to the degree of complexity of the task; that is, a *lower* level of D is *more* advantageous for the performance of more complex tasks. In this respect, D is just the opposite of g. The g loading of tasks increases with task complexity, and persons who score highest in the most g-loaded tests are more successful in dealing with complexity. From what research has taught us about D and the Yerkes-Dodson Law, one would not predict high-D persons to perform like high g persons as a function of task complexity. In humans, changes in drive and arousal are reflected in pupillary dilation. Ahern and Beatty (1979) measured the degree of pupillary dilation as an indicator of effort and autonomic arousal when subjects are presented with test problems. They found that (a) pupillary dilation is directly related to level of problem difficulty (as indexed both by the objective complexity of the problem and the percentage of subjects giving the correct answer), and (b) subjects with higher psychometrically measured intelligence show *less* pupillary dilation to problems at any given level of difficulty. (All subjects were university students.) Ahern and Beatty concluded:

> These results help to clarify the biological basis of psychometrically-defined intelligence. They suggest the more intelligent individuals do not solve a tractable cognitive problem by bringing increased activation, "mental energy" or "mental effort" to bear. On the contrary, these individuals show less task-induced activation in solving a problem of a given level of difficulty. This suggests that *individuals differing in intelligence must also differ in the efficiency of those brain processes which mediate the particular cognitive task.* (1979, p. 1292; emphasis added)

Neurophysiological Correlates of Hick Variables

My search of the literature has turned up only two investigations of physiological correlates of Hick parameters, both based on the average (cortical) evoked potential (AEP), using an auditory stimulus (a "click"). An index of "neural adaptability" (NA), derived from the amplitude of the AEP, which was found to be correlated with IQ in previous studies using subjects of average and superior intelligence, was found to be correlated both with psychometric g and with certain Hick parameters in a group of 54 severely retarded adults (Jensen et al., 1981). The index of neural adaptability showed the following correlations with Hick parameters (in parentheses are the correlations of the Hick parameters with g factor scores derived from 15 psychometric tests):

Median RT:	$-.02$ n.s.	$(-.13$ n.s.$)$
Median MT:	$-.16$ n.s.	$(-.18$ n.s.$)$
RTσ_i:	$-.24, p < .05$	$(-.44, p < .01)$
MTσ_i:	$-.38, p < .01$	$(-.57, p < .01)$

Remarkably, the correlation between the two sets of correlations is $+.94$; that is, the correlation of the Hick variables with psychometric g is closely paralleled by their correlation with the index of neural adaptability. The sum of the standardized Hick variables together with NA yields a shrunken multiple R of .54 ($p < .001$) with psychometric g.

A further investigation of the relation between the AEP and Hick's Law was made by Schafer, Amochaev, and Russell (1982), who engaged eight normal young adults in the Hick task with set sizes 1, 4, and 8 (using Jensen's RT-MT apparatus) while measuring their cortical responses evoked by the visual stimuli in the Hick task. The results showed that the amount of information (bits) conveyed by the evoking stimuli affects not only the RT (i.e., Hick's Law), but also the latency of the cortical evoked potential (EP). The EP latencies also manifested Hick's Law, the EP latencies increasing linearly as a function of bits. EP amplitude, interestingly, showed a *negative* relation to bits, *decreasing* linearly from 0 to 3 bits. This is especially interesting because amplitude is also inversely related to IQ. The average fit of the RTs to Hick's Law (calculated from data provided by Dr. Schafer) is $r = .958$; of the EP latencies, $r = .933$; of the EP amplitudes, $r = (negative) -.997$. Hence both the latency and amplitude of the cortical potential evoked by stimuli conveying varying degrees of information appear to manifest Hick's Law to about the same degree as overt RT. The rank-order correlations between RTs and the late cortical EP latencies (i.e., the N417 and P553 components) were .58 and .65. These results should encourage further investigations of the relationships between RT variables, evoked cortical potentials, and psychometric g. It seems most probable that it is from this sphere of research at the interface of brain and behavior that a scientifically adequate theory of individual differences in intelligence will eventually take shape.

REFERENCES

Ahern, S., & Beatty, J. (1979). Pupillary responses during information processing vary with Scholastic Aptitude Test scores. *Science, 205,* 1289–1292.

Ananda, S. M. (1985). *Speed of information processing and psychometric abilities in later adulthood.* Unpublished doctoral dissertation, University of California, Berkeley.

Barrett, P., Eysenck, H. J., & Lucking, S. (1986). Reaction time and intelligence: A replicate study. *Intelligence, 10,* 9–40.

Blank, G. (1934). Brauchbarkeit optischer Reaktionsmessungen. *Industrielle Psychotechnik, 11,* 140–150.

Braden, J. P. (1985). *The relationship between choice reaction time and IQ in deaf and hearing children.* Unpublished doctoral dissertation, University of California, Berkeley.

Carlson, J. S., & Jensen, C. M. (1982). Reaction time, movement time, and intelligence: A replication and extension. *Intelligence, 6,* 265–274.

Carlson, J. S., Jensen, C. M., & Widaman, K. F. (1983). Reaction time, intelligence, and attention. *Intelligence, 7,* 329–344.

Cohn, G. J., Carlson, J. S., & Jensen, A. R. (1985). Speed of information processing in academically gifted youths. *Personality and Individual Differences, 6,* 621-629.

Cronbach, L. J. (1951). Coefficient alpha and the internal structure of tests. *Psychometrika, 16,* 297-334.

Donders, F. C. (1969). Over de Snelheid van psychische Processen. In W. G. Koster (Ed. and Trans.), *Attention and performance II, Acta Psychologica, 30,* 412-431. (Originally published in 1868-1869.)

Eysenck, H. J. (1967). Intelligence assessment: A theoretical and experimental approach. *British Journal of Education Psychology, 37,* 81-98.

Fairweather, H., & Hutt, S. J. (1978). On the rate of gain of information in children. *Journal of Experimental Child Psychology, 26,* 216-229.

Forsyth, R. A., & Feldt, L. S. (1969). An investigation of empirical sampling distributions of correlation coefficients corrected for attenuation. *Educational and Psychological Measurement, 29,* 61-71.

Gulliksen, H. (1950). *Theory of mental tests.* New York: Wiley.

Hemmelgarn, T. E., & Kehle, T. J. (1984). The relationship between reaction time and intelligence in children. *School Psychology International, 5,* 77-84.

Hendrickson, A. E. (1982). The biological basis of intelligence. Part I: Theory. In H. J. Eysenck (Ed.), *A model for intelligence.* Berlin: Springer-Verlag.

Hick, W. E. (1952). On the rate of gain of information. *Quarterly Journal of Experimental Psychology, 4,* 11-26.

Hyman, R. (1953). Stimulus information as a determinant of reaction time. *Journal of Experimental Psychology, 45,* 188-196.

Jensen, A. R. (1979). g: Outmoded theory or unconquered frontier? *Creative Science and Technology, 2,* 16-29.

Jensen, A. R. (1982a). Reaction time and psychometric g. In H. J. Eysenck (Ed.), *A model for intelligence.* Berlin: Springer-Verlag.

Jensen, A. R. (1982b). The chronometry of intelligence. In R. J. Sternberg (Ed.), *Advances in research on intelligence* (Vol. 1). Hillsdale, NJ: Erlbaum.

Jensen, A. R. (1985). Methodological and statistical techniques for the chronometric study of mental abilities. In C. R. Reynolds & V. L. Willson (Eds.), *Methodological and statistical advances in the study of individual differences.* New York: Plenum.

Jensen, A. R. (1987a). The g beyond factor analysis. In J. C. Conoly, J. A. Glover, & R. R. Ronning (Eds.), *The influence of cognitive psychology on testing and measurement.* Hillsdale, NJ: Erlbaum.

Jensen, A. R. (1987b). Process differences and individual differences in some cognitive tasks. *Intelligence, 11,* 107-136.

Jensen, A. R. (in press). Speed of information processing and population differences. In S. H. Irvine (Ed.), *The cultural context of human ability.* New York: Cambridge University Press.

Jensen, A. R., & Munro, E. (1979). Reaction time, movement time, and intelligence. *Intelligence, 3,* 121-126.

Jensen, A. R., Schafer, E. W., & Crinella, F. M. (1981). Reaction time, evoked brain potentials, and psychometric g in the severely retarded. *Intelligence, 5,* 179-197.

Kirby, N. (1980). Sequential effects in choice reaction time. In A. T. Welford (Ed.), *Reaction times.* New York: Academic Press.

Larson, G. E., & Rimland, B. (1984). *Cognitive speed and performance in basic electricity and electronics (BE&E) school* (Report No. TR85-3). San Diego, CA: Navy Personnel Research and Development Center.

Larson, G. E., & Saccuzzo, D. P. (1985). *Modifying Jensen's reaction time task for microcomputer presentation: The role of potential reponse errors.* Manuscript submitted for publication.

Lawley, D. N. (1963). On testing a set of correlation coefficients for equality. *Annals of Mathematical Statistics, 34,* 149.

Lemmon, V. W. (1927). The relation of reaction time to measures of intelligence, memory, and learning. *Archives of Psychology, 15*, 5–38.

Marascuilo, L., & Levin, J. R. (1983). *Multivariate statistics in the social sciences: A researcher's guide.* Monterey, CA: Brooks/Cole.

Merkel, J. (1885). Die zeitlichen Verhältnisse der Willensthähigkeit. *Philosophische Studien, 2,* 73–127.

Nettelbeck, T. (1985). What reaction times time. *Behavioral and Brain Sciences, 8,* 235.

Nettelbeck, T., & Kirby, N. H. (1983). Measures of timed performance and intelligence. *Intelligence, 7,* 39–52.

Paul, S. M. (1984). *Speed of information processing: The Semantic Verification Test and general mental ability.* Unpublished doctoral dissertation, University of California, Berkeley.

Peak, H., & Boring, E. G. (1926). The factor of speed in intelligence. *Journal of Experimental Psychology, 9,* 71–94.

Roth, E. (1964). Die Geschwindigkeit der Verarbeitung von Information und ihr Zusammenhang mit Intelligenz. *Zeitschrift für Experimentelle und Angewandte Psychologie, 11,* 616–622.

Schafer, E. W. P., Amochaev, A., & Russell, M. J. (1982). Brain response timing correlates with information mediated variations in reaction time. *Psychophysiology, 19,* 345.

Sen, A., Jensen, A. R., Sen, A. K., & Arora, I. (1983). Correlation between reaction time and intelligence in psychometrically similar groups in America and India. *Applied Research in Mental Retardation, 4,* 139–152.

Shannon, C. E., & Weaver, W. (1949). *The mathematical theory of communication.* Urbana, IL: University of Illinois Press.

Smith, G. A. (1980). Models of choice reaction time. In A. T. Welford (Ed.), *Reaction times.* New York: Academic Press.

Spearman, C. (1927). *The abilities of man.* New York: Macmillan.

Teichner, W. H., & Krebs, M. J. (1974). Laws of visual choice reaction time. *Psychological Review, 81,* 75–98.

Telzrow, C. F. (1983). Making child neuropsychological appraisal appropriate for children: Alternative to downward extension of adult batteries. *Clinical Neuropsychology, 5,* 136–141.

Vernon, P. A. (1981a). *Speed of information-processing and general intelligence.* Unpublished doctoral dissertation, University of California, Berkeley.

Vernon, P. A. (1981b). Reaction time and intelligence in the mentally retarded. *Intelligence, 5,* 345–355.

Vernon, P. A. (1983). Speed of information processing and general intelligence. *Intelligence, 7,* 53–70.

Vernon, P. A., & Jensen, A. R. (1984). Individual and group differences in intelligence and speed of information processing. *Personality and Individual Differences, 5,* 411–423.

Vernon, P. A., Nador, S., & Kantor, L. (1985). Reaction times and speed-of-processing: Their relationship to timed and untimed measures of intelligence. *Intelligence, 9,* 357–374.

Vernon, P. A., & Kantor, L. (1986). Reaction time correlations with intelligence test scores obtained under either timed or untimed conditions. *Intelligence, 10,* 315–330.

Wade, J. P. (1984). *The relationships among intelligence and six chronometric paradigms with academically able students.* Unpublished doctoral dissertation, Arizona State University.

Welford, A. T. (1980). Choice reaction time: Basic concepts. In A. T. Welford (Ed.), *Reaction times.* New York: Academic Press.

Woodworth, R. S., & Schlosberg, H. (1956). *Experimental psychology* (revised ed.). New York: Holt.

Yerkes, R. M., & Dodson, J. D. (1908). The relation of strength of stimulus to rapidity of habit formation. *Journal of Comparative Neurology and Psychology, 18,* 458–482.

CHAPTER 5

What Does Reaction Time Tell Us About Intelligence?

Douglas K. Detterman
Case Western Reserve University
and
Air Force Human Resources Laboratory

Reaction time is one of the oldest and most extensively studied tasks in experimental psychology. It has been used to investigate general principles of behavior and to assess individual differences. Simple reaction time was one of the measures used by Galton (1883) to index individual differences. And every student of psychology has heard an account of how personal equations were proposed as an adjustment for differences in astronomers' reaction times.

Though reaction time received early attention, it was quickly abandoned. More complex measures were adopted in the belief that a simple measure of performance would never be useful in understanding complex behaviors. This trend was particularly true of individual differences research. Complex tests like those currently used on intelligence tests were favored over simpler measures of more elementary processes.

Some experimental psychologists continued to study reaction time (Smith, 1968) in the hope of discovering general principles of behavior. But individual difference researchers ignored it for the major part of this century, with a few notable exceptions (Baumeister & Kellas, 1968; Welford, 1980). Within the last several years, however, there has been a resurgence of interest in the relationship between reaction time and human intelligence. The purpose of this chapter is to consider this recent interest in reaction time, particularly with respect to how reaction time experiments might clarify theories of intelligence.

I will attempt to accomplish three things in this chapter. First, I will specify the potential classes of theories of human intelligence and indicate how choice reaction time measures are related to each class of theory. Second, I will present a brief, biased review of the literature and data from three new experiments in support of my theoretical biases. Third, factors which must be explored before the relationship between reaction time and human intelligence are understood will be discussed. I believe it will be clear from this discussion that choice reaction time is not a simple process reflecting a unitary aspect of human intelligence. It is, instead, a complex set of processes, some of which are a part of human intelligence.

THEORIES OF INTELLIGENCE AND
THEIR RELATIONSHIP TO CHOICE REACTION TIME

There are three classes of possible theories of human intelligence (Detterman, 1980, 1982, 1984a, 1984b, 1986). Each of these theories has a different implication for the relationship of reaction time to intelligence. However, before discussing this relationship it is important to specify just what reaction time measures will be discussed.

Choice Reaction Time
Choice reaction time task.   Choice reaction time tasks discussed in this chapter are similar, if not identical, to the choice reaction time task described by Jensen (1979, 1982a). A diagramatic representation of this task is shown in Figure 1. The implementation of the task which I have used in my research uses a computer screen, and subjects make all responses by touching the screen. The left panel of Figure 1 shows what the subject sees in this task. The right panel indicates what the subject must do.

At the beginning of each trial, a semicircular display of empty windows appears on the computer screen. The display shown in Figure 1 has eight windows, but a trial could have 1, 2, 4, 6, or 8 windows. At the bottom center of the screen is a small bar. To begin the trial, the subject presses the bar and keeps pressing the bar. The subject watches the screen until, after some variable interval, one of the windows lights up. When the subject sees the lit window, he or she responds by moving his or her finger from the bar and touching the lit window as quickly as possible. When the subject makes the correct response, the screen goes blank and, after a brief interval, a new trial begins.

The task I have used consists of 120 trials of the type described above. Each set size gets 24 trials. Trials are generally blocked by set size. That is, all trials

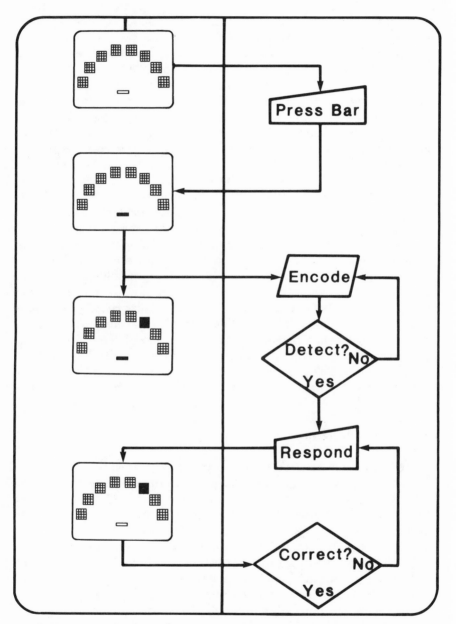

FIGURE 1. A flow diagram of the choice reaction time task with computer video screen changes shown in the left panel and subjects responses in the right panel.

with one alternative (i.e., window) are presented together, all two-alternative trials are together, etc. Trial blocks of different set size are presented in ascending order. Subjects always receive 24 trials of 1, 2, 4, 6, and 8 alternative trials in that order.

Choice reaction time measures. There are a number of measures which can be obtained during each trial. Carroll (1980) has recommended that reaction time be divided into decision time and movement time. Decision time is the amount of time from stimulus onset to response initiation. In the paridigm described above, decision time is the time the subject keeps his or her finger on the bar at the bottom of the screen *after* one of the windows has lit up. Movement time is the amount of time required to execute a response. It is measured as elapsed time from when the subject lifts his or her finger from the bar until the lighted window is touched.

Other measures of interest include number of errors, total amount of time for each trial, and measures with the potential to show systematic change over trials or conditions. One measure which has received a great deal of attention is the slope of decision time over set size. As the number of alternatives which a subject must scan gets larger, an increase in reaction time is expected. Hick (1952) proposed that reaction time was a linear function of the log(base 2) of number of choices, since the log of number of choices represents the amount of information in the display. Unlike Hick, who was most interested in the ability of information theory to generally describe human behavior, individual differences researchers are most interested in whether differences in slope for individuals are related to intelligence. It would be expected that less intelligent persons should have relatively more difficulty as the number of alternatives increases. So steeper slopes should indicate lower IQs.

Theories of Intelligence

One of the most persistent debates in psychology has been how to characterize intelligence. Spearman (1904, 1927) characterized intelligence as a single thing which he called g. On the other hand, Thurstone (1935, 1938) attempted to show that intelligence consisted of a small number of separate abilities. Still others (Humphreys, 1979; Thomson, 1939) have characterized intelligence as a large, perhaps infinite, number of separate components.

Which ever of these theories is correct, there are some undeniable empirical findings for which any theory will have to account. One is that complex tests of intelligence demonstrate what Spearman called "positive manifold"; all mental tests are positively correlated. The size of this interrelationship in any particular set of tests can be summarized by the proportion of variance accounted for by the unrotated first principal component. This is what

Spearman defined as g. Though I will adopt this as the empirical definition of g, it does not mean that I agree with Spearman's theoretical explanation of why g exists. It is impossible, I think, to deny the empirical reality of the phenomenon, but there can be many possible theoretical explanations for it. In fact, it is really the implication that reaction time has for theories of intelligence and understanding g in particular that makes it such an interesting topic.

Another important empirical relationship is that tests of basic cognitive abilities tend to have lower correlations with IQ than do more complex tests. How does a theory of intelligence explain this difference across levels of complexity?

Intelligence as a single thing. It is tempting and, indeed, parsimonious to believe that intelligence is a single thing. Although it has seldom been explicitly stated, one of the reaons for increased interest in reaction time is that mental speed would appear to be a good candidate for the single variable defining intelligence (e.g., Eysenck, 1982). It would certainly provide major support for this theoretical position to find a simple, almost biologically-based test that would be completely predictive of g.

In fact, finding a single variable which would predict the g-loadedness of different tests is a major requirement to support this theoretical position, because the theory postulates just such a relationship. In addition, the differences in the size of intercorrelations among tests is accounted for by postulating that some tests are more g-loaded than others. In other words, they include more of the single variable in what they measure.

What this particular theoretical position should therefore predict is that, if it were possible to obtain a "pure" measure of the single variable that is g, then the correlation between this pure measure and factor scores of g extracted from less pure measures of intelligence should be nearly perfectly correlated. This is the hope for measures of mental speed such as choice reaction time or electrophysiological measures of related processes. In fact, measures of averaged evoked potentials obtained by some investigators (A. Hendrickson, 1982; D. Hendrickson, 1982) come very close to this goal.

As will be seen in the following discussion, even if it is possible to show that a single measure from a simple task is highly correlated with g, it still must be shown that the measure is of a single process and is not, itself, a measure of a number of complex processes. This would require a sophisticated understanding of the task purported to yield a single, simple measure of g. Certainly, neither choice reaction time nor averaged evoked potentials are sufficiently well understood to conclude that any measures they yield reflect the operation of a single variable.

Intelligence as a small set of independent elements. Another theoretical possibility is that intelligence is composed of a small number of separate abilities or processes. Any mental task consists of a subset of these processes. The more complex the task, the more processes that will be required to perform it.

According to this position, tasks are interrelated to the extent they both use the same processes. IQ tests are highly correlated with each other because they consist of complex items and involve all of the basic processes in each test. Simpler tasks have lower intercorrelations with each other because each task has fewer of the basic processes and, therefore, two tasks are likely to have fewer processes in common.

Even though simple tasks have lower correlations with intelligence, they can be combined to predict all of the variance in the more complex IQ tests. All that is necessary is that the simple tests be selected so that they contain, in combination, all of the processes contained in the more complex test. Ideally, each of the simple tests would have a small correlation with IQ but be uncorrelated with any of the other simple tests.

In fact, a test of this theoretical position is the degree to which it is possible to obtain independent measures of the postulated separate processes. If it is possible to combine measures so that increments in prediction accrue beyond what would be expected due to the unreliability of the combined measures, then the different simple tasks must contain different processes.

Further, it is to be expected that simple tasks will have low correlations with IQ. If there are 10 basic processes involved in intelligence, and each accounts for the same amount of variance, then it should be expected that a pure measure of one of these processes would account for 10% of the variance, and that its correlation with a perfectly reliable IQ test would be .33. The more processes constituting intelligence, the smaller the correlations of basic processes with intelligence should be.

What are the implications of this theoretical position for the relationship between choice reaction time and intelligence? If there are relationships between IQ and choice reaction time measures, these relationships would obviously be interpreted much differently than they would be if intelligence was the result of a single variable. It would be expected that choice reaction time measures would correlate with intelligence to the extent the measures include the same processes as intelligence. Different choice reaction time measures would be uncorrelated if they did not contain common processes.

Since correlations do exist between simple cognitive tasks, this position would explain those correlations as resulting from the presence of common processes. That is, even what appear to be very simple tasks are not pure representations of basic processes. If two simple tasks were reflections of pure processes, they would be uncorrelated. Not surprisingly, according to this position current measures of choice reaction time would be regarded as fairly complex.

Intelligence as a large set of elements.   A third theory of intelligence owes its beginning to Thomson (1939). It is sometime called "bond theory." In this theory, intelligence is conceived of as a large, approaching infinite, set of elements. Tests are intercorrelated to the extent they share common elements.

In fact, all correlations can be explained on the basis of shared elements. IQ tests are complex and, therefore, consist of a larger number of elements. Since these elements comprise a large portion of the total number of elements, it is likely that two IQ tests of high complexity will share a large number of elements and will, consequently, be highly correlated.

Basic cognitive tasks will include a smaller number of elements. They will accordingly share fewer common elements with more complex IQ tests, and will have lower correlations than IQ tests have with each other. Basic cognitive tasks also will have lower intercorrelations with each other for the same reason.

It is difficult to empirically distinguish this theoretical position from the position which regards intelligence as a single thing. The reason for this is that, if a large sample is drawn from a larger population, the expected value of the sample approaches a constant equal to the mean of the population as the sample size approaches the population size or as sample size gets very large. This means that a sample of elements could seem as if a single element were operating having a numerical value equal to the mean of the population.

Given the small number of subjects usually used in psychological research, it is very likely that it is impossible to distinguish whether results are due to a single variable or a large sample of elements. Therefore, for all practical purposes the two positions can be regarded as equivalent. If it is not possible to show that a small number of independent elements can account for intelligence and g especially (as in the second theory discussed above), then it would be necessary to distinguish the two possibilities represented by the first and third positions.

In summary, there are three possible theoretical explanations of intelligence. Intelligence as a single thing, and intelligence as a very large collection of elements, are indistinguishable alternatives and can be regarded as a single alternative at least for the time being. For convenience, I will refer to this combined alternative as the explanation of intelligence in terms of a single variable (or, simply, Model 1). The other position discussed will be called the separate elements position (or Model 2).

Both Model 1 and 2 provide different explanations for general intelligence and, more specifically, for g. Both models also account differently for the correlations of basic cognitive tasks with intelligence and with each other. Because of these differences between the two theoretical positions, basic cognitive tasks, like choice reaction time, take on special meaning to those interested in obtaining a better understanding of human intelligence.

CHOICE REACTION TIME DATA

Others' Data

In this brief review of the literature, the major emphasis will be on determining exactly what is known about individual differences in reaction time. There is a long history of research on reaction time that is unconcerned with individual differences time but that, instead, attempts to develop a general (or nomothetic) model of reaction time (e.g., Grice, Nullmeyer, & Spikes, 1982; Pachella, 1974; Smith, 1968). Though this work is interesting, it is largely irrelevant to understanding individual differences in reaction time. Models based on group data have no necessary relationship to individual differences on the same task.

The literature on reaction time research can be divided into roughly three periods. The first period was discussed above, and consisted of the early efforts to use reaction time to assess individual differences. The second period began in the early 1960s within the field of mental retardation. The third period covers the last 10 years, and has been led by researchers (particularly A. Jensen) concerned with theoretical explanations of intelligence.

Earlier data.   An overriding concern in mental retardation research has been to discover defective processes that might explain intellectual differences. Researchers explored a wide range of processes in search of deficits. One process examined was mental speed. The results of this research have been well summarized by Baumeister and Kellas (1968), who, along with Berkson, were the major contributors of much of this work.

The major findings of this research program are clear (though there are, of course, many secondary findings). The first finding is that mentally retarded subjects are, on the average, slower than their intellectually average peers. The second finding is that mentally retarded persons are more variable in their responding than intellectually average persons. In fact, mentally retarded subjects' fastest responses are no different than intellectually average subjects', but they make many more longer responses.

Several other lines of research have continued with the rationale employed in the choice reaction time research with the mentally retarded. Inspection time, defined as the amount of time required to make a simple discrimination, has been shown to be longer in the mentally retarded (Lally & Nettelbeck, 1977; Nettelbeck, 1980; Nettelbeck & Kirby, 1983; also see Raz & Willerman, 1985; Raz, Willerman, Ingmundson, & Hanlan, 1983 for the auditory equivalent to inspection time). Keating and Bobbitt (1978) related a number of cognitive measures, including speed measures, to developmental level. Though a review of related research is beyond the scope of this chapter, the findings from this work can be summarized as tending to reinforce choice reaction time results which show a relationship between intelligence and speed.

Recent data. The resurgence of interest in choice reaction time has been kindled by a deeper interest in theoretical explanations of intelligence. Proponents of *g* as a single thing have attempted to find a measure of a very basic process which would be correlated with intelligence. Tasks examined as potential candidates were those that would seem to be related to important processes like mental speed. Choice reaction time was a natural candidate for examination, because it appeared to be a very simple task and because it could be argued to be a measure of mental speed.

In a series of studies, Jensen and his colleagues (Carlson & Jensen, 1982; Cohn, Carlson, & Jensen, 1985; Jensen, 1979, 1980, 1982a, 1982b, 1984; Jensen & Munro, 1979; Vernon, 1981, 1983; Vernon & Jensen, 1984) have made a case for the relationship of choice reaction time to *g*. They have found that choice reaction varies systematically across groups differing in IQ. Variability also has been shown to be related to IQ. An attempt has been made to argue that the slope of the line fit to decision time as a function of bits of information (number of alternatives or set size) in the display is related to IQ. While there has been some criticism of this research (Longstreth, 1984), the major findings are consistent with the research done with the mentally retarded. However, the conclusions regarding slope are based on group data and are, therefore, less readily accepted. Nevertheless, Jensen and Vernon (1986) come to the conclusion that slope is correlated about $-.30$ with IQ in the population.

Jensen's choice reaction time results have been supported in their essential details by other investigators (e.g., Barrett, Eysenck, & Lucking, 1986; Hemmelgarn & Kehle, 1984). But just because aspects of choice reaction time can be shown to be related to intelligence does not mean that intelligence can be equated with neural speed or efficiency, as some have suggested (e.g., Eysenck, 1982). The case, however, has been made stronger by neurophysiological data.

Averaged Evoked Potentials (AEPs) have been shown, when appropriately measured, to be highly related to intelligence (Haier, Robinson, Braden, & Williams, 1983; A. Hendrickson, 1982; D. Hendrickson, 1982). AEPs also vary by IQ level in a fashion similar to choice reaction time measures (Jensen, Schafer, & Crinella, 1981).

There are at least two findings from Jensen's choice reaction time research that are difficult to square with a single-cause explanation of *g*. First, when choice reaction time measures are combined to predict intelligence, the multiple correlation is .50 (Jensen & Vernon, 1986). Since the highest correlation between IQ and a choice reaction time parameter is under .40, it can only be concluded that there are at least two sources of variance contributing to this multiple correlation. It would take at least two variables to explain the relationship between choice reaction time and intelligence.

The second finding inconsistent with *g* as a single thing is that the relationship between choice reaction time and IQ increases with complexity of the choice reaction time task. The relationship between task complexity and intelligence is incontestable. Lashley (1929) pointed it out in rats, and Tirre (1986) has shown it with reaction time data. It would seem most reasonable to conclude that this relationship occurs because, as a task becomes more complex, more of the basic processes of intelligence are required to perform the task.

New Data

The following studies have been conducted during the last 5 years with the help of Jack Mayer, David Caruso, Peter Legree, and Fran Conners. All of the studies used the basic methodology previously described and shown in Figure 1. But, in each case, there were modifications to this procedure.

Mentally retarded/college students. The initial study involved two groups of subjects: 20 mentally retarded young adults enrolled in special education classes, and 20 college students. Because this was the first attempt at obtaining choice reaction time measures, everything was done in an experimentally correct fashion.

Trials were block-randomized so that a subject received a single trial of each set size before getting another trial of any set size. The set size on each trial was apparent because when a trial began, an appropriate number of empty "windows" appeared. The positions used were counterbalanced orders of the eight possible locations. So a trial having a set size of one could have the stimulus window appear in any one of the eight locations. In addition, each of the eight possible positions was equally often tested for each set size. There were 24 trials for each of the set sizes (1, 2, 4, 8), for a total of 96 trials. The choice reaction time task was given with a set of other cognitive tasks, so subjects were experienced with the apparatus. Instructions were given by a voice synthesizer and all responses were made by touching the touch-sensitive screen. The experimenter answered any questions the subject had after instructions had been presented and ensured that the subject used only his index finger.

Results. The results of the choice reaction time task are shown in Table 1. Reliabilities are split-half correlations of alternate trials. The IQ test used was the WAIS-R and the Full Scale IQ from this test was correlated with various parameters obtained from the task.

Decision time is the amount of time required for the subject to remove their finger from the home position. Slope of DT is the slope of the line fit for each subject to mean decision time for a set size and log to the base 2 of that set

TABLE 1
Choice Reaction Time Measures for a Combined Sample of
20 Mentally Retarded and 20 Intellectually Average Subjects
(Time in Seconds, (Correlations) Corrected for
Restriction in Range)

Measure	Mean	SD	Rel.	r(IQ)
DT	.46	.21	.99	$-.47(-.29)$
Errors	5.27	5.57	.98	
DT Slope	$-.002$	.014	.30	$-.05(-.03)$
DT Int.	.464	.21	.93	$-.48(-.29)$

size. Thus, each subject has four pairs of scores on which slope and intercept were computed. Correlations for DT slope and intercept with IQ were obtained by correlating the slope and intercept value obtained for each subject with the subject's IQ score.

Because the correlations are based on extreme groups of subjects (mentally retarded and college-student), the combined data have an inflated standard deviation. A correction for attenuation will have the effect of appropriately reducing the obtained correlation to the correlation that would be expected in the full population. It is this corrected correlation that should be consistent over experiments.

Examination of Table 1 indicates that mean decision time is correlated with IQ about $-.29$. This agrees with what has been found by other investigators. However, several aspects of the data are not in agreement with previous results.

A first problem is that the average slope is negative. This means that subjects were actually faster on trials with more alternatives. That is, the more information in the display the faster the subject responds. This makes little sense. However, an examination of the data indicated that mentally retarded subjects were producing the negative slopes and, in general, were highly variable in their performance. This variability is reflected in the low reliability of the slope measure. With regard to slope measures of choice reaction time, perhaps the best conclusion is that the measure is not very reliable but that, when standard experimental controls are employed, the slope measure approaches 0. Hick's law may be useful in describing data for a group, but it does not appear to be useful in understanding individual differences. The intercept measure, on the other hand, does appear to be reliable and correlates with IQ, so it is difficult to argue that the task is somehow a poor one.

The use of standard experimental controls may or may not have been the reason for the slope results. It is important to remember that trials were randomized, so any trial could be of any set size. Some subjects could have found this confusing. It also would be possible to randomly present blocks of trials of different set sizes. For example, a subject might receive a sequence of

6-trial blocks, each trial within the block having a set size of 1, 8, 4, 2, 6, 8, 2, 6, 1, and 4. This would randomly mix order but would give subjects successive trials on a fixed set size. These results do indicate that order effects in the choice reaction time task are far from well understood.

High school students. Because of problems in the previous study, the choice reaction time task was modified to more closely correspond to the methodology used by Jensen. A six-alternative block of trials was added increasing total number of trials to 120. Trials were presented in an ascending, blocked format (sets of 1, 2, 4, 6, and 8 alternatives were presented in that order). In addition, the position of alternatives was fixed. Alternatives were always presented in the positions closest to the top center of the semicircular array of "windows." Additional measures of performance including trial time (TT) were collected. TT was the total amount of time to complete a trial.

Subjects for this experiment were randomly selected from the graduating class of a large suburban high school until a sample of 141 had agreed to participate. The sample contained mentally retarded subjects who had met the requirements for a certificate of attendance. The range of WAIS-R IQ scores was from 50 to 150, and the mean of the sample was 108, with a standard deviation of 15. The IQ scores of subject's in the sample were almost perfectly normally distributed. Because this sample so closely approximated the population, no correction for attenuation was applied.

Results. Full results are shown in Table 2. As in the previous study, decision time was correlated with IQ about − .32. Movement time showed the same correlation. The DT slope and intercept measures also replicated the results of the previous study. DT slope increased by about 20 milliseconds as each bit of information was added. Though group data are very consistent in showing Hick's law, individual data are far less reliable and show only a

TABLE 2
Choice Reaction Time Measures for a Sample of 141
High School Students (Time in Seconds)

Measure	Mean	SD	Rel.	r(IQ)
DT	.44	.08	.94	− .32
MT	.22	.05	.90	− .32
SD of DT	.21	.14	.66	− .16
DT Slope	.02	.03	.34	− .04
DT Int.	.41	.10	.84	− .24
MT Slope	.007	.02	.65	− .01
MT Int.	.20	.05	.82	− .30
TT	3.85	.90		− .09
SD of TT	2.52	1.22		.13

$-.04$ correlation with IQ ($-.07$ corrected for unreliability). The reliability of .34 is unacceptably low, but was approximately the same as was obtained in the previous study and in the research of others.

Despite differences in sample characteristics, there are a number of striking similarities between this and the last study. DT and MT are about the same, and MT is about half of DT in both studies. The slope of DT is the same in both studies, and DT correlates with IQ about the same in both studies. Indeed, it can be concluded that this study replicates the last in all essential details. These results are also in agreement with those reported by Jensen and Vernon (1986).

Air Force Enlistees. This study was a replication of the previous one, with a few modifications. Most importantly, touch screens were not used for response input. Instead, subjects used the computer keyboard. To begin a trial, they touched the space bar and made a response by pressing the appropriately numbered key. Each "window" in the display had a number above it to indicate the appropriate response. Windows always had the same number above them, which was their serial order (from the left) in the full set of alternatives. Instructions were written on the computer screen instead of spoken by a voice synthesizer. All subjects were administered the test in a computer laboratory with 30 stations.

Subjects were 860 Air Force enlistees. All subjects had taken the Armed Service Vocational Aptitude Battery (ASVAB), which is a heavily *g*-loaded, group-administered written test. Correlations of choice reaction time measures were computed with the General composite from the ASVAB. (The results are not appreciably different if factor scores from the first principal component of the ASVAB subtests are used in place of the General composite.) The General composite score is regarded, for present purposes, as an IQ score. It should be noted that, unlike the previous two studies, the ASVAB was not administered concurrently but could have been given as much as a year before the subjects completed the choice reaction time task.

A definite problem with this sample is that it has undergone explicit selection. Almost no person in the sample is below the 40th percentile on national norms, and proportionally fewer subjects are included at the high end of the enlistee distribution. Irregularities in the obtained sample were corrected by weighting cases. Explicit selection was corrected for by applying the appropriate correction for restriction in range.

Results. Results are shown in Table 3. What is immediately apparent is that using a keyboard in place of a touch screen had a substantial slowing effect on both DT and MT. Interestingly, DT is still about twice as long as MT. It would appear that the use of the keyboard has not differentially affected separate components of this task.

DT correlates $-.33$ with IQ after correction for selection. From the three

TABLE 3
Choice Reaction Time Measures for 860 Air Force Enlistees
(Time in Seconds, (Correlations) Corrected for
Restriction in Range)

Measure	Mean	SD	Rel.	r(IQ)
DT	.68	.12	.88	−.18(−.33)
MT	.31	.10	.88	−.08(−.16)
DT Slope	.04	.07	.59	.04(.07)
DT Int.	.61	.18	.64	−.15(−.28)
MT Slope	.018	.06	.72	.07(.13)
MT Int.	.28	.16	.77	−.10(−.18)
Errors	2.30	2.78	.55	.07(.12)
SD of DT	.18	.15	.64	.17(.31)
TT	5.34	.29	.82	−.16(−.29)
SD of TT	1.01	.36	.69	−.10(−.18)

studies presented here and research done by others, there can be little question about the relationship between DT and intelligence. The correlation is about −.30 in the general population.

When the various measures obtained from the choice reaction time task are combined to predict g (unrotated first principal component factor scores), the multiple correlation, corrected for attenuation and unreliability, is .46. This compares favorably with the .50 obtained by Jensen and Vernon (1986). This consistency argues for similarity of the tasks.

Another finding consistent with my previous findings (but not Jensen's) is that slope measures for individual subjects do not correlate with measures of intelligence. In all three studies reported here, the correlation of slope with intelligence was nearly 0. Previous reports of slope relationships to intelligence have been based on mean slope values for groups of different IQ levels. Correlating mean IQ with mean slope differences for groups of subjects would produce larger correlations than those existing among individual subjects in the population as a whole. The results obtained on a task similar to Jensen's do not support his conclusions concerning the slope–IQ correlation of −.30 in the general population, but do support his conclusions concerning the relationship of IQ and other measures of choice reaction time.

A serious qualification is that the slope of DT has not yielded a highly reliable measure even with the liberal split-half procedures used here. An extensive effort was made to make the slope measure as reliable as possible but with little success. Statistical corrections for unreliability were not applied, because there is substantial doubt whether such corrections would reflect anything even remotely attainable in practice. Even if the correlations obtained are corrected for unreliability, they would still be small—all less than −.15.

From the results obtained here, it would appear that derived measures like slope and intercept are much more difficult to make acceptably reliable than direct measures like latency or errors. But there would have to be much more compelling reasons before beginning an effort to make them reliable. Evidence so far obtained suggests that, even if perfect reliability were achieved, a slope measure would provide very little important information about individual differences.

If slope measures are unimportant, is there any useful purpose for a choice reaction time task that varies the number of alternatives? Table 4 shows data for each number of alternatives. Though mean DT and MT change systematically, correlations with IQ do not increase as set size increases. In fact, for movement time the correlation with IQ would appear to decrease as set size increases.

Reliability was computed by comparing the first 12 trials to the last 12 trials for each set size. Across blocks of increasing set sizes (which were administered in ascending order), reliability generally increases for both DT and MT. This suggests that subjects become more consistent with practice. Because of this trend, it is possible to speculate that the DT × IQ correlation may be produced by different processes in early and late set size blocks. Trials with only one alternative administered first may correlate with IQ because subjects are learning about the task and the faster they learn about the task the better their performance. On the other hand, in the last block of trials in which there are eight alternatives, the DT correlation with IQ may reflect differential response to complexity.

It should be remembered that this study used a large number of subjects (N = 860). Further, the procedures used have gone through an extensive development process to ensure that the parameters obtained from the task are as reliable as they could be made. If these factors are taken in conjunction with the observation that the results of this study replicate the general findings of the two previous studies, there would seem to be little doubt concerning the relation of reaction time to IQ.

TABLE 4

Decision Time and Movement Time for Each Choice Set Size
for 860 Air Force Enlistees (Time in Seconds, (Correlations)
Corrected for Restriction in Range)

	Decision Time			*Movement Time*		
Set Size	*Mean*	*Rel.*	*r(IQ)*	*Mean*	*Rel.*	*r(IQ)*
1	.63	.59	− .29	.30	.70	− .18
2	.63	.77	− .22	.27	.66	− .12
4	.69	.83	− .27	.30	.71	− .15
6	.72	.82	− .28	.33	.78	− .06
8	.74	.85	− .27	.35	.78	− .08

General Conclusions

There are a number of conclusions that can be drawn about choice reaction time as a measure of individual differences. First, there can be little doubt that decision time is correlated $-.30$ with IQ. Whether this is regarded as a small or large relationship is a subjective judgement. Further, there are many potential explanations of this relationship.

A second conclusion to be drawn is that the slope of decision time appears to have little relationship to individual differences in intelligence. Though Hick's law may (and does in the data presented) hold for group data, individual variations in slope do not account for intellectual differences. This conclusion can be tempered slightly by the fact that a highly reliable measure of slope is difficult to obtain and was not obtained in the data reported here.

A third conclusion is that movement time has a variable but significant relationship to intelligence. In some studies, the relationship was as high as the relation of DT to IQ while in others it was substantially lower. The simple model presented earlier does not explain why this should be so.

Generally, it would appear that a rather simple, direct picture of the relationship of intelligence to choice reaction time emerges from the research presented here. Making a case that decision time is a measure of mental speed, and the single variable defining g, would not be difficult. That argument, however, would not explain a number of the more complex relationships obtained in these data and in other studies.

IS CHOICE REACTION TIME A SIMPLE TASK?

Those who argue that choice reaction time measures reflect mental speed which is the single variable producing g make a major assumption. They assume that, because choice reaction time appears to be a simple task, it actually is simple, and that the parameters obtained from it are pure measures of unitary processes. Though Jensen and Vernon have not explicitly argued that g is a unitary process, they have been definite in their assertion that choice reaction time (which they call the Hick paradigm) is a very simple task:

> This [the relationship between choice reaction time measures and g-loaded tests] is of major theoretical interest, because the Hick paradigm involves no knowledge content, no reasoning, no problem-solving, no "higher mental processes," in the generally accepted meaning of these terms, and it has about as little resemblance to conventional unspeeded psychometric tests as one could possibly imagine. (Jensen & Vernon, 1986, p. 156)

Is this the case? I will argue that it almost certainly is not, that choice reaction time is far more complicated than it appears on the surface.

Processes That Should Be Investigated

In the course of conducting the research reported here, a number of things that may be important to understanding the processes involved in choice reaction time have suggested themselves. Some are supported by data either from this research or the research of others, while others are based only on observation and anecdote.

Understanding Instructions. Even slight differences in understanding instructions could have substantial impact on the results. It is probably unreasonable to assume that subjects develop equivalent mental representations of the choice reaction time task even with fairly extensive instructions.

Even though subjects may fully understand how to perform the task after instruction, they may come to very different conclusions about aspects of the task not included in the instructions. For example, different subjects may select to hold their heads at different distances from the computer monitor screen. This would affect the portion of the screen that falls on the fovea, which would, in turn, affect perceptual sensitivity. Subjects also might interpret the instructions to make their response as quickly as possible.

In the work with Air Force enlistees it was found that early blocks were less reliable than later blocks (see Table 4). Since reliability was assessed by comparing first to last half of each block, this result indicates that subjects became more consistent in their performance over trials. Subjects might be more variable on early trials because they are experimenting with various ways of doing the task, including holding their heads at different distances from the screen and trying different degrees of speededness. This experimentation is almost required of subjects in experimental tasks they are given, since instructions are generally brief and there is little effort to ensure that subjects have equivalent instantiations of what is instructed.

Familiarity with equipment. A subject who has familiarity with a typewriter keyboard might have an advantage over an inexperienced subject, if responses are made on the keyboard. On the other hand, if responses can only be made with the index finger and they use a small set of keys (as was the case in my research), subjects with typing skills might experience interference. At an even more basic level, subjects with little or no exposure to computers might react quite differently to computer-administered tasks than subjects who had some experience. This could be an obvious factor in cross-cultural research, but could also affect the performance of retarded subjects who have less computer experience.

Motivation. Little attention has been given to the effects of motivation on individual differences in reaction time. While higher levels of motivation would probably have little effect on the fastest reaction times they might well influence variability. One easy way to increase motivation on the choice reaction time task would be to provide subjects with feedback. As the task is currently structured (and most other basic cognitive tasks for that matter), there is no way for a subject to know if he or she is doing well or not. This certainly must have some impact on performance.

Surprising as it may seem, subjects ordinarily report that they enjoy the choice reaction time task so feedback may be unimportant for motivation. As an experiment, I modified the reaction time task to provide scoreboard feedback like that provided in many video games. Although this version of the task has not been used extensively enough for conclusive evaluation, it does seem to have a much more game-like quality which encourages more intense attention to performance on each trial.

Sensory acuity. Sensory variables have been given little or no attention as causative factors in individual differences in choice reaction time. However, it is well known that visual defects are more common among the mentally retarded. Certainly sensitivity to stimulus change depends in part on sensory acuity. Sensory acuity also could have secondary effects on such processes as search strategy, eye movements, and other perceptually related parts of the task.

Speed-accuracy tradeoff. There is almost certainly a relationship between speed and accuracy in choice reaction time. In the data presented above, errors showed a negative correlation with IQ. However, Brewer and Smith (1984) have provided a more substantial demonstration. The task they used was somewhat different in that several fingers were used to make a response. Each subject completed literally thousands of trials on this task. When an error occurred, performance before and after the error trial was systematic. Before an error, a subject would become progressively faster but after an error was committed a dramatic slowing of responding would occur. This slowing was much greater for lower IQ subjects.

This research suggests that subjects actively seek an optimum level of responding which maximizes speed and minimizes errors. It also explains why mentally retarded subjects are more variable. Because they make larger corrections in speed after an error but do respond as quickly as other subjects on their fastest trial, they are more variable overall. Findings from this research indicate that any model which fails to consider trial to trial changes in performance in incomplete. Clearly, the model shown in Figure 1 cannot be a complete description of performance on the task, because no memory for past trials is included.

Attention. How long it takes a subject to notice stimulus onset is at least partially a function of attentional mechanisms. By head movement, a subject could select how much of the display is to be kept in foveal vision. Different subjects might also select very different criteria for deciding when stimulus onset has occurred. The degree or intensity of attention might have considerable effect on performance, although there is no way to judge this from current data.

Memory factors. There are a number of ways that memory factors could affect performance on a choice reaction time task. Differences in memory for previous trials could affect the criterion subjects set, or how willing they are to risk an error. Memory differences also could affect how well instructions are remembered, and the degree to which experiences on previously done similar tasks are used. In a task which employs responses not made directly to the stimulus as on a computer key board, the subject must remember the correct response while searching for the place to make that response. This could produce memory problems for some subjects.

Search strategy.   In a choice reaction time, the way in which alternatives are searched for stimulus onset could have a significant impact on decision time. Though some attention has been given to search strategies (e.g., Welford, 1980), there is still not adequate information concerning individual differences. Mentally retarded subjects are generally poorer at search tasks and at devising and using strategies. As common as such behaviors are among low IQ subjects, it would seem highly unlikely that search strategy in choice reaction time would not vary across IQ levels.

Response selection.   An introspectively important component of choice reaction time is response selection. Complicating the response component can make choice reaction time a much more difficult task. A comparison of Tables 2 and 3 show that, when the method of response changed from touch screen to keyboard, it took twice as long not only to respond (MT) but also to decide to respond (DT). Evidently, response complexity affects decision processes.

Response execution and use of feedback.   Most models of choice reaction time suggest that, once a response is selected, the selected response is simply executed. This sort of model would suggest that, if the response had to be changed in the middle of execution, it would not be possible to do it. In order to modify a response, some form of feedback (or parallel processing) would be needed during response execution. The subject would have to be continually verifying the validity of his response.

Such a feedback process must almost certainly occur. It seems highly unlikely that, once a subject lifts his or her finger from the home key indicating response selection, it would be impossible for him or her to change his or her response. Rather, observation of subjects and introspection while doing the task would seem to indicate that the response being executed is continually being monitored for correctness.

That subjects monitor their responses is no small point. It means that many of the processes that subjects use in initiating the response are used also while making the response. This would make the response execution phase an extremely complex one. It also would explain why movement time can be correlated with IQ.

Additional evidence.   Karrer (in press) has reported a series of extremely interesting studies of simple reaction time tasks with mentally retarded and intellectually average subjects. What is particularly interesting about his research is that electrophysiological measures were combined with behavioral measures to slice a reaction-time task into smaller components. For example, finger muscle recording could be used to time response initiation, and AEPs could be utilized to mark the onset of central processing. The conclusions Karrer is able to come to, using this finer-grained measurement, are surprising.

First, the major source of slowness in simple motor tasks like simple reaction time is the process of response initiation or beginning a motor act. Second, and perhaps even more significant, was the finding of "differences in the patterning of neural activity across the brain regions in the retarded that could be associated with differences in structures or in strategies of task performance" (ms. p. 24). Third, it was possible to show that mentally retarded were like intellectually normal peers on some task components, but differed on others. These findings hardly support the conclusion that simple reaction time is a simple task. Taken with the possibilities discussed in the previous paragraphs, it would take tremendously strong evidence to convince me that choice reaction time is as simple a task as it initially appears.

A Possible Model of Choice Reaction Time

It is clear that the simple model shown in Figure 1 lacks sufficient detail to account for observed performance on the choice reaction time task. Although it might not be possible or even useful to attempt to develop a model complete enough to include all of the factors discussed above, it is possible to specify the general form such a model might take. Two general types of changes would have to be made to current models: existing processes would have to be elaborated and new processes would have to be added.

The elaboration of processes might include the sorts of divisions Karrer has developed using electrophysiological measures. There are also other possibilities, such as the use of eye movements to observe visual search strategy. Refinement of process description will require refinement in measurement.

The processes to be added to current models include a motivational and attentional component, a component representing the functional set of instructions, and a memorial representation of speed–accuracy tradeoff functions and strategic knowledge, to name a few. Choice reaction time will not be completely understood until these sorts of processes are understood. For example, it would be difficult to interpret cross-cultural choice reaction time research without a more adequate knowledge of these processes.

Relation of Model to IQ

The complexities of understanding choice reaction time and its relationship to intelligence are really no different than the problems in understanding any basic cognitive task. A reasonable model of the task must be developed. Ways to measure the parameters of the model as reasonably independent of other parameters as possible must be developed. The independent parameters of the model can then be correlated with g to see which are most involved in intellectual functioning. But perhaps most important of all, the parameters found in any one basic cognitive task must be shown to be used in other tasks or the particular parameter has no convergent validity and is of little theoretical use.

If all of these steps are accomplished, the relationship between choice reaction time parameters and intelligence would be clear. A list of the processes employed in choice reaction time and the proportion of variance each contributes to general intelligence could be specified. This, of course, assumes that the preceding analysis is correct.

What if g is actually caused by a single variable? The problem is that this will be very difficult to demonstrate, even in the unlikely case that it is true. In fact, it is very much like attempting to prove the null hypothesis, with the exception that, if all other things are equal, parsimony prevails. But before parsimony decides the issue, it would be necessary to provide a precise theory of mental speed (or the single explanatory variable, whatever it is) which accounts for all of the relationships between intelligence and choice reaction time measures. No such model has yet been offered.

A Proposed Research Strategy

Research with the choice reaction time task can make a valuable contribution to our understanding of intelligence. However, it is unlikely to fulfill its entire potential if it is investigated alone. Establishing convergent and discriminant validity demands that findings from choice reaction time research be reinforced by similar research with other basic tasks. Any systematic research effort should, therefore, include at least two basic tasks.

The need for additional refinement of parameters will require the introduction of increasingly sophisticated measurement methods. With computers it is now possible to simultaneously acquire behavioral, motor, eye movement, and electrophysiological data. Obtaining such data would make it possible to divide the choice reaction time task into much smaller stages.

Just refining measurement will not produce insight. Refinement in measurement must be driven by more sophisticated theory. With few exceptions, individual difference researchers have made all too little use of mathematical modeling and simulation techniques to develop plausible models of intelligence and basic cognitive tasks which could explain the relationship between the two. There needs to be much greater effort to develop mathematically explicit models.

Finally, research on individual differences has been plagued by small sample sizes and by samples drawn from poorly specified populations. It is difficult to come to any firm conclusions with a small number of subjects. Though large sample sizes are expensive and difficult to obtain, they are extremely important for good individual differences research.

What is required, then, is a research program which uses multiple basic tasks, employs extremely sophisticated measurement techniques to collect data for each task, begins from a precise model of performance on each task, makes predictions supported by simulation, and uses ample sample sizes in the experimental confirmation of predictions. When such a research program is launched, we will be well on our way to understanding the important relationship between choice reaction time measures and intelligence.

REFERENCES

Baumeister, A. A., & Kellas, G. (1968). Reaction time and mental retardation. In N. R. Ellis (Ed.), *International review of research in mental retardation: Vol. 3*, New York: Academic Press.

Barrett, P., Eysenck, H. J., & Lucking, S. (1986). Reaction time and intelligence: A replicate study. *Intelligence, 10*, 9–40.

Brewer, N., & Smith, G. A. (1984). How normal and retarded individuals monitor and regulate speed and accuracy of responding in serial choice tasks. *Journal of Experimental Psychology: General, 113*, 71–93.

Carlson, J. S., & Jensen, C. M. (1982). Reaction time, movement time, and intelligence: A replication and extension. *Intelligence, 6*, 265–274.

Carroll, J. B. (1980). *Individual difference relations in psychometric and experimental cognitive tasks*. Chapel Hill, NC: L. L. Thurstone Psychometric Laboratory, University of North Carolina.

Cohn, S. J., Carlson, J. S., & Jensen, A. R. (1985). Speed of information processing in academically gifted youths. *Personality and Individual Differences, 6*, 621–629.

Detterman, D. K. (1980). Understand cognitive components before postulating metacomponents. *Brain and Behavioral Sciences, 3*, 589.

Detterman, D. K. (1982). Does 'g' exist? *Intelligence, 6*, 99–103.

Detterman, D. K. (1984a). 'g'-Whiz. *Contemporary Psychology, 29*, 375–376.

Detterman, D. K. (1984b). Understand cognitive components before postulating metacomponents, etc.: Part II. *Behavioral and Brain Science, 7*, 289–290.

Detterman, D. K. (1986). Human intelligence is a complex system of separate processes. In R. J. Sternberg & D. K. Detterman (Eds.), *What is intelligence? Contemporary viewpoints on its nature and definition*. Norwood, NJ: Ablex Publishing Corp.

Eysenck, H. J. (Ed.). (1982). *A model for intelligence*. New York: Springer-Verlag.

Galton, F. (1883). *Inquiries into human faculty and its development*. London: Macmillan.

Grice, G. R., Nullmeyer, R., & Spikes, V. A. (1982). Human reaction time: Toward a general theory. *Journal of Experimental Psychology: General, 111*, 135–153.

Haier, R. J., Robinson, D. L., Braden, W., & Williams, D. (1983). Electrical potentials of the cerebral cortex and psychometric intelligence. *Personality and Individual Differences, 4*, 591–599.

Hemmelgarn, T. E., & Kehle, T. J. (1984). The relationship between reaction time and intelligence in children. *School Psychology International, 5*, 77–84.

Hendrickson, A. E. (1982). The biological basis of intelligence. Part I: Theory. In H. J. Eysenck (Ed.), *A model for intelligence* (pp. 151–196). New York: Springer-Verlag.

Hendrickson, D. E. (1982). The biological basis of intelligence. Part II: Measurement. In H. J. Eysenck (Ed.), *A model for intelligence* (pp. 197–228). New York: Springer-Verlag.

Hick, W. (1952). On the rate of gain of information. *Quarterly Journal of Experimental Psychology, 4,* 11–26.

Humphreys, L. G. (1979). The construct of general intelligence. *Intelligence, 3,* 105–120.

Jensen, A. R. (1979). *g*: Outmoded theory or unconquered frontier? *Creative Science and Technology, 2,* 16–29.

Jensen, A. R. (1980). Chronometric analysis of mental ability. *Journal of Social and Biological Structures, 3,* 103–122.

Jensen, A. R. (1982a). Reaction time and psychometric *g*. In H. J. Eysenck (Ed.), *A model for intelligence* (pp. 93–132). New York: Springer-Verlag.

Jensen, A. R. (1982b). The chronometry of intelligence. In R. J. Sternberg (Ed.), *Advances in the psychology of human intelligence: Vol. 1.* Hillsdale, NJ: Erlbaum.

Jensen, A. R. (1984). Test validity: *g* versus the specificity doctrine. *Journal of Social and Biological Structures, 7,* 93–118.

Jensen, A. R., & Munro, E. (1979). Reaction time, movement time, and intelligence. *Intelligence, 3,* 121–126.

Jensen, A. R., Schafer, E. W. P., & Crinella, F. M. (1981). Reaction time, evoked brain potentials, and psychometric *g* in the severely retarded. *Intelligence, 5,* 179–197.

Jensen, A. R., & Vernon, P. A. (1986). Jensen's reaction time studies: A reply to Longstreth. *Intelligence, 1986, 10,* 153–179.

Keating, D. P., & Bobbitt, B. (1978). Individual and developmental differences in cognitive processing components of mental ability. *Child Development, 49,* 155–169.

Karrer, R. (in press). Input, central and motor segments of response time in mentally retarded and normal children. In M. G. Wade & T. Tjossem (Eds.), *Motor skill acquisition of the mentally handicapped.* Advances in Psychology. Amsterdam, Netherlands: North Holland Publ.

Lally, M., & Nettelbeck, T. (1977). Intelligence, reaction time, and inspection time. *American Journal of Mental Deficiency, 82,* 273–281.

Lashley, K. S. (1929). *Brain mechanisms and intelligence.* Chicago, IL: University of Chicago Press.

Longstreth, L. E. (1984). Jensen's reaction time investigations of intelligence: A critique. *Intelligence, 8,* 139–160.

Nettelbeck, T. (1980). Factors affecting reaction time: Mental retardation, brain damage, and other psychopathologies. In A. T. Welford (Ed.), *Reaction times.* New York: Academic Press.

Nettelbeck, T., & Kirby, N. H. (1983). Measures of timed performance and intelligence. *Intelligence, 7,* 39–52.

Pachella, R. G. (1974). The interpretation of reaction time in information-processing research. In B. Kantowitz (Ed.), *Human information processing: Tutorials in performance and cognition.* Hillsdale, NJ: Erlbaum.

Raz, N., & Willerman, L. (1985). Aptitude-related differences in auditory information processing: Effects of selective attention and tone duration. *Personality and Individual Differences, 7,* 71–90.

Raz, N., Willerman, L., Ingmudson, P., & Hanlan, M. (1983). Aptitude-related differences in auditory recognition masking. *Intelligence, 7,* 71–90.

Smith, E. E. (1968). Choice reaction time: An analysis of major theoretical positions. *Psychological Bulletin, 69,* 77–110.

Spearman, C. E. (1904). "General intelligence" objectively determined and measured. *American Journal of Psychology, 15,* 201–293.

Spearman, C. E. (1927). *The abilities of man: Their nature and measurement.* London: Macmillan.

Thomson, G. H. (1939). *The factorial analysis of human ability.* London: University of London Press.

Thurstone, L. L. (1935). *Vectors of mind.* Chicago, IL: University of Chicago Press.

Thurstone, L. L. (1938). Primary mental abilities. *Psychometric Monographs* (No. 1). Chicago, IL: University of Chicago Press.

Tirre, W. C. (1986, January). *Information processing correlates of intelligence: New information from computer administered tests.* Paper presented at the meeting of Southwest Educational Research Association, Houston, Texas.

Vernon, P. A. (1981). Reaction time and intelligence in the mentally retarded. *Intelligence, 5,* 345–355.

Vernon, P. A. (1983). Speed of information processing and general intelligence. *Intelligence, 7,* 53–70.

Vernon, P. A., & Jensen, A. R. (1984). Individual and group differences in intelligence and speed of information processing. *Personality and Individual Differences, 5,* 411–423.

Welford, A. T. (Ed.). (1980). *Reaction time.* New York: Academic Press.

AUTHOR NOTE

I wish to thank D. Caruso, J. Mayer, P. Legree, and F. Conners for their help in collecting the data included here. I would also like to thank the staff of the Air Force Human Resources Laboratory for their help. This work was supported by NICHHD, Office of Mental Retardation (Grants HD07176 and HD15518), the Air Force Office of Scientific Research (AFOSR) and the Brooks Air Force Base Human Resources Laboratory, Project LAMP.

CHAPTER 6

A Context for Understanding Information Processing Studies of Human Abilities

John Horn
University of Southern California

DIFFICULTIES IN DISTINGUISHING HUMAN ABILITIES

Much is known about human abilities, but much more is not known. That which is known appears under many headings in the scientific literature. It is difficult to summarize it in an organized system. The information can be organized in different ways.

One way to organize the information is in terms of the magnitudes of intercorrelations among different ability measures (Cf. Cronbach, 1970; Horn, 1968, 1972, 1986b). Seen in this way, abilities range from very broad to very narrow. A broad ability is one for which the average of the intercorrelations among different measures of the ability is small, although significantly different from zero. A narrow ability is one for which the average of the intercorrelations among different measures of the ability is large, although somewhat smaller than the reliabilities of the measures.

A fairly narrow ability is indicated by the following measures:

- Visual Matching . . . Under constraints to respond quickly, the subject must find 1-to-5-digit numbers that are the same among a list of six such numbers.

- Spatial Relations . . . Under constraints to respond quickly, the subject must determine which two or three shapes among six choices (in a two-dimensional plane) fit together to form a displayed whole.
- Visual Scanning . . . Working as quickly as possible over a short period of time (e.g., 2-minute trials), find as many letter ds as possible on a sheet of paper filled with the letters of the alphabet.

This ability is often referred to as (visual) Perceptual Speed (P), and thereby identified with a primary ability—i.e., factor among what has become known as the 24 well-replicated common factors of cognitive performances (Ekstrom, French, & Harmon, 1979). The intercorrelations among different measures of Perceptual Speed are typically in the .65 to .75 range when the reliabilities of the measures are of the order of .75 to .85.

What a test measures depends in part on the way it is administered. This can be seen in the Spatial Relations test of the P factor. If this test is given with liberal time limits (without constraints to work quickly) and the items are of sufficient difficulty, it measures a Visualization, Vz, primary ability, rather than P (Ekstrom, French, & Harman, 1979). The same test given under different conditions measures a different ability.

At the other end of a continuum from narrow are broad measures of general intelligence, often symbolized as IQ or g or G. The breadth of a measure of IQ varies greatly from one study to another, reflecting the fact that different batteries of tests involve more and fewer tests of different abilities (Horn & Goldsmith, 1981). IQ tests can be narrow, but, often, researchers, counsellors, and people in general suppose that general intelligence is broad—a diverse collection of abilities. Let us consider some examples of broad measures of g (i.e., IQ).

IQ might be measured by summing the 12 Cognitive Ability subtest scores of the Woodcock-Johnson Psycho-Educational Battery (WOJ; Woodcock & Johnson, 1977), or the 10 Mental Processing subtests of the K-ABC (Kaufman & Kaufman, 1983a,b), or the 17 subtest scores of the McCarthy Scales of Children's Abilities (McCarthy, 1972). The following labels indicate the breadth of IQ measures formed in these ways.

Subtests of the WOJ

Cognitive Abilities (CA)		Test of Achievements (TOA)	
CA	Picture Vocabulary	TOA	Humanities
CA	Antonyms-Synonyms	TOA	Social Studies
CA	Quantitative Concepts	TOA	Science
CA	Verbal Analogies	TOA	Applied Problems
CA	Analysis-Synthesis	TOA	Calculations
CA	Concept Formation	TOA	Letter-Word
CA	Visual Auditory	TOA	Dictation
CA	Memory for Sentences	TOA	Proofing

Subtests of the WOJ (continued)

CA	Spatial Relations	TOA	Passage Comprehension
CA	Visual Matching		
CA	Blending		
CA	Numbers Reversed		

Subtests of the K-ABC

Mental Processing Subtests (MPS)		Tests Of Achievements (TOA)	
MPS	Matrix Analogies	TOA	Riddles
MPS	Spatial Memory	TOA	Reading Decoding
MPS	Photo Series	TOA	Reading Understanding
MPS	Gestalt Closure	TOA	Expressive Vocabulary
MPS	Number Recall	TOA	Faces and Places
MPS	Triangles	TOA	Arithmetic
MPS	Magic Window		
MPS	Face Recognition		
MPS	Hand Movements		
MPS	Word Order		

Subtests of the McCarthy

Block Building	Imitative Action
Conceptual Grouping	Verbal Memory
Number Questions	Draw-a-Design
Opposite Analogies	Picture Memory
Counting & Sorting	Numerical Memory
Word Knowledge	Verbal Fluency
Puzzle Solving	Draw-a-Child
Leg Coordination	Tapping Sequences
Arm Coordination	

A measure formed by combining the CA subtests of the WOJ is narrower than a measure obtained by summing both the CA and TOA of this test. Both the narrower and the broader measure are referred to as IQ or *g*. A very broad measure might be obtained by summing all the subtest scores of both the WOJ and the K-ABC or the K-ABC and the McCarthy or a combination of the subtests of all three of these tests. Even broader measures of *g* can be envisioned (Humphreys, 1979, Jensen, 1984).

While measures of *g* are usually broad indeed, measures of what is called *g* can be narrow, too. The measure obtained with the matrices test is narrow, for example. The best known example of such a measure is obtained with the Raven Progressive Matrices (Raven, 1977). This narrow measure is regarded by some psychologists as a quite good indicator of *g* (Jensen, 1973).

We see, then, that the breadth of measure of a cognitive ability is a function of the extent to which different kinds of component abilities — different subtest measures — are included in the measure. As diversity increases, the average of the intercorrelations among components of the measure decreases. Typically, the intercorrelations among different components of a multi-subtest measure of IQ are about .45, but, if measures of artistic abilities, musical abilities, or athletic abilities are among the components, the average of the correlations (still almost always positive) can drop below .20, perhaps to .15, depending on the number of measures of each kind of ability, the heterogeneity of the battery, the evenness of the distribution across different kinds of abilities, and other factors (e.g., the reliabilities, the age of the subjects).

We see, then, that human abilities can be defined partly in terms of breadth (broad-to-narrow) and partly in terms of conditions of administration (high-to-low constraints to work quickly). Many other such parameters of description have been used. Guilford (1967) has attempted to develop a taxonomy by exhaustively identifying such parameters. The following labels indicate the major categories of Guilford's system:

Contents:		Products:	
F	Figural	U	Units
S	Symbolic	C	Classes
M	Semantic	R	Relations
B	Behavioral	S	Systems
		T	Transformations
		I	Implications

Operations:	
E	Evaluation
N	Convergent Production
D	Divergent Production
M	Memory
C	Cognition

In Guilford's system, an ability test is defined by a particular combination of one operation, one content and one product. For example, a multiple choice vocabulary test is described as "Cognition of Semantic Units, CMU." "Cognition is [defined as] awareness, immediate discovery or rediscovery, or recognition of information in various forms. Units are relatively segregated or circumscribed items of information having 'thing' character. . . . Semantic information is the form of meanings to which words commonly become attached . . . although we must recognize [also] that much semantic information is nonverbalized" (Guilford, 1967, pp. 71, 227).

There are $4 \times 5 \times 6 = 120$ different three-way combinations of four contents, five operations and six products. This is the number of tests one might construct on the basis of Guilford's system. Does this correspond to the number of distinct abilities humans possess?

There are two answers to this question. First, 120 is probably an underestimate of the number of separable human intellectual abilities; second, it is doubtful that the 120 abilities of the Guilford system are reliably and validly distinct. Let us examine the basis for this last statement.

The Guilford system derives partly from logic, and partly from the evidence of empirical research. The main research support for the system is indicated in the Ekstrom et al. (1979) integration of results from first-order factor analytic studies. That integration of results indicates 24 well-replicated ability factors, and some 13 factors for which there is some, but not well replicated, evidence. Brief descriptions of these abilities are provided in Table 1.

It can be seen in the table that roughly 25–30 of the three-way combinations of Guilford's system are associated with abilities for which there is empirical evidence from factor analytic studies. This concordance comes about partly because Guilford based his system, post hoc, on these factor analytic findings. The theory of the system is not supported by these findings: it is an outgrowth of them.

Unfortunately, the studies (by Guilford and his coworkers) designed to add to this evidence have been hampered by lack of objectivity (Carroll, 1972; Horn, 1967; Horn & Knapp, 1973, 1974; Humphreys, 1962; Undheim & Horn, 1977). The results from this work indicate that there is not a good basis for retaining many of the major hypotheses of Guilford's system. Some of the three-way combinations of the Guilford system represent empirically based distinctions between established primary mental abilities, but many of the combinations are only logical indications of ways to construct tests, not indications of distinct human abilities. They do not indicate distinctly different processes of thinking such as are linked together when a person solves a problem. As Humphreys (1962, p. 476) pointed out, the facets of the Guilford system "are not psychological as defined. They should be useful to the test constructor, [but] they do not need to make a behavioral difference."

The difficulties with the Guilford structure of intellect system obtain as well for other efforts to provide an empirically sound basis for distinguishing among different human abilities. There is no thoroughly acceptable system. Distinctions drawn on the basis of different contents or operations or products can be useful, but they are not sharp (Horn, 1972).

Consider the problem of making sharp distinctions. Look at a test designed to measure Spatial Orientation, S, as an example. This represents an hypothesis that humans differ in a cognitive process of perceiving (comprehending, seeing) differences among similar spatial objects. In a test to measure this ability, one must explain to people what they are to do, and individuals differ in abilities of understanding explanations. A test to measure the S ability thus involves, to some extent, a measure of Verbal Comprehension, V. This is true, not only because V facilitates understanding the instructions one must understand in order to do well on spatial tasks, but also because performance on spatial tasks can be (in some people) facilitated by verbalizing and using the ability of V. It is true, also, because both S and V can spring from the same determiners (genetic and/or environmental). There are many reasons why measures of S and V cannot be entirely independent.

Different levels of breadth of abilities also are not sharply distinguished. A

TABLE 1
FIRST-ORDER (PRIMARY) MENTAL ABILITIES
After Ekstrom, French, and Harman (1979)

SHORT-TERM APPREHENSION AND RETRIEVAL ABILITIES	Guilford Symbol	French Symbol	Well Replicated
Associative Memory. When presented with one element of previously associated but otherwise unrelated elements, recall associated element.	MSR	Ma	Yes
Span Memory. Immediately recall a set of elements after one presentation.	MSU	Ms	Yes
Meaningful Memory. Immediately recall a set of items that are meaningfully related.	MSR	Mm	?
Chunking Memory. Immediately recall elements by categories into which elements were classified.	MMC		No
Memory for Order. Immediately recall the position of an element within a set of elements.	MSS		No

LONG-TERM STORAGE AND RETRIEVAL ABILITIES.

Associational Fluency. Produce words similar in meaning to a given word.	DMR	Fa	Yes
Expressional Fluency. Produce different ways of saying much the same thing.	DSS	Fe	Yes
Ideational Fluency. Produce ideas about a stated condition or object — e.g., a lady holding a baby.	DMU	Fi	Yes
Word Fluency. Produce words meeting particular structural requirements — e.g., ending with a particular suffix.	DMR	Fw	Yes
Originality. Produce "clever" expressions or interpretations — e.g., titles for a story plot.	DMT	O	Yes
Spontaneous Flexibility. Produce diverse functions and classifications — e.g., uses for a pencil.	DMC	Xs	Yes
Delayed Retrieval. Recall material learned hours before.			No

VISUALIZATION AND SPATIAL ORIENTATION ABILITIES.

Visualization. Mentally manipulate forms to "see" how they would look under altered conditions.	CFT	Vz	Yes
Spatial Orientation. Visually imagine parts out of place and put them in place — e.g., solve jigsaw puzzles.	CFS	S	Yes
Speed of Closure. Identify Gestalt when parts of whole are missing.	CFU	Cs	Yes
Flexibility of Closure. Find a particular figure embedded within distracting figures.	NFT	Cs	Yes
Spatial Planning. Survey a spatial field and find a path through the field — e.g., pencil mazes.	CFI	Ss	Yes
Figural Adaptive Flexibility. Try out possible arrangements of elements of visual pattern to find one arrangement that satisfies several conditions.	DFT	Xa	Yes

TABLE 1 *(Continued)*

VISUALIZATION AND SPATIAL ORIENTATION ABILITIES	Guilford Symbol	French Symbol	Well Replicated?
Length Estimation. Estimate lengths or distances between points.		Le	Yes
Figural Fluency. Produce different figures using the lines of a stimulus figure.	DFI		No
Seeing Illusions. Report illusions of such tests as Muller-Lyer, Sanders, and Poggenforff.	DFS		No
ABILITIES OF LISTENING AND HEARING.			
Listening Verbal Comprehension, Va. Show understanding of oral communications.			No
Temporal Tracking, Tc. Demonstrate understanding of sequence of auditory information — e.g., reorder a set of tones.			No
Auditory Relations, AcoR. Show understanding of relations among tones — e.g., identify separate notes of chord.			No
Discriminate Patterns of Sounds, DASP. Show awareness of differences in different arrangements of tones.			No
Judging Rhythms, MaJR. Identify and continue a beat.			No
Auditory Span Memory, Ma. Immediately recall a set of notes played once.			No
Perception of Distorted Speech, SPUD. Demonstrate comprehension of language that has been distorted in several ways.			No
ACCULTURATIONAL KNOWLEDGE ABILITIES.			
Verbal Comprehension. Demonstrate understanding of words, sentences and paragraphs.	CMU	V	Yes
Sensitivity to Problems. Suggest ways to deal with problems — e.g., improvements for a toaster.	EMI	Sep	Yes
Applying Conventional Logic. Given stated premises draw logically permissible conclusions even when these are nonsensical.	EMR	Rs	Yes
Number Facility. Do basic operations of arithmetic quickly and accurately.	NSI	N	Yes
Verbal Closure. Show comprehension of words and sentences when parts are omitted.			No
Estimation. Use incomplete information to estimate what is required for problem solution.	CMI		No
Behavioral Relations. Judge interaction between people to estimate how one feels about a situation.	CBI		No
Semantic Relations: Esoteric Concepts. Demonstrate awareness of analogic relationships among abstruse bits of information.	CMR IMR		No
Mechanical Knowledge. Information about industrial arts — mechanics, electricity, etc..		Mk	?

(Continued)

TABLE 1 *(Continued)*

ACCULTURATIONAL KNOWLEDGE ABILITIES	*Guilford Symbol*	*French Symbol*	*Well Replicated?*
General Information. Knowledge about letters, arts and sciences.		Vi	Yes
General Information: Science, Humanities, Social Sciences, Business.		Vi	
ABILITIES OF REASONING UNDER NOVEL CONDITIONS.			
Induction. Discover a principle of relationships among elements.	NSR	I	Yes
General Reasoning. Find solutions for problems having an algebraic quality.	CMS	R	Yes
Figural Relations. Demonstrate awareness of relationships among figures.	CFR		?
Semantic Relations: Common Concepts. Demonstrate awareness of relationships among common pieces of information.	CMR IMR		No
Symbolic Classifications. Show which symbol does not belong in a class of several symbols.	CSC		No
Concept Formation. Given several examples of a concept, identify new instances.	CFC		No
SPEED OF THINKING ABILITIES.			
Perceptual Speed. Under highly speeded conditions, distinguish similar visual patterns and find instances of a particular pattern.	ESU	P	Yes
Correct Decision Speed, CDS. Speed of finding correct answers to intellectual problems of intermediate difficulty.			No
Writing and Printing Speed. As quickly as possible, copy printed or cursive letters or words.			No

test designed to measure a narrow ability of Span Memory (Ms), for example, involves broader abilities such as short-term Acquisition and Retrieval (SAR). This is true because memory for elements (in Ms) can be facilitated or inhibited by memory for components of which the elements are a part (as measured in SAR), and because other influences, such as those associated with recency or primacy, operate at both levels.

In sum, then, a test designed to measure at one level of breadth always measures, to some extent, narrower and broader abilities, and a test designed to measure one kind of capacity—a cognitive operation, say—always measures, to some extent, other capacities. Abilities are not different in the same sense that marbles and apples are different. The distinctions among abilities are as shades of gray.

INFORMATION PROCESSING IN HUMAN ABILITIES

What has just been said about difficulties in distinguishing different capacities applies as well to distinguishing between different intellectual processes. It is difficult to separate different features of apprehending the information of problems, and different features of converting information into what might constitute solutions to problems. But a description of such features, however difficult it may be to define them, has come to be known as a description of information processing.

Thus, studies of information processing focus on what a person does in solving a particular kind of problem, usually a problem of apprehension and short-term retention. A way of demonstrating what a person does is referred to as a paradigm. A paradigm is much the same as a test, but often in information processing studies a paradigm is not used to measure individual differences, whereas the word "test" usually refers to operations for measuring such differences. A paradigm thus may indicate only how people on the average perform on different aspects of a problem, but the history of study of human abilities is rich in conversions of paradigms into tests to measure individual differences. This is certainly true of the most recent period of study of abilities (as illustrated in this volume).

To illustrate the concept of information processing paradigms, consider a well known paradigm developed by S. Sternberg (1975). There are many versions of this paradigm. In one version, subjects are shown sets of from 3 to 8 different letters and then asked to judge whether or not a particular letter was among the set of letters to which they had been exposed. Reaction times to make correct judgements are recorded, and plotted along the ordinate relative to the number of letters in the exposure set. A bivariate plot of such data has the following form:

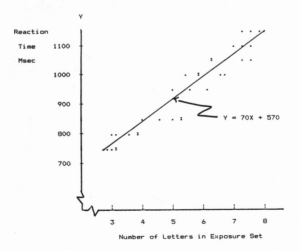

An equation for a straight line is fitted to this scatter-plot. The slope for this equation is interpreted as indicating a process of scanning immediate memory to ascertain whether or not the presented letter is among the letters stored in that memory. The intercept is interpreted as indicating a melange of processes such as are required to get oriented toward the stimuli and generate a response (after one has scanned to determine if an element is present). For the results illustrated in the figure, the slope is 70 msec. This indicates that, on the average over several people, it takes about 70 msec to scan from one letter to another in order to find whether or not a previously presented letter (now in immediate awareness) is in the presented set. This slope remains the same as the number of elements is increased, as does the time to activate the collection of processes represented by the intercept (about 560 msec).

The results illustrated in the figure thus indicate that, for any person, the time to locate a particular element in memory is a direct function of the number of elements in a memory set that contains the element. But individuals can differ notably in the amount of time it takes to scan from one element to another (the slope), or in the time required for the processes represented by the intercept of an equation fitted to their trials on the S. Sternberg paradigm. Recent work using such paradigms has been aimed at describing such individual differences and showing how they relate to test measures that have been around for some time (e.g., Cooper, 1976; Egan, 1979; Chase, 1973; Horn, 1978; Hunt, 1983; Pellegrino, 1983, and this volume). Such approaches have been used with tests of several different contents – spatial, semantic, mathematical (Carpenter & Just, 1986; Poltrock & Brown, 1984; Hayes, 1973; Horn, Donaldson, & Engstrom, 1981; Hunt, Lunneborg, & Lewis, 1975; Mulholland, Pellegrino, & Glaser, 1980; Pellegrino & Kail, 1982; R. J. Sternberg, 1977) – and with the aim of describing abilities such as g and Verbal Comprehension. For the most part, these studies can be viewed as efforts to describe relatively broad abilities in terms of narrower abilities. The narrower abilities are then often called "components," in which case the approach may be referred to as componential (R. J. Sternberg, 1977).

Very commonly, the narrow abilities of information processing or componential studies are measured in terms of reaction times (RT) to make a decision that can be judged to be correct. Our example of the S. Sternberg paradigm illustrates this. RT measures should be carefully distinguished from other measures that can be obtained from a paradigm or test. A well-known paradigm of Shepard & Metzler (1971) can be used to illustrate distinctions between RT measures and other measures of abilities.

The Shepard-Metzler spatial rotation paradigm requires a subject to judge whether or not one of two figures is a rotation of the other. Different amounts of rotation, Rj, are represented in j = 1, 2, . . ., n different sets of figures. A subject's reaction times (Tj) to make correct judgments (of whether or not one figure is a rotation of the other) are plotted along the axis of ordinates in a bivariate Cartesian system, and the Rj degrees of rotation of different figures are plotted along the axis of abscissas. A good-fit straight line of the form Tj = mRj + k is fitted to the plotted points to represent the relation between RT and amount of rotation. As in the S. Sternberg paradigm, the slope of this line is interpreted as indicating a cognitive process, in this case a process of visual scanning, and the intercept is interpreted as indicating a mixture of processes such as those of coordinating muscles in pressing a lever (to respond), focusing on the figures, encoding the figures into immediate awareness, etc.

A test designed to measure the Spatial Orientation primary ability, S, can be comprised of the items of the Shepard-Metzler paradigm (French, 1951), but the scoring of the items is not for reaction time but for accuracy — i.e., whether or not one figure is correctly judged to be a particular rotation (e.g., a flip-flop) of the other. The scoring difference between RT & accuracy is frequently the defining characteristic for distinguishing a study said to represent cognitive processing and other kinds of studies of abilities: the tasks of two studies can be very similar, but, in the study said to represent processing, RT measures are obtained, while, in the other study, the basic measures are for accuracy.

This is not always the case, however. What is called cognitive processing may involve accuracy measures for simple or very homogeneous tasks or features of tasks. Often in studies of this kind, the simple tasks are used to help describe the variance in accuracy scores for complex tasks. Measures derived from serial recall tasks illustrate this approach to defining cognitive processes.

In a serial recall task the subject is presented with a series of elements — say, words — in a particular order and, after a lapse of time (usually very short), asked to recall the elements in the order in which they were presented. If several sets of elements are presented (or the same set is presented over several trials) and the scorer accumulates (over presentations) the elements correctly recalled and their serial positions, typically a curve such as the following is indicated. This figure illustrates what are called primacy and recency processes (Glanzer & Cunitz, 1966; Murdock, 1960). Primacy is indicated by the finding that an element presented early in a series is more likely to be recalled than an element presented in the middle of the series; recency is indicated by the finding that an element presented near the end of a (fairly long) series is more likely to be recalled than an element presented either early or in the middle of the series.

In one kind of cognitive process study using these measures (Horn et al., 1981), primacy and recency measures of individual differences were obtained as accuracy scores for the elements early-presented and late-presented. These measures were then used in multiple, part, and partial correlational analyses to demonstrate the extent to which elementary processes could account for

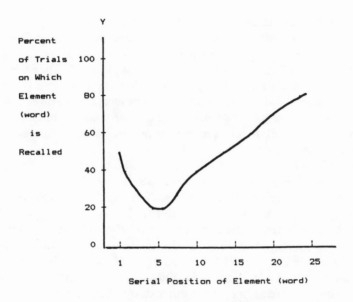

Serial Position of Element (word)

the variance in accuracy measures of the kind that have been said to indicate *g*. In this work recency was said to indicate a process of holding elements of information in immediate awareness, as required in comparing elements in a reasoning task; primacy was said to indicate nascent comprehension of the kind that is needed for encoding information. Both of these processes were found to account for some (by no means all) of the variance in a broad *g*-like measure labeled Gf. Perhaps more important, the processes were implicated in adulthood age differences in Gf (Horn et al., 1981). These findings will be discussed in a later section of this chapter.

There is considerable evidence to suggest that the component abilities indicated by reaction time measures are different from the component abilities indicated by accuracy scores. Egan (1979), for example, looked carefully at speed and accuracy processes of thinking, using the Shepard-Metzler task and a clock-position test developed by Guilford (1967). He found that the speed of rotation (slope) measures correlated near zero with number-correct (i.e., accuracy) scores on the Shepard-Metzler and Guilford tests. The slope measures also correlated near zero with measures of pilot-training perform-ances that were expected to indicate spatial abilities. These findings are con-sistent with the overall pattern of findings for many measures in other studies (Horn, 1978; Horn et al., 1981).

It is difficult to obtain reliable measures of slopes and intercepts for indi-vidual subjects. It is possible that Egan's results mainly reflect this problem. If slope measures do not have substantial reliability — above .7 — they cannot correlate substantially with another variable, and small correlations can not be seen to be significant in "smallish" samples (e.g., Ns less than 100). Problems of obtaining adequate reliabilities for slope and intercept measures have been important in many studies of information processing (e.g., Carpenter & Just, 1978; Horn et al., 1981; Hunt, et al., 1975; R. J. Sternberg, 1977).

Virtually an entire new field of cognitive processing studies has been opened by advances in microcomputer technology. RT measures are easily obtained with this technology, but so are other measures. We have only just begun to look through the window into human thinking that has been opened by measurements derived from microcomputer presentations. This volume attests to the promise of quite interesting findings yet to come.

The remainder of this chapter is devoted to sketching an indication of broad abilities that need to be understood in terms of detailed analyses of the kind that now can be undertaken in cognitive processing studies.

A HIERARCHY OF HUMAN ABILITIES

The system I will describe is empirically based. There have been hundreds of studies of the intercorrelations and linear structures (e.g., common-factor, simple structure) for human abilities. This work has been collated and summarized (by, for example, Cattell, 1971; Ekstrom et al., 1979; French, 1951; French, Ekstrom, & Price, 1963; Guilford, 1967; Guilford & Hoepfner, 1971; Hakstian & Cattell, 1974, 1978; Horn, 1968, 1972, 1982a, b, 1985, 1986a, b, c; Horn & Donaldson, 1980; Pawlik, 1966, 1978). The results have led to an understanding (with provisos, Carroll & Horn, 1981) of different kinds and different levels of narrowness of human abilities. I will outline this understanding in the sections that follow.

In describing levels of narrowness of abilities, it is useful to move from the general to the specific. It would be reasonable, also, to do it the other way, and go from the narrow to the broad. But it seems that often, at least, adults prefer to think in terms of broad concepts for which there can be particular instances. Also, broad concepts of general intelligence (and there are several, Horn, 1986a) have been in vogue for roughly 80 years, in consequence of which many people readily assume that it is most useful to think in terms of such an ability before (if ever) thinking in terms of narrower abilities.

To make the presentation fairly concrete, I will use the subtests of a popular test—the WOJ—to illustrate the kinds of component abilities that are parts of major abilities. Many of the WOJ subtests represent primary abilities indicated by replicated research, as summarized by Ekstrom et al. (1979). This relationship is suggested in Table 2. We shall see that some of the major abilities indicated by existing research are not well represented in the WOJ. In describing those abilities, I will refer to subtests of other popular tests, such as the K-ABC and McCarthy.

TABLE 2
WOODCOCK-JOHNSON TESTS CLASSIFIED IN TERMS OF
The Primary Ability Best Measured With a Test

Test No.	CA or TOA	Subtest Name	Symbol	Primary Ability Name	Second Order
1	CA	Picture Vocabulary	V	Verbal Comprehension	Gc
8	CA	Antonyms-Synonyms	EMR	Evaluation of Semantic Relations	Gc
22	TOA	Humanities	Vi	General Information	Gc
21	TOA	Social Studies	Vi	General Information	Gc
20	TOA	Science	Vi	General Information	Gc
15	TOA	Passage Comprehension	MMC	Chunking Memory	Gc
17	TOA	Applied Problems	Sep	Sensitivity to Problems	Gq
6	CA	Quantitative Concepts	R	General Reasoning	Gq
16	TOA	Calculations	N	Number Facility	Gq
12	CA	Verbal Analogies	CMR	Cognition of Semantic Relations	Gf
9	CA	Analysis-Synthesis	CFR	Cognition of Figural Relations	Gf
11	CA	Concept Formation	CFC	Concept Formation	Gf
4	CA	Visual Auditory Learning	ACoR	Auditory Relations	Gf,Ga
13	TOA	Letter-Word Identification	CMR	Semantic Relations	Vf*
18	TOA	Dictation	DASP	Discriminate Patterns of Sounds	Vf,Ga
19	TOA	Proofing	EMU	Evaluation of Semantic Units	Vf
14		Word Attack	Tc	Temporal Tracking	Vf,Ga
5	CA	Blending	SPUD	Distorted Speech Comprehension	Ga
3	CA	Memory for Sentences	Mm	Meaningful Memory	SAR
10	CA	Numbers Reversed	Ms	Span Memory	SAR
2	CA	Spatial Relations	Vz	Visualization	Gv
7	CA	Visual Matching	P	Perceptual Speed	Gs

Very Broad Abilities

The ability that might be measured by a linear combination of all the measures of the WOJ or K-ABC—those listed as cognitive or process abilities, as well as those referred to as measures of achievement—is broader than most measures of IQ or g. Call this measure G1. A somewhat less broad G2 measure could be obtained by summing over the 12 measures of cognitive abilities in the WOJ, or the 10 measures of processes in the K-ABC. These G2 measures are comparable in breadth to a total-score G2 measure obtained as the sum of the subtest scores of the cognitive subtests of the McCarthy (1972) test. Each of these G2 measures has a somewhat different mixture of component abilities, but they are comparable in terms of breadth. A G3 measure might be a linear combination of the measures (sum of subtest scores) obtained with the tests of achievement in the WOJ or K-ABC. These measures, too, would be comprised of somewhat different component abilities, and both would be narrower than the G2 measures, but they would be comparable in terms of breadth.

The G3 measure would be roughly as broad as the total IQ measure of the Wechsler tests (Matarazzo, 1972; Wechsler, 1981), although the primary factor compositions of the indicated G3 measures are different from the primary factor composition of Wechsler IQ measures. The G2 and G3 measures would in each case be broader than the measure obtained as Stanford-Binet IQ, although this conclusion must be guarded because the Stanford-Binet provides a broader measure at young ages than at older ages (see Horn, 1972, 1976, 1977 for review of some of the relevant evidence).

In a test intended for applied work, it might be wise to provide the user with a basis for using a broad-to-narrow hierarchy of ability measures. Such a hierarchy would permit flexibility in use. A broad-to-narrow hierarchical system permits one to skirt issues that seem to divide investigators such as Horn (1985, 1986a), on the one side, and Jensen (1984, 1985) and Eysenck (1985), on the other, while at the same time retaining the major concepts of these different investigators. Features of a potentially useful hierarchy will be illustrated in subsequent sections.

Second-Order Abilities

For several reasons of theory and practice, it is useful to step down in a hierarchy of breadth from very broad measures referred to as IQ (or the like) to measures that are less broad. This helps indicate lawful relations that are clouded if only a concept of general intelligence is used (Horn, 1986a); it helps mitigate confusion generated by the fact that IQ has been so variably defined.

One of the major problems with the literature pertaining to IQ is that different measures of what is said to be the same attribute involve different collections of basic abilities having different construct validities (Cronbach, 1971; Horn, 1972, 1976, 1986a, b; Horn & Goldsmith, 1981). This condition leads to unproductive arguments about whether or not a test "really measures *g*" (arguments seen in the Harnad, 1985, collection of essays pertaining to a piece by Jensen). The arguments are unproductive for reasons adumbrated previously: the melange of abilities an IQ test measures is an arbitrary function of the nature and breadth of the subtests used in the total measure. Although Jensen (1984) contends that the broad measure obtained with the K-ABC tests is not a good measure of IQ, in fact his argument boils down to an opinion that short-term memory and visualization abilities (called by other names in Kaufman & Kaufman, 1983) do not best exemplify his ideas about what should be measured in an IQ test. (As pointed out by Horn & Goldsmith, 1981, these ideas change from one to another of Jensen's writings). Kaufman and Kaufman, on the other hand, argue that the abilities they measure are the sine qua non of what should be measured in an IQ test. What we presently know about human abilities does not consistently support or refute either party in this kind of controversy. Different mixture-measures are useful for different purposes.

What the extant evidence does indicate is that abilities less broad than *g* indicate important lawful relations that are not well represented in theories of general intelligence. The interrelationships among diverse samples of ability measurements are not explained by g; distinctly different abilities are required to explain these relationships. More important, these distinctly different abilities have different lawful relationships with variables that indicate the development and function of cognitive capacities. These broad abilities, and the measures of the WOJ that fit within a system of these abilities, will be described next.

Acculturation knowledge or crystallized intelligence, Gc. The tests of the WOJ capture the breadth of this ability better than any published test of which I am aware. The tests that measure Gc are found both among the cognitive abilities (CA) and tests of achievement (TOA) of the WOJ. Listed in order of strength of relationship to Gc, these abilities are:

Verbal knowledge — i.e., Picture Vocabulary and Antonyms-Synonyms, each measured in CA.

Science Information, measured in TOA.

Social Science Information, measured in TOA.

Humanities Information, measured in TOA.

Reasoning, measured (in CA) with a verbal analogies test. The correlation expected between verbal knowledge and verbal analogies is roughly .65. The correlation will be smaller than this estimate if the words of the analogies are very common, but the relations among the words are quite abstract. To the extent that this condition obtains, the correlation between verbal analogies and Gc decreases and the correlation between verbal analogies and fluid intelligence (Gf, as will be described shortly) increases (Horn, 1968, 1972; Horn & Cattell, 1966).

Applied Problems, measured in TOA. Given a verbally developed problem and information of possible relevance for solving the problem, use the information to achieve a solution.

Passage Comprehension, measured in TOA. Provide an appropriate word to complete an incomplete statement.

Quantitative Concepts, measured in CA. This test extends to problems of algebra (e.g., solve equations), trigonometry (determine perimeters, areas), and the calculus (differentiation, integration). It can be expected to measure Gf as well as Gc.

Calculations, measured in TOA. Do addition, subtraction, division and multiplication calculations, some involving fractions and decimals.

A very broad version of the Gc ability involves knowledge in most areas of scholarship—the humanities, business, the social sciences, the physical sciences, and mathematics. This ability may be what most people mean when they use the term "intelligence" (Humphreys, 1979; Sternberg, Conway, Ketron, & Bernstein, 1981).

Broad reasoning or fluid intelligence, Gf. The reasoning of Gf involves many mental operations—identifying relations among events, drawing inferences, forming concepts, recognizing concepts, identifying conjunctions, recognizing disjunctions, etc. Abilities of the WOJ that indicate the ability, listed in order of their relationship to the ability, are the following:

Analysis-Synthesis, measured in CA. The task is to apply abstract rules of relationships among black, yellow and blue squares. For example, the rule might be that two arrows, one pointing from a black square to a yellow square and the other pointing the opposite way, represent the same thing as a black square alone. The subject must understand the double-arrow relationship well enough to be able to apply it in other instances in which colors of the squares vary.

Concept Formation, measured in CA. In this test the subject must figure out a rule that indicates why one drawing of colored squares or circles is an instance of a concept.

Visual Auditory Learning, measured in CA. Comprehend and use a code that involves transforming English words into symbols.

Reasoning, measured with verbal analogies in CA, (discussed in describing Gc). This is a good measure of Gf when the words of the analogies are equally familiar or equally esoteric for all examinees and only the relationships among the words introduce variance in individual differences in correctly solving the problems.

Quantitative Concepts, measured in CA. Again, to the extent that the items require reasoning rather than the knowledge of Gc or Gq (to be discussed shortly), this test will measure, Gf.

Calculations, measured in CA. To the extent that the items involve reasoning but do not emphasize mathematical knowledge, per se, this test will be mainly indicative of Gf rather than Gc or Gq.

Numbers Reversed Memory, measured in CA. Presented with a series of several numbers, repeat the series in the reverse of the order presented.

Other well known measures of Gf are Blocks (of the WAIS) and Matrices.

In the WOJ battery, not unlike other batteries, there is considerable overlap in the measures of Gf and Gc. Such overlap is difficult to avoid. This is true partly because it is difficult to devise tasks that measure reasoning but are not also prominent indicators of acculturation knowledge, and vice versa. Nevertheless, Gf and Gc are usually distinguishable even in batteries that are not well designed to show the distinction; the two have distinct relationships to age in adulthood, and different predictive relationships with a number of outcome variables, both in childhood and adulthood.

Broad speediness, Gs. WOJ abilities that are most indicative of Gs were identified earlier in describing the difference between narrow and broad abilities. As indicated in that discussion, speediness is indicated by the following measures.

> Visual Matching, measured in CA. This test has been studied in many previous investigations.
> Spatial Relations, measured with under highly speeded conditions in CA.
> Letter-Word Identification, measured in TOA. Under constraints to work rapidly, correctly pronounce common English words.

Almost any test can be made into a measure of Gs by decreasing the demands for knowledge and reasoning, and increasing the demands for working quickly. Also, most speeded tests involve, to some extent, the Gs ability. Thus measures such as Quantitative Concepts, Analogies and Dictation should correlate with Gs because they involve emphasis on speed of performance.

Short-term acquisition and retrieval, SAR. The phenomena studied in most of the research on information processing are closely similar to the phenomena measured in SAR. Thus, much of what has been learned from studies of information processing pertains most directly to this broad ability. The tests of the WOJ that mainly indicate SAR include the following:

> Numbers Reversed Memory, measured in CA, described briefly in the discussion of Gf.
> Digit Span, measured in the SLS.
> Tone Span, measured in the SLS.
> Location Span, measured in the SLS.
> Word Span. To the extent that this task measures individual differences in familiarity with words, it will indicate Gc rather than SAR. If the words are equally familiar to all respondents (or equally obscure), the task will mainly indicate SAR.
> Memory For Sentences, measured in CA. Repeat a sentence immediately after it has been spoken.
> Blending. Given spoken syllables, such as "win" and "dough" put them together to make a word — "window."
> Visual-Auditory Learning, measured in CA. Learn to associate familiar spoken words with unfamiliar visual symbols so that sentences in the symbols can be translated into words. The test is thus a symbol-word

paired associate memory measure. Performance on this task can be indicative of Gv (to be discussed shortly), rather than SAR – if there is emphasis on visualization and not much demand for retention of unrelated material.

SAR should not be confused with Long-term Storage and Retrieval, TSR, one of three broad abilities indicated by several lines of research but not in the WOJ. The other two abilities are Visual Intelligence, Gv, and Auditory Intelligence, Ga. Because the WOJ does not provide for good measurement of these abilities, it is less comprehensive than it might be. This means that the WOJ has a different composition than somewhat similar tests that do measure TSR, Gv and/or Ga. For example, the K-ABC, compared with the WOJ, is heavily weighted with measures of Gv.

Long-term storage and retrieval, TSR. This ability is often confused with SAR. It is true that the manner in which information is organized at the time of encoding for memory storage (i.e., SAR) is indicative of the manner in which the information is retrieved at a later date (i.e., TSR) – even if much time intervenes between acquisition and retrieval (Norman, 1979). But it is clear, also, that individual differences in immediate apprehension and retrieval over short periods of time, measured in SAR, are independent of (although correlated with) individual differences in the facility with which information can be retrieved from quasi-permanent storage, as measured in TSR. It can be difficult to distinguish TSR from SAR, if the memory tasks for TSR do not tax the ability to retrieve information stored at least several minutes before, and preferably several hours or days before.

Tests such as the following are indicative of TSR.

Retention of Learning After Several Minutes or Hours. Tasks of short-term memory can be used to measure this ability if recall is measured long after the short-term memory testing has been completed. The measure best indicates TSR rather than SAR if the subject is not led to expect that recall will be asked for after a long lapse of time.

Expressional Fluency, a facility for coming up with appropriate and different expressions for an idea.

Ideational Fluency, a facility for finding different ways to interpret and write or talk about a particular event – e.g., a woman boarding a bus.

Associational Fluency, retrieving words that are connotatively similar to a given word. This should be measured with fairly liberal time limits, in order to give subjects a chance to exhaust the elements in a category of association.

Memory Acquisition. The task is to memorize, verbatim, a page of words. It can be difficult to distinguish TSR from Gc if the TSR tasks do not emphasize fluent recall of knowledge, in contrast to breadth of knowledge as such. If the task mainly requires that one recite passages learned several minutes previously, then performances will be mainly indicative of TSR. The tasks should not be highly speeded. It is not known whether or not time to reach a particular criterion in verbatim learning of verbal material is a good measure of this ability. My guess is that such a measure is more indicative of Gc or SAR than of TSR. If so, Memory Retention and Relearning will not be a good measure of TSR, but instead will best measure Gc. This hypothesis is based on very little evidence.

Broad visual intelligence, Gv. Gv might be referred to as visual fluency. It represents an ease of visualizing how things appear from different perspectives, and how they change as they move in space. It is not analytic, however, in the sense that Gf is analytic: one doesn't so much analyse how objects will look as they move in space, as merely "see" this intuitively (Poltrock & Brown, 1984). This is illustrated in the following examples of measures of Gv.

- Visual Manipulation, as measured in Paper Folding, a test that has been studied in many previous investigations. The task is to perform mental operations that simulate the folding of a piece of paper, punching a hole through the folded paper, unfolding the paper, and identifying how the holes would appear.
- Visual Constancy. This can be measured with an accuracy score based on the Shepard and Metzler test. In most studies of Gv and its components, correctness of response is the measure, and this is obtained under only moderately speeded conditions. Studies of the visual abilities of pilot and navigator trainees in the U.S. Air Force (Guilford & Lacy, 1947) indicate that Gv is not so much the speed of visualizing as it is the ease or fluency of visualization.
- Analytic Perception, as measured in the Gottschaldt or Hidden Figures test. In addition to being used as a measure of visualization, this test has been regarded as an indicator of Field Independence (Witkin & Goodenough, 1981). Field Independence was measured initially with Rod-and-Frame and Tilting-Room tests. These measures indicate inclination to use cues from one's own body, rather than environmental cues surrounding an object, as a basis for locating the object in space. Witken and his coworkers have presented evidence suggesting that Field Independence is associated with being male, not female. Work by Bock and Kolakowski (1973) suggests that individual differences in Gv stem from a sex-linked major-gene influence.
- Gestalt Closure. This test has been used in many previous studies. The ability is one of closing gaps to complete a view that is obscure, as when objects must be seen through a fog.
- Design Memory. Although intended to measure short-term memory, this test is likely to be a good indicator of Gv if the task for the subject is

one of visualizing the steps in drawing a figure or if performance is facilitated by ability to visualize how lines are put together to create a figure.

It can be difficult to distinguish Gv from Gf if visualization tasks can be solved by analytic reasoning, or if there are few requirements for fluent visual thinking.

Broad auditory intelligence, Ga. This ability represents a facility in "chunking" streams of sounds, keeping these chunks in awareness, and anticipating an auditory form that can develop out of such streams. It is not heavily dependent on auditory acuity, which is a quite separate capacity (Horn & Stankov, 1982).

For centuries, there has been recognition that auditory genius is not necessarily aligned with other forms of intelligent behavior, but a clear operational distinction between Ga and other broad intellectual abilities was not made until recently (Horn, 1973; Horn & Stankov, 1982; Stankov, 1978; Stankov & Horn, 1980). In the studies where this distinction was drawn, first-order abilities were identified within a catholic sampling of auditory tasks; factoring these primary abilities, along with first-order indicators of Gc, Gf, and Gv, then isolated Ga and a separate auditory acuity dimension. The tasks that indicate Ga involve detection, transformation, and retention of tonal patterns.

The following are some of these tasks.

Discrimination among Sound Patterns (DASP). In Tonal Classifications, one of the marker tests of DASP, the task is to identify which one of five chords does not belong with the others. Other markers require one to identify changes in patterns of notes. Dewar, Cuddy, and Mewhart (1977) interpreted an ability similar to DASP as "sensitivity to relational cues in sounds."

Maintaining and Judging Rhythms (MaJR). The tasks that best indicate MaJR require one to join in a beat, as provided by a metronome, and correctly continue the beat after the beat-setter (metronome) has stopped. An incomplete words test similar to Blending in the WOJ also indicates the ability. In this task, one must identify a spoken word when particular sounds have been left out in the pronunciation. The suggestion is that the ability is important in understanding the rhythms of language.

Temporal Tracking of Sounds (Tc). The ability of Tc is one of holding sound patterns of past and present in mind while anticipating patterns of the future. Hearnshaw (1956) and Pollack (1969) have referred to this as "temporal integration." In a prominent task of the ability one must retain nonsense syllables in awareness for several seconds, while a new pronunciation of nonsense syllables is going on, and identify just where in the newly pronounced set the first-pronounced syllables are located.

Auditory Cognition of Relations (ACoR). This ability is analogous to visual Gestalt Closure. In the Chord Decomposition task that helps define the ability one must identify separate notes that were heard in a chord. A factor indicating this ability had been identified in early work (French, 1951; Shuter, 1968).

Auditory Immediate Memory (Msa). This is only a weak indicator of Ga. Msa represents a finding that span memory for sounds is different from span memory for visual patterns, including visually-presented words and paralogs. It seems that Msa enables one to hold sound patterns in mind while performing cognitive manipulations of the kind expressed in the other abilities of Ga. This function of Msa in Ga is similar to the function of span memory in Gf (Horn, 1970; Horn & Cattell, 1966).

It can be seen in these examples that the abilities of Ga require, in different ways, holistic comprehension of patterns among sounds. As in the case of Gv, Ga is best indicated when the tasks do not emphasize the reasoning of Gf or the comprehension of Gc, but, instead, require that one fluently perceive the flow of sounds.

Little has been done to show how Ga is important for understanding development and achievement. The bits of evidence now in hand suggest that it is indeed important, not only for understanding achievements in music, but also for understanding language development and academic achievement in the early years of schooling (Anastasi, 1976; Atkin, Bray, Davidson, Hertzberger, Humphreys, & Selzer, 1977a, b; Minton & Schneider, 1980). A measure of Ga probably should be included in test batteries designed for use in research.

Summary of outline of major abilities.   At a general level, then, important "intelligences" of humans can be described as follows:

Gc: A broad pattern of the achievements and knowledge that are emphasized in acculturation.

Gf: A broad pattern of reasoning, seriating, sorting, and classifying.

TSR: A facility in retrieving information stored in what might be called long-term memory.

SAR: A broad pattern of immediate awareness, alertness and retrieval of material apprehended a short time before.

Gv: A facility for visualizing figures and responding appropriately to spatial forms.

Ga: A pattern of skills of listening and responding appropriately to auditory information.

In Figure 1, I have outlined a structural model and an information processing hierarchy for these abilities. The intelligences are represented by circles; some of the directed arrows extended outward from these circles point to

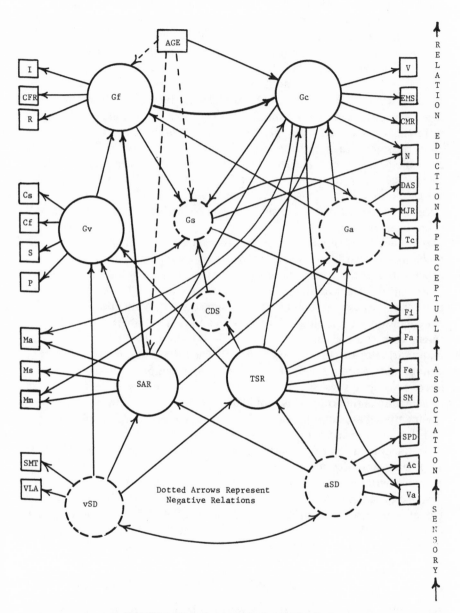

FIGURE 1 Function organizations of intellect.

squares representing the manifest variable indicators of the intelligences. The squares correspond to primary factors (tests) one would use in structural model analyses to enable the intelligences to be distinguished. (The two dimensions in dotted circles at the bottom of the figure and CDS have not been discussed previously in this chapter: vSD and aSD represent elementary capacities for attaining awareness of stimuli — visual (vSd) and auditory (aSD) — as discussed insightfully by Broadbent, 1966. CDS represents Correct Decision Speed. These abilities will be discussed in considering ability differences associated with age. The arrows running from bottom to top along the right in the figure represent the idea that information first enters the psychological system as elementary awarenesses, which then are linked in associations, which then form perceptual gestalts, which then can be understood in terms of relations and correlates. Eduction of relations and correlates has been regarded as the sine qua non of intelligence (as in Spearman's near-classic theory).

In bringing these intelligence factors to your attention my purpose is not so much to argue for particular interpretations as to suggest that information processing theories need to take account of such broad abilities. The factors represent consistent findings from a number of studies. They are hardy in the sense that they can be found (in well designed studies) under notably different conditions of sampling of subjects and marker variables. They have different construct validities (Cronbach, 1987) — i.e., their correlations with many variables are consistently different. The factors obtained in samples of young children are similar to factors obtained in samples of adults. Such evidence adds up to suggest that different intellectual processes exist at a broad level in human thinking. This should be kept in mind when information processing studies are done on one kind of task or a few tests. A law indicated for one intelligence need not be applicable to other intelligences.

To illustrate a few of the ways in which these broad abilities are different empirically and in terms of construct validity, I will turn to consideration of evidence pertaining to adult development. In this work the aim has been to describe broad abilities in terms of components that not only indicate individual differences but also indicate individual differences associated with age differences across what I like to refer to as the "vital years of adulthood" (Horn, 1982a) — i.e., the period from age 20 to age 60 years.

SOME DEVELOPMENTAL FINDINGS

The results of Figure 2 illustrate how mixture models of intelligence, coupled with an assumption that the same g is measured in different mixtures, can create confusion. From young adulthood to old age, there is (on the average across many individuals) monotonic decrease in some intellectual abilities, and monotonic increase in other abilities. Each of these kinds of abilities is a part of first principal component measures of g and other (IQ) mixture-

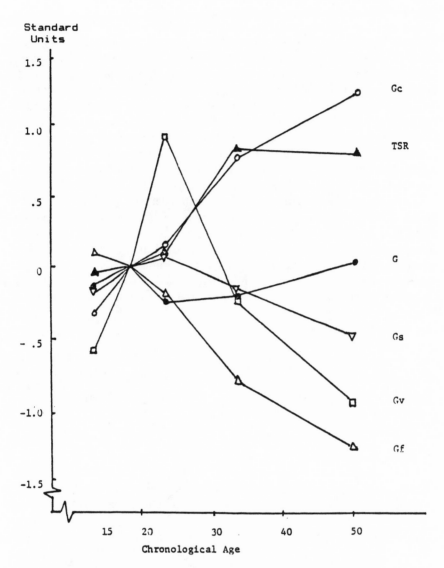

FIGURE 2   Adulthood age differences in dimensions of human intellect.

measures of "general intelligence." If a mixture-measure happens to be loaded with the abilities that decline with age, then investigators using that measure will find that "intelligence" declines with age in adulthood; if most of a mixture-measure is made up from abilities for which there is aging increase, those who use that measure will find that "intelligence" increases with age in adulthood; if the two kinds of abilities are about equally weighted in a mixture, then the pronouncement can be that "intelligence" reaches a plateau of development in adulthood.

Several variations on these themes have been played in the published literature, with resulting controversy and effort to explain the "contradictory" results. For example, many pages in the literature of adult development have
been devoted to explanations for a belief that cross-sectional studies show
aging decrease in intelligence while longitudinal results do not. This charac-
terization of results is wrong on several counts (Horn & Donaldson, 1980),
but one important count is that the apparent contradiction is created, at least
in part, by the use of different mixture-measures; the mixture-measures of
longitudinal studies have been heavily loaded with Gc and TSR, but the
mixture-measures of cross-sectional studies have been most loaded with Gf
and SAR. The use of mixture-measures can create many subtle confusions.

The results of Figures 3 through 6 indicate independence among rather elementary abilities which, however, have some claim to being regarded as
among the intellectual abilities of intelligence.

The rationale for the analyses of the studies of Figures 3 through 6 is suggested by considering Figure 3. In this figure a prima facie case is indicated
for a claim that the aging decline of intelligence is due to aging loss of simple
capacities, such as a capacity for making visual discriminations (vSD), a ca-

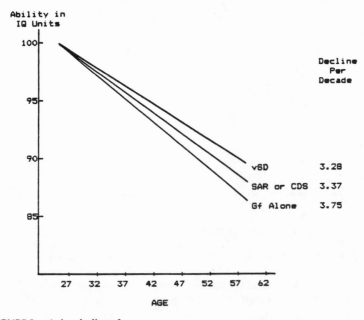

FIGURE 3   Aging decline of

vSD:	Visual Sensory Detectors
SAR:	Short-term Acquisition-Retrieval
CDS:	Correct Decision Speed
Gf:	Fluid Reasoning Abilities

pacity for speed in making correct decisions (CDS), or a capacity of short-term memory (SAR).

Consider the visual discrimination factor, vSD. Measured using procedures developed by Broadbent (1966), this indicates the breadth of a person's immediate awareness of stimuli. It is reasonable to suppose that if such awareness were lacking, there would be consequent distortion of perception in problems of the kind one must solve in order to score well on measures of "intelligence" — in particular, measures of Gf. Thus, if loss of visual discrimination capacities occurred with aging, then this might be the underlying cause for any corresponding loss seen in Gf. The curve for decline of vSD, as shown in Figure 3, establishes this prima facie case. Since the decline of vSD is about the same as the decline for Gf, it appears that the decline of the latter could result from the decline of the former.

Missing in such reasoning, however, is a demonstration that the decline of vSD accounts for the decline of Gf. When this missing link is introduced by removing vSD decline from Gf decline, the results illustrated in Figure 4 are obtained. These results provide no support for an hypothesis that loss of sensory function is responsible for loss of the intellectual capacities represented by Gf. Eliminating the part of Gf decline that is estimated by decline of vSD does not bring about a significant change in the curve of decline for

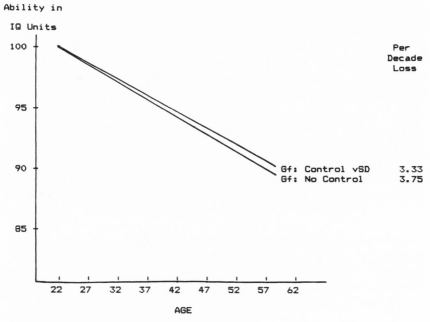

FIGURE 4   Aging decline of Gf after control of

vSD = visual sensory detection

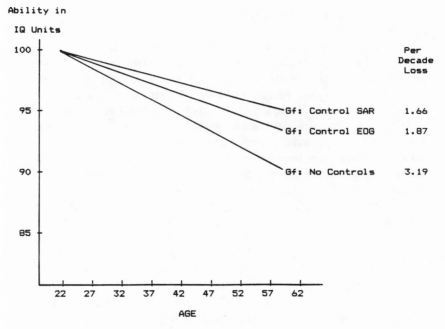

FIGURE 5   Aging decline of Gf after control of

SAR = short-term acquisition and retrieval
EOG = encoding organization

Gf: the change from 3.75 to 3.33 units of decline per decade is not significant. This same kind of result was obtained with a measure of auditory sensory discrimination.

Shown in Figure 5 are results suggesting that when there is control for short-term memory (SAR), and/or nuclear abilities of SAR (e.g., organizing information in encoding, EOG, as measured using a paradigm developed by George Mandler, 1968), the decline curve for Gf is significantly reduced (from 3.19 to 1.66, for SAR, or 1.87, for EOG, units of decline per decade). Such results support an hypothesis that individual and aging differences in Gf involve, in part, the immediate memory of SAR and encoding organization of EOG.

The results for EOG and SAR are not independent: control for EOG or SAR produces roughly the same reduction in the decline curve for Gf (varying a bit from one study to another, as seen in Horn et al., 1981), but adding one of these controls to the other does not significantly increase the effect. The suggestion is that EOG is the essential element of SAR associated with the aging decline of Gf. This is not to say, however, that EOG accounts for all the variance in SAR or all the aging decline of SAR. EOG accounts for only the part of SAR in Gf that declines with age, and only about one-half the aging decline of SAR, as such.

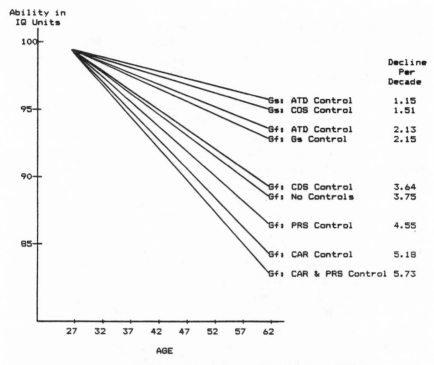

FIGURE 6   Aging decline of Gf and Gs after control of particular variables:

CDS:	Correct Decision Speed
Gs:	Inspection Speediness
ATD:	Attention Division
COS:	Concentration on Slowness
PRS:	Persistence
CAR:	Carefulness

Several findings are illustrated by the results summarized in Figure 6. First, the results indicate the extent to which the decline of Gf can be described in terms of aging changes in speed of performance.

An interesting finding of our studies is that speed in obtaining correct answers to problems of nontrivial difficulty (CDS) has very little relation to the level of difficulty with which one copes in measures of Gf. The results depicted in Figure 6 tell this story in terms of development; removal of decline of Gf that can be predicted by decline of CDS has very little influence on the decline curve for Gf (the change is from 3.75 to 3.64 units of decline per decade, which is not significant).

In contrast to control for CDS, control for a simple factor of inspection speediness, Gs, *does* account for some of the aging decline of Gf. The change from 3.75 to 2.15 units of decline per decade is significant.

But speediness per se may not be the culprit responsible for the loss of Gf that is associated with Gs. As shown in the top part of Figure 6, most of the aging decline of Gs itself is accounted for by control of capacities for maintaining close concentration (COS) and dividing attention (ATD). When COS and ATD are controlled in Gf, there is control also for the decline of Gs and the associated decline of Gf. Moreover, the part of Gf decline that is associated with Gs is accounted for by decline of capacities represented by COS and ATD.

The summary of Figure 6 also illustrates results suggesting that the decline of Gf does not result because older adults are more careful and persistent than younger adults. To the contrary.

We find that older adults work longer than younger adults before abandoning a difficult problem — the PRS (persistence) variable of the figure. Also, older adults give fewer incorrect answers to problems of nontrivial difficulty — the CAR (carefulness) variable of the figure. CAR and PRS are reflected in slowness of performance in timed tests, particularly if the respondent is given no opportunity to "abandon" a problem for which no solution is found (i.e., give no answer). But when carefulness and persistence are used to estimate the decline of Gf, and this estimated part is removed, the decline of Gf not reduced; it is increased, as can be seen in the results of the figure. Such findings indicate that carefulness and persistence are qualities that enable older adults to perform better on untimed Gf tasks than they would perform if these qualities were not allowed to operate. When advantages associated with carefulness and persistence are removed by statistical control, there is significant increase in the aging decline of Gf.

Table 3 contains a summary of results from analyses in which several different sets of variables were controlled in studying the aging decline of Gf. One important conclusion derived from these analyses is that different sets of three or four control variables produce essentially the same result — i.e., account for the same amount of aging loss of Gf. This suggests that many ostensibly different variables measure the same basic intellectual processes. For example, although Gs, inspection speediness, is operationally independent in measurement from COS, concentration on slowness, and SAR, all of these

TABLE 3
PROCESSES OF GF THAT ALSO RELATE TO AGING
Based on Horn, Donaldson, and Engstrom (1981)

COS:	Concentration: Maintaining close attention, as in very slow tracing.
EOG:	Encoding Organization: Classifying incoming information in ways that facilitate subsequent recall.
ICM:	Incidental Memory: Remembering small things that would seem to be insignificant.
EIR:	Eschewing Irrelevancies: Not attending to what has proved to be irrelevant.
ATD:	Dividing Attention: Attending to other things while remembering a given thing.
MSB:	Working Memory: Holding several distinct ideas in mind at once.
HYP:	Hypothesizing: Forming ideas about what is likely.
Gs:	Inspection Speediness: Speed in "finding" and "comparing."

variables involve a common process — e.g., attentiveness — that is implicated in Gf decline: they do not carry entirely independent variance in accounting for the aging loss of Gf. The same can be said for several combinations of the variables shown in the table. And there are several ways to talk about the three or four basic processes that are implicated in aging losses of intellectual abilities. These matters are discussed in other papers (Horn, 1982a, 1985; Horn et al., 1981).

Our results indicate that no combination of the variables of Table 3 will account for all the observed decline of Gf. The precise proportion of the decline that is accounted for by different variables varies with the reliabilities of the measures and the extent of the variability in the subject sample, but, roughly, only about one-half of the aging loss of Gf can be reliably accounted for with variables of the kind that are illustrated in the table.

SUMMARY OF MAJOR POINTS

The review of this chapter illustrates a componential approach to analyzing individual differences in any important (broad) ability. Results from this componential analysis show that Gf, for example, is made up of distinct processes, or capacities, that are associated with aging differences and changes. Gf is merely one of several different intelligences that can be analysed in this way. It is operationally distinct from Gc, which has a different course of development over the vital years of adulthood. Gc, too, is comprised of different processes, different elementary components. Both Gf and Gc are developmentally different from Gv, visual intelligence, Ga, auditory intelligence, SAR, short period apprehension and retrieval, TSR, long-term storage and retrieval, and perhaps two forms of speed of thinking. A componential information processing account can be given for each of these intelligences. Each account would be different.

The domain of intellectual abilities can be described at any of several different levels of abstraction. In considering which level is "best," objectives should be carefully considered. In some work, rather narrow concepts and measures should be used. In other work broad concepts, such as the intelligences of this essay, will be of most value. For the next few years, particularly in developmental psychology, probably it will be most worthwhile to work with broad concepts. As the overall picture begins to be seen clearly, it will become most useful to explore the details of particular cognitive processes.

Figure 7 represents another view of the model that was outlined previously in Figure 1. Two hierarchies are now suggested; one on the right, one on the left: a processing hierarchy (referred to earlier) and a developmental hierarchy. The latter represents the idea that the abilities derive from different

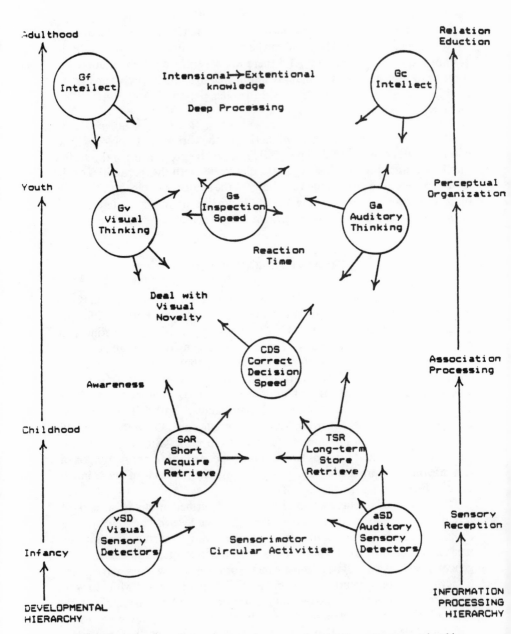

FIGURE 7 Broad abilities within developmental and information processing hierarchies.

232

TABLE 4
ABBREVIATIONS USED IN FIGURES 1 AND 7

Abbreviation:	Meaning
I	Inductive Reasoning
CFR	Cognition of Figural Relations
R	Quantitative Reasoning
Gf	Fluid Eduction
V	Verbal Comprehension
EMS	Evaluation of Semantic Systems
CMR	Cognition of Semantic Relations
Gc	Acculturated Knowledge
Cs	Speed of Closure
Cf	Flexibility of Closure
S	Spatial Orientation
P	Perceptual Speed
Gv	Broad Visual Comprehension
Gs	Broad Speediness
CDS	Correct Decision Speediness
DAS	Discrimination Among Sound Patterns
MJR	Maintaining and Judging Rhythms
Tc	Temporal Tracking
Ga	Broad Auditory Comprehension
Ma	Associational Immediate Memory
Ms	Span Immediate Memory
Mm	Meaning Paired Associates Immediate Memory
SAR	Short-term Apprehension and Retrieval
Fi	Ideational Fluency
Fa	Associational Fluency
Fe	Expressional Fluency
SM	Semantic Memory over Minutes
SMT	Sperling Matrix Awareness
VLA	Visual Location Address
vSD	Visual Sensory Detection
SPD	Speech Perception under Distraction
Ac	Auditory Acuity
Va	Auditory Valence Recall
aSD	Auditory Sensory Detection

environmental and genetical determinants and have different implications for refined predictions of outcomes. The organizations of the lower part of the figure emerge early in development, before emergence of the organizations of the upper part of the figure. Componential analyses of information processing should be directed at helping us to understand these matters.

It seems that Gf and Gc derive from separate sets of genes, the influences of which are manifested early in development (Horn, 1985; 1986). Piaget may have identified such early manifestations in his descriptions of assimilation and accommodation. From an early age, it seems, some individuals are best structured to readily bring information into their cognitive systems, whereas other individuals are best structured to mull and reorganize information that (less readily) enters their systems. Such predilections shape individual development from infancy onward, produce differences in the ways individuals process information and thus bring about the distinction we see, only crudely, in Gc and Gf.

Masses of environmental influences augment genetic factors to help shape abilities. Individual differences in these influences help bring about the separate distributions of different abilities. The independence of Gf, Gc, Gv, Ga, SAR, TSR, Gs, and CDS reflects the independence of environmental influences, as well as the independence of genetic determiners.

Genetical and environmental determiners work together. A genetically determined readiness to bring information into cognitive structures makes one "ready", as it were, for the acculturational formation of Gc. A readiness to mull the information that gets into one's cognitive system facilitates extended development of Gf.

Other factors are important in this development. Different nutritional and physical injury factors, for example, will affect different basic predispositions in different ways and to different extents. Existing evidence indicates, for example, that neurological injuries in childhood have a more enduring effect on Gc than do similar injuries in adulthood. Neurological injuries in childhood may produce greater effects on Gf than on Gc, as in adulthood, but the implications are different. These matters are complex. Much interesting work remains to be done.

Thus, each of the broad abilities indicated in Figure 7 has different genetic underpinnings and a different course of development over the life span. SAR, for example, stems from genetic factors that are different from those that affect TSR. The different genetical determiners chart different courses of optimal and typical development for SAR and TSR. This is true for the other abilities of the figure.

The influences suggested in Figure 7 are multidirectional. Just as the influences of the lower part of the figure produce the effects represented high in the figure, so abilities of the upper section determine the abilities of the lower part of the figure; broad abilities influence narrow abilities, and vice versa.

There is much to learn. How best to go about this? A suggestion of this chapter is that researchers break bonds that bind work to concepts of general intelligence and recognize the distinct distributions of different intelligences. Studies of information processing should be organized in accordance with the evidence that indicates broad, important abilities that are independent in fundamental ways. Architectonic construction of new information should be organized around such concepts. Valuable technology, as well as scientific understanding can derive from theory constructed in this way.

REFERENCES

Anastasi, A. (1976). *Psychological Testing* (4th ed.). New York: Macmillan.

Atkin, R., Bray, R., Davidson, M., Herzberger, S., Humphreys, L. C. & Selzer, V. (1977a). Cross-lagged panel analysis of sixteen cognitive measures at four grade levels. *Child Development, 21,* 78–81.

Atkin, R., Bray, R., Davidson, M., Herzberger, S., Humphreys, L. C. & Selzer, V. (1977b). Ability factor differentiation, grades 5–11. *Applied Psychological Measurement, 1,* 65–66.

Bock, R. D. & Kolakowski, D. (1973). Further evidence of sex-linked major-gene influence on human spatial visualizing ability. *The American Journal of Human Genetics, 25,* 1–14.

Broadbent, D. E. (1966). The well-ordered mind. *American Educational Research Journal, 3,* 281–295.

Carpenter, P. A. & Just, A. M. (1978). Eye fixations during mental rotation. In J. W. Senders, D. F. Fisher & R. A. Monty (Eds.), *Eye movements and the higher psychological functions.* Hillsdale, NJ: Erlbaum.

Carpenter, P. A. & Just, M. A. (1986). Spatial ability: an information processing approach to psychometrics. In R. J. Sternberg (Ed.), *Advances in the psychology of human intelligence.* Hillsdale, NJ: Erlbaum.

Carroll, J. B. (1972). Stalking the wayward factors. *Contemporary Psychology, 17,* 321–324.

Carroll, J. B. & Horn, J. L. (1981). On the scientific basis of ability testing. *American Psychologist, 36,* 1012–1020.

Cattell, R. B. (1971). *Abilities: Their structure, growth and action.* Boston: Houghton-Mifflin.

Chase, W. G. (Ed.), (1973). *Visual information processing.* New York: Academic Press.

Cooper, L. A. (1976). Individual differences in visual comparison processes. *Perception & Psychophysics, 19,* 433–444.

Craik, F. I. M. (1977). Age differences in human memory. In J. E. Birren & K. W. Schaie (Eds.), *Handbook of the psychology of aging.* New York: Van Nostrand-Reinhold.

Cronbach, L. J. (1970). *Essentials of psychological testing* (3rd Ed.). New York: Harper and Row.

Cronbach, L. J. (1987). Construct validation after thirty years. In R. Linn (Ed.), *Intelligence: Measurement, Theory and Public Policy.* Urbana, IL: University of Illinois Press.

Dewar, K. M., Cuddy, L. L., & Mewhart, D. J. K. (1977). Recognition memory for single tones with and without context. *Journal of Experimental Psychology: Human Learning and Memory, Vol. 3, 1,* 60–67.

Egan, D. E. (1979). Testing based on understanding: Implications from studies of spatial ability. *Intelligence, 3,* 1–15.

Ekstrom, R. B., French, J. W., & Harman, M. H. (1979). Cognitive factors: Their identification and replication. *Multivariate Behavior Research Monographs, 79.2.*

Eysenck, H. J. (1985). The nature of cognitive differences between blacks and whites. *The Behavioral and Brain Sciences, 8,* 229.

French, J. W. (1951). The description of aptitude and achievement tests in terms of rotated factors. *Psychometric Monographs*, No. 5.

French, J. W., Ekstrom, R. B., & Price, L. A. (1963). *Manual and kit of reference tests for cognitive factors*. Princeton, NJ: Educational Testing Services.

Glanzer, M. & Cunitz, A. R. (1966). Two storage mechanisms in free recall. *Journal of Verbal Learning and Verbal Behavior, 5*, 351–360.

Guilford, J. P. (1967). *The nature of human intelligence*. New York: McGraw-Hill.

Guilford, J. P. & Hoepfner, R. (1971). *The analysis of intelligence*. New York: McGraw-Hill.

Guilford, J. P. & Lacy, J. I. (Eds.) (1947). Printed classification tests (Research Report No. 5), Army Air Force Aviation Psychology Program.

Hakstian, A. R. & Cattell, R. B. (1974). The checking of primary ability structure on a broader basis of performances. *British Journal of Educational Psychology, 44*, 140–154.

Hakstian, A. R. & Cattell, R. B. (1978). Higher stratum ability structure on a basis of twenty primary abilities. *Journal of Educational Psychology, 70*, 657–659.

Harnad, S. (Ed.) (1985). *The behavioral and brain sciences*. New York: Cambridge University Press.

Hayes, J. R. (1973). On the function of visual imagery in elementary mathematics. In W. G. Chase (Ed.), *Visual information processing* (pp. 167–196). New York: Academic Press.

Hearnshaw, L. S. (1956). Temporal integration and behavior. *Bulletin of the British Psychological Society, 9*, 1–20.

Herrnstein, R. J. (1973). *IQ in the meritocracy*. Boston: Little, Brown.

Horn, J. L. (1967). On subjectivity in factor analysis. *Educational and psychological measurement, 27*, 811–820.

Horn, J. L. (1968). Organization of abilities and the development of intelligence. *Psychological Review, 75*, 242–259.

Horn, J. L. (1970). Organization of data on life-span development of human abilities. In L. R. Goulet & P. B. Baltes (Eds.), *Lifespan development in psychology* (pp. 423–466). New York: Academic Press.

Horn, J. L. (1972). The structure of intellect: primary abilities. In R. M. Dreger (Ed.), *Multivariate personality research* (pp. 451–511). Baton Rouge, LA: Claitor.

Horn, J. L. (1973). Theory of functions represented among auditory and visual test performances. In J. R. Royce (Ed.), *Contributions of multivariate analysis to psychological theory* (pp. 203–239). New York: Academic Press.

Horn, J. L. (1976). Human abilities: a review of research and theory in the early 1970s. *Annual Review of Psychology, 27*, 437–485.

Horn, J. L. (1977). Personality traits and concepts of ability. In B. B. Wolman (Ed.), *International encyclopedia of neurology, psychiatry, psychoanalysis and psychology* (Vol. 8) (pp. 315–320), New York: Aesculapius Press and Van Nostrand-Reinhold.

Horn, J. L. (1978). Human ability systems. In P. B. Baltes (Ed.), *Life-Span development and behavior* (pp. 211–256). New York: Academic Press.

Horn, J. L. (1982a). The aging of human abilities. In B. B. Wolman (Ed.), *Handbook of developmental psychology* (pp. 847–870). New York: Prentice Hall.

Horn, J. L. (1982b). The theory of fluid and crystallized intelligence in relation to concepts of cognitive psychology and aging in adulthood. In F. I. M. Craik & S. E. Trehum (Eds.), *Aging and cognitive processes* (pp. 237–278). Boston: Plenum.

Horn, J. L. (1985). Remodeling old models of intelligence: Gf-Gc theory. In B. B. Wolman (Ed.), *Handbook of intelligence* (pp. 462–503). New York: Wiley.

Horn, J. L. (1986). Intellectual ability concepts. In R. J. Sternberg (Ed.), *Advances in the psychology of human intelligence* (Vol. 3) (pp. 35–77). Hillsdale, NJ: Erlbaum.

Horn, J. L. (1987a). Models for intelligence. In R. Linn (Ed.), *Intelligence: measurement, theory and public policy*. Urbana, Illinois: University of Illinois Press.

Horn, J. L. (1987b, in press). Thinking about human abilities. In J. R. Nesselroade (Ed.), *Handbook of multivariate psychology*. New York: Academic Press.

Horn, J. L. & Cattell, R. B. (1966a). Refinement and test of the theory of fluid and crystallized intelligence. *Journal of Educational Psychology, 57,* 253–270.

Horn, J. L. & Cattell, R. B. (1966b). Age differences in primary mental ability factors. *Journal of Gerontology, 21,* 210–220.

Horn, J. L. & Cattell, R. B. (1982). Whimsey and misunderstandings of Gf-Gc theory. *Psychological Bulletin, 91,* 623–633.

Horn, J. L. & Donaldson, G. (1980). Cognitive development in adulthood. In O. G. Brim & J. Kagan (Eds.), *Constancy and change in human development* (pp. 445–529). Cambridge, MA: Harvard University Press.

Horn, J. L., Donaldson, G., & Engstrom, R. (1981). Apprehension, memory and fluid intelligence decline in adulthood. *Research on Aging, 3,* 33–84.

Horn, J. L. & Goldsmith, H. (1981). Reader be cautious: Bias in mental testing by Arthur Jensen. *American Journal of Education, 89,* 305–329.

Horn, J. L. & Knapp, J. R. (1973). On the subjective character of the empirical base of Guilford's structure-of-intellect model. *Psychological Bulletin, 80,* 33–43.

Horn, J. L. & Knapp, J. R. (1974). Thirty wrongs do not make a right: Reply to Guilford. *Psychological Bulletin, 81,* 502–504.

Horn, J. L. & Stankov, L. (1982). Auditory and visual factors of intelligence. *Intelligence, 6,* 165–185.

Humphreys, L. G. (1962). The organization of human abilities. *American Psychologist, 17,* 475–483.

Humphreys, L. G. (1979). The construct of general intelligence. *Intelligence, 3,* 105–120.

Hunt, E. (1983). The nature of intelligence. *Science, 219,* 141–146.

Hunt, E., Lunneborg, C., & Lewis, J. (1975). What does it mean to be high verbal? *Cognitive Psychology, 7,* 194–227.

Jensen, A. R. (1973). *Educability and group differences.* New York: Harper & Row.

Jensen, A. R. (1984). Test Validity: g versus the specificity doctrine. *Journal of Social and Biological Structures, 7,* 93–118.

Jensen, A. R. (1985). The nature of the black-white difference on various psychometric tests: Spearman's hypothesis. *The Behavioral and Brain Sciences, 8,* 193–219.

Kaufman, A. S. & Kaufman, N. L. (1983). *Kaufman assessment battery for children (K-ABC).* Circle Pines, MN: American Guidance Service.

Kaufman, A. S. & Kaufman, N. L. (1983). *Kaufman assessment battery for children: interpretive manual.* Circle Pines, MN: American Guidance Service.

Mandler, G. (1968). Organized recall: Individual functions. *Psychonomic Science, 13,* 230–236.

McArdle, J. J. & Horn, J. L. (1983). Structural equation modeling the adulthood aging of Gf and Gc dimensions of intellect. *Technical Report,* Psychology Department, University of Denver.

Matarazzo, J. D. (1972). *Wechsler's measurement and appraisal of adult intelligence* (5th Ed.). Baltimore, MD: Williams and Wilkins.

McCarthy, D. (1972). *McCarthy scales of children's abilities.* New York: The Psychological Corporation.

Minton, H. L. & Schneider, F. W. (1980). *Differential psychology.* Prospect Heights, IL: Waveland.

Mulholland, T. M., Pellegrino, J. W., & Glaser, R. (1980). Components of geometric analogy solutions. *Cognitive Psychology, 12,* 252–284.

Murdock, B. B. (1960). The immediate retention of unrelated words. *Journal of Experimental Psychology, 60,* 222–224.

Norman, D. A. (1979). Perception, memory and mental processes. In L. C. Nilsson (Ed.), *Per-*

spectives in memory research (pp. 132–168). Hillsdale, NJ: Erlbaum.

Pawlik, K. (1966). Concepts and calculations in human abilities. In R. B. Cattell (Ed.), *Handbook of multivariate experimental psychology* (pp. 535–556). Chicago: Rand McNally.

Pawlik, K. (1978). Faktoranalytische personlichkeits-forschung, In G. Strube (Ed.), *Die Psychologie des 20 Jahrhunderts* (pp. 23–68). Zurich: Kindler.

Pellegrino, J. W. (1983). Individual Differences in Spatial Ability: The Effects of Practice on Components of Processing and Reference Test Scores. Paper presented at the annual meetings of the American Educational Research Association, Montreal, Canada.

Pellegrino, J. W. & Kail, R. (1982). Process analyses of spatial aptitude. In R. J. Sternberg (Ed.), *Advances in the psychology of human intelligence* (Vol. 1, pp. 137–159). Hillsdale, NJ: Erlbaum.

Pollack, R. H. (1969). Ontogenetic changes in perception. In D. E. Elkind & J. H. Flavell (Eds.), *Studies in cognitive development* (pp. 346–378). New York: Oxford University Press.

Poltrock, S. E. & Brown, P. (1984). Individual differences in visual imagery and spatial ability. *Intelligence, 8*, 93–138.

Raven, J. C. (1977). *Raven Progressive Matrices*. San Antonio, TX: The Psychological Corporation.

Shephard, R. N. & Metzler, J. (1971). Mental rotation of three-dimensional objects. *Science, 171*, 701–703.

Shuter, R. (1968). *The Psychology of Musical Ability*. London: Methuen.

Stankov, L. (1978). Fluid and crystallized intelligence and broad perceptual factors among 11 to 12 year olds. *Journal of Educational Psychology, 70*, 324–334.

Stankov, L. & Horn, J. L. (1980). Human abilities revealed through auditory tests. *Journal of Educational Psychology, 72*, 21–44.

Sternberg, R. J. (1977). *Intelligence, Information Processing and Analogical Reasoning: The Componential Analysis of Human Abilities*. Hillsdale, NJ: Erlbaum.

Sternberg, R. J., Conway, B. E., Ketron, J. L., & Bernstein, M. (1981). People's conceptions of intelligence. *Technical Report*. New Haven, Connecticut: Yale University, Department of Psychology.

Sternberg, S. (1975). Memory scanning: New findings and current controversies. *Quarterly Journal of Experimental Psychology, 27*, 1–32.

Undheim, J. O. & Horn, J. L. (1977). Critical evaluation of Guilford's structure-of-intellect theory. *Intelligence, 1*, 65–81.

Wechsler, D. (1981). *WAIS-R: Wechsler Adult Intelligence Scale Revised* New York: Psychological Corporation.

Witkin, H. A. & Goodenough, D. R. (1981). *Cognitive studies: essence and origins*. New York: International Universities Press.

Woodcock, R. W. & Johnson, M. B. (1977). *Woodcock-Johnson Psycho-Educational Battery*. Boston: Teaching Resources Corporation.

CHAPTER 7

Cognitive Processing, Cognitive Ability, and Development: A Reconsideration

Daniel P. Keating and Darla J. MacLean
University of Maryland Baltimore County

To an overwhelming extent, adults outperform children on a wide variety of the cognitive tests and tasks in which they have been observed. Similarly, but less strongly, older children and adolescents outperform younger children. In addition, within-age comparisons of children's or adults' intellectual performance reveal substantial intercorrelations: Individuals tend to perform generally near the top, middle, or bottom of the appropriate age-comparison group.

Researchers have long sought basic explanations for these pervasive developmental and individual differences in intellectual performance. For both the general age-gradient of task performance, and the within-age "positive manifold" of task intercorrelations, psychologists have assumed, or perhaps merely hoped, that one or a few basic mechanisms might suffice.

Over the course of this century, it has proved a difficult task. In this paper, we will briefly review some of these earlier attempts, in order to suggest why a "componential" approach, using parameters of basic cognitive processing as component elements, has been viewed as a possible way out of the impasse. Second, we will review several of the current attempts to link basic cognitive processing with developmental and individual differences in cognitive ability. Note that we are using "ability" as a shorthand term, and do not thereby mean to imply an particular theoretical stance. What we mean by ability in this paper is the reliably measured performance—whatever its origin—on tests or tasks requiring complex cognitive activity for their solution. Such performance, or ability, comprises the descriptive reality we seek to explore further.

This review of the set of contemporary approaches broadly labeled "cognitive processing accounts" reveals some substantial interpretive and methodological difficulties with the assumptions of those models. At the conclusion of the empirical review, we summarize the major threats to validity of such cognitive componential attempts. In the third and final section, we conclude by suggesting possible routes for future research, both more traditional approaches, which entail either further rigorization of the model-testing procedures, or the addition of different level "components," or both; as well, we consider briefly a developmental and historical agenda which we have termed "reconstruction" in cognitive development (Keating & MacLean, in press). Overlaps between these two approaches are then also briefly examined.

Conceptual Background

The range of performance on tasks requiring complex cognitive activity is undoubtedly great. Even restricting our consideration to the range of the population within which significant organic impairment is neither suspected nor likely, there exists overwhelming evidence of vast developmental and individual differences. The regularity of normative age trends on many cognitive ability tasks is well documented, from tasks as simple as digit span recall, to the complexities of logical and scientific reasoning (Keating, 1980). When individual differences are taken into account, the range is even more impressive. Even on extremely challenging tests designed for older adolescents or adults, such as the Scholastic Aptitude Test (SAT) or the Advanced Progressive Matrices (APM), substantial numbers of younger children (11 to 13 years old) outperform 95% to 98% of much older individuals—5 or more years older in chronological age (Keating, 1976).

Both these phenomena—the regularity and range of developmental (that is, age) differences, and the range and intraindividual consistency of individual differences—have been recognized virtually since the inception of standardized testing for cognitive ability. Indeed, theories designed to account for these observed patterns have comprised a generically defined "psychometric agenda." We briefly review the history and outcome of that agenda, in order to understand better the logic leading to a componential approach.

Psychometric Attempts to Explain Cognitive Ability.   It would be incorrect to argue that there is a single clear agenda within the research tradition of psychometrics. We focus here on those aspects of that tradition which involve theoretical statements about the nature and structure of human mental abilities. It is assumed that humans are capable of dealing with complex information, understanding relationships, solving intellectual problems, and so on, because of an underlying structure of mental ability or abilities. Uncovering and explaining this structure has been a common goal of diverse psychometric theories of ability.

Though not a history of these attempts, this discussion is aided by a distinction drawn from the history of mental testing: the different traditions associated with Galton and with Binet (Cairns, 1983). Galton's claims regarding a single, overriding intellective function, differentially distributed across individuals and resting squarely on a potentially identifiable physiological base, are the foundation of the theoretical arguments within psychometric theory. Contrasted with this, Binet generally eschewed foundational claims about intelligence and cognition (questions of developmental origin or teleology were explicitly not a part of his agenda), and focused instead on the use of information regarding the performance of children on standardized tasks as the basis for targeted intervention to change such performance skills.

Thus the Galton/Binet contrast historically constitutes a continuing debate: Do "intelligence" measures tell us something fundamental about the competence/capacity of the individual, something which "explains" differences in performance, or do they instead give a "reading" of current levels of developmental acquisition with respect to performance, but justify no internal-subjective attributions? From the former position, theoretical and empirical clarification as to the nature and structure of the underlying intellect is a fundamental goal; from the latter position, the *practical* improvement of performance is the validity criterion.

Historically, much of the confusion within psychometrics can be traced to Terman's conflating of these two perspectives. Galtonian in theoretical orientation, Terman adopted Binet's method of standardized assessment with the conviction that it gave rather direct access to the presumed underlying distribution and structure of ability. With a handy but largely unanalyzed tool ("IQ"), a movement of enormous social importance was launched: mass testing of "intelligence," a movement which dominated the educational research agenda for over a half-century (Farnham-Diggory & Nelson, 1984).

Not until the late 1970s was there a sustained attempt to explain the obtained IQ (or IQ-like) variance in less ambiguous and less arbitrary *cognitive* psychological analyses (Keating, 1984). The Galtonian goal returned with an impressive array of new methods, and efforts to understand and explain ability variance, primarily through theoretical moves of a reductionist tendency — either to physiology or to cognitive elements — have advanced the theoretical issues considerably. A complete history of these theoretical developments is an important task, but beyond the scope of this chapter, and unnecessary for our argument. Instead, the reasons for turning to cognitive processing components as explanatory factors will be highlighted.

The starting point for any discussion of psychometric theory must be "What do we do with *g* (general intelligence)?" This means different things to different theorists, but the fundamental issue is whether or not there is some single entity or aspect of mind which is at the core of human intellectual functioning. As noted above, this was Galton's claim, and it has remained influential. A succinct current statement of the Galtonian notion can be found in Eysenck (1984):

> Intelligence A . . . is the underlying physiological structure of the nervous system that enables individuals to behave intelligently and that causes individual differences in intelligence. Intelligence B is the application of this innate ability in everyday life. Intelligence C is the attempt to measure, by means of IQ tests, intellectual functioning. (p. 290)

This is a clear set of claims endorsed in more or less similar terms by theorists from Spearman (1904) to Jensen (1979). This purest, physiological *g* is at the beginning of the causal chain; although it gets entangled along the way with educational, cultural, personality, and other factors, it is assumed to be the essence of human intelligence. What are the empirical supports for such a claim?

Note at the outset that supporting this claim empirically is an admittedly difficult task. Because we can observe only "Intelligence C" — that is, performance on some collection of tasks — the inference to an underlying structure must make clear and testable assertions about the rules for inference. Unfortunately, this has not generally been the case. When such tests have been done, for example for Spearman's one-common-factor theory, the support for the claims has been weak (Horn, 1984).

At the more global level of argument (e.g., Jensen, 1984), there are three sets of correlational evidence used to support the notion of *g*: (a) the ubiquity and magnitude of the first principal component for virtually any collection of cognitive tasks; (b) the differential loadings of types of tasks on this first principal component; and (c) the relationship of complex performance to more elemental features which might be "purer" measures of physiological *g*, especially reaction time (Jensen, 1984) or evoked potential (Eysenck, 1982, 1984).

Horn (1984) has marshalled many of the key arguments against the use of the first principal component to infer *g*. Most central is the problem of arbitrariness: "Different collections of tests . . . measure different principal components. A principal component is not a stable indicator of any particular common factor. It represents arbitrary collections" (Horn, 1984, p. 7). The problem of arbitrariness can be extended to include the collections of test-takers as well as tests. In the absence of a clearly stated theory with specific claims, such correlational patterns *can not speak* to the generic notion of *g*.

When such specific claims have been tested, they have been found wanting. Horn (1984) summarizes:

> In spite of the prevalence of belief in general intelligence, in spite of the emotional intensity with which this belief is held, and despite the fact that this belief is proclaimed as true by some of the high priests of our science, the belief should be cast out. (p. 12)

As we will see, Horn hopes to make a better case for a multi-factor theory of intelligence. We defer consideration of that theoretical issue to consider the next claim for g, the *interpretation* of differential factor loadings.

Even if it can not sustain the claim for g, the ubiquity of the first principal component seems to constitute an intuitive or "face validity" claim for something like general intelligence. On every occasion when we construct some new test of what we believe to tap "intelligence," it inevitably loads significantly on the first principal component – or, more colloquially, it correlates with IQ. Further, there also seems to be a pattern across studies such that the more one seeks to construct content-free and thus "culture-fair" measures, such as Raven's Progressive Matrices, the *higher* the loading of such tests on the g factor. Thus, diminished cultural loading seems to accurately reflect higher "Intelligence A" loading. Should we not regard the convergent findings of a highly replicable positive manifold, together with differential loadings for less acculturated tasks, as establishing the claim for some sort of general intelligence?

Not necessarily, and for two straightforward reasons, both of which introduce the problem of ambiguity of interpretation. First, this evidence does not establish a boundary around an intellective domain. Again, Horn (1984): "Many nonintellectual performances are included in this manifold. . . . Positive correlations do not indicate the boundaries for a domain of human intellect" (p. 10). That is, interpreting the manifold as intellective requires that *anything* falling into the manifold must *also* be interpreted as part of g, unless we advance some theory to distinguish between those variables which "belong" and those which do not. Such a distinction might *yield* a theory, but it would need to be validated in some other way. Face validity is not enough.

Second, the belief that the pattern of differential loadings reveals "purer g" is of course an interpretation. We and others have proposed an alternative (Keating & MacLean, in press; Keating, 1984; Olson, 1984): Rather than "culture-free" or "culture-fair," tests such as Raven's matrices tap highly formal and specific school skills related to text processing and decontextualized rule application, and are thus the *most systematically* acculturated tasks typically employed for intellectual assessment. Some cross-cultural evidence would support such a claim (e.g., Sharp, Cole, & Lave, 1979; Luria, 1979). Note that this turns g as physiology on its head (or perhaps helps to get its feet on the ground): the first factor is now interpretable as *the degree of acculturation to the mainstream school skills of Western society.* Perhaps this is the wrong interpretation. (We suspect not.) But note the central problem: *Each* view is an interpretation based on pre-scientific, unstated assumptions. Choosing between the interpretations is impossible on the basis of additional analyses of task performance alone: It is undecidable at this level, within these (psychometric) methods. It is clear, then, that the notion of *g* cannot be supported with existing psychometric evidence, and that neither the ubiquity nor the loading patterns of first principal components provide support for such a claim.

Eysenck (1982, 1984) contends that psychometric methods have not yet adequately addressed the real scientific question, the assessment of Intelligence A. Because practical intelligence testing built on the work of Binet, the theoretical questions raised by Galton have been inappropriately muddied. Pursuing a directly reductionist argument, he proposes the use of indices more closely tied to this Intelligence A, or physiological *g*. One candidate is reaction time (which Jensen, 1984, views as being composed substantially of differential rates of "neural oscillation"), though there are performance confounds in this as well. Eysenck's better candidate is evoked potential – the cranial-surface electrical changes in response to a simple stimulus – which, when measured in certain ways, correlates quite highly with IQ (.82 in one notable example). Assuming that this could be rigorously replicated (and there may be significant technical problems in doing so), would we be safe in inferring the capture of our reticent factor, *g*?

Even granting evoked potential's centrality within the positive manifold, we are still unable to use it to define the meaning of the manifold. As a correlational pattern, it is still open to a variety of interpretations, and deciding among them must move to another level of analysis. But isn't this doing just that? Isn't this a physiological measure, and thus capable of *defining* the meaning of the manifold?

It serves such a role in definition only if we already assume the existence of the very conceptual element we have set out to locate empirically. Recall that the criterion of its importance is again IQ (or some other performance-based index of the positive manifold). This variance can serve as criterial *only* if we already assume it to be a reasonable (if muddy) index of "intelligence" to begin with. Otherwise, disruptive alternative interpretations intrude.

Let us take note of two. First, evoked potential can be viewed as an index of physiological *g* only if it is a stable characteristic of the person, and *not* mere state variability. Note further that simple test-retest reliability is insufficient to remove this concern: The context of assessment may elicit differential states in different individuals. (This is not a facetious suggestion. For persons accustomed to succeeding easily in challenging test-like situations, such a "brain" assessment situation may elicit different cognitive activity than for those who have not had such success.) Second, even if this problem could be dealt with, there is no way of knowing — other than through neo-natal assessment, and perhaps not then, given intrauterine environmental variability — whether such differences reflect "innate" differences in "accuracy of neural transmission" (Eysenck, 1984), or the effect of developmentally acquired differences. *All* the evidence thus advanced to date for "explaining" intellectual performance differences by correlation with physiological indices (evoked potential and others) is similarly compromised by this interpretive ambiguity. Of course, the strength, replicability, and generalizability of even these findings is far from well-established.

Along with Horn (1984), we wonder why the strength of belief in g as the psychological explanation of individual differences in intellectual performance manages to persist despite such failures. He suggests that "emotionally-based beliefs can have a curious staying power" (p. 8). The emotional basis itself deserves inquiry; perhaps it is bound up in the power/knowledge nexus (Foucault, 1984) of our social practices. Locating "failure" within the person is less socially destabilizing than seeking it in the social practices themselves. Such blinders are evident as well in the use of g (IQ) correlations with real world criteria as "validity" evidence: This belief must presume that the "real world" is *not* similarly biased, when compared with tests (Keating, 1984).

As noted above, Horn's (1984) critique of g (general intelligence) models was advanced in part to create theoretical space for a more sophisticated multi-ability theory. His elaboration of the fluid vs. crystallized intelligence notion (Horn, 1980, 1982, 1984) has the advantages of specificity and intuitive appeal. Further, Horn claims that many of the key features of the model are empirically testable, and that such attempts have yielded results compatible with the Gf/Gc distinction (as well as other specific features of the model).

Though a theoretically advanced development relative to g models, Horn's interpretation of psychometric evidence is itself subject to the very critiques he has used against the earlier formulations. Most central again are the problems of arbitrariness and ambiguity (Sternberg, 1977).

In addition to the ways noted above in which factor analytic evidence is arbitrary, the move to multiple-ability models introduces another: How many factors do we need or want? Here, the Guilford–Horn exchange is instructive (Guilford, 1980; Horn & Cattell, 1982). The "subjective character" of this debate is self-evident; it can not be decided on the evidence, since different prior assumptions dictate the outcome. Horn views Guilford's 120-factor structure-of-intellect as "forcing" unnecessary distinctions; Guilford views Horn's analysis as ignoring necessary distinctions. The preference is in principle arbitrary.

The Gf/Gc interpretation is ambiguous in precisely the same way as noted earlier. In contrast with some colloquial uses of the terms, "fluid" is not meant as free-floating resources; rather, it represents incidental or casual learning as opposed to systematic acculturation (as in education). But another interpretation is possible, that the Gf tasks tap skills which are the *most* systematically acculturated. The face validity acceptance of Gf tasks as incidental learning merely moves the claim to another ground; to address this question would require an extensive understanding of the socialization practices which impinge on cognitive development (Keating & MacLean, in press). Otherwise, the distinction and its interpretation rest on a superficial assumption that we already know well enough what the important features of cognitive acculturation are, an assumption difficult to maintain in the face of careful analyses (e.g., Bronfenbrenner & Crouter, 1983; Cole & Means, 1981).

Horn (1980) readily admits how ill-defined the distinction is, but argues that there is a "latent" structure which it approximates:

> The Gc dimension is only a rough, fallible indicator of a complex latent attribute of intelligence. The Gf dimension is no less fallible as an indicator of the latent attribute referred to as fluid intelligence. (p. 295)

It is noteworthy that the "latent" nature of the dimensions implies a new attempt to go beyond arbitrariness and ambiguity, by using causal modeling (Horn, 1984). The well-known goal of causal modeling is to supplement or replace a posteriori interpretations of covariance analyses with the testing of covariance patterns against an a priori specified model. But clearly this merely moves the problem one step further back: What generates the a priori models? If they are merely restatements of previously observed empirical relationships, then the location of the "latent" attributes is in the network of empirical associations, and the demonstration is tautological. And unless the models are *complete,* there is the risk of ignoring important causal contributions. Horn's (1984) analyses, for example, give prior status to psychological elements and their genetic grounding. In the absence of *fully* specified models, including all possible socialization influences and interactions with unintended organismic variance, rapid but unfounded inferences proliferate; for example (Horn, 1984):

> It is well-established that girls learn language earlier and more readily than do boys. An essential determinant of the differences between boys and girls is genetic—the Y chromosome. (p. 28)

Thus, a highly likely connection between a physical basis and the psychological development is implied. Though used by Horn to contradict a different assumption (that Gf is genetic, and Gc isn't), the example is doubly revealing. First, consider the claim "earlier *and more readily*": What is the added meaning of the emphasized phrase? "More readily" is inferred *because* it is earlier. The intent, though, is clear: The earlier learning is presumptively caused by an internal intellective characteristic, a "readiness." Second, the statement reveals its own implicit causal model, that the Y-chromosome effect is (at least partly) direct. But we also know that XX-chromosome persons (i.e., mothers) are the primary caretakers of children whose language acquisition has been studied, and that many aspects (social, emotional, cognitive, behavioral) of the relationship between mothers and children varies with the child's gender (e.g., Chodorow, 1978). Without all of *this* information is the causal model, we may miss the fact that the Y-chromosome effect is only indirect, that is, through different maternal relationships with daughters versus sons.

Causal models can thus be as easily misleading as informative. For purposes of "explaining" intelligence, such modeling could only be meaningful after the inclusion of all socialization and developmental factors. *That* agenda, however, presumes an understanding of social practices which we have not even undertaken (Bronfenbrenner & Crouter, 1983). To the extent that the constraints of causal modeling force such attention to ontogentic history and social/culture practices, this would be a welcome and progressive development. To the extent that it is used to reflexively validate already held assumptions about the nature of human intelligence, it merely contributes to the long-standing problems of arbitrariness and ambiguity of "objectively determined factor analyses" (Horn, 1980, p. 295).

Largely because of these problems, psychometric theorists have recognized that the validity of any model of ability can not be decided within specifically psychometric methods. In an important multivariate modeling analysis, Baltes, Nesselroade, and Cornelius (1978) showed that obtained data structures of psychometric performance variance, *including* developmental patterns, could be generated with simple assumptions, using either purely environmental models, purely genetic models, or mixed models of several sorts. What does this imply for conclusions about underlying "causes" derived solely from the performance data matrix? Clearly, it suggests that the inferences are unwarranted. These multivariate data matrices of performance are no less robust because of this; rather, they have a different theoretical status. "It is not only desirable, therefore, but operationally possible to consider multivariate constructs such as [psychometric] factors as dependent variables" (Baltes et al., 1978). In these terms, "validity" has a different meaning from its traditional and colloquial one: It is not the credibility of the inferences about ability, but instead whether the data structures are robust enough to be used as reasonable dependent variables. Understanding *how* inter- and intraindividual differences in performance come to exist thus lies beyond psychometric theory, and requires a different approach.

Seeking to validate ability theories using underlying cognitive processes as the elements of explanation represents one such attempt. The logic of such analyses, reviewed in more detail below, is that appropriately detailed estimates of online cognitive processing could overcome the limitations of a purely psychometric approach. Ideally, such estimates would be unambiguous, at least relative to composite test scores, which have often been viewed as representing the products rather than the processes of intellectual activity. Obtaining unambiguous estimates, or parameters, of ongoing cognitive activity is, of course, problematic, but the availability of well-analyzed experimental tasks from the information-processing literature has been seen as a possible route around this impasse (Keating & Bobbitt, 1978; Keating, 1984). In addition, the relationship of the processing accounts to the target abilities would be nonarbitrary. That is, rather than relying on post hoc interpretations of empirically derived factors, componential analysis permits (we would contend that it *requires*) some level of a priori theorizing about how the proposed processes in fact relate systematically to the complex cognitive skill, or ability.

Note carefully these two issues for later discussion. Componential analyses, relative to psychometric factor analyses, demonstrate potential theoretical superiority by virtue of being less ambiguous and less arbitrary. When either or both of these criteria are *not* met, then the value of using processing accounts to explain ability variance—that is, for the purpose of construct validation—is compromised or lost. These concerns are focal for our review of contemporary approaches to componential validation of ability models.

Developmental versus individual differences.   Before proceeding to that empirical review, there is one additional conceptual distinction of considerable importance. The use of processing accounts to explain performance on complex cognitive tasks has not been restricted to psychometric or ability theorists. Indeed, researchers interested in intraindividual change (that is, development) in cognitive activity have shown a similar interest in basing their explanations upon changes in cognitive processing.

Piaget (1954; Inhelder & Piaget, 1958), for example, used extensively the notion of logical "operations" as explanations of changes in the performance of quite complex cognitive tasks. These operations were viewed as the elemental components—albeit constructed elements—of cognitive activity. Piaget's processing account of cognitive development encounters its own set of validity problems, particularly on the questions of isolating *logical* operations as central, and of across-domain consistency of the hypothesized cognitive structures (Keating, 1980). The "core" performance theory may in fact be a less significant contribution of Piagetian theory (Keating, 1984, 1986) compared to other features. In any case, performance on Piagetian tasks has become the target of more basic processing accounts, in a fashion similar to that of performance on psychometric tests (Keating, 1980).

The relationship between developmental and individual differences has occasionally been a source of conceptual confusion in the cognitive processing literature, and some clarification is useful at this point. Two questions provide a useful focus for this clarification. First, what is the goal of identifying developmental differences in speed of processing? Second, is it necessary to consider developmental changes when examining individual differences in cognitive processing?

In general, both the purpose and the methodology for examining developmental differences in cognitive processing have been quite similar to the componential approach for examining individual differences. As individuals develop, their cognitive processing may undergo fundamental shifts in speed, efficiency, or capacity. If this is the case, then such changes might account for some of the commonly observed age-gradient in performance on complex tasks. Case (1978), for example, has argued that discrete shifts in the capacity of working memory (M-space) are responsible for a significant proportion of the developmental changes in performance on Piagetian and other complex tasks.

Beyond similarity of goals, the study of developmental changes in cognitive processing also shares similarity of methodology with individual differences research strategies (Keating, 1979). Although the investigation of *intra*individual change ultimately requires observations across time (as in longitudinal, cross-sequential, or short-term microgenetic designs), virtually all "developmental" cognitive processing research is in reality cross-sectional. Such designs are in fact correlations of *age* with performance, and hence share the same experimental logic, and are subject to the same validity concerns, as more explicitly interindividual research strategies.

It is helpful to bear these similarities in mind when considering more generally the validity of claims about the role of cognitive processing in intellectual performance. Many of the issues which are somewhat confusing in the context of an individual differences research strategy become clearer in the age-correlation approach, and vice versa. As but one example, to which we return in greater detail below, consider the role of knowledge, both procedural and content, in performance on presumably "processing" tasks. Roth (1983) studied experts and novices in chess; some of each group were adults, and some children. His goal was to separate – by means of subject selection – the role of knowledge from that of age. He notes that we often confound these effects, because age is, in effect, a surrogate for numerous other variables besides "development" – for example, specific procedural or content knowledge. Inferring fundamental developmental differences on the basis of age effects, even when they are consistent, does not therefore avoid this confounding. this is a frequently mentioned (although often ignored) critique, which applies sui generis to studies of individual differences in general. Until we have controlled in some convincing way for background, experience, and socialization differences among the research participants, inferences about fundamental differences in the nature or quality of basic cognitive processing are potentially confounded.

Cole and Means (1981) provide a useful compendium of the inferential pitfalls possible in studies which compare how people think. As we shall see below, it is often difficult to specify in advance which particular sources of confounding need to be guarded against. Knowledge differences between groups and individuals may crop up in their overall approach to the task, their understanding of the instructions, their experience with related cognitive activities, and so on. Thus, the validity concerns summarized later are pertinent both to componential approaches seeking to explain individual differences, and to developmental studies of cognitive processing.

One exception to this would be investigations of whether there are developmental differences in speed or efficiency of isolated cognitive processes, regardless of whether or not those processes are meaningfully related to differences in the performance of complex cognitive tasks. From the perspective of this question, the contradictory conclusions of Wickens (1974) and Chi (1977) on whether there are *overall* developmental (that is, age) differences in speed of processing represent a fundamental question: Do such differences exist in some absolute sense? It is somewhat difficult, however, to understand the import of this question standing alone. It seems likely in fact, that, across the years of childhood and adolescence, there exist many seemingly "absolute" differences on many variables. But if those differences (in, say, speed of finger-tapping) are *unrelated* to performance on more meaningful tasks, their theoretical value is, at best, unclear. We suspect that there is something of the aptly named "jingle" fallacy at work here: If a parameter is derived from a task given a cognitive processing "name," then it must somehow be important to cognitive activity. At a minimum, it is incumbent upon researchers to specify the connections between their experimental parameters and some meaningful domain of real cognitive activity (Morrison, Lord, & Keating, 1984).

Of course, establishing absolute developmental differences in an isolated cognitive process is problematic. Chi's (1977) point, in response to Wicken's (1974) review, is pertinent. Knowledge differences are almost certainly highly correlated with age differences on many cognitive experimental tasks. Children are, in general, novices at many things. Careful partialling out of this knowledge factor is central to the logic of inferring fundamental developmental differences in processing. Whether such partialling out can be accomplished in practice remains to be seen. The current literature is replete with examples (e.g., MacLean & Keating, 1986) of rather straightforward knowledge manipulations having a major impact on the elimination or attenuation of generally accepted claims about developmental differences in cognitive processing.

This brings us rather directly to the second question above. If the study of developmental differences in processing is so difficult, because of the confounding of knowledge and experience with age, why consider it at all in componential approaches? Precisely because when we examine individual differences *without* reference to the developmental histories of the participants, we are likely to capture the same confounding factors, but simply be unaware of it. One might well make the case, in fact, that the study of development is an overarching validity requirement for theories of human intelligence. The likelihood of overlooking or dismissing significant cognitive socialization factors when not employing a developmental perspective is distressingly high (Keating & MacLean, in press).

Cognitive Ability and Development: Processing Accounts

With this conceptual background as our basis, we can now consider several of the current attempts to explain cognitive ability in terms of underlying cognitive processes. The research programs were selected for review as representing the diversity of approaches, a diversity which has increased rapidly in the past decade. As well, each of the research programs reviewed has encountered significant and similar construct validity difficulties. By reviewing a representative range of empirical attempts, we may draw some general inferences about validity guidelines. Note also that we do not exhaustively review the empirical studies within the selected approaches. Instead, we focus on what we view as the key issues in each approach, and draw on its empirical evidence as needed to clarify those issues.

As we noted earlier, a key goal of this chapter is to elucidate systematically the threats to construct validation of componential approaches. In response to these difficulties, one might seek to make the empirical investigations even more rigorous. Alternatively, one might seek to reframe the original question, which might well lead to different methods of investigation (Keating & MacLean, in press). Although preferring the latter, we do see considerable value in the former course as well. In either case, systematic evaluation of construct validity concerns will be, we hope, a useful contribution.

General Accounts: To g or not to g?   As was historically the case with psychometric ability theories, the simplest and most straightforward version of a cognitive processing explanation for ability differences is to focus on a mechanism to explain general intelligence (g). In this model, some (as yet unknown) cognitive processing function, probably neurally based, varies systematically among individuals. This function is believed to affect performance on a wide range of cognitive tasks—indeed, in virtually any cognitively demanding situation. Two implications follow from this most basic model. First, it is argued that this processing variance both accounts for and validates the general factor, g, in intellectual performance. If such variance exists in the neural substrate for cognitive processing, then it is to be expected that activities requiring processing, such as tests or tasks, will also show a pattern of intraindividual consistency in performance. Second, because it is fundamental to performance, it should be possible to isolate its operation in a variety of experimental contexts. That is, convergent identification of parameters tapping this processing should be feasible.

This perspective has been the basis of a number of recent empirical studies (Carlson, Jensen, & Widaman, 1983; Jensen & Munro, 1979; Vernon, 1983; Vernon & Jensen, 1984; Vernon, Nador, & Kantor, 1985). Although the details across such studies vary somewhat, the componential logic is quite consistent. On the basis of performance on carefully timed experimental tasks, parameters are derived which are presumed to reflect rather directly the underlying variance in general cognitive processing efficiency. These parameters are then correlated in some fashion with measures of general cognitive ability (such as Raven's matrices). In most cases, these researchers have reported moderate to substantial intercorrelation of the parameters of general processing speed or efficiency, and the measures of general cognitive ability. Substantial factor loadings of the experimental parameters on ability-defined general factors are interpreted as support both for the existence of a general factor of intelligence, and for its explanation as a function of individual differences in cognitive processing efficiency. In this section, we examine two such studies (Carlson et al., 1983; Vernon, 1983) in closer detail, in order to raise some questions about the validity of these general conclusions.

Carlson et al. (1983) studied 105 seventh-grade children on two experimental tasks of cognitive processing, and three psychometric tasks. The first experimental task is the frequently used paradigm developed by Hick (1952) to assess the rate of gain of information. Specifically, subjects are required to respond as quickly as possible when a light comes on, by pushing a button beneath the light. The number of possible lights which can come on is then varied in such a way as to increase the "bits" of information which must be processed in order to respond. A standard experimental finding is that response time increases in a regular fashion related to the increase in bits of information. Thus, the slope of the increase of reaction across bits can be interpreted as a measure of processing efficiency: More efficient processing should result in shallower slopes. Carlson et al. (1983), as have others, also separated response time from movement time. The subject has his or her finger resting on a home button before any lights come on. The elapsed time from onset of the stimulus (i.e., the light coming on) until the lifting of the finger is measured as reaction time (RT); the time from lifting until pushing the appropriate button is movement time (MT). This separation permits a finer-grained analysis of the online processing of bits of information. The second experimental task was designed to measure attention, by having subjects generate random numbers at 1-second intervals (to the beat of a metronome). The measure of attention (or vigilance) was the degree of departure from actual random generation. The ability tasks were Raven's Standard Progressive Matrices, a reading comprehension scale, and standardized academic achievment data (CTBS) from school records.

On the basis of the componential logic, the two key parameters of processing would seem to be the slope of RT from the Hick's (1952) task, and the attention variable from the random number generation (RNG) task. (What processes the RNG task is in fact tapping is a point to which we return below). In Table 1 from Carlson et al. (1983, p. 336), the correlations of RT slope with the three psychometric measures (Raven's, reading, and CTBS) are .09, .03, and $-.00$; the correlations of attention with these measures are $-.02$, .14, and .07. None of these correlations is significantly different from zero. One the face of it, this would appear to be rather striking evidence of disconfirmation of the processing basis of general ability. Indeed, the authors note that the absence of a correlation between RT slope and ability is "problematic (p. 341)."

Carlson et al. (1983) proceed, however, by defining latent variables among the processing and among the psychometric variables in order to further explore the relationships. They define a common RT factor which includes both Total RT and the intra-individual variability of RT (SD RT), along with RT slope. They construct a similar common MT factor. The three psychometric indices define a g factor, and the attention task together with the reading comprehension performance defines an attention factor. They then examine several different structural models of the relationships among these latent variables. As well, they include in them the relationships of these models to unique factors, such as reading. On the basis of the relationships among the variables specified in the most preferred model, Carlson et al. (1983, pp. 339–340) draw several conclusions. First, g and attention are essentially uncorrelated, although attention is a key factor in the RT relationship to g. Second, the RT and MT latent variables are substantially correlated. Third, the MT latent variable is essentially unrelated to g or to attention. Finally, the strong RT relationship to the unique reading factor, and with attention, suggests an important speediness component: "It is this speediness component, in addition to *quality* of processing (or general intelligence), that correlates significantly with RT" (Carlson et al., p. 341). The final picture, based on the more sophisticated structural modeling, is the reemergence of a speed of processing component as significantly related to ability, although this relationship is to some extent moderated by an attention factor. The attention factor may be either neurally based, or voluntary; on the basis of these findings, Carlson et al. (1983, p. 343) suggest that it is not possible to judge.

In reviewing the evidence from the Carlson et al. (1983) study, we suspect that this is a case in which structural modeling has obscured as much as it may have revealed. The key problems seem to be in the specification of the original common factors for the structural modeling, and in the consequent absence of any interpretation of the more straightforward zero-order correlations. Let us consider each issue.

In order to initiate the structural modeling, Carlson et al. (1983) specify common factors for RT and MT, as described above. This seems to run counter to the original componential logic. The advantage of the experimental paradigm is *not* that we can get dependent variables defined in milliseconds rather than number correct on a test. Rather, it is that the parameters are derived from the experimental procedures in such a way as to be theoretically interpretable. In this case, the RT slope is the obvious choice. As already noted, it is uncorrelated with any ability measure, and is further uncorrelated with any other experimental parameter except SD RT. Proceeding to combine it with other RT measures may in some sense "define" a latent variable of overall RT, but it obscures the particular logic of the experimental paradigm. The fact that general measures of reaction time correlate with general measures of ability does not advance our understanding much, if at all. It is precisely the opportunity to derive parameters which represent specific, analyzed cognitive processes that is the major advance of a componential approach. Embedding such analyzed parameters within a general factor comprised equally (or more than equally) of *unanalyzed* reaction time defeats the logic of the approach.

In so doing, a more interesting story apparent from the zero-order correlations is mostly overlooked. Carlson et al. (1983, p. 343) argue that there is little in their data to permit the distinction between neurophysiological interpretations of the "attention" factor, versus an interpretation which would see the attention factor as representing voluntary, sustained effort. Returning to the original correlations, however, it seems clear that the latter interpretation is more plausible on the basis of these findings. Recall that the key variables, RT slope and attention, were entirely uncorrelated with the ability measures. It would seem quite difficult for a general processing theory to account for this lack of correlation, especially for RT slope, which is theoretically the clearest parameter of processing efficiency. The ability measures, however, are somewhat correlated with other parameters derived from the Hick (1952) task. The intra-individual variability of both RT (SD RT) and MT (SD MT) are each significantly correlated with all of the ability measures (Raven's, reading, and CTBS). That is, six out of six correlations of intraindividual variability are significantly correlated with ability (ranging from .19 to .40).

One might argue that this is consistent evidence, though unexpectedly, of a processing basis for general ability. Before accepting this, however, we might question what is the interpretation of the SD RT and SD MT parameters. The processing explanation might invoke regularity of neural oscillation (Jensen, 1984) or accuracy of neural transmission (Eysenck, 1982). But such processing explanations *must* also account for the failure of RT slope to correlate at all.

An alternative interpretation, suggested but not explored by Carlson et al. (1983) in these data, seems able to deal with the entire data set. The SD RT and SD MT measures tap into consistency of performance. This consistency, however, is more easily interpreted as the result of how much voluntary, sustained effort the subjects are willing to put into the tasks. Subjects who try hard throughout the tasks, to get the very best times, will have low variability and fast response times; subjects who try hard sometimes, but not always, will be more variable and, on the average, slower. Particularly for movement time, this pattern seems easily interpretable as voluntary, sustained effort. This pattern of high, sustained, voluntary effort on experimenter-defined tasks is obviously likely to be of value in the performance of school-related tasks as well; but the connection need not be at the level of cognitive processing efficiency.

In this new interpretation, then, we would expect substantial intercorrelations of variability measures with total response times (both within and between RT and MT); consistent correlations between variability, as the best experimental index of effort, and school-related performance (that is, the ability measures); and no necessary correlation of slope RT with anything, because that most accurately assesses actual processing differences, about which the "effort" interpretation remains silent. This is, in fact, the precise pattern shown in the Carlson et al. (1983) data. The "effort" parameters from the experimental task are substantially intercorrelated: All are significant at the $p < .01$ level, and average about .45. The ability/variability intercorrelations are noted above: All are significant at the $p < .05$ level, and average about .25. Finally, except for the possibly artifactual correlations (of RT slope with the same data set, that is, Total RT and SD RT), RT slope is uncorrelated with anything else, averaging about .03. The single problematic finding for this new interpretation is the failure of the explicit attention measure, RNG, to correlate with the ability measures. As an index of attention, whether of the voluntary, sustained type, or of a more basic processing type, it should correlate with ability performance. This task, however, does not clearly tap only, or primarily, aspects of attention. Subjects must also remember what numbers they have generated, and understand clearly the notion of "randomness." This seems a tall order for seventh-graders. Carlson et al. (1983) provide no additional analyses of performance on this task, but it seems quite possible that it tapped memory factors, and knowledge of numbers and of the notion of randomness, as much or more as it tapped "attention."

Because many of the same issues arise in a study reported by Vernon (1983), it will be analyzed more succinctly. Subjects in this study were 100 college students. They participated in a series of five experiments, from which a number of cognitive processing parameters were derived. In addition, they also were administered the Raven's, and the full-scale Wechsler Adult Intelligence Scale (WAIS). The principal analyses were multiple regressions, with the IQ measures as criteria and the processing parameters as predictors. The consistent finding is that the multiple R prediction of IQ is substantial across different combinations of processing variables: .46 for mean RTs and intraindividual variability of RT (SD RT); .43 for mean RTs alone; .43 for SD RTs alone; and .37 when using only derived parameters, such as slopes or RT differences (Vernon, 1983, p. 65). The principal conclusions are based on these and similar findings from other analyses. First, "the speed with which persons can perform different cognitive processes is significantly and quite highly related to their intelligence" (p. 68). Second, "it is not only the speed with which a person can perform mental operations that is related to higher performance on tests of mental ability, but also the consistency with which he can perform at the same level over a period of time. . . . Speed and consistency of response were highly correlated and appeared to be joint aspects of an individual's information-processing capability" (p. 68–69). Finally, Vernon (1983) notes that the majority of the relationship between IQ and reaction time is accounted for by the psychometric g factor, rather than by speediness or other specific factors, and hence g variance is attributable to variance in the efficiency of the execution of a few specific basic cognitive processes. Further, it is proposed that the apparent role of knowledge and strategic differences is not that they explain IQ, but rather that they are the *result* of differences in these basic processes operating over time: "Over a period of time—the years of formal education, for example—faster cognitive processing may allow more information to be acquired" (Vernon, 1983, p. 69).

Several concerns overlap with those in the Carlson et al. (1983) study described above. First, the fact that consistency of processing was just as predictive as speed of processing can be interpreted differently than Vernon (1983) suggests. Vernon apparently regards this consistency as part of the individual's information-processing "capability." But that is, of course, an assumption. Inconsistency of performance might arise because of processing limitations, but it might just as easily reflect voluntary, sustained effort, as described earlier. In that case, the equivalence of the relationships of these two "parameters" with ability becomes more difficult to interpret clearly.

In any case, neither of these multiple regressions—of mean RT or SD RT—is consistent with the logic of the experimental tasks. Both sets represent confounded, and thus difficult to interpret, parameters. Indeed, Vernon (1983) acknowledges this explicitly: "Mean reaction times per se do not provide as good a measure of specific cognitive processes as do the differences between reaction times on some of the tests and the slopes of reaction times on the others " (p. 65). The multiple regression to predict IQ from the set of seven derived parameters, as noted, is also quite substantial (.37). Zero-order correlations between the derived parameters and IQ are unfortunately not reported, and thus more detailed analysis of the findings is difficult.

There are some interpretive problems, however, with the set of derived parameters as predictors of g. First, the multiple regression model can of course make no distinction among well-designed and poorly-designed parameters. (In this case, we mean parameters which are relatively unambiguously interpretable versus those which are potentially confounded). Several of the tasks are complicated variants of the name identity–physical identity task developed by Posner (Posner & Mitchell, 1967). In these analyses, Vernon (1983) uses the straightforward difference between RT's in different conditions (physical identity versus synonym/antonym judgments of word pairs). Even for simple letter match judgments, the "RT difference" parameter is quite difficult to interpret clearly (Bisanz, Danner, & Resnick, 1979; List, Keating, & Merriman, 1985). When the material is as complex as synonym/antonym judgments, it is not at all apparent that the RT difference parameter (comparing the rapidity of such judgments to those for physical identity) is directly interpretable as a "processing" parameter. This parameter may easily tap into strategic and knowledge differences among the subjects. The mixing of such potentially confounded parameters with relatively clearer parameters in a single multiple regression does not allow more fine-grained understanding of the processing basis of ability performance. Another issue is whether *any* combination of processing parameters which predict IQ is as good as any other. That is, if the ability/processing connection rests on a fundamental psychological reality (that is, g as speed of processing), would we not also expect to find a replicable *pattern* of relationships among parameters and ability measures? Thus, it is not only the size of the relationship, but also the pattern of the relationship which serves to establish construct validity. We return to this issue briefly below. Finally, the intercorrelation of the parameters themselves does not seem to support easily the notion of fundamental variance in speed of processing: The processing parameters do not converge. Excluding the artifactual cases in which the same variable participates in the derivation of two different parameters, the average intercorrelation of the *derived* processing parameters is about .10. Included in this figure is the slope of intraindividual variability across bits of information; that is, the degree to which the subject becomes *more* variable in performance as the amount of information to be processed increases. As argued above, this is open to multiple interpretations. Subjects who maintain a high level of consistent performance on the hard items might do so because of superior processing equipment *or* because of a willingness to continue to exert effort. Thus, even the extremely modest convergence of parameters includes several ambiguous measures.

To summarize, the evidence on behalf of fundamental variation in processing efficiency as the explanation of differences in *g* suffers from a number of construct validity weaknesses. Although composite predictions reveal moderate to substantial connections, these connections often incorporate unanalyzed as well as analyzed parameters. When the details of the connections are examined, it is clear that alternative interpretations—such as consistency of sustained, voluntary effort—can not easily be dismissed. In order to establish the construct validity of processing/ability connections, it seems necessary to have more specified and clearer tests.

Cognitive Correlates: From processes to abilities. The logic of investigating the connections between processing and mental ability has been used in a wide variety of studies, not just those which have presumed a *g* model. The pioneering work of Hunt (1978; Hunt, Lunneborg, & Lewis, 1975; Lansman, Donaldson, Hunt, & Yantis, 1982) and his colleagues helped to establish the research paradigms to study such connections. From its inception, Hunt's approach did not presume to be related necessarily to *g*. Instead, its goal was to study the connections between cognitive processing and specific abilities, such as performance on verbal ability tasks (Hunt, 1978).

The study by Lansman et al. (1982) carries this research paradigm further by explicitly looking for the *pattern* of relationships within and between a battery of experimentally derived parameters of processing and a battery of psychometric tests. The ability tests were selected so as to form factors frequently found in the psychometric literature, specifically crystallized (Gc) and fluid (Gf) intelligence, spatial visualization (Gv), and clerical speed and accuracy (CPS). A series of confirmatory factor analyses of the data from 91 college students who took 16 psychometric tests and six processing tasks (three each in computerized format and paper and pencil format) revealed the four psychometric factors already mentioned, and also permitted the extraction of the common variance from a series of 18 parameters drawn from the processing tasks. The processing variance was separated into the processes involved in the three tasks: mental rotation, letter matching, and sentence verification. Relating the psychometric and processing factors to each other, Lansman et al. (1982) report that mental rotation speed was strongly correlated with Gv (.78); letter matching speed was correlated with CPS (.69); and sentence verification speed was correlated with both Gc (.28) and CPS (.38). They argue that the most important finding from this study is the specificity of the relationships between the processing measures and the psychometric ability factors. They note further that the absence of any relationship between the processing factors and Gf ($-$.10, .02, and .00) might be viewed as troublesome, but contend Gf measures a specific ability of inductive reasoning. In any case, the pattern is argued to be interpretable, especially in the connection between mental rotation and Gv, and the (weaker) connection between sentence verification and Gc: "The experimental results complement the psychometric studies by connecting them to a literature that explicates the details of the processes of memory referencing and visual image manipulations " (Lansman et al., 1982, p. 379).

Note, however, that the connections between processing and ability in this study are reported exclusively in terms of the correlations between derived factor scores from each domain. In order to understand these relationships more completely, it is necessary to know how these factors, especially the processing factors, were established. In describing this procedure, they note that:

> Within each experimental task, the correlations between RT measures based on the computerized version and number correct on the paper and pencil version were quite high. However, the correlations between corresponding derived measures (i.e., slope of the RT function for the mental rotation tasks, the NI-PI difference in the letter matching tasks, and negation time in the sentence verification task) were low. *For this reason, we did not use these derived measures in defining the general factors. . . . Little information was lost by omitting the derived scores, since correlations involving derived measures showed the same pattern as correlations involving mean RT and error scores.* (Lansman et al., 1982, p. 369; emphasis added).

In other words, the "derived" parameters, which are the primary means of "explicating" the details of processing potentially involved in the performance of the more complex tasks, are *not included* in the processing factors. Instead, the processing factors are, to borrow Horn's (1984) phrase, a "miscellaneous collection" of indices from several tasks which are only coincidentally experimental in nature. That the derived parameters show the same "pattern" of correlations is difficult to interpret; whether the *magnitudes* are at all similar to the reported factor correlations can not be determined.

What exactly these "processing" factors are capturing is thus unclear. There are several reasons, however, to suspect that much more than simple processing is incorporated into the processing factors. As but one example, consider the reported error rates on the computerized version of the mental rotations task (Lansman et al., 1982, Figure 2, p. 357). They range from near zero errors at 20-degree rotation, to 15%–20% errors at 140- and 180-degree rotations. Across tasks (computerized to paper and pencil), the correlations of percent errors with slope is about .20. What this suggests is a quite substantial speed–accuracy trade-off, and it may well be that differential strategies of overall approach to the task are embedded in the "processing" factors, hence further confounding the processing/ability connections.

Lansman et al. (1982) seem to come close to dismissing the original logic of the cognitive correlates approach. The use of derived parameters as less ambiguous and less arbitrary variables with which to discover the underlying components of complex performance is dismissed, in favor of an empirically more promising, but analytically undefined, "processing" factors approach.

They argue, in fact, that "it is naive to expect individual differences in broad aspects of intelligence to be 'accounted for' by information processing rates, let along any single rate measure" (p. 379). Not only are the "processing" factors undefined, they are probably undefinable, in the same way that psychometric factors are unable to establish underlying validity on the basis of correlations among performance indices.

It would seem more informative to retain the original logic of theoretically derived parameters, and to investigate them in an explicit construct validation model. Following a series of investigations into developmental and individual differences in cognitive processing, Keating, List, and Merriman (1985) undertook such an investigation. Much of the work on which this is based is conceptually similar to that described above, and has been reviewed elsewhere (Keating, 1984). Here, we briefly describe only the logic and outcome of the most complete of the validation studies.

The study was designed as a two-tiered convergent/discriminant validity investigation. It was similar conceptually to the Lansman et al. (1982) research described above, although it included an age factor as well — eighth graders and college students. We investigated the two domains of verbal and spatial ability (Keating et al., 1985). The psychometric factors were defined by a set of group and individual tests drawn from these two domains. At the processing level, each subject participated in six experiments. Three of these experiments were designed to tap long term memory retrieval access, and three investigated mental rotation. We derived one key parameter from each experiment, which was theoretically the one most related to the hypothesized cognitive process. For retrieval, these were NI-PI differences (Posner & Mitchell, 1967) from both simultaneous and sequential presentations, and the response time to judge whether an item belonged to a specified category, calculated as the slope of RT across (dimensionally scaled) levels of salience (e.g., bird-robin versus bird-turkey). For rotation, the reaction time to judge whether objects were shown as normal or mirror image, calculated as slopes of RT across degrees of rotation, for schematic faces, and for alphabetic characters with and without advance information as to orientation.

The logic of this validity study is straightforward. At the level of processing, differently derived parameters of retrieval efficiency should converge more closely with each other than with parameters of mental rotation efficiency, and vice versa. This is the first tier of convergent/discriminant validity. On the second tier, the rotation parameters should predict the spatial ability composite more accurately than the verbal ability composite, and the retrieval parameters should reverse this pattern.

This is precisely what did *not* occur (Keating et al., 1985). The processing parameters showed no particular convergence within the hypothesized constructs, nor did they predict the appropriate ability domain. In fact, in a series of multiple regressions, the sets of processing parameters were as likely to predict the inappropriate ability domain as the expected one. We regarded these data as rather striking disconfirmation of a quite plausible validity model relating cognitive processing, and its development, to psychometric ability. In restricting the investigation to explicitly specified parameters, so as to retain the desirable features of nonarbitrariness and nonambiguity, what was discovered was the lack of any interpretable processing/ability relationship.

Hunt (1985) viewed these conclusions as an overreaction to a disappointing data set. Rather than a dispute over empirical findings, however, what we wish to emphasize here is the necessity of clear statements about validity criteria. It is no doubt possible to obtain empirically robust relationships among some measures derived from some experimental tasks, and psychometric ability scores. What is proving more difficult is to do so while retaining the advantages of the experimental, analytic approach. As we noted above, the value of using experimental parameters is not the tasks in which they happen to be embedded, but rather the theoretical specification of the relevant processing mechanisms. In this sense, the use of "composite" processing factors seems to make little analytic sense. When such precautions are taken, the construct validity of the processing/ability connection is elusive.

Componential Models: From skills to processes.   Early in the search for processing bases of cognitive ability, Sternberg (1977) proposed an alternative approach: the "componential" model. Rather than trying to identify unconfounded parameters of basic cognitive proceesses, and then relating these to ability measures, Sternberg proposed analyzing existing measures of complex performance (i.e., ability tests), and identifying the relevant processes required for that performance. In an ingenious methodological approach, Sternberg "decomposed" performance on complex tasks into simpler elements, by having subjects perform the task with greater or lesser amounts of the needed information specified on different trials. For example, on analogies of the form A : B: : C : D, Sternberg (1977) showed one, two, or three of the terms for a subject-controlled "encoding" period, and then showed the remaining terms (with a forced choice between a D and a D' option), with instructions to respond as quickly as possible. By contrasting performance across conditions using a series of multiple regressions, he was able to estimate the contributions of various specified components.

This thoughtful proposal has confronted some significant difficulties. Since these have been commented on extensively (Sternberg, 1980, and associated commentaries), we only briefly summarize them here. In addition, Sternberg (1984) has implicitly rejected some of the assumptions of the original componential model, and has expanded the model to include "metacomponents" and social/cultural components, at least partly in response to some of the problems noted below.

First, the modeling procedure of task decomposition seems to work best—

and perhaps only—on discrete and more easily specified tasks. Thus, picture/piece analogies, which involve only a small set of items reiterated frequently through the task, are more easily modelled than are the more open-ended verbal analogies (Sternberg, 1977). Second, when the derived parameters—estimated from the multiple regression beta weights—are correlated with overall task performance, it is the unanalyzed components (e.g., the residual) which show significant correlations. This is the recurring problem noted above: Unanalyzed reaction time composites may correlate highly, but these correlations can not be meaningfully interpreted. Third, some ambiguity of interpretation is evident in some presumably specific components. For example, Sternberg (1977) named the amount of time subjects took in the self-controlled part of the analogies task "encoding," and reported the unexpected finding that subjects who took *longer* to process the initial terms did better on the overall task. Of course, this is easily reinterpreted not as a specific measure of encoding processing, but rather a strategically driven (since it was under the subject's control) estimate of extracting useful information from the initial terms—something like "study time."

For these and other reasons, Sternberg first supplemented his theory by the inclusion of metacomponents (1980), which are strategic and learning aspects of task performance, which in turn coordinate the processing components, and then later by the inclusion of social/cultural or context components (Sternberg, 1984). The componential core of the theory is somewhat submerged under these higher levels of the "triarchic" model. Further, it is not immediately apparent whether strategy, knowledge, and culture are easily or productively investigated as psychological components similar to basic processing. It is apparent that, however submerged, the fundamental of the theory is still at the internal processing level.

> The critical question for a theorist of intelligence to ask is that of how those differences in knowledge came to be. Certainly, sheer differences in experience are not perfectly correlated with levels of expertise. . . . Individual differences in knowledge acquisition have priority over individual differences in knowledge. (Sternberg, 1984, p. 285).

Of course, one might have a different theory about knowledge acquisition than the accumulation of "sheer experience" (e.g., Keating & MacLean, in press). In any case, this assertion needs to be looked at empirically, which will necessarily involve more careful attention to developmental histories, a goal which we applaud.

Factorial Developments: Processing changes as factor validity. As with other psychometrically derived models of intelligence, Horn's (1980) theory claims to explain individual and developmental differences in intellectual behavior by positing an underlying mental ability. In Horn's model, cultural effects are taken into account by factor analyzing the underlying ability into two sub-abilities—Gc (crystallized intelligence) and Gf (fluid intelligence). As noted above, this distinction is an ambiguous one.

The strongest version of Horn's claim vis a vis developmental differences is that Gf shows substantial decline through the adult years, that this decline is real (Horn & Donaldson, 1976), and that it is largely but not wholly accounted for by declines in specific cognitive processes characterized as involving attentiveness, incidental learning, alertness, and organization in short-term memory.

How does Horn arrive at this list of mental processes? He uses a part-correlation strategy to isolate statistically some of the key tasks, and hence inferred intellectual processes, which contribute to the change functions over the adult years in Gc and Gf. This strategy is analogous to the componential approach of Sternberg (1977) or the cognitive correlates approach of Hunt (1978) or Keating (1984), except that, in this case, the inferences are based on the *reduction* of the construct–validity correlations. That is, when intellectual "process" factors are partialled out of the age-Gf or the age-Gc correlations, the magnitude of the correlations is presumably reduced in proportional degree that these factors (i.e., "process" marker tasks) are accounting for the age changes in the Gf or Gc dimensions. In Horn (1982, Figure 7, p. 267) these age change claims are depicted. In brief, Gf is shown as declining about 3.7 IQ point-equivalents per decade of the adult years, while Gc rises a similar magnitude. For Gc, the key process variables identified (and therefore those variables most responsible for Gc increases with age) are the factors:

TSR: tertiary storage and retrieval—which is defined by tasks such as the *number* of associations generated by subjects in response to a target word; and

USES: defined by the *number* of uses for common objects generated by subjects.

Horn (1982) interprets this factor pattern as indicating more flexible access to a greater store of information in long-term memory, for older as compared to younger adults.

In contrast, the Gf decline is best initially explained by four factors. These are (Horn, 1982, p. 264):

EOG: Organization at the stage of encoding in memory (which accounts for much of the short-term memory involvement in GF decline)

COS: Concentration-attentiveness, as in trying to trace very slowly (which also accounts for much short-term memory decline in Gf as well

as Gf decline in ability to divide attention and maintain clerical-perceptual speediness)
EIR: Eliminating irrelevancies in concept attainment (which accounts for much of the incidental memory involvement in Gf decline)
HYP: Hypothesis formation in the 20-questions game (which, like EIR, accounts for much of the incidental memory involvement in Gf decline).

Partialling out any three of these four factors accounts for about half of the Gf decline. The remainder of this section examines three critiques directed to this set of claims.

A thorough critique of specific tasks and their interpretations is beyond the scope of this review; nevertheless, an important general question is whether a consistent and meaningful alternative interpretation can be advanced for the factor patterns and associated "processes" described above. In other words, is the inferred criterion of what is considered "fluid" intelligence in the Cattell-Horn model the only reasonable way of interpreting this evidence? As discussed above, in terms of overall construct validity, it is not clear that any interpretation can be determined as being most accurate on the basis of the psychological performance data alone.

Given our interpretation of "fluid intelligence," how does this impact on the interpretation of the age-change data? In other words, do Horn's "processing" markers for age change serve to validate the original factor model? This would only be true if the "processing" markers were themselves relatively unambiguously interpretable. We would cite two concerns in this regard—task meaning and practice effects.

The meaning of the task, and the performance-based inferences about competence, may themselves vary with age. As one specific example, the 20-questions game, the key task for HYP (as described above) may rest upon a different set of cognitive schemata for the 20-year-old science major as compared to the elderly retiree—and not merely as a "poorer" set of schema for the latter. For example, given the older adults' generally broader knowledge base, they may form substantive hypotheses earlier in the questioning. Although this is not as useful a strategy in the constraints of this artificial task as highly abstract "categorical narrowing" would be, it is likely a highly efficient strategy in analogous real-world tasks. Indeed, Chi, Glaser, and Rees (1982) review a substantial amount of the expert/novice literature, and conclude that experts do in fact move to substantive hypothesis formation at an earlier point than do novices. Older adults, then, may not be employing less efficient strategies or have deficient HYP processing, but are inappropriately applying highly effective strategies from their own experience. College students, in contrast, may be characterized as in a "learning" phase, in which being an "expert at being a novice" is at a premium in their cognitive activity.

A somewhat narrower but still crucial concern is the effect on performance of practice directly with tasks or tests used to measure "non-systematically-acculturated" ability. This is of greatest concern for tasks used to experimentally infer underlying cognitive processes thought to be more or less independent of learning or transfer (Salthouse, 1982). In a review of this literature, Salthouse (1982) contends that performance on many such experimental tasks is highly susceptible to practice effects. If this is the case, then attempts to infer decline in "basic" cognitive processes are likely to be difficult as well.

In summary, then, it is clear that serious doubts can be raised with respect to the claim that fluid abilities show an invariant and necessary decline. A consideration of the criterion of intelligence employed, the models of development assumed, and the prevalence of practice effects, calls into question these claims. We wish to point out once more, however, that alternative views are not validated by merely raising these doubts. In this case, however, it is not clear that the appeal to "processing" as the basis for validity is entirely successful, since the processing parameters are themselves open to multiple interpretations.

Summary: Threats to construct validity.   Throughout our selective, but we believe representative, review of the empirical literature on the connections between cognitive processing and cognitive ability, we have stressed the validity concerns specific to each research paradigm. What is evident from this review is the striking similarity of the potential threats to validity across these diverse approaches. Here, we briefly restate in summary fashion those key concerns. These validity concerns do not comprise an exhaustive list, of course; rather, they are those which are most relevant to the specific goal of accounting for cognitive ability variance in cognitive processing terms.

These issues divide neatly into two general categories, which we can identify as principally psychometric concerns versus principally experimental concerns. In uniting correlational and experimental methodologies, there are both risks and benefits (Keating, 1984). The major risk is that the results are vulnerable to both internal and external validity threats.

Within the psychometric category, three major items are to be addressed: convergent and discriminant validity issues; subject selection; and procedures adopted in accounting for ability variance. First, the psychometric necessity for establishing both convergent and discriminant validity by using a variety of tests presumed to measure a range of abilities is well established. Unfortunately, such concern is relatively more rare when it comes to cognitive processing parameters. It can not simply be assumed that even carefully specified parameters from well-analyzed tasks are isomorphic with the hypothesized process (Morrison, Lord, & Keating, 1984). Convergent parameters from different tasks would be a major advance on this front.

Second, it is advisable to consider carefully the range and representativeness of subjects included in such studies. Cognitive processing parameters are typically not robust, often being measured in differences of less than 50 milliseconds across conditions. Contrasting retarded and nonretarded populations, for example, for the purposes of inferring a processing basis of ability differences might be quite misleading. The absolute differences on the experimental tasks between the populations may be attributable to a wide range of noncognitive as well as cognitive differences.

Third, there seems to be an emerging pattern within this literature that the more carefully specified and rigorously validated the processing parameters become, the *less* cognitive ability variance they account for. Indeed, it may be "naive," as Lansman et al. (1982) argue, to expect otherwise. In some not too distant future, it may well be possible to do meta-analytic reviews of the connection between processing variance and ability variance. If, in that analysis, those studies employing only carefully defined processing parameters are separately considered, it seems likely that they would be substantially less related to ability variance; that is, greater rigor = less variance accounted for. Given this, the temptation is to increase the variance accounted for by using more general, albeit confounded, parameters (e.g., total RT), or to embed the carefully analyzed parameters in some compound variable (latent or otherwise) which will correlate better with the ability measures. We contend that this is a temptation to be resisted. Otherwise, the signal advantage of seeking a processing basis for ability is compromised or lost. What we have, instead, is a replay of the same difficulties of interpreting factor structures post hoc, which undermined psychometric theory – and which componential analysis was originally designed to overcome (Keating & Bobbitt, 1978).

The threats to internal validity – the category of experimental validity concerns – are more interrelated and can be briefly described. These revolve around the issue of unambiguous interpretation of the derived parameters from the processing tasks. The major concern is that such parameters may capture more than just processing variance; indeed, they may often be partly or wholly confounded with other, nonprocessing aspects of performance. When group (e.g., age) or individual comparisons are being made, this risk is enhanced (Cole & Means, 1981; Roth, 1983). A convenient way of codifying these concerns is to explore thoughtfully the other major categories of the processing "system" which might confound speed or efficiency interpretations (Keating, 1984): differential content knowledge, or differential familiarity with the stimulus materials or other features of the experimental task (MacLean & Keating, 1986); differential procedural knowledge, or strategic knowledge (sometimes referred to as "control process," Roth, 1983); and differential motivation or willingness to participate at high levels of arousal throughout the experimental task. This last is clearly difficult to ascertain, but the internal evidence from some processing investigations suggests that it is nontrivial (e.g., Carlson et al., 1983). One strategy is to attempt to equate for these pre-existing differences among subjects by using processing parameters from that portion of the curve *after* subjects have reached asymptote (Salthouse, 1982). There are very few such studies which use these parameters to account for ability variance, but if they were successful, they would be quite convincing.

From Cognitive Reduction to Developmental History

We have organized this empirical and conceptual review, though highly critical, with what we hope to be a constructive goal in mind. A rigorous analysis of the validity requirements of investigations which seek to use cognitive processing to account for cognitive ability differences, both developmental and individual, should be helpful in future research. Although space constraints permit only the briefest discussion of these research directions, we would like to include some suggestions.

The validity issues embedded in the review and summarized above are likely to be of most immediate use in research which carries forward some version of the original componential agenda. It may well be that the approach has not been sufficiently explored. Detterman (1984), in criticizing what he regarded as Sternberg's (1984) too-rapid abandonment of a componential agenda, noted cogently that the mathematical requirements of a componential model are in fact quite modest. Even a small number of component parameters, each of which correlates, say, .10 with a target ability, might account for a substantial portion of the total ability variance, if they each make independent contributions. Of course, in this case it would be necessary to obtain robust replications not only of the magnitude of the multiple Rs, but also of their *patterns*, but the possibility should not be dismissed. On the other hand, such traditional componential approaches do need, at a minimum, to make the theoretical claims to valid processing explanations of ability clear enough to be testable. As we have noted in this review, inattention to this critical issue can generate seemingly substantive findings which, upon inspection, rest on somewhat shaky or ambiguous foundations.

Alternatively, one might expand the componential notion to include novel components, as in Sternberg's (1984) metacomponents of learning and transfer, and "context" components of social and cultural background. In these cases, it is even more critical to be clear about the theoretical status of these novel components. Short-term memory processing efficiency, for example, has the advantage of clarity, even if it turns out to account for little ability variance. Whether "cultural context" can be meaningfully studied as an individual psychological component is less immediately obvious.

A final alternative we note here is a loosely defined research program we have described in some detail elsewhere as "reconstruction in cognitive development" (Keating & MacLean, in press). We argue that both explicit and implicit structural models – psychometric, Piagetian, and componential – have given too short shrift to other methods of investigating cognitive activity and cognitive development. We propose there the incorporation of theories and methods which more consciously address questions of the individual's developmental history. This can be approached both through reconsideration of extant empirical findings—as illustrated in several examples above—and through research directly on the cognitive socialization experiences of children and adults.

Of course, such socialization investigations rely on well-developed models of cognitive activity. If, as we suspect, the empirical findings such as those reviewed here are more useful as highly sensitive indicators of knowledge differences, rather than underlying processing differences, then those methods and techniques are crucial to a socialization, or knowledge acquisition, perspective. Indeed, appropriate use of structural models, whether conceived initially as seeking to remove confounds from processing interpretations, or as seeking to explore the construction of a knowledge or skill domain, might well discover themselves to be on a single path after all.

REFERENCES

Baltes, P. B., Nesselroade, J. R., & Cornelius, S. W. (1978). Multivariate antecedents of structual change in development: A simulation of cumulative environmental patterns. *Multivariate Behavioral Research, 13,* 127–152.

Bisanz, J., Danner, F., & Resnick, L. B. (1979). Changes with age in measures of processing efficiency. *Child Development, 50,* 132–141.

Bronfenbrenner, U., & Crouter, A. C. (1983). The evolution of environmental models in developmental research. In P. Mussen (Ed.), *Handbook of child psychology* (Vol. 1, pp. 357–414). New York: Wiley.

Cairns, R. B., (1983). The emergence of developmental psychology. In P. Mussen (Ed.), *Handbook of child psychology, Vol. 1.* New York: Wiley.

Carlson, J. S., Jensen, C. M., & Widaman, K. F. (1983). Reaction time, intelligence, and attention. *Intelligence, 7,* 329–344.

Case, R. (1978). Intellectual development from birth to adulthood: A neo-Piagetian approach. In R. S. Siegler (Ed.), *Children's thinking: What develops?* Hillsdale, NJ: Erlbaum.

Chi, M. T. H. (1977). Age differences in the speed of processing: A critique. *Developmental Psychology, 13,* 543–544.

Chi, M. T. H., Glaser, R., & Rees, E. (1982). Expertise in problem solving. In R. J. Sternberg (Ed.), *Advances in the psychology of human intelligence, Vol. 1.* Hillsdale, NJ: Erlbaum.

Chodorow, N. (1978). *The reproduction of mothering.* Berkeley, CA: University of California Press.

Cole, M., & Means, B. (1981). *Comparative studies of how people think.* Cambridge, MA: Harvard University Press.

Detterman, D. K. (1984). Understand cognitive components before postulating metacomponents, etc., part 2. *Behavioral and Brain Sciences, 7,* 289–290.

Eysenck, H. J. (1982). *A model for intelligence.* Berlin: Springer Verlag.

Eysenck, H. J. (1984). Intelligence versus behavior. *Behavioral and Brain Sciences, 7,* 290–291.

Farnham-Diggory, S., & Nelson, B. (1984). Cognitive analyses of basic school tasks. In F. J. Morrison, C. Lord, & D. P. Keating (Eds.), *Applied developmental psychology, Vol. 1* (pp. 21–74). Orlando, FL: Academic Press.

Foucault, M. (1984). Truth and power. In P. Rabinow (Ed.), *The Foucault reader* (pp. 51–75). New York: Pantheon.

Guilford, J. P. (1980). Fluid and crystallized intelligences: Two fanciful concepts. *Psychological Bulletin, 88,* 406–412.

Hick, W. E. (1952). Rate of gain of information. *Quarterly Journal of Experimental Psychology, 4,* 11–26.

Horn, J. L. (1980). Concepts of intellect in relation to learning and adult development. *Intelligence, 4,* 285–317.

Horn, J. L. (1982). The theory of fluid and crystallized intelligence in relation to concepts of cognitive psychology and aging in adulthood. In F. I. M. Craik & S. E. Trehub (Eds.), *Aging and cognitive processes* (pp. 237–278). Boston: Plenum.

Horn, J. L. (1984, March). *Remodeling models of intelligence.* Paper presented at the Gatlinburg Conference on Theory and Research in Mental Retardation, Gatlinburg, TN.

Horn, J. L., & Cattell, R. B. (1982). Whimsy and misunderstandings of Gf-Gc theory: A comment on Guilford. *Psychological Bulletin, 91,* 623–633.

Horn, J. L., & Donaldson, G. (1976). On the myth of intellectual decline in adulthood. *American Psychologist, 31,*701–792.

Hunt, E. (1978). Mechanics of verbal ability. *Psychological Review, 85,* 109–130.

Hunt, E. (1985). Marching forward on the IQ front. *Contemporary Psychology, 30,* 607–608.

Hunt, E., Lunneborg, C., & Lewis, J. (1975). What does it mean to be high verbal? *Cognitive Psychology, 7,* 194–227.

Inhelder, B., & Piaget, J. (1958). *The growth of logical thinking from childhood to adolescence.* New York: Basic Books.

Jensen, A. R. (1979). *g*: Outmoded theory or unconquered frontier? *Creative Science & Technology, 2,* 16–29.

Jensen, A. R. (1984). Mental speed and levels of analysis. *Behavioral and Brain Sciences, 7,* 295–296.

Jensen, A. R., & Munro, E. (1979). Reaction time, movement time, and intelligence. *Intelligence, 3,* 121–126.

Keating, D. P. (Ed.). (1976). *Intellectual Talent.* Baltimore, MD: Johns Hopkins University Press.

Keating, D. P. (1979). Toward a multivariate life-span theory of intelligence. In D. Kuhn (Ed.), *Intellectual development beyond childhood* (pp. 25–40). San Francisco: Jossey-Bass.

Keating, D. P. (1980). Thinking processes in adolescence. In J. Adelson (Ed.), *Handbook of adolescent psychology* (pp. 211–246). New York: Wiley.

Keating, D. P. (1984). The emperor's new clothes: The "new look" in intelligence research. In R. J. Sternberg (Ed.), *Advances in the psychology of human intelligence, Vol. II* (pp. 1–35). Hillsdale, NJ: Erlbaum.

Keating, D. P. (1986, May). *Structuralism, deconstruction, reconstruction: The limits of reasoning.* Paper presented at the Annual Meeting of the Jean Piaget Society, Philadelphia, PA.

Keating, D. P., & Bobbitt, B. L. (1978). Individual and developmental differences in cognitive-processing components of mental ability. *Child Development, 49,* 155–167.

Keating, D. P., List, J. A., & Merriman, W. E. (1985). Cognitive processing and cognitive ability: A multivariate validity investigation. *Intelligence, 9,* 149–170.

Keating, D. P., & MacLean, D. J. (in press). Reconstruction in cognitive development: A poststructuralist agenda. In P. B. Baltes, D. L. Featherman & R. M. Lerner (Eds.), *Life-span development and behavior, Vol. 8.* Hillsdale, NJ: Erlbaum.

Lansman, M., Donaldson, G., Hunt, E., & Yantis, S. (1982). Ability factors and cognitive processes. *Intelligence, 6,* 347-386.

List, J. A., Keating, D. P., & Merriman, W. E. (1985). Differences in memory retrieval: A construct validity investigation. *Child Develolpment, 56,* 138-151.

Luria, A. (1979). *Cognitive development: Its cultural and social foundations.* Cambridge, MA: Harvard University Press.

MacLean, D. J., & Keating, D. P. (1986, April). *Adult recall and recognition performance: Knowledge versus age.* Paper presented at the Biennial Conference on Human Development, Nashville, TN.

Morrison, F. J., Lord, C., & Keating, D. P. (Eds.). (1984). *Applied developmental psychology, Vol. 1.* New York: Academic Press.

Olson, D. (1984). *Intelligence and literacy: On the relations between intelligence and the technologies of representation and communication.* Unpublished manuscript, Ontario Institute for Studies in Education, Toronto, Ontario.

Piaget, J. (1954). *The construction of reality in the child.* New York: Basic Books.

Posner, M. I., & Mitchell, R. F. (1967). Chronometric analysis of classification. *Psychological Review, 74,* 392-409.

Roth, C. (1983). Factors affecting developmental changes in the speed of processing. *Journal of Experimental Child Psychology, 35,* 509-528.

Salthouse, T. A. (1982). *Adult cognition: An experimental psychology of human aging.* New York: Springer Publishers.

Sharp, D. W., Cole, M., & Lave, C. (1979). Education and cognitive development: The evidence from experimental research. *Monographs of the Society for Research in Child Development, 44,* Serial No. 178.

Spearman, C. (1904). "General intelligence" objectively determined and measured. *American Journal of Psychology, 15,* 201-293.

Sternberg, R. J. (1977). *Intelligence, information processing, and analogical reasoning: The componential analysis of human abilities.* Hillsdale, NJ: Erlbaum.

Sternberg, R. J. (1980). Sketch of a componential subtheory of human intelligence. *Behavioral and Brain Sciences, 3,* 573-584.

Sternberg, R. J. (1984). Toward a triarchic theory of human intelligence. *Behavioral and Brain Sciences, 7,* 269-315.

Vernon, P. A. (1983). Speed of information processing and general intelligence. *Intelligence, 7,* 53-70.

Vernon, P. A., & Jensen, A. R. (1984). Individual and group differences in intelligence and speed of information processing. *Personality and Individual Differences, 5,* 411-423.

Vernon, P. A., Nador, S., & Kantor, L. (1985). Group differences in intelligence and speed of information-processing. *Intelligence, 9,* 137-148.

Wickens, C. D. (1974). Temporal limits of human information processing: A developmental study. *Psychological Bulletin, 81,* 739-755.

CHAPTER 8

The Role of
Mental Speed in Intelligence:
A Triarchic Perspective

Diana B. Marr and Robert J. Sternberg
Yale University

The notion that mental speed is an important aspect of intelligence dates back to psychology's earliest inquiries into the nature and expression of intelligence, usually with the proviso that intelligence is related to the individual's speed of *cognitive processing,* as distinct from his or her general temporal style or preference (e.g., Spearman, 1927). However, distinguishing between capacity and preference for speed is a tricky business. Unless the perceived relevance of mental speed in a given task is equivalent for all individuals, measures of mental speed may be confounded by differential motivation to perform quickly. At the same time, individual differences in experience with any given task are likely to produce individual differences in speed of performance, independent of any general capacity or preference for mental speed. In addition, different levels of analysis are likely to result in very different estimates of an individual's "mental speed" (e.g., overall speed of performance vs. speed of specific component processes). Thus, to understand the relationship between mental speed and intelligence, it is necessary to understand the perceived *relevance* of speed for any given task, the individual's prior *experience* with the task, and the *information-processing components* that are involved in task performance.

Although the relationship between speed and intelligence spans a broad range of cognitive tasks and behaviors, in this chapter we shall limit our discussion to speed in the execution of three classes of behavior: *habituation,* because it is one of the earliest behaviors for which a relationship between speed and intelligence has been found; *automatization,* because of its applicability across task domains and behaviors; and *choice reaction time,* because of the impressive results and intense controversy produced by research in this area. We shall begin with a very general overview of the apparent relationship between intelligence and speed within each of these three classes of behavior. Then, following a brief description of Sternberg's (1985) triarchic theory of intelligence, we shall reevaluate the evidence within the framework of that theory, and present our own view of the value and limitations of mental speed as an indicator of intelligence.

EVIDENCE FOR THE RELATIONSHIP
BETWEEN INTELLIGENCE AND MENTAL SPEED

From early infancy through adulthood, individual differences in the speed of at least some cognitive responses appear to be related to individual differences in intelligence. For example, studies of infant habituation rate (i.e., the amount of exposure to a new stimulus that is required for the infant to respond to that stimulus as if it were an old, familiar stimulus) have suggested that more intelligent infants habituate more quickly than do less intelligent infants. McCall and Kagan (1970) found significant correlations between infant habituation rate and concurrent measures of cognitive ability. More recently, research by Fagan and McGrath (1981) has found correlations between the speed with which infants habituated to new visual stimuli at 5 to 7 months of age, and their vocabulary scores at 7 years of age. Lewis and Brooks-Gunn (1981) have found similar correlations between habituation at 3 months, and Bayley intelligence test scores at 24 months, of age.

Insofar as habituation depends primarily upon the cognitive processes necessary to transform the initially novel stimulus into something more familiar, habituation rate may be considered a reflection of cognitive processing speed. However, habituation rate almost certainly depends upon a great deal more than cognitive processing speed. For example, Fagan and McGrath (1981) have suggested that individual differences in habituation rate may reflect individual differences in infant recognition memory; for habituation to occur after repeated exposures to the stimulus, the infant must recognize that the stimulus is the same stimulus presented in previous trials. If more intelligent infants have superior recognition memory, this superiority would almost certainly result in faster habituation. Individual differences in habituation rate also may reflect differential motivation or interest in novel stimuli (e.g., Berg & Sternberg, 1985), or differences in attentional capacity. If we assume that the individual's information processing is limited by competing demands upon his or her attentional resources (e.g., Hunt & Lansman, 1982;

Kahneman, 1973), then the infant who allocates attention to nonstimulus properties of the experimental condition (or to his or her internal state) will have fewer attentional resources available for the habituation stimulus, and will be likely to habituate more slowly. Even if attentional capacity is *not* a limited resource, the development of effective strategies and skills of divided attention appear to require extensive practice with the specific attentional tasks (e.g., Spelke, Hirst, & Neisser, 1976), so individual differences in prior experience may influence habituation rate when divided attention is necessary. Although the speed with which an infant achieves an habituated response probably is an indication of intelligence, the processes through which that response is achieved are far from clear. *Speed of response* is not necessarily a sign of *mental speed*; although a pure cognitive speed factor may play an important role in determining habituation rate, so may memory, motivation, interest, attention, and prior experience.

Intelligence also has been related to the speed with which individuals automatize repetitive sequences of mental operations (e.g., Lansman, Donaldson, Hunt, & Yantis, 1982; see also Hunt, Frost, & Lunneborg, 1973). The source of this correlation is open to speculation, but, here again, a pure cognitive speed factor seems unlikely. Perhaps more intelligent individuals are simply more aware of the advantages of automatizing their behavior. Indeed, academically superior students have been found to differ substantially from their less able counterparts in their ability to recognize how particular characteristics of a task contribute to that task's difficulty, and to adjust their strategies accordingly (Bransford, Stein, Vye, Franks, Auble, Mezynski, & Perfetto, 1982). In other words, the correlation between intelligence and automatization speed may be grounded in higher level strategic processes, and not in mental speed, per se. Alternatively, motivational variables may influence both automatization speed (limiting the individual's willingness to invest the additional effort required for rapid automatization) and performance on psychometric measures of intelligence.

Some of the most controversial findings relating mental speed to intelligence come from studies of choice reaction time. Reaction-time research has a long and often embarrassing history, but the theoretical commitment and methodological rigor of recent investigators have brought this field back into the mainstream of psychological theory and research. Although we do not agree with all of their conclusions, researchers such as Jensen (1980a, b, 1982a, b) and Vernon (1981, 1983) have done impressive work, and their findings have been a source of intellectual stimulation for psychologists.

In Jensen's choice reaction-time procedure (Jensen & Munro, 1979), the subject sits with one finger resting on the "home" button of an apparatus with eight lights; the subject's task is to remove the finger from home base as soon as a light is turned on, and to move the finger to a button directly below that light, pressing the button to turn off the light. The subject's reaction

time, or *initiation time* (IT), is the interval between onset of the light and removal of the finger from home base. *Movement time* (MT) is the interval between leaving home base and pressing the button to turn out the light. Typically, a subject will first receive a series of trials using one light, followed by a
second series of trials with two lights, a third with four lights, and a fourth
with eight lights (with any unused lights and buttons covered by a template).
In the one-light condition, stimulus location is fixed, and the only uncertainty in the task is temporal onset of the stimulus; as the number of uncovered lights increases, stimulus location becomes increasingly uncertain.

Jensen has found that IT, intraindividual variability (standard deviation)
of IT, and slope of IT across set sizes all show significant negative correlations with psychometric measures of intelligence (e.g., Jensen 1980a, b,
1982a, b; Jensen & Munro, 1979). Similar results have been obtained by
Vernon (1981, 1983) in studies of mentally retarded individuals and of
university students. Jensen also claims that, as task complexity (i.e., set size)
increases, so does the correlation of IT with psychometric measures of
intelligence.

What do these findings tell us about mental speed and intelligence? As
compelling as some of the results may appear to be, it probably is too early to
make any definitive statements about the nature of the relationship between
choice reaction time and intelligence. Do the measures really reflect capacity
for mental speed, or are they, like most other measures, subject to contami-
nation by individual differences in information-processing strategies, perceptual skills, motivation, and attention? Jensen has interpreted the fact that
IT increases with set size as evidence that the subsequent motor response is
programmed during the IT phase: Presumably, the greater stimulus uncertainty at larger set sizes requires more (and more complex) response programming. Hence, the speed of complex response programming might account for
much of the relationship between IT and intelligence. However, Longstreth
(1984) has found that modifying the task so that subjects were not required to
program a motor response produced only a slight reduction in the slope of IT
over set size. Thus, it appears that the increase in IT with set size cannot be
adequately explained by Jensen's response preparation/programming
hypothesis.

If response preparation does not account for the relationship among IQ,
IT, and task complexity, what else might be involved? Perhaps motivational
and attentional factors come into play. Jensen (1980a) has argued against a
motivational explanation, noting that the IT response occurs prior to the individual's *conscious* awareness of the stimulus, and that subjects are unable
to "fake" a slower response without falling seven or eight standard deviations
below their normal response speeds (Jensen, 1982a). However, although this
apparent insensitivity of the measure to conscious effort might seem to preclude *direct* motivational influences on reaction time, motivation may never-

theless play an indirect role, mediated by the allocation of attentional resources to the task. As set size and task complexity increase, so do the attentional requirements of the task. The unmotivated subject may be more likely to divide his or her attention between the reaction-time task and other features of the experimental environment, and this divided attention may produce slower reaction times. Similarly, anxiety (and any number of other emotional or physiological conditions) may divert necessary attentional resources from the task as the subject attends to changes in his or her internal state.

Finally, reaction time (particularly choice reaction time) is notoriously unstable over time and over different stimulus modalities (Jensen, 1982b; McCall, 1979). Is this instability a function of reaction-time measures, or does the problem lie in the construct itself? Although the source of reaction-time instability is not clear, evidence that transient changes in physiological state may affect reaction time across a variety of different measures (e.g., Church, 1984; Kamiya, 1961; Meck, 1983; Woodworth & Schlosberg, 1954) suggests at least the possibility that the construct itself may be unstable. Unless general intelligence is correspondingly unstable (which seems not to be the case), instability of reaction-time measures may pose theoretical as well as practical problems; but, even if the instability is merely a measurement problem, it seriously limits the practical utility of reaction time as a measure of individual intelligence.

In conclusion, there seems to be little doubt that the speed of cognitive *response* is related to performance on many psychometric *measures* of intelligence, at least within certain populations in Western society. But is the speed of response an accurate reflection of mental processing speed, and are our measures of intelligence accurate reflections of intelligence? These questions will be addressed in the remainder of this chapter, within the framework of the triarchic theory.

AN OVERVIEW OF THE TRIARCHIC THEORY OF INTELLIGENCE

The triarchic theory of human intelligence defines intelligence as the mental activity underlying purposive adaptation to, shaping of, and selection of real-world environments relevant to one's life (Sternberg, 1985). The triarchic theory consists of three subtheories: a contextual subtheory, a componential subtheory, and an experiential subtheory.

The *contextual subtheory* relates intelligence to the requirements of the individual's environment, limiting the domain of intelligence to that subset of mental activity that is *relevant to effective interaction with one's external real-world environment*. Thus, even if a particular mental capacity is a universal component of intelligence, the intelligent expression of that ability may vary from culture to culture (and, within any culture, may vary from environment to environment). Different environments not only give rise to different definitions of intelligence, but also may shape that intelligence in somewhat different ways. Rewards for the exercise and development of particular cognitive abilities will vary from one environment to another, as will the opportunities to exercise and develop these abilities.

Because intelligence is defined in terms of environmental adaptation, a rich understanding or assessment of intelligence can be achieved only through the use of contextually relevant tasks. The problem, of course, is that adaptive behavior for any given time or culture is not necessarily adaptive for another. To the extent that the contextual relevance of these tasks varies substantially for different individuals, assessment should vary accordingly.

Whereas the contextual subtheory relates intelligence to the external world of the individual, the *componential subtheory* describes the internal mental processes that are likely to be involved in intelligence across different environments. The componential subtheory proposes that three classes of information-processing components underlie intelligent functioning: metacomponents, performance components, and knowledge-acquisition components. In this chapter, we shall discuss only the first two classes, metacomponents and performance components. (For a discussion of knowledge-acquisition components, see Sternberg, 1985.)

Metacomponents are higher order processes that are used to plan, monitor, and evaluate one's task performance. They allow the individual to (a) identify the nature of the problem, (b) determine the appropriate mental representation for the problem, (c) select the necessary operations for problem solution, (d) choose a strategy for combining these operations, (e) decide how to allocate mental resources, and (f) monitor one's problem-solving performance. These metacomponents, which are used across a wide variety of tasks, are believed to be largely responsible for general intelligence, or *g*. *Performance components* are the lower order processes that are invoked to perform the necessary problem-solving operations. These components are used to encode, combine, compare, and respond to stimuli. The relative importance of these two classes of components will vary from task to task and, for any given task, will vary as a function of prior experience. When a task is relatively novel, metacomponents will be of primary importance; when a task is fully automatized, performance components will play a larger role.

Although these components may be universal, it is clear that their degree of involvement in any given task may vary from culture to culture and from environment to environment. Tasks that are essential to environmental adaptation are apt to be practiced to the point of automatization, whereas totally irrelevant tasks are not. Thus, if the same task is used to measure intelligence among individuals from widely divergent environments, it is rather unlikely that this task will measure the same thing for all individuals. For individuals who are extremely experienced with the task, success may depend primarily upon the use of performance components; for those who are extremely inexperienced with the task, success may depend primarily upon metacomponents. Clearly, this difference makes cross-cultural comparisons problematic.

Even within a single culture or environment, we are faced with the problem of deciding the relative contributions of metacomponents and performance components to intelligent performance on any given task. How novel or familiar should a task be in order to provide the best estimate of intelligence? The *experiential subtheory* addresses this question, specifying optimal points on the familiarity–novelty continuum for the expression and assessment of intelligent behavior. Tasks that are extremely novel are apt to be relatively poor measures of intelligence. If the task requirements lie too far outside of the individual's prior experiences, he or she may get stuck in the early stages of metacomponential processing and be unable to apply his or her full range of abilities to the problem. If, for example, the individual spends all of his or her time trying to determine the appropriate mental representation for the problem, task performance will provide a poor indication of the individual's functioning on other metacomponents or performance components. On the other hand, if the task is already automatized, performance will depend primarily upon the speed and accuracy of a preselected sequence of performance components, with only a negligible contribution from metacomponents. Thus, the best overall measure of intelligence will be obtained by using a task that is relatively (but not extremely) novel or a task that is in the process of becoming automatized.

In summary, the contextual subtheory relates intelligence to successful interaction with the external environment; the componential subtheory relates intelligence to the internal processes that underlie effective person–environment interaction; and the experiential subtheory specifies the optimal level of task novelty for the assessment of intelligence. In the remainder of this chapter, we shall consider some of the evidence for and against mental speed as a central aspect of intelligence, and evaluate this evidence in light of the triarchic theory of human intelligence.

THE CONTEXTUAL SUBTHEORY: HOW RELEVANT IS MENTAL SPEED?

Relevance of the Construct

The emphasis on mental speed in western societies is evident in our popular notions of what it means to be intelligent. We commonly refer to those we consider intelligent as "quick" and to those we consider unintelligent as "slow." The young child who learns very quickly is often judged to be more intelligent by teachers and parents than the child who learns very slowly, even if the quick learner forgets almost as quickly as he or she learns and the slow learner never forgets. Similarly, the child who is always the first in the class to come up with reasonably correct answers to the teacher's questions is apt to be considered "brighter" than the child who takes slightly longer to formulate more precise answers. At least within academic environments in which it is consistently rewarded, mental speed would appear to be advantageous to environmental adaptation. But is mental speed equally adaptive outside of the classroom?

Empirical evidence for the value placed upon mental speed outside of academic settings has been found in studies of the factors underlying the conceptions of intelligence held by widely diverse groups of individuals in this society (e.g., Berg & Sternberg, 1984; Sternberg, Conway, Ketron, & Bernstein, 1981). In these studies of people's "implicit theories of intelligence," individuals were asked to list what they considered to be particularly characteristic attributes of exceptionally intelligent individuals. The hundreds of specific and general attributes that were generated in this fashion were then compiled into a single list. All of the listed behaviors were rated by subjects, who indicated the extent to which they considered each behavior to be characteristic of exceptionally intelligent individuals. These ratings showed that individuals at all ages (college-age through post-retirement years) and all walks of life (students, psychologists, housewives, professionals, white-collar, blue-collar, and unemployed workers) considered behaviors that explicitly referenced cognitive speed (e.g., "learns rapidly") to be somewhat characteristic of intelligence. It should be noted, however, that the relative importance of these behaviors differed somewhat from group to group, and for no group were they the most important characteristics of intelligence. Furthermore, when the ratings were factor analyzed to identify the factors underlying people's implicit theories of intelligence, no "mental speed" factor emerged, and factor loadings of speed-related behaviors were relatively low on all factors for all groups except psychologists. And even among psychologists, the only factor loading higher than .60 was the loading of "learns rapidly" (loading .61 on a verbal intelligence factor).

What do these results tell us about the contextual relevance of mental speed? The ratings of speed-referenced behaviors suggest that mental speed (or, at the very least, certain instantiations of mental speed) is considered by many people in our society to be moderately indicative of intelligence. To the extent that the individuals who provided these ratings considered intelligence to be an adaptive constellation of abilities, and not merely an irrelevant construct created by educators and psychologists, these ratings suggest that mental speed probably serves an intelligently adaptive function in dealing with certain aspects of the external environment.

However, it is not clear that mental speed is equally relevant across different cultures and subcultures. In fact, there is strong reason to believe that certain minority subcultures differ dramatically in their views of time in general,
and of speed in particular. For example, Heath (1983) has noted that the prevailing attitudes about time in a lower-class black community were dramatically different from attitudes in a lower-class white community. Whereas the
activities of lower-class white youngsters are constrained by fairly rigid time
schedules (a time to eat, a time to sleep, etc.), the flow of time for the lower-
class blacks is flexible and unscheduled (eat when hungry, sleep when tired,
etc.). Thus, attention to temporal constraints and schedules develops early
for the white youngsters; for the black youngsters, such constraints and
schedules seem arbitrary and irrelevant.

Jones (1984) and Jones and Block (1984) have suggested that white Americans generally live their lives according to *linear time* (i.e., events are measured "by the clock"), but that black Americans tend to use *nonlinear time*
(i.e., the passage of time is measured by the flow of events). Jones and Block
argue that a primary value of linear time is the prediction and control of future events. For generations, black Americans had little opportunity to control their own futures, rendering linear time largely irrelevant to their lives.
Mental speed, of course, is a function of linear time, and its perceived value
or intelligence is apt to be constrained by the limited relevance of linear time.
Assuming that individuals are to some extent motivated to perform "intelligently" in testing situations, those with nonlinear temporal orientations may
be less likely to view attention to linear time (and to optimization of mental
speed) as intelligent. Thus, even if these individuals are fully capable of high-
speed performance, they may deliberately choose not to use this ability.

The cultural differences in temporal attitudes are also evident when we
compare western and non-western cultures. For example, in the agricultural
Kipsigi culture of rural Kenya, infants are in constant contact with their
mothers, who are thus able to attend to their needs as they arise (Super &
Harkness, 1980). With infants carried by their mothers in a sling during the
day, and sleeping in their mother's bed at night, there is no need to impose
any external temporal schedule. Whenever infants are tired, they can sleep;
whenever they are hungry, the mother is there to feed them. Under these circumstances, there is little need for the developing youngster to attend to time
as an external and relevant entity. As the child matures, of course, time becomes more important to his or her life, but the relevant units of time for
measuring and predicting life events are larger and less precise than the relevant units of time in Western society.

This is not to say that mental speed is *entirely* irrelevant in certain cultural
or subcultural milieux. In fact, it is difficult to conceive of an environment in
which the capacity for rapid cognitive processing would not be adaptive, if
only in coping with sudden emergency situations. However, the extent to

which the capacity is adaptive will depend upon the environmental frequency and importance of such situations. Furthermore, even in environments in which the capacity for mental speed is of paramount importance to survival, the "intelligence" of maximizing mental speed in any given task will depend upon the perceived consequences of high-speed performance. If the individual sees no particular payoff for attending to the speed of his or her performance, then speed of performance might be a more accurate reflection of the individual's preferred temporal style than of his or her capacity for speed. Thus, insofar as different environments vary in the degree to which they encourage certain temporal styles and preferences, capacity and preference are apt to be confounded.

This problem has not gone unnoticed by those who propose mental speed as a universal determinant of intelligence. For example, Jensen (1980a) has argued that racial differences in temporal style or preference are minimal, and are unrelated to choice reaction-time measures of cognitive speed. However, the data upon which this conclusion rests are somewhat dubious. Temporal style or preference (i.e., "personal tempo") was assessed using a task in which subjects were given a grid consisting of 300 empty squares and were instructed to draw Xs in as many squares as possible within a fixed period of time. Instructions were varied to emphasize or to de-emphasize the importance of speed, and results were compared for black and white subjects. Under both instructional conditions, results showed large individual differences but no significant racial differences on the Making Xs test. Jensen takes this finding as evidence that racial differences in personal tempo are virtually nonexistent, and concludes that racial differences on measures of cognitive speed are therefore uncontaminated by temporal preference or style.

This optimistic conclusion, however, presupposes that the Making Xs Test is an adequate measure of temporal preference. Unfortunately, there seems to be little evidence that this is the case. Because the test was designed to assess personal tempo, independent of cognitive speed, it obviously was necessary to use a task in which the cognitive demands were practically nil. In so doing, however, one must implicitly accept two premises: (a) the individual's personal tempo (or temporal preference) is invariant across cognitive and noncognitive situations and task domains; and (b) the specific task selected to assess personal tempo is appropriate for this purpose. There seems to be little or no evidence to support either of these premises, and considerable reason to question them both.

First, is personal tempo really invariant across situations and task domains? Is preference for rapid motor response (e.g., making Xs) perfectly correlated with preference for rapid cognitive response? The answer to these questions requires comparison of cognitive and noncognitive preference but, apart from reflexive responses, we find it difficult to conceive of a purely noncognitive task. Furthermore, even if such a task could be found, it would be necessary to compare it with a measure of preference for cognitive speed (which surely would be confounded with cognitive capacity).

Second, is the Making Xs Test an appropriate instrument for assessing personal tempo? Does this test really assess temporal preference *independent of cognitive abilities?* Probably not. In fact, making Xs seems no less cognitive than many reaction-time measures. Certainly, the kinds of cognitive demands are different (attention to spatial dimensions and fine motor coordination in making Xs vs. attention to temporal onset and spatial location in Jensen's choice reaction-time task), but the relative magnitude of these demands is unclear. To what extent do individual differences in performance on this task reflect strategic differences, differences in simple motor speed, differential speed/accuracy tradeoffs, etc.? At present, we simply do not know.

In conclusion, the capacity for rapid cognitive processing probably is adaptive, relevant, and intelligent. However, the extent to which any given expression of that capacity is intelligent is apt to vary across cultures, situations, and task domains. Thus, the assessment of mental speed necessarily requires that the particular instantiations of mental speed that are tapped by our measurement instruments be equally relevant for all examinees.

Relevance of Measures of Mental Speed

Even if mental speed per se were found to be equally relevant to intelligent environmental adaptation across all cultures and subcultures, it would still be necessary to demonstrate the relevance of the specific tasks used to assess that speed. In the case of early infancy habituation studies, relevance may not be much of an issue. One of the major tasks facing the infant is the transformation of the initially novel elements of his or her environment into something more familiar and comprehensible. Thus, any habituation stimulus may be relevant to the infant simply because of its novelty, and habituation to almost any stimulus may be intelligent. In fact, Raaheim (1974) *defines* intelligence as the ability to transform what is relatively novel into something more familiar.

Although task relevance may not be at issue in infant habituation, it appears to pose a particularly sticky problem for automatization studies. On the one hand, if the task is high in contextual relevance (i.e., is genuinely important to environmental adaptation), it is likely that at least some subjects will have had prior experience with variants of the task (if not with the specific task itself). If the prior experience is approximately equal for all subjects, the consequences may be minimal: The behavior of interest may already be partially automatized, so that the obtained rate of automatization will reflect only the latter portion of the automatization curve. If, however, individuals differ in their prior experience, the behavior may be partially automatized for some individuals and not for others, in which case the interpretation of individual differences in the time required to achieve full automatization becomes problematic. On the other hand, if the task is low in contextual relevance, it may not be particularly intelligent to automatize performance. Indeed, even some relevant behaviors are best left unautomatized, because of the loss of responsive flexibility that necessarily accompanies automatized performance. Fortunately, contextual relevance often can be established within a specialized context that is relatively distinct from the individual's larger environment. If an individual knows that he or she will have to repeat a particular behavior 2000 times in a laboratory experiment, then automatization becomes relevant even if the task itself is totally irrelevant. Thus, the best measures of automatization are apt to be extremely novel, seemingly irrelevant tasks that must be performed rapidly for a long enough period of time to make automatization itself relevant and intelligent. Within any particular experimental context, the relevance of rapid automatization of a task is not necessarily dependent upon the contextual relevance of the task itself.

The same probably can not be said about typical choice reaction-time measures. Whereas automatization has the advantage of ultimately reducing the cognitive demands on the subject, millisecond improvements in choice reaction time may offer no particular advantage to the examinee. Of course, relevance might be established by offering rewards for rapid performance, but a deliberate emphasis on extrinsic motivation (possibly at the expense of any pre-existing intrinsic motivation) introduces a new set of complications that most of us would rather avoid. So, it appears that the relevance of these measures must be established by providing tasks in which high-speed performance is naturally advantageous. Most existing choice reaction-time measures fall somewhat short of this ideal.

Is relevance really essential in these studies, given the evidence that reaction times are not subject to conscious control, and hence are presumably unaffected by any perceptions of task relevance or irrelevance? We believe that it is, for a number of reasons. Although Jensen's (1980a) finding that instructing subjects to "try harder" or to "take it easy, don't try so hard" has no effect on performance is encouraging from some points of view, we do not find it to be compelling evidence that performance is unaffected by attentional factors. Indeed, these instructions keep the subjects' attention focused on the task at hand. If whistling "Dixie," listening to Berlioz, or counting backwards from 100 while performing the task could be shown to produce no change in reaction times, we would be inclined to agree that allocation of attentional resources (deliberate or otherwise) plays no role in task performance. In the absence of such evidence, insofar as relevance may affect attention to the task, some consideration of relevance seems essential.

Conclusions

In summary, mental speed appears to be adaptive and intelligent for at least some segments of western society on at least some tasks. A review of the contextual relevance of mental speed suggests that mental speed may be relevant for "all of the people, some of the time." However, any given measure of that speed is probably only relevant for some of the people, some of the time. If this is true, then theoretical understanding of the role of mental speed in intelligence, and the practical assessment of that speed, require knowledge of the specific kinds of mental speed that are relevant to specific groups or individuals in specific situations or conditions. In particular, it is likely that different cultural (and subcultural) attitudes about time and speed may lead to cultural (and subcultural) differences in the perceived relevance and intelligence of any specific instantiation of mental speed. However, despite these cultural variations, the capacity for mental speed is probably at least somewhat relevant and somewhat intelligent in virtually all cultures.

The relevance of our measures of that speed, however, is a bit more problematic. Many infant habituation and adult automatization paradigms provide a sort of de facto relevance because of their unique subject characteristics or because of the intrinsic advantages of speed within the specific experimental context. In infant habituation studies, the special characteristics of infants may provide some assurance that almost any novel stimulus will be of some relevance to the infant, if only because it is novel. And, given the extraordinary amount of initially novel information that every infant must process in order to make sense of this confusing new world, rapid processing is certainly an adaptive (and intelligent) behavior. In automatization studies that require subjects to perform the same task repeatedly over long periods of time, the task itself may be irrelevant but automatization is likely to be very relevant (and intelligent) because it will serve to reduce the cognitive demands of the task. Thus, although careful attention to the relevance of the tasks and stimuli employed in studies of habituation or automatization is desirable, it may not be essential. However, task or stimulus relevance is apt to play a substantial role in performance on measures of choice reaction time.

The relevance of speed in typical choice reaction-time paradigms is unclear. There is no obvious intrinsic advantage to high-speed responses, and the tasks themselves are of questionable relevance for most subjects. The relatively high correlation between choice reaction time and intelligence (e.g., Jensen, 1980b, 1982a; Vernon, 1981, 1983) suggests that the choice reaction-time tasks are tapping *something* that is related to measures of general intelligence. But is that something actually cognitive processing speed? Perhaps, but in the absence of convincing evidence against motivational or attentional explanations, such a claim seems premature.

THE COMPONENTIAL SUBTHEORY: SPEED OF WHAT?

Up to this point, we have described mental speed merely as speed of cognitive processing. But exactly what *kind* of cognitive processing is involved in the relationship between mental speed and general intelligence? According to the componential subtheory, metacomponential processing should account for much of the "intelligence" of mental speed. This view is consistent with the current evidence that strategic (i.e., metacomponential) differences are often associated with differences in intellectual ability. And, because different strategies lead to different combinations of lower order information-processing components (i.e., performance components), they almost certainly will produce differences in overall speed of performance. This is not to say that differences in the speed with which the performance components are executed are totally irrelevant to intelligence. However, we expect that these differences account for only a small proportion of the total variance in intelligence.

Mental Speed and Metacomponents

What is the evidence for individual differences in metacomponential processing, and how might these differences be related to mental speed and intelligence? One especially fruitful line of research has examined individual differences in information-processing *strategies*. Individual differences in solution strategies have been found for a wide variety of tasks, including the Raven Progressive Matrices (Hunt, 1974), sentence-picture verification (MacLeod, Hunt, & Mathews, 1978), linear syllogistic reasoning (Sternberg & Weil, 1980), mental rotation (Pellegrino & Kail, 1982), and visual comparison and representation (Cooper, 1982). Furthermore, many of these strategic differences appear to be related to individual differences in specific cognitive abilities, general intelligence, or both. For example, MacLeod, Hunt, and Mathews (1978) have found that the strategies subjects use on sentence-picture verification tasks can be predicted from their relative verbal and spatial abilities; Sternberg and Weil (1980) found a similar relationship for the use of linguistic vs. spatial strategies in the solution of linear syllogisms. In fact, Baron (1978) and Hunt (1978) have suggested that individual differences in global problem-solving strategies may account for a major portion of the variance in intelligence.

Additional evidence for the relationship between metacomponents and intelligence has been found in studies of analogical reasoning. For example,

Sternberg (1977) has found that more intelligent individuals are more consistent in their use of a systematic strategy for problem solution. Sternberg (1981) also has found that more intelligent individuals spend relatively more time on global planning (i.e., developing a strategy that will be applicable to a group of problems) and relatively less time on local planning (i.e., developing a specific strategy for each problem).

There also appear to be ability-related differences in the allocation of attentional resources. For example, Bransford et al. (1982) found that, in learning new information, attentional allocation was determined by the difficulty of the information for academically superior fifth-grade students, whereas difficulty had little or no effect on the attentional allocation of less able students. And in a study of executive processes in reading, Wagner and Sternberg (in press) found that more skilled readers were more likely to adjust their allocation of attentional resources to achieve specific reading objectives than were less skilled readers.

Individual differences in metacomponential processing have obvious implications for measures of mental speed. For example, if some strategies are faster than others, then individual differences in processing speed may be confounded with individual differences in strategy. Similarly, individual differences in attentional allocation may have a profound effect on problem-solving speed. For example, Marr and Sternberg (1986) found that, when intermediate-school students were required to incorporate novel information into an otherwise familiar verbal analogies task, intellectually gifted students allocated significantly more attention to relevant novel information than to irrelevant novel information; their nongifted peers, on the other hand, actually gave more attention to irrelevant than to relevant information. If mental speed were assessed using only the irrelevant condition, the results would indicate that gifted students were faster information processors than nongifted students. On the other hand, if mental speed were assessed using only the relevant condition, the results would indicate that gifted students were no faster than nongifted students.

Given that such metacomponential differences do exist and are related to other measures of intelligence, how might these differences be reflected in measures of habituation, automatization, and choice reaction time? We believe that metacomponents are likely to play a major role in all three phenomena. Furthermore, we believe that the correlation between intelligence and mental speed in these behaviors is largely a function of individual differences in the quality (and not just the speed) of metacomponential processing.

Little is known about the specific cognitive processes involved in infant habituation to novel stimuli. As mentioned earlier, Fagan and McGrath (1981) have argued that habituation rate is largely a function of recognition memory, rather than of simple processing speed. We are inclined to agree with this explanation, but with a metacomponential emphasis on the *strategic* aspects of memory transfer, storage, and retrieval. For any given stimulus, only a selected subset of stimulus properties can be committed to memory, so selective abstraction and encoding of the most useful and relevant properties is essential. The selection of an optimal subset of stimulus properties and optimal storage and retrieval cues will play a major role in the subsequent accessibility and utility of the information. If, as we suspect, the relationship between intelligence and differential attention to relevant vs. irrelevant information (Marr & Sternberg, 1986) begins to develop in infancy, then more intelligent infants will be likely to identify and attend to a small, relevant subset of stimulus characteristics, whereas less intelligent infants may devote more of their attention and processing resources to irrelevant stimulus characteristics. As a result of this strategic difference, more intelligent infants may actually engage in less (but more useful) information processing. Because they are committing only relevant information to memory, habituation will occur more rapidly than for less intelligent infants, even if there are no differences in memory capacity or in the speed of individual component processes.

The role of metacomponential processing in automatization is somewhat more obvious. At the very least, the individual must (a) identify the specific problem requirements; (b) select a solution strategy and a set of performance components to carry out that strategy; (c) monitor task performance and, if necessary, modify the preselected strategy; (d) discover which sequence (or sequences) of performance components are constant over problems or task repetitions; (e) determine the point at which the advantages of metacomponential monitoring are outweighed by its costs; and (f) relinquish metacomponential control of processing. It is easy to see how individual differences in these metacomponential processes could be related to individual differences in both speed of automatization and intelligence. Inaccuracy in identifying the problem (Stage 1) or inefficiency in the selected strategy (Stage 2) will lead the individual into a time-consuming feedback-correction loop (Stage 3), which must be terminated before the individual can determine which processes might be targeted for automatization (Stage 4). Furthermore, if Stages 1–3 are terminated prematurely, an inappropriate strategy will be carried over into the later stages, requiring additional metacomponential monitoring and altering the cost–benefit ratio of this monitoring in Stage 5. (For a discussion of premature termination of information processing sequences, see Sternberg & Rifkin, 1979, and Sternberg & Nigro, 1980.) Thus, the speed of automatization is probably less dependent upon the speed of metacomponential processing than on the accuracy of that processing.

Choice reaction time appears to be less metacomponential than habituation or automatization. As we noted earlier in this chapter, Jensen (1980a, 1982b) and Vernon (1981) have reported that no learning occurs as a result of repeated practice on the choice reaction-time task. Jensen (1980a) has also found that subjects are unable to estimate their own performance at better than chance levels, and are unable to increase or decrease their reaction times when instructed to do so. This evidence, combined with the fact that the choice reaction-time response may occur prior to the subject's conscious awareness of the stimulus, would seem to rule out any major role, at least at the conscious level, for metacomponents. At the same time, Jensen's claim that the correlation between reaction time and intelligence increases as a function of task *complexity* (albeit with a rather low ceiling on complexity) suggests that metacomponents probably are involved. We believe that these apparent contradictions can be resolved, and that metacomponential processing accounts for much of the reaction-time/intelligence correlation.

The claim that no practice effects occur over trials certainly seems to argue against extensive metacomponential solution monitoring or correction. Longstreth (1984) has criticized the methods by which practice effects were assessed (generally across sessions rather than within sessions), and has attempted to demonstrate that practice effects do, in fact, exist. However, Longstreth's experiments were conducted using a substantially modified version of Jensen's apparatus. Instead of simple lights, Longstreth's stimuli were digits (1-4), each displayed in the center of a video screen. Whereas Jensen's response buttons were directly adjacent to the stimulus lights, the buttons in Longstreth's apparatus were placed on a separate response console. Longstreth did find practice effects, but his modification of the original procedure introduces new transformations (digits) and memory requirements (location and assignment of response buttons) that were not present in the original task. Thus, it is not clear that Longstreth's results can be generalized to Jensen's measures of choice reaction time.

Perhaps Jensen and Vernon are correct, and practice effects do not occur. What might this absence of practice effects tell us about the choice reaction-time task? Possibly that the task is already automatized when subjects enter the laboratory. Considering the nature of the task, this may not be an entirely unreasonable assumption. The signal light–button press pairing occurs so frequently in our daily experience (in video games, multiline telephones, automated cameras, and a vast array of electronic equipment) that some degree of automatization seems almost inevitable. However, even if the task is already automatized, individual differences in metacomponential processing may shape task performance in at least two ways: through individual differences in allocation of attentional resources or in the particular response strategies that previously have been automatized.

Mental Speed and Performance Components

Obviously, individual differences do exist in the speed and efficacy with which performance components are executed. And even if metacomponents are the major determinants of intelligence, performance components undoubtedly have some impact on intelligence, if only because the metacomponents depend upon prompt and accurate feedback from the performance components. For most of these performance components, faster processing tends to be related to higher scores on psychometric measures of intellectual ability (Sternberg, 1977). In fact, Sternberg and Gardner (1983) have found correlations as high as .8 between certain component scores and scores on psychometric tests of inductive reasoning.

However, for at least one of these performance components (encoding), speed of execution is *negatively* correlated with measures of intellectual ability. Thus, even at the level of the performance components, high processing speed may not necessarily be indicative of intelligence. We suspect, however, that the relatively longer time spent on encoding by more intelligent individuals is a consequence of metacomponential strategy rather than simple processing speed. More intelligent individuals may well be encoding each bit of information more rapidly than their less intelligent counterparts, but they may be encoding more bits of information. Alternatively, more intelligent individuals may set a higher criterion for encoding accuracy, processing and reprocessing each bit of information until this criterion is reached. In other words, we believe that the capacity for rapid execution of performance components is likely to be related to intelligence, but that the metacomponential ability to employ that speed *selectively* is of far greater importance.

Although detailed information-processing models have not been developed for habituation, automatization, or choice reaction-time measures, the general performance components of encoding, combination, and comparison are certainly involved in all three tasks. Given the cognitive complexity of habituation and automatization (and the resulting metacomponential investment), we would expect the general speed with which performance components are executed to play a relatively minor role. However, within-task variability in speed across performance components may have substantial effects, particularly in the case of feedback mechanisms. For example, if high-speed execution of a performance component is coupled with relatively slow feedback from the performance component to the relevant metacomponents, there may be little opportunity for metacomponential corrections to occur; by the time an error is detected, the individual may already have moved on to another performance component.

This view of the effects of temporal variability is consistent with findings (e.g., Jensen, 1982a) that more intelligent individuals show less variability in choice reaction time (suggesting, perhaps, that metacomponential feedback and correction do play a role in choice reaction-time measures). However, as mentioned previously, the early onset of the response (possibly prior to conscious awareness of the stimulus) and the apparent absence of learning or practice effects suggest that much of the response may be automatized long before the individual is exposed to the specific experimental procedure.

Thus, the speed with which performance components are executed probably makes a larger contribution here than in habituation or automatization. In fact, many of the problems with choice reaction-time measures may result from the fact that performance on these measures depends so heavily upon the speed with which performance components are executed. In particular, it may account for the instability of reaction times and for the disturbing racial differences that typically are found on these measures (e.g., Jensen, 1982a).

Why should choice reaction-time measures be so unstable over time? Jensen (1982a) has suggested that this instability is an "intrinsic organismic phenomenon," and does not reflect measurement error in the instrumental sense. But what might account for this organismic temporal instability? Perhaps the answer may be found in the noncognitive correlates of reaction time. Kamiya (1961), for example, found that reaction time is affected by body temperature, which naturally fluctuates throughout the day. Woodworth and Schlosberg (1954) found evidence that reaction time also varies in response to various neuroactive drugs. Furthermore, both reaction time and the accuracy of temporal judgments (e.g., estimates of interval duration) have been shown to be related to anxiety, nutritional factors (i.e., relative amounts of proteins vs. carbohydrates in the diet), psychoactive drugs, and body temperature (e.g., Church, 1984; Meck, 1983). Given the nature of reaction-time measures, we can speculate that these noncognitive variables are likely to act at the level of the performance components. Given the nature of the noncognitive variables involved, their effects are likely to contribute not only to intra-individual variability (i.e., standard deviation of IT), but also to interindividual and intergroup variability (i.e., racial differences in IT).

Conclusions

In conclusion, it appears likely that the relationship between mental speed and intelligence is largely dependent upon individual differences in the use and outcomes (but not necessarily in the speed) of metacomponential processing. For example, the efficient use of metacomponential functions may increase the speed of infant habituation by reducing the amount of information that must be processed by the performance components (perhaps by identifying and directing attention to particularly relevant stimulus properties). In the case of automatization, accurate metacomponential processing may increase speed by facilitating the early selection and revision of appropriate processing strategies, allowing the individual to minimize the amount of time spent in costly feedback-correction loops. Metacomponents also may play a major role in choice reaction-time measures. Even if much of the task has already been automatized, speed of performance may depend as much upon the efficiency of the automatized strategy as on the actual speed of the individual performance components, thus providing an indirect indication of the quality of metacomponential processing that was involved in automatizing the task; in addition, attentional allocation may be an important determinant of choice reaction time.

Metacomponents probably do not tell the whole story. Just as metacomponential accuracy may contribute to mental speed and intelligence, the speed and accuracy with which performance components are executed may also play a role. In particular, the metacomponents can only function in response to prompt and accurate feedback from the various performance components. In general, the speed of task performance probably depends less upon the absolute speed of performance components than upon the variability of that speed, and the accuracy of the feedback the performance components supply.

In addition to the theoretical and empirical evidence, there are strong practical reasons for concentrating on metacomponents rather than performance components. In particular, the lower-order performance components are more likely to be affected by transient changes in the internal state of the organism (e.g., temperature, diet, anxiety). The relatively high sensitivity of performance components to these transient internal states may account for much of the instability in reaction-time measures (which probably are influenced more than any other measures by the absolute speed of performance components). Metacomponents, by contrast, are likely to be relatively stable and insensitive to such changes.

THE EXPERIENTIAL SUBTHEORY: PRACTICE MAKES PERFECT?

According to the experiential subtheory, the best measures of intelligence will be obtained from tasks that are either relatively novel or in the process of becoming automatized. Obviously, measures of habituation and automatization satisfy this criterion. Typical choice reaction-time tasks, however, do not appear to be particularly novel, and the apparent absence of practice effects (e.g., Jensen, 1980b) might seem to suggest that these tasks are not in the process of being automatized. And yet, relatively high correlations are consistently found between choice reaction-time and psychometric measures of intelligence. If the experiential subtheory is correct (and we believe, of course, that it is), how can we account for these results? We believe that the answer to this question lies in the nature of typical psychometric tests of intelligence.

The most obvious source of the reaction time–intelligence correlations would appear to be the shared emphasis on speed. However, the fact that the psychometric tests were administered *without* time constraints in Jensen's studies seems to argue against this explanation. It is conceivable that the correlation reflects, in part, a shared overemphasis on performance components, but this also seems unlikely. First, the fact that the correlation increases as the reaction-time task becomes more complex suggests that metacomponents play a major role. Second, given what we have said about the relative stability of metacomponents and performance components, an overemphasis on performance components (particularly on speed of performance components) would appear to be inconsistent with the relatively high test-retest reliabilities of most psychometric tests. Instead, we believe that the high correlations may reflect metacomponential consequences of the relative locations of the psychometric and reaction-time measures on a novelty-familiarity continuum.

Most psychometric intelligence test items are not particularly novel; nor are they in the process of being automatized. To be sure, they are not fully automatized either, but most test items depend upon the strategic selection and application of previously automatized sets of performance components. In general, even the strategic (metacomponential) requirements of the task are quite familiar to examinees. Thus, test scores are likely to depend heavily upon (a) the efficiency of previously automatized behaviors (reflecting the quality of the metacomponential processing employed in the automatization process); (b) the generalization of previously automatized behaviors to a new problem situation; (c) the appropriate selection, combination, and application of these automatized behaviors; and (d) optimal allocation of attentional resources to the current problem. We believe that these four determinants of test performance are also likely to be involved in choice reaction-time measures (although selection and combination probably play a much smaller role in the choice reaction-time paradigm).

In other words, neither psychometric intelligence tests nor reaction-time measures assess intelligence at an optimal point on the novelty–familiarity continuum (cf. Davidson & Sternberg, 1984). Both err in the direction of familiarity, and therefore invoke certain shared processes that are common to a variety of familiar tasks. These two kinds of tests probably measure similar subsets of intelligent behavior, and ignore many of the same higher level metacomponential aspects of intelligence.

SUMMARY

In this chapter, we have examined the relationship between mental speed and intelligence within the framework of Sternberg's (1985) triarchic theory of human intelligence. The triarchic theory (a) limits the domain of intelligence to that subset of mental activity that is relevant to the individual's successful interaction with the external environment (the *contextual subtheory*); (b) defines the classes of internal mental processes governing intelligent behavior (the *componential subtheory*); and (c) specifies optimal points on a novelty–familiarity continuum for the assessment of intelligence (the *experiential subtheory*).

A review of previous research on mental speed and intelligence suggests that the capacity for rapid cognitive processing probably is somewhat adaptive and intelligent across most, and possibly all, environments. However, the degree to which mental speed is adaptive and intelligent may vary across tasks and across individuals, so that measures of the *capacity* for mental speed are likely to be confounded by differences in *preference* for mental speed. Thus, understanding and assessment of intelligent mental speed depend upon knowledge of the specific kinds of mental speed that are relevant to specific groups of individuals in specific kinds of situations.

It appears likely that the relationship between mental speed and intelligence is largely dependent upon individual differences in the accuracy (but not necessarily in the speed) of metacomponential processing. The speed and accuracy with which performance components are executed undoubtedly contribute to intelligence, but their contribution is probably relatively small in relation to higher level metacomponential processes. In fact, we believe that individual differences in performance on most measures of mental speed are determined more by differences in the quality of metacomponential processing than by differences in the speed of performance components.

Speed of performance is an uncommonly attractive and convenient dependent variable. It is easily measured, often consequential, and clearly a product of cognitive functioning. Measures of mental speed appear to offer an elegant simplicity that has been lacking in so many other measures of intelligence. However, mental speed probably is not a simple construct, but rather the product of many complex mental processes, only some of which are related to intelligence. Thus, further advances in our understanding of intelligence may depend upon our ability to isolate and understand the specific component processes that contribute to the relationship between intelligence and mental speed.

REFERENCES

Baron, J. (1978). Intelligence and general strategies. In G. Underwood (Ed.), *Strategies in information processing.* London: Academic Press.

Berg, C. A., & Sternberg, R. J. (1984). *Implicit theories of intelligence across the adult life-span.* Unpublished manuscript, Yale University Department of Psychology, New Haven, CT.

Berg, C. A., & Sternberg, R. J. (1985). Continuity versus discontinuity in the developmental course of intelligence. In H. W. Reese & L. P. Lipsitt (Eds.), *Advances in child development and behavior* (Vol. 19). New York: Academic Press.

Bransford, J. D., Stein, B. S., Vye, N. J., Franks, J. J., Auble, P. M., Mezynski, K. J., & Perfetto, G. A. (1982). Differences in approaches to learning: An overview. *Journal of Experimental Psychology: General, 111,* 390–398.

Church, R. M. (1984). Properties of the internal clock. In J. Gibbon & L. Allen (Eds.), *Timing and time perception: Annals of the New York Academy of Sciences, Volume 423.* New York: New York Academy of Sciences.

Cooper, L. A. (1982). Strategies for visual comparison and representation: Individual differences. In R. J. Sternberg (Ed.), *Advances in the psychology of human intelligence* (Vol. 1). Hillsdale, NJ: Erlbaum.

Davidson, J. E., & Sternberg, R. J. (1984). The role of insight in intellectual giftedness. *Gifted Child Quarterly, 28,* 58–64.

Fagan, J. F., & McGrath, S. K. (1981). Infant recognition memory and later intelligence. *Intelligence, 5,* 121–130.

Heath, S. B. (1983). *Ways with words.* New York: Cambridge University Press.

Hunt, E. (1974). Quote the raven? Nevermore! In L. W. Gregg (Ed.), *Knowledge and cognition.* Hillsdale, NJ: Erlbaum.

Hunt, E. (1976). Varieties of cognitive power. In L. B. Resnick (Ed.), *The nature of intelligence.* Hillsdale, NJ: Erlbaum.

Hunt, E. (1978). Mechanics of verbal ability. *Psychological Review, 85,* 109–130.

Hunt, E., Frost, N., & Lunneborg, C. (1973). Individual differences in cognition. In G. Bower (Ed.), *The psychology of learning and motivation: Advances in research and theory* (Vol. 7). New York: Academic Press.

Hunt, E., & Lansman, M. (1982). Individual differences in attention. In R. J. Sternberg (Ed.), *Advances in the psychology of human intelligence* (Vol. 1). Hillsdale, NJ: Erlbaum.

Jensen, A. R. (1980a). *Bias in mental testing.* New York: Free Press.

Jensen, A. R. (1980b). Chronometric analysis of mental ability. *Journal of Social and Biological Structures, 3,* 103–122.

Jensen, A. R. (1982a). The chronometry of intelligence. In R. J. Sternberg (Ed.), *Advances in the psychology of human intelligence* (Vol. 1). Hillsdale, NJ: Erlbaum.

Jensen, A. R. (1982b). Reaction time and psychometric *g.* In H. J. Eysenck (Ed.), *A model for intelligence.* New York: Springer-Verlag.

Jensen, A. R., & Munro, E. (1979). Reaction time, movement time, and intelligence. *Intelligence, 3,* 121–126.

Jones, J. M. (1984). TRIOS: An approach to understanding black culture. *Social Science Newsletter, 69,* 2.

Jones, J. M., & Block, C. B. (1984). Black cultural perspectives. *Clinical Psychologist, 37,* 58–62.

Kahneman, D. (1973). *Attention and effort.* Englewood Cliffs, NJ: Prentice-Hall.

Kamiya, J. (1961). Behavioral, subjective, and psychological aspects of drowsiness and sleep. In D. W. Fiske & S. R. Maddi (Eds.), *Functions of varied experience.* Homewood, IL: Dorsey.

Lansman, M., Donaldson, G., Hunt, E., & Yantis, S. (1982). Ability factors and cognitive processes. *Intelligence, 6,* 331–345.

Lewis, M., & Brooks-Gunn, J. (1981). Visual attention at three months as a predictor of cognitive functioning at two years of age. *Intelligence, 5,* 131–140.

Longstreth, L. E. (1984). Jensen's reaction-time investigations of intelligence: A critique. *Intelligence, 8,* 139–160.

MacLeod, C. M., Hunt, E. G., & Mathews, N. N. (1978). Individual differences in the verification of sentence-picture relationships. *Journal of Verbal Learning and Verbal Behavior, 17,* 493–507.

Marr, D. B., & Sternberg, R. J. (1986). Analogical reasoning with novel concepts: Differential attention of intellectually gifted and nongifted students to contextually relevant and irrelevant novel information. *Cognitive Development, 1,* 53–72.

McCall, R. B. (1979). Individual differences in the pattern of habituation at 5 and 10 months of age. *Developmental Psychology, 15,* 559–569.

McCall, R. B., & Kagan, J. (1970). Individual differences in the infant's distribution of attention to stimulus discrepancy. *Developmental Psychology, 2,* 90–98.

Meck, W. H. (1983). Selective adjustment of the speed of internal clock and memory processes. *Journal of Experimental Psychology: Animal Learning Processes, 9,* 171–201.

Pellegrino, J. W., & Kail, R. (1982). Process analyses of spatial aptitude. In R. J. Sternberg (Ed.), *Advances in the psychology of human intelligence* (Vol. 1). Hillsdale, NJ: Erlbaum.

Raaheim, K. (1974). *Problem-solving and intelligence.* Oslo: Universitetsforlaget.

Spearman, C. (1927). *The abilities of man.* New York: Macmillan.

Spelke, E., Hirst, W., & Neisser, U. (1976). Skills of divided attention. *Cognition, 4,* 215–230.

Sternberg, R. J. (1977). *Intelligence, information processing, and analogical reasoning: The componential analysis of human abilities.* Hillsdale, NJ: Erlbaum.

Sternberg, R. J. (1981). Intelligence and nonentrenchment. *Journal of Educational Psychology, 73,* 1–6.

Sternberg, R. J. (1985). *Beyond IQ: A triarchic theory of human intelligence.* New York: Cambridge University Press.

Sternberg, R. J., Conway, B. E., Ketron, J. L., & Bernstein, M. (1981). People's conceptions of intelligence. *Journal of Personality and Social Psychology, 41,* 37–55.

Sternberg, R. J., & Gardner, M. K. (1983). Unities in inductive reasoning. *Journal of Experimental Psychology: General, 112,* 80–116.

Sternberg, R. J., & Nigro, G. (1980). Developmental patterns in the solution of verbal analogies. *Child Development, 51,* 27–38.

Sternberg, R. J., & Rifkin, B. (1979). The development of analogical reasoning processes. *Journal of Experimental Child Psychology, 27,* 195–232.

Sternberg, R. J., & Weil, E. M. (1980). An aptitude x strategy interaction in linear syllogistic reasoning. *Journal of Educational Psychology, 62,* 226–239.

Super, C. M., & Harkness, S. (1980). The infants' niche in rural Kenya and metropolitan America. In L. L. Adler (Ed.), *Issues in cross-cultural research.* New York: Academic Press.

Vernon, P. A. (1981). Reaction time and intelligence in the mentally retarded. *Intelligence, 5,* 345–355.

Vernon, P. A. (1983). Speed of information processing and general intelligence. *Intelligence, 7,* 53–70.

Wagner, R. K., & Sternberg, R. J. (in press). Executive processes in reading. In B. Britton (Ed.), *Executive control processes in reading.* Hillsdale, NJ: Erlbaum.

Woodworth, R. S., & Schlosberg, H. (1954). *Experimental Psychology.* New York: Holt, Reinhart, & Winston.

AUTHOR NOTES

This chapter was prepared while Diana Marr was a National Science Foundation predoctoral fellow at Yale University. Preparation of the chapter was facilitated by Contract N0001483K0013 from the Office of Naval Research and Army Research Institute.

CHAPTER 9

Inspection Time and Intelligence

T. Nettelbeck
University of Adelaide

This is the problem whether high speed in the performance of easy tasks can be taken as indicative of the ability to perform more difficult tasks without pressure of time. (Thurstone, 1937, p. 249)

1. INTRODUCTION

The construct *inspection time* (IT) described in this chapter is derived from a model for comparative judgment formulated by Vickers (1970, 1979), which assumes that processing leading to a decision begins with a series of covert, discrete samples or "inspections" from sensory input. Each inspection occupies a small, constant period of time. Thus, IT is one of a class of variously named constructs reflecting evidence that there is some temporal limitation to the rate at which information is taken in for processing, so that separate elements of information falling within some minimum duration are processed simultaneously. This concept of perceptual periodicity has a long history in psychology (James, 1890) but detailed experimental investigation of it appears to date from Stroud (1955).

The procedure for measuring IT proposed by Vickers, Nettelbeck, and Willson (1972) involves what would be a very simple visual discriminative judgment for almost anyone, across very wide ranges of age and of visual intellectual abilities, except that duration of the test figure is restricted to a brief exposure. This restriction results in a wide range of individual differences in the accuracy of performance, even within fairly homogeneous groups. We may note here that no differences have been found between the sexes in a number of different IT tasks (Longstreth, Walsh, Alcorn, Szeszulski, & Manis, 1985; Nettelbeck, 1973a; Nettelbeck & Kirby, 1983a; Raz, Willerman, Ingmundson, & Hanlon, 1983).

Much IT research has been concerned predominantly with comparisons between mildly retarded adults and nonretarded children and adults, these studies invariably demonstrating a marked deficiency among retarded adults that is equivalent to a lag in mental age (MA) of at least 4 years. This work has been reviewed elsewhere (Nettelbeck, 1985a) and will not be discussed further here, except in so far as it pertains specifically to issues under consideration.

In practice, IT is the target duration necessary for discriminative performance in a task like that devised by Vickers et al. (1972) to be virtually free from error. The possibility that individual differences in IT may reflect differences in measured intelligence (IQ) was first suggested by Nettelbeck and Lally (1976). However, it has largely been the initiative of Brand (1981, 1984; Brand & Deary, 1982) to give this idea theoretical substance.

Consideration of the problem referred to in the epigram opening this chapter, a quotation from Thurstone, begins in Section 2 with a discussion of the relevance of *mental speed* to an understanding of intelligence. Next, in Section 3, a rationale underlying the definition of IT is outlined, together with a description of different procedures for estimating IT. However, an evaluation of assumptions behind these procedures is left until Section 5, since the discussion of these assumptions is mainly relevant to the issue of an association between IT and IQ, research into which is therefore first reviewed in Section 4. Section 5 focuses on issues relevant to the reliability of different measures of IT and on whether IT provides an index of perceptual speed. Additional theoretical difficulties for the interpretation of IT not considered previously are also introduced in this section. Finally, an interpretation of available data, in the light of these various considerations, is made in Section 6. Throughout the chapter, possible directions for future research are suggested where these seem called for.

2. MENTAL SPEED

The intuition that there is a relationship between intelligence and some kind of mental quickness — both constructs being assumed to be relatively permanent individual attributes — also has an enduring history in psychology. Attempts to test this relationship may be said to have begun with Galton (1883), and in the 40 years following this pioneering initiative a substantial body of research was directed to the issue (McFarland, 1928). Although early research was largely either unsuccessful in demonstrating any association between speed and ability (Wissler, 1901), or highly problematical (Beck, 1933), a belief in some such relationship nonetheless generally prevailed. No comment has yet appeared in the literature on this topic (so far as I am aware) as to why this belief should have proved so resilient. Reasons can only be speculated about, but may include the desirability to an emerging behavioral science of the exact, ratio properties offered by timing events, when compared with the available, less precise, methods for estimating ability. Be that as it may, speed of intellectual functioning remained an important component of influential theories of intelligence developed by Thorndike (1926) and Thurstone (1938), and practical tests of abilities and aptitudes have traditionally allowed credit for faster performance.

Research evidence supporting an association between ability and mental speed exists, although it is by no means unambiguous. While individuals who produce correct solutions more quickly to test problems tend to get more items correct than slower performers, irrespective of time constraints (Dibner & Cummins, 1961; Heim, 1947; Heim & Batts, 1948; Heim, Watts, & Simmonds, 1974), more able individuals have not always been found to be faster in every situation than those less able (Jensen, 1982). Although correlations between various measures of reaction time (RT) and IQ have most commonly been negative, as predicted by a speed–intelligence hypothesis, they have usually been small and seldom more than −.3 (Hunt, 1980). Jensen (1979, 1982) has reported a stronger relationship when various parameters of RT from different tests are regressed on to IQ, but the strength of association has varied considerably across studies involving subjects of different age, education, ability, and race, and with different parameters of RT. Further, there are difficulties in accepting Jensen's interpretation of his results (Longstreth, 1984; Nettelbeck, 1985b; Nettelbeck & Kirby, 1983a), there being grounds on which to challenge the assertion that RT reflects only fundamental processes not influenced by higher-order cognitive skills.

Despite these doubts, it does appear from Jensen's results that IQ and some aspects of RT in these investigations could share from between about 10% to 40% of variance in performance. However, it is not clear from these studies what the nature of mental speed is or whether such speed is unitary (Jensen, 1979).

Cattell's view is that mental speed is not unitary. Thus, Cattell (1971) has pointed to empirical evidence for the existence of at least seven kinds of mental speed, these being expressed in different test situations. *Perceptual speed* and *speed of closure* are identified as primary abilities contributing to a broad, secondary "capacity" factor termed *power of visualization* (g_v), rather than to either of the major broad factors *fluid general intelligence* (g_f) or *crystallized general intelligence* (g_c). Three other kinds of speed, reflecting in turn cortical alertness, motivation, and aspects of personal tempo, are essentially personality characteristics but can influence abilities, contributing to a broad secondary factor termed *general cognitive speed* (g_s).[1] This is held to influence stages of information processing concerned with perceptual encoding, memory retrieval and executive control in relatively routine tasks or where some time stress is involved. Another primary speed ability, *motor speed,* relates to coordination rather than to intellectual abilities. Finally, Cattell discusses a seventh conceptualization which "corresponds to each and every ability, primary or secondary" (Cattell, 1971, p. 108). Although he appears to doubt the theoretical utility of such a general speed factor, he nonetheless identifies it as the "intellectual speed" defined by Furneaux (1960), linking it to "power intelligence" and loaded by g_f rather than by g_s.

The significant contribution of Cattell to this issue notwithstanding, the nature and extent of an association between mental speed and ability is still not known, despite a century of research directed to the possibility, as Berger's (1982) thorough review makes clear. In part, this is because limitations to the method of factor analysis make it incapable of unequivocally resolving theoretical dispute (Eysenck, 1967; Sternberg, 1977); but also because, as yet, few experimental psychologists have attempted to develop a theoretical framework adequate to sustaining a thorough analysis of mental speed (Berger, 1982). There have been exceptions, however.

Recent attempts to specify the nature of mental speed in relation to intelligence appear to stem from Eysenck's (1953, 1967) concern to direct the study of intelligence towards an experimental framework, as an adjunct to the prevailing correlational approach. As recounted by White (1982), Eysenck was responsible for initiating the investigations that Furneaux (1952, 1960), White (1973, 1982), and others have carried out to elucidate the significance of speed of performance in intelligence tests. Furneaux's work in particular influenced Eysenck's brief theoretical outline, which emphasized a dual variable termed "quality," constituted from "speed" and "power," as the major determinant of intellectual differences. Eysenck's model also allowed for some contribution from the mental processes and test materials involved, similar to Guilford's "structure-of-intellect" model (cf. "operations" and "contents," Guilford, 1956). Further, Eysenck recognized the influence on actual test performance of noncognitive personality variables identified by Furneaux as "accuracy" (an error-checking mechanism for rejecting incorrect solutions) and "continuance" (persistence in the face of task difficulty

---

[1]Hakstian and Cattell (1978) make some changes to the terminology of Cattell's (1971) theory, for example *general cognitive speed* being replaced by *general perceptual speed* (Gps). The two authors express somewhat different interpretations of this factor, Hakstian emphasizing that closure (i.e., "completing the gestalt"), in addition to speed, is involved. They also introduce a speculative third-stratum factor, *capacity to concentrate,* involving visualization and long-term retention capacities as well as Gps. However, these issues are not crucial to the present discussion.

rather than abandonment). Although the nature of speed and power were not spelled out, the quality of intellectual activity was assumed ultimately to be determined by the biological efficiency of nerve conduction.

This formulation has now been further developed in the light of work by Hendrickson and Hendrickson (1980; see also A. E. Hendrickson, 1982, and D. E. Hendrickson, 1982). Their theory seeks to explain their finding strong correlations between IQ and the average total length of the trace of evoked potential waveforms, obtained by electroencephalographic recording (EEG). This measure of EEG is hypothesized to reflect the activity of "chains" of "pulse trains" as information is processed by the brain. According to this model, those aspects of the brain responsible for intellectual performance do not differ significantly among normal individuals with respect to anatomy; the number of pulses within a train is constant; memory capacity is constant. However, characteristic, inherent variations in temporal intervals between pulses are held to exist between individuals; these variables introduce unreliability into information conveyed by the pulse train and IQ differences are the consequence of differences in the extent to which such error is present. In this view, mental speed, as revealed when performance is timed, is not a primary characteristic of brain activity but, rather, a secondary consequence of neural efficiency, inaccurate information processing resulting in slower transmission time (Eysenck, 1982, 1984). Thus, ambiguity in the earlier version of the theory about the relationship between power and speed is resolved; power derives from the capacity of the central nervous system to process information accurately, the speed of such processing reflecting that capacity.

Somewhat different theoretical formulations to Eysenck's have been advanced by Jensen (1979, 1982) and by Brand (1984; Brand & Deary, 1982). In part, however, differences between these three theories reflect the different experimental procedures used to collect the data bases from which the theories have been constructed, and substantive differences between them may be limited to Jensen's interpretation of mental speed. All three hold in common that mental speed is strongly associated with general intelligence (g); this concept of speed is therefore equivalent to Cattell's broad speed factor, rather than being limited to relatively narrow, specific domains of cognitive activity.

Jensen (1982) provides the most detailed account to date of his model for a relationship between RT and g. The brain is conceived as an information processor of limited capacity with respect to (a) the amount of information dealt with and the number of operations performed at any one point in time; and (b) the duration of short-term retention without the transformation required for long-term storage. Thus, rapid encoding and storage operations permit more accurate processing within a limited period of time, with individual differences in speed producing more profound effects with increasing processing complexity. As in Eysenck's theory, neural efficiency is assumed in normal cases to be an innate variable, the number of neural elements activated by a given level of stimulus energy being dependent upon the level of "noise" within the system. Although not stated explicitly, a basic assumption in this theory is that differences in IQ are in part the consequence of differences in chronic levels of internal noise. However, individual differences in mental speed are central to Jensen's theory and not simply the outcome of inaccurate processing. In addition to the ratio of signal to noise elements activated, periodicities in these elements in oscillation between excitation and refractoriness contribute to RT. Jensen does not specify in detail how speed is transformed into power, other than to speculate about relative advantage from the cumulative effect of more rapid processing over very long periods of time. His model does not distinguish between the speed of different operations or stages within the overall process, although his discussion of capacity limitations (Jensen, 1982) suggests that he is essentially concerned with central aspects of processing, rather than with peripheral input or response execution stages.

The theory advanced by Brand (1984; Brand & Deary, 1982) specifies that it is initial *speed of apprehension* during the early stages of perception that determines the development of general intelligence. "Speed of apprehension" and "perceptual speed" are used synonymously to mean the speed "of the brain's immediate reaction to sensory input — in the absence of any requirement for 'thought'." (Brand & Deary, 1982, p. 134). Thus, while "quick on the uptake," a person having high IQ will not necessarily appear to respond quickly, since many everyday situations will involve higher-level complex post-perceptual decisions, and the need to translate such decisions into action. This model therefore avoids what Sternberg (1984) has termed the "smart as fact" fallacy (p. 283), by distinguishing between speed of input at the beginning of stimulus encoding that cannot be influenced by conceptual or personality variables, and the speed of subsequent processes, which can be so influenced.

The capacity to take in information more quickly is held to increase with ontogenetic development. Brand's theory also allows the possibility that normal development sets some maximum ceiling rate to perceptual processing, which would eventually result in an asymmetrical, less spread distribution of speed compared to the IQ distribution. For this reason, and because g_f is held to exert greater influence than g_c on performance at younger levels of MA, Brand argues that the speed–ability relationship should be more discernible at younger MA. Thus, although speed of apprehension provides the basis for intellectual development, additional genetic and environmental variables not directly determining this speed increasingly come to influence intellectual functioning. Individual differences with respect to such genetic determinants permit the possibility also that some persons having higher IQ will not also have above-average speed of apprehension; i.e., high speed of apprehension may be a sufficient but not a necessary condition for high adult IQ.

Brand's theory is specifically concerned with speed of intake as fundamental to g, being derived directly from research into an association between IT and IQ. However, the theory is not inconsistent with Eysenck's, insofar as Brand considers that differences in mental speed may derive from differences in general neurological reliability, rather than from specific mechanisms that determine temporal functioning.

3. THE MEASUREMENT OF INSPECTION TIME (IT)

3.1 Rationale

Vickers et al. (1972) described an early version of Vickers' "accumulator model" for discriminative judgment, which provided a theoretical rationale for estimating IT, conceptualized as a fundamental temporal limitation to the capacity of early perceptual processing. The summary of the theoretical context which follows is limited for the present to procedures for measuring IT, but will be expanded in Section 5.2(d), where limitations to the rationale for these measurement procedures will be discussed. The assumption held either explicitly or implicitly in most research to be reviewed in this chapter, viz., that IT does provide a valid measure of perceptual speed, will be evaluated in Section 5.3(c).

Briefly, the accumulator model assumes that sensory representation of stimulation relevant to the required discrimination is accumulated over time as it enters the processing system. This accumulation occurs against a background of existing *neural noise* arising from various external and internal sources. Evidence favouring alternative decisions is summated in separate memory registers, one for each alternative outcome. Accumulation proceeds as a sequence of discrete inspections, each contributing some variable quantity of information to the decision but occupying a constant period of time (i.e., IT). A decision is made when evidence favouring one outcome summates to a predetermined level that reflects the *degree of caution* adopted by the individual for that particular judgment on that occasion. Thus, outcome is the consequence of a race between the contents of alternative counters; for a 2-choice discrimination task, the accumulation process may be conceptualized as two unidirectional random walks (Vickers, 1979). The overall time taken when making a response is therefore mainly determined by the level of caution adopted by the individual beforehand together with the individual's IT, according to the following equation:

$$L = (N \times IT) + t, \text{ where } L = \text{response latency};$$
$$N = \text{total number of inspections made to reach a decision};$$
$$IT = \text{inspection time};$$
$$t = \text{residual nondecision time associated with sensory delay and motor performance.}$$

According to this formulation, IT could be measured in a task requiring only a single inspection, providing that the initial inspection favoured the correct response and that t was eradicated. Vickers et al. (1972) argued that these requirements were satisfied by a discrimination task involving two lines of different length, the difference between these being equivalent to 0.8° of visual angle. This value was more than 2.58 times 0.3°, their estimate of the likely upper limit of noise in the human visual system, derived from their reanalysis of data from elderly persons.[2] Provided that the observer had the opportunity to make one inspection of the sensory data, this task should result in virtually error-free performance. By varying the exposure duration of the discriminanda, it should be possible to estimate the minimum period required for error-free performance, independently from the time taken to register a response. This procedure should therefore exclude the effects of t, and also of conceptual factors related to motivation and caution which, in the case of RT measures, would be expected to result in more than a single inspection.

The theoretical significance of this last point has not been acknowledged by all researchers adopting the IT construct. Thus, Sen and Goswami (1983) followed a lines-discrimination procedure without restricting access to short-term visual storage, in line with Brand and Deary's (1982) opinion that backward masking (see below) may not be critical. However, although it may prove possible to develop a method for measuring IT outside of a masking procedure (an option considered further in Section 6), for the methods described in Section 3.2 some kind of restriction is essential to prevent (or at least to minimize) intrusion by subjective cognitive variables determining caution. The theoretical standing of IT as a precognitive variable rests on this restriction. Similarly, tasks used by Mackenzie and Bingham (1985) and Irwin (1984) introduce problems of interpretation. The former task required that subjects scan the screen to locate the target, therefore introducing the

---

[2]Vickers et al. (1972) defined noise as the standard deviation of a distribution of magnitude in sensory effect from stimulation. Thus, the expected probability of error following one inspection from a difference corresponding to 0.8° would be less than .005.

likelihood that more than one inspection would be necessary, so that strategy differences could arise. Irwin's task, involving the identification of an alphabet character, is arguably sufficiently difficult to require several inspections in order to offset levels of internal noise.

Vickers et al. (1972) achieved precisely restricted target exposure by using a backward masking procedure to overwrite the target stimulus, thereby preventing additional processing beyond the duration between target onset and mask onset ("stimulus-onset-asynchrony" or SOA). An estimate (λ) of IT was objectively defined as the target stimulus duration that was found empirically to coincide with 97.5% accuracy.[3] This point could be determined, by interpolation if necessary, from the theoretical function best describing the relationship between target stimulus duration and the accuracy of responding. Vickers et al. (1972) argued that, although this function should be linear and described by $0.5(1 + f)$, where f is the ratio of target exposure duration to IT, sources of random error would produce a negatively accelerated function conforming to the top half of a cumulative normal distribution with a mean of zero (i.e., zero duration at 50% accuracy).

Subsequent experiments to test assumptions underlying the measurement of IT suggested that these assumptions were justified. Thus, response accuracy as a function of target exposure conformed closely to the theoretical normal ogive, as shown in Figure 1 (Lally & Nettelbeck, 1977; Vickers et al., 1972). Repeated measures of IT found little difference (mean λ approximately 100 ms on each occasion), with a correlation of 0.8 between measures (Vickers et al., 1972). Estimates of noise from the same subjects ranged from 0.26° to 0.48° with a mean of 0.30°, clearly of the order expected on the proposed rationale (Nettelbeck, 1972, 1973b; Vickers et al., 1972). Although Nettelbeck (1972) also found that noise measures could be more than doubled to 0.66° by stress (occasioned by the expectation of electric shock), this did not appear to pose difficulties for the procedure, since subsequent measures of λ with a stimulus difference equivalent to 1.6° (i.e., twice as large as the difference employed by Vickers et al.) were not discernibly different from initial estimates (Nettelbeck & Lally, 1976; Lally & Nettelbeck, 1977).

3.2 Procedure

A variety of discrimination tasks involving different stimuli in different modalities, and following various masking procedures, with different means of presentation, number of trials, accuracy criteria, and forms of response, have been used to measure IT (Brand & Deary, 1982; Nettelbeck, 1982,

---

[3]The symbol of λ is reserved throughout for estimates of IT defined in terms of 97.5% accuracy. At other levels of accuracy the term SOA is used. This distinction makes it clear when direct comparisons can be made between different measures of IT using the common metric λ.

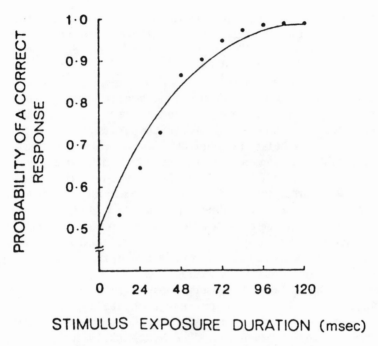

STIMULUS EXPOSURE DURATION (msec)

FIGURE 1.   Probability of a correct response as a function of stimulus exposure duration. (After Vickers et al., 1972, Figure 9a).

1985a). Alternative versions have, for example, required discrimination between two or more lights, or lines in different locations, identifying the temporal order of two tones or two vibrators, or the relative pitch of two tones, or the recognition of various symbols and alphabet characters. There will be further discussion about these alternatives in sections to follow. The most frequently used task has required discrimination between two lines of different length, as described in the previous section. Typically, the difference between these lines has been between 0.8° and 1.6°, with the target exposed continually up to the time of mask onset and employing a pattern mask to limit exposure. Figure 2 illustrates a form of this task, used commonly by Nettelbeck and others in Adelaide, and hereafter referred to as the "2-lines" version.

This procedure results in "central" masking, as defined by Turvey (1973). Turvey demonstrated two kinds of masking, the effect occurring either peripherally (not capable of binocular integration) or centrally (binocular integration), depending on the form of the mask and the relative intensities of target and masking figures. Although there is controversy about whether two separate processes are involved, as opposed to the same process in different conditions (Felsten & Wasserman, 1980), the demonstration of two types of

a   **b**

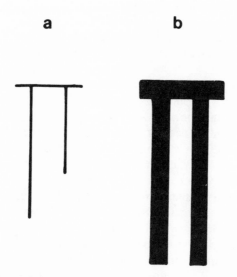

FIGURE 2.   The 2-lines discrimination task for measuring inspection time: (a) target figure; (b) masking figure.

masking can pose a problem for interpreting results obtained by different procedures from subjects differing in age or ability, unless locus of masking is known to be the same.

To date, two studies have defined locus of masking in the IT task. Nettelbeck, Hirons, and Wilson (1984, Experiment 1) used a dichoptic procedure with a 2-lines task to present target and mask to separate eyes, so that masking could only occur centrally. Individual measures of λ from the same six mildly mentally retarded and six nonretarded adult subjects remained essentially the same as when made with the usual binocular procedure. Nettelbeck and Wilson (1985, Study 1) have confirmed this finding for two samples of 10 normal children aged about 8 and 12 years respectively, compared with 10 university undergraduates. Not only were within-group measures of IT essentially the same for binocular and dichoptic conditions but the same outcome was obtained when a variable interval was introduced between target offset and mask onset (ISI), within both binocular and dichoptic conditions. These manipulations confirmed constant SOA for a given level of accuracy, irrespective of target duration, and therefore conformed to Turvey's "additive rule" (Turvey, 1973, Experiment V), established by him as a functional test for central masking. Nettelbeck et al. (1984, Experiment 2) also obtained results consistent with the additive rule for eight mildly retarded and six nonretarded young adults, but using a different task requiring a judgment about which of two lights in different positions was turned on momentarily before backward masking by a bank of lights. (This procedure was devised by Smith, 1978, and is referred to here as the "2-lights" task). Thus, it can reasonably be assumed that, at least for the 2-lines and 2-lights tasks as used in Adelaide, the masking effect is equivalent across a wide range of MA and IQ.

Although procedural details have been different, virtually all investigations have used some version of one of two basic psychophysical procedures to vary target duration. The *method of constant stimuli* (MCS) incorporates a fixed number of trials at each of several specific target exposure durations (i.e., SOAs), selected from within a wide range which includes the expected level of IT. Most commonly, different target durations are presented within a quasi-random sequence, but, even when target durations are constant within blocks of trials, markedly similar results may be obtained, at least for mildly retarded and nonretarded adults (Nettelbeck, Kirby, Haymes, & Bills, 1980). Different versions of the *method of limits* have been applied, with those investigators who have access to computer-controlled technology preferring some form of the *adaptive staircase* version. Under this method, testing begins at a long SOA, and subsequent exposures are reduced or lengthened as required, each change being determined by the accuracy of responding at a given SOA. The aim is to determine SOA coincident with a specified level of accuracy. Typically, the staircase method results, within a small number of trials, in a level of accuracy close to that required. Those trials that then follow involve judgments that "home in" on the SOA finally determined as reflecting IT. This method therefore has the advantage of controlling for individual differences in the extent of practice required before achieving a specified level of accuracy, an important consideration when comparing different age or ability groups. The version used in Adelaide, and the one for which most reliability data are available (see Section 5.1) was derived from the algorithm termed "Parameter Estimation by Sequential Testing" (PEST), developed by Taylor and Creelman (1967). However, the adaptive methods used by others are similar (e.g., Irwin, 1984; Mackenzie & Bingham, 1985).

4. INSPECTION TIME (IT) AND IQ

Research on this topic is summarized in Tables 1, 2, and 3 according to whether a verbal ability test was used (Table 1), or some combination of the Performance subscales from the Wechsler Adult Intelligence Scale (WAIS) (Table 2), or a test of general intelligence (Table 3). This scheme follows Muñiz and Lubin (1985), but extends their presentation by including additional research, together with data from some studies that are not available from the published versions of those studies. Further, a common estimate of IT (λ) has been employed throughout, thereby permitting the direct compari-

son of different results.[4] Those studies that have reported WAIS Verbal IQ
(VIQ) and Performance IQ (PIQ) separately from Full Scale IQ (FSIQ) are to
be found in all three tables. However, the tables are not comprehensive and
some studies considered below have not been included, either because insufficient details were available or because details were too complex to be summarized in this way.

4.1 IT and Verbal Ability

Nettelbeck and Lally's (1976) finding of a strong correlation between IT and
WAIS-PIQ but not VIQ suggested that some basic limitation in rate of perceptual sampling might particularly influence outcome in tasks, like the PIQ
subtests, where time limits apply and which involve visual organization and
integration. Evidence that masking in the IT task interrupts some central decision network (Section 3.2) suggested that the limitation was centrally located. This conclusion was supported by the reported correlation between IQ
and an alternative version of the IT measure for auditory discrimination
(Brand & Deary, 1982). Thus, if similar results were obtainable in more than
one modality, IT must involve more than just peripheral visual limitations.

The notion of some central limitation that is not general, but applies only
in situations under specific time constraints, does not accord with Brand's
theory (Section 2) that IT reflects general intellectual capacity. Instead,
Brand argued that IT should be found to correlate with tests loading on *g,*
including tests of verbal abilities which, although obviously reflecting education and culture to some extent, are also known to load strongly on the g factor. Brand and Deary (1982) advanced evidence in support of this position.

The various results shown in Table 1 do not resolve this issue. Among those
from adult subjects, two are questionable because of small samples that have
included mentally retarded persons together with subjects of high ability
(Deary, 1980; Nettelbeck & Lally, 1976). Such combinations were queried by
Mackintosh (1981), and have since been demonstrated to inflate correlation,
individuals with IQ lower than about one standard deviation (SD) below average performing too differently in timed tasks to be regarded as being from
the same population as average to above-average subjects (Nettelbeck &
Kirby, 1983a,b).

---

[4]It is possible to compare different absolute measures of SOA obtained from different levels
of accuracy directly, if it is assumed that the function relating response accuracy to SOA conforms to the top half of a cumulative normal ogive that passes through zero duration at 50% accuracy. As outlined in Section 3.1, this assumption is justified. Thus, λ (SOA at 97.5% accuracy)
can be calculated from any other SOA (say at 85% accuracy) by multiplying the latter by the ratio
of Z scores defining the 97.5 and 85th percentiles under the normal curve; in this case 1.96 ÷ 1.04
= 1.88, so that λ = SOA at 85% accuracy × 1.88.

TABLE 1
IT(λ) and Verbal Ability

Author	Subjects	Age (years)	n	Task	Psychophysical procedure
Nettelbeck & Lally[b] (1976)	University students and retarded adults	16–22	10	1. 2-lines[c] 2. 2-lines	MCS MCS
Hartnoll (1978)[d]	School children	11–12	18	1. Animal names (visual)	Method of limits (ascending)
				2. Animal pictures	Method of limits (ascending)
Grieve (1979)	Adults	16–28	10	2-lines	adaptive/MCS
Deary (1980)	Retarded and nonretarded adults	17–25	17	1. 2-lines 2. 2-tones	adaptive/MCS adaptive/MCS
Nettelbeck (1982)	University students	19–48	45	2-lights	PEST
Sharp (1982)	Adolescents and adults	15–36	12	2-lines	adaptive/MCS
Hulme & Turnbull (1983)	School children	6–7	65	2-lines	MCS
Smith & Stanley (1983)	School children	12–13	107	2-lines	MCS
Vernon (1983)	University students	18–34	50	2-lines	adaptive
Irwin (1984)	School children	11–13	47	1. 2-alphabet characters (visual) 2. 2-tones	adaptive adaptive
Nettelbeck (1985c)	Nonretarded adults	17–40	1. 43 2. 40	2-lines 2-lines	MCS PEST
Mackenzie & Bingham (1985)	University students	18–48	1. 16[h] 2. 13	2-lines[i]	adaptive

Notes:
[a]Published results have been converted where necessary to λ (i.e. SOA at 97.5% accuracy; see Footnote 4). Weights applied are Hartnoll, Grieve, 1.19; Deary (1.) 1.53; Sharp, 1.19; Hulme & Turnbull, 1.53; Vernon, 1.19; Irwin, 3.56; Mackenzie & Bingham, 3.56.
[b]A further breakdown is shown in Nettelbeck (1982, Appendix 1).
[c]Vertical lines as in Figure 2 unless stated otherwise.
[d]Reported by Brand & Deary (1982, Table 1).
[e]Australian Council for Educational Research.
[f]Brief form; Dr. C. Hulme, personal communication, December, 1985, February, 1986.
[g]Correlations between IT and verbal ability tests.
[h]1. Strategy users; 2. Strategy non-users.
[i]Horizontal lines, screen placement varied.

Mean, (SD), range	λ (ms)[a]	Test	Mean, (SD), range, IQ	Correlation IT-IQ	p (one-tailed)
–	98–554	WAIS VIQ	82, (22), 49–124	1. – .32	n.s.
–	100–804			2. – .41	n.s.
–	48–131	Vocabulary + verbal reasoning + verbal fluency	"normal"	1. – .54	< .05
–	36–83			2. + .20	n.s.
99, (24)	71–143	Mill Hill Vocabulary	101, (15), 81–125	– .88	< .01
–	31–1071	Mill Hill Vocabulary	98, (21), 59–135	1. – .69	< .01
–	6–160			2. – .66	< .01
98, (–)	50–173	Verbal reasoning[e] (ACER-AL)	127, (–), 104–135	– .34	< .05
45, (12)	30–71	AH4 Vocabulary	"normal"	– .69	< .01
164, (30)	107–268	WISC-R VIQ[f]	116, (18), 75–152	– .08	n.s.
104, (88)	12–460	1. Reading comprehension	(See table 3)[g]	1. + .04	n.s.
		2. Vocabulary		2. + .12	n.s.
127, (30)	61–224	WAIS-VIQ	122, (9), 103–137	+ .02	n.s.
646, (422)	–	Mill Hill Vocabulary	99, (11)	1. – .09	n.s.
696, (641)	–			2. – .32	< .01
80, (52)	37–336	WAIS-R VIQ	117, (14), 87–142	1. – .34	< .05
83, (44)	41–259		116, (14), 87–142	2. – .38	< .01
236, (41)	–	WAIS VIQ	118, (9)	1. + .06	n.s.
288, (48)	–		117, (9)	2. – .18	n.s.

Grieve (1979) and Sharp (1982) strongly support the hypothesis of an IT-verbal ability correlation, although Grieve's result is due entirely to six subjects in the IQ 81–105 range (reported by Brand & Deary, 1982, Table 1), so that sampling error is a possibility. Three sets of results from Nettelbeck (1982, 1985c) also support this hypothesis, although the former study did use a verbal reasoning test to which time constraints apply. However, the similarity of outcome for three separate measures of IT, with samples of 40 or more for both the lines and lights tasks and with different psychophysical procedures, does provide reliability for these results, the mean r from which is $-.35$.[5] However, Vernon (1983) and Mackenzie and Bingham (1985) have found no evidence of correlation between IT and WAIS-VIQ. Vernon's method does not appear to be distinguishable from others employing the same procedure (see also Nettelbeck, 1982, Appendix 1). Although his sample had well above average IQ scores, this was equally the case for Nettelbeck's 1982 study. Mackenzie and Bingham's result is not necessarily as critical to the hypothesis as Vernon's, however. The outcome among their subjects, using a detection strategy based on apparent movement (i.e., group 1 in Table 1), should be discounted, since this group has introduced a cognitive variable not systematically operative in other studies. The possible influence of strategies on IT will be discussed in Section 5.7, but it should be noted here that the effect of this particular apparent movement strategy would be to reduce correlation (Egan, 1985). With respect to Mackenzie and Bingham's group 2, measures of λ calculated from their data are substantially longer than is typically found for nonretarded adults in a 2-lines task (refer to Tables 1, 2, 3, and Nettelbeck, 1982, Appendix 1). This outcome may reflect the relative difficulty of their task, which involved two horizontal lines presented in different and unpredictable screen locations, so that individual differences in visual scanning could have influenced the accuracy of performance.

A recent study by Cooper, Cumberland, and Downing, not included in Table 1, should also be considered here. (Details have been provided by N. J. Mackintosh, personal communication August, 1985; see also Brand, 1984, p. 59). Cooper et al., found a correlation of $-.17$ between IT for 2-lines and vocabulary scores among 45 secondary school students aged 15 and 16 years, whose IQ ranged from 91 to 128. (IQ was measured by the Cattell Culture Fair Test, but has here been converted to the WAIS equivalent). Including this outcome with the other seven sets of results for adult subjects (Grieve, 1979; Sharp, 1982; Mackenzie & Bingham, 1985; Nettelbeck, 1982, 1985c, two sets; Vernon, 1983), the mean correlation between IT and verbal ability is $-.29$; the median value is $-.34$.

---

[5]Wherever mean correlations have been calculated from samples of different size, coefficients have been transformed to Fisher's z and weighted according to the degrees of freedom for each sample before averaging, as described by Guilford (1965, pp. 348–349).

Among the investigations involving children, Hartnoll (1978, reported by Brand & Deary, 1982) provides strong support for the hypothesis of a correlation between IT and verbal ability in one condition but not in the other. Further, since this task involved identifying animal names and pictures, the outcome is also consistent with a word-knowledge explanation. Sen and Goswami (1983) have also reported correlations of − .56 and − .48 (age partialled out) between two versions of IT and a Hindi translation of the Peabody Picture Vocabulary Test (PPVT) among 48 Indian schoolchildren aged 6 to 11 years. However, since this study did not employ a masking procedure to limit processing subsequent to target exposure, MA differences in cognitive strategies cannot be excluded. Support from Irwin (1984) is equivocal, although the results from this study should also be viewed with caution. Irwin's visual task required distinguishing between dot-matrix versions of a lower case *o* and an umlauted *ü*; since means and SDs for λ in this study were inordinately large and measurement distributions markedly skewed, it is possible that some participants did not understand what was required. Similarly, results for the auditory task suggest that some subjects encountered considerable difficulty in making the discrimination, although results here favoured some association between IT and verbal ability.

Although the remaining two studies in Table 1 (Hulme & Turnbull, 1983; Smith & Stanley, 1983) found no correlation between IT and verbal ability, these results are consistent with an IT–MA association. Both studies followed similar procedures, so that comparison is justified. Mean λ among the younger children (Hulme & Turnbull) is significantly longer (z = 4.72); furthermore, reanalysis of Smith and Stanley's IT data has found significantly slower λ among 12- than 13-year-olds ($p < .01$).[6] Direct evidence that IT becomes faster with ontogenetic development, at least until 11 to 13 years of age, is provided by a series of investigations by Wilson (1984). The major study (which appears in the dissertation as Experiments 2.1 and 2.2) employed a cross-sectional design to compare IT among children aged 6 to 12 years and adults, together with a longitudinal follow-up on most children, so as to distinguish maturation effects on IT from effects due to cohort and practice. Longitudinal change after 1 year could not be explained as resulting from practice, and cross-sequential analyses established that IT became shorter with increasing age, independently of cohort. The correlation between IT and MA (PPVT) during the first year of the study was − .43 (n = 70),[7] a result comparable to Scallon's test with a similar sample (reported by Brand, 1984, p. 60). Since MA and chronological age (CA) were confounded in these studies, Wilson (1984, Experiment 6) made a second experiment,

---

[6]I am grateful to Dr. Glen Smith for providing me with the IT data from this study.

[7]A published account of this study is to be found in Nettelbeck & Wilson (1985, Study 3). However, this does not include correlations between IT and ability measures.

comparing children at different IQ levels (Raven Coloured Progressive Matrices) while controlling for MA. IT was measured for two MA groups (8 and 11 years), each consisting of below-average but nonretarded (IQ 80–90), average (IQ 95–114), and above-average (IQ 122–135) subsets (n = 8). Consistent with other experiments in her thesis, Wilson found significantly slower IT in the MA-8 group but, within MA groups, IT did not correlate significantly with IQ. This finding indicates that, if retarded persons are excluded, then, until adult levels of performance are reached, it is MA that correlates with IT. The general developmental trend discernible from Wilson's experiments is shown in Figure 3. The hypothetical extension of this curve prior to age 6 is supported by Hosie's (1979) measure of IT for 4-year-olds (see Table 3, below) and by Lasky and Spiro's (1980) assessment of processing speed in infants aged 5 months, using a backward masking procedure. The forward extension of the function to old age reflects results from Nettelbeck (unpublished, reported by Nettelbeck, 1985a) and Wenger (1975-78). Briefly, this work has found a significant increase in IT beyond 50 years of age, but with a more marked increase beyond age 60, and with IT among persons more than 70 years about 90% longer than measures among young adults.

Wilson's results are broadly consistent with Brand's theory, pointing to a change with maturation in some central processing mechanism. Similarly, Nettelbeck's (1982, 1985c) finding of moderate correlations between IT and verbal ability support the notion of some relationship between IT and g. However, Brand's theory also predicts individual differences in IT with wide ability differences within a given age cohort during childhood, with such dif-

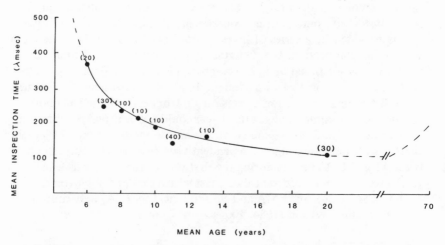

FIGURE 3.   Relationship of inspection time to age. (After Wilson, 1984, Figure 7.1; see also Nettelbeck, 1985a, Figure 2). The numbers of subjects in each group are shown in brackets.

ferences more pronounced at younger MAs, particularly where the ability test loads on g_f. Although the VIQ scales employed by Hulme and Turnbull (1983) would be expected to load more on g_c, and their sample combined 6- and 7-year-olds without age comparisons, this study does appear to have included an adequate sample-size and a sufficiently wide IQ range to provide some kind of test of this prediction. However, mean VIQ (Table 1) confirms that the sample had unusually high average ability,[8] so that ceiling effects in IT were a possibility. Therefore, that these results do not support Brand's theory is not necessarily critical to his position.

In summary, the question of an IT–verbal ability correlation remains unresolved, with some evidence consistent with this proposal but some not. Future researchers should note, however, that the wide variety of tasks and procedures adopted by various investigators makes interpretation of studies to date a risky business. There is a need for agreement on common ways for measuring IT if comparable research findings are to accumulate.

4.2 IT and PIQ

As shown in Table 2, a statistically significant IT-PIQ correlation has been found in all studies except two (Smith & Stanley, 1983; Vernon, 1983). The low correlation found by Mackenzie and Bingham (1985) among subjects using a detection stragegy based on apparent movement (i.e., group 1 in Table 2) should be discounted for the reasons already discussed in Section 4.1. Similarly, results from Nettelbeck and Lally (1976), who employed a mixed retarded and nonretarded sample, should be removed from consideration.

A possible explanation for the near-zero correlations found by Smith and Stanley lies in the fact that their subjects were not practiced in the task beforehand (Smith & Stanley, 1983, p. 361), which could result in a degree of unreliability. This suggestion is supported by the large SDs shown in Tables 2 and 3, these values being about twice what has commonly been found with a mean of this order (Nettelbeck, 1982, Appendix 1). Dr. Smith has also confirmed (personal communication, January, 1986) that about 17% of all cases tested were lost because goodness-of-fit between data and the theoretical function (described in section 3.1) was unsatisfactory. However, even among the remaining studies in Table 2, the range of correlations is still wide; from $-.24$ to $-.71$ for retarded adults, and from $+.15$ to $-.72$ for nonretarded adults and children. The means from these instances provide the only estimate available concerning the strength of the IT-PIQ association; for nonretarded and retarded subjects separately, the means are $-.33$ and $-.45$, respectively. Thus, the IT–PIQ relationship appears to be stronger among retarded samples, as has been noted previously (Brand & Deary, 1982; Hulme

---

[8] I am grateful to Dr. M. Anderson for drawing this to my attention.

TABLE 2
IT(λ) and PIQ

Author	Subjects	Age (years)	n	Task	Psychophysical procedure
Nettelbeck & Lally[b] (1976)	University students and retarded adults	16–22	10	1. 2-lines[c] 2. 2-lines	MCS MCS
Lally & Nettelbeck[d] (1977)	1. University students 2. Nonretarded adults 3. Retarded adults	17–24 17–22 17–26	16 16 16	2-lines 2-lines 2-lines	MCS MCS MCS
Nettelbeck, Cheshire & Lally (1979)	Retarded adults	18–30	14	2-lines	MCS
Lally & Nettelbeck (1980)	Retarded adults	17–25	20	1. 2-lines 2. 2-lines	MCS MCS
Hulme & Turnbull (1983)	School children Retarded adults	6–7 22–44	65 8	2-lines 2-lines	MCS MCS
Smith & Stanley (1983)	School children	12	58	2-lines	MCS
Vernon (1983)	University students	18–34	50	2-lines	adaptive
Nettelbeck (1985c)	Nonretarded adults	17–40	1. 43 2. 40	2-lines 2-lines	MCS PEST
Mackenzie & Bingham (1985)	University students	18–48	1. 16[g] 2. 13	2-lines[h] 2-lines	adaptive adaptive

Notes:
[a]Published results have been converted where necessary to λ. Weights applied are Hulme & Turnbull, 1.53; Vernon, 1.19; Mackenzie & Bingham, 3.56.
[b]A further breakdown is shown in Nettelbeck (1982, Appendix 1).
[c]Vertical lines as in Figure 2 unless stated otherwise.
[d]The overall correlation with three groups combined was $-.80$; for combined nonretarded groups it was $-.25$; results are as reanalysed by Nettelbeck & Kirby (1983a).
[e]Brief form; Dr. C. Hulme, personal communication, December, 1985, February, 1986.
[f]Correlations between IT and WISC-R subtests shown.
[g]1. Strategy users; 2. Strategy nonusers.
[h]Horizontal lines, screen placement varied.

& Turnbull, 1983). Although the high $-.72$ from Mackenzie and Bingham (1985) should be treated cautiously, bearing in mind the nature of their task, as discussed in Section 3, the sample is small and including this result makes little difference to the mean.

4.3 IT and General Intelligence

Problems for the interpretation of results from Smith and Stanley (1983) and Irwin (1984), as discussed in Sections 4.1 and 4.2, are equally applicable

Mean, (SD), range λ (ms)[a]		Test	Mean, (SD), range, IQ	Correlation IT-IQ	p (one-tailed)
–	98–554	WAIS PIQ	86, (22), 51–123	1. – .92	<.01
–	100–804			2. – .89	<.01
93, (43),	49–174	WAIS PIQ	120, (6), 116–130	– .17	n.s.
90, (42),	40–189	WAIS PIQ	106, (6), 90–115	– .54	<.05
207, (47),	94–284	WAIS PIQ	69, (7), 57–81	– .45	<.05
210, (70),	90–392	WAIS PIQ	75, (10), 60–95	– .24	n.s.
264, (63),	171–378	WAIS PIQ	69, (8), 51–83	1. – .41	<.05
225, (55),	146–371			2. – .51	<.05
164, (30),	107–268	WISC-R PIQ[e]	114, (18), 86–155	– .29	<.05
283, (119),	122–536	WAIS PIQ[e]	64, (13), 41–86	– .71	<.05
126, (103),	16–460	PC (WISC-R)	(see table 3)[f]	.00	n.s.
		BD (WISC-R)		+ .18	n.s.
		Mazes (WISC-R)		+ .17	n.s.
127, (30),	61–224	WAIS-PIQ	118, (12), 97–146	+ .15	n.s.
80, (52),	37–336	WAIS-R PIQ	114, (15), 77–138	1. – .49	<.01
83, (44),	41–259		114, (15), 77–138	2. – .55	<.01
236, (41)	–	WAIS PIQ	114, (9)	1. – .20	n.s.
288, (48)	–		109, (10)	2. – .72	<.01

here, and IT–IQ correlations from these studies have therefore not been considered in the analyses that follow. These omissions leave only two studies involving children (Hosie, 1979; Hulme & Turnbull, 1983), one finding a high correlation from a small sample and the other a low correlation in a large sample. Clearly, a study involving adequate samples from different cohorts, with each cohort representing a normal distribution of IQ, is required to resolve this discrepancy.

Table 3 contains 17 sets of results from nonretarded adults, disregarding Mackenzie and Bingham's strategy users for the reason given in Sections 3.1 and 4.1, and three studies in which nonretarded and retarded subjects have been mixed (Anderson, 1977; Deary, 1980; Nettelbeck & Lally, 1976). Seven other sets of results can be considered; a correlation of – .44 between Cattell Culture Fair IQ and IT measured for 2-lines, from a sample of 45 secondary school students aged 15 and 16 years (Cooper et al., reported by N. J. Mackintosh, personal communication August, 1985); a correlation of – .31 between Raven Advanced Progressive Matrices and IT measured for 2-lines,

TABLE 3
IT(λ) and Measures of General Intelligence

Author	Subjects	Age (years)	n	Task	Psychophysical procedure
Nettelbeck & Lally (1976)	University students and retarded adults	16–22	10	1. 2-lines[b] 2. 2-lines	MCS MCS
Nettelbeck (1973b)[c]	University students	17–28	40	2-lines	MCS
Anderson (1977)	Retarded and nonretarded adults	16–26	1. 13 2.12 3.12	2-lines 3-lines 4-lines	adaptive/MCS adaptive/MCS adaptive/MCS
Grieve (1979)	Nonretarded adults	16–28	10	2-lines	adaptive/MCS
Hosie (1979)	Nursery infants	4	12	2-lines (colored)	method of limits (descending)
Deary (1980)	Retarded and nonretarded adults	17–25	17	1. 2-lines 2. 2-tones	adaptive/MCS adaptive/MCS
Nettelbeck (1982)	University students	19–48	46	2-lights	PEST
Hulme & Turnbull (1983)	School children	6–7	65	2-lines	MCS
Nettelbeck & Kirby (1983a)	1. University students 2. Trade apprentices 3. Retarded adults	(mean = 24, (SD = 7) (mean = 18, SD = 2) (mean = 21, SD = 3)	59 82 41	1. 2-lights 2. 2-vibrators 1. 2-lights 2. 2-vibrators 1. 2-lights 2. 2-vibrators	PEST PEST PEST PEST PEST PEST
Vernon (1983)	University students	18–34	50	2-lines	adaptive
Smith & Stanley (1983)	School children	12–13	107	2-lines	MCS
Irwin (1984, Exp. I)	School children	11–13	48	1. 2-alphabet characters (visual) 2. 2-tones	adaptive adaptive
Irwin (1984, Exp. II)	School children	11–13	25	2-alphabet characters (visual)	adaptive

316

Mean, (SD), range λ (ms)[a]		Test	Mean, (SD), range, IQ	Correlation IT-IQ	p (one-tailed)
–	98–554	WAIS FSIQ	83, (22), 47–119	– .70	<.05
–	100–804			– .63	<.05
101, (22),	74–156	Verbal & number reasoning (ACER-AL/AQ)[d]	125, (–), 112–135	– .13	n.s.
–	18–262	Cattell Culture Fair[e] or	94, (20), 44–121	– .87	<.01
–	83–238	Stanford-Binet	98, (14), 69–121	– .78	<.01
–	107–214			– .66	<.01
99, (24)	71–143	Cattell Culture Fair[e]	103, (7), 91–114	– .61	< .05
1020, (166),	510–1530	Coloured Progressive Matrices	102, (33), 95–125	– .78	<.01
–	31–1071	Standard Progressive Matrices	100, (24), 55–125	– .72	<.01
–	6–160			– .70	<.01
98, (–),	50–173	Advanced Progressive Matrices[f]	127, (–), 116–132	– .20	n.s.
164, (30),	107–268	WISC-R FSIQ[g]	117, (17), 89–150	– .20	n.s.
89, (26),	47–167	Advanced Progressive Matrices[f]	124, (7), 109–136	– .23	n.s.
115, (34)	56–184			– .17	n.s.
102, (30),	55–186	Standard Progressive	109, (10), 85–129	– .23	<.05
152, (56),	68–416	Matrices		– .22	<.05
185, (133),	43–714	WAIS	68, (10), 43–82	– .26	<.05
396, (199),	150–921	FSIQ		– .27	<.05
127, (30),	61–224	WAIS FSIQ	121, (9), 100–142	+ .10	n.s.
104, (88),	12–460	Cattell Culture-Fair[e]	101, (11), 74–126	– .12	n.s.
646, (422)		Standard Progressive Matrices	100, (14)	– .27	<.05
696, (641)				– .23	<.05
1. 606, (263)		Standard Progressive	97, (8)	– .06	n.s.
2. 398, (154)		Matrices		+ .04	n.s.

(Continued)

TABLE 3 *(Continued)*

Author	Subjects	Age (years)	n	Task	Psychophysical procedure
Irwin (1984, Exp. III)	Students	17–52	27	2-lines	adaptive
Edwards (1984)	Nonretarded adults	20–40	30	1. 2-lines	PEST
			30	2 . 2-lights	PEST
			29	3. 2-tones	PEST
			30	4. 2-vibrators	PEST
Sharp (1984)	Secondary students	14–16	24	2-lines	adaptive
Nettelbeck (1985c)	Nonretarded adults	17–40	43	1. 2-lines	MCS
			40	2. 2-lines	PEST
Mackenzie & Bingham (1985)	University students	18–48	1.16[h]	2-lines[i]	adaptive
			2.13	2-lines	adaptive

Notes:

[a]Published results have been converted where necessary to λ. Weights applied are Anderson, Grieve, 1.19; Hosie, 2.55; Deary, (1.) 1.53; Hulme & Turnbull, 1.53; Vernon, 1.19; Irwin (Expts. I & II), 3.56; Irwin (Expt. III), 3.21; Mackenzie & Bingham, 3.56.

[b]Vertical lines as in Figure 2 unless stated otherwise.

[c]Reported by Nettelbeck (1982).

[d]Australian Council for Educational Research.

[e]The Cattell test has a mean of 100 and SD of 24; not known whether values shown have been converted to WAIS equivalents.

[f]Estimated from APM scores by converting to z after estimating normative sample SD from Tables APMXII and APMXIV, ACER manual for APM.

[g]Brief form; Dr. C. Hulmes, personal communication, December, 1985, Feburary, 1986.

[h]1. Strategy users; 2. Strategy nonusers.

[i]Horizontal lines, screen placement varied.

from a sample of 25 university students (Jensen, 1982, p. 120);[9] biserial correlations of − .49 and − .41 between Cattell Culture Fair scores (IQs either around 132 or 98)[10] and two measures of recognition threshold (c.f. IT) for 2-tones, from 20 university students (Raz et al., 1983, Experiment II); correlations of − .48 and − 51 between scores on the Armed Forces Qualification Test (IQs either around 115 or 90) and IT measured for 2-tones and 2-lines, respectively, from the same sample of U.S. Navy servicemen (n = 20 and 22, respectively), (Brand, 1984 pp. 58–59); a correlation of − .44 between IT and IQ (Cattell Culture-Fair, adjusted to WAIS equivalents, 81 to 125, mean =

[9]Enquiries to Dr. P. A. Vernon (personal communication, July, 1985) have confirmed that these subjects were not included in Vernon (1983).

[10]IQs measured with the Cattell test, which has a mean of 100 and SD of 24, have been adjusted to WAIS equivalents.

Mean, (SD), range λ (ms)[a]		Test	Mean, (SD), range, IQ	Correlation IT-IQ	p (one-tailed)
137, (27)		Advanced Progressive Matrices[f]	120, (8), 97–131	−.17	n.s.
99, (38),	45–197	Advanced Progressive Matrices[f]	121, (8), 102–135	−.41	<.05
78, (31),	34–156			−.28	n.s.
117, (116),	11–399			−.38	<.05
153, (66),	36–284			+.02	n.s.
		Standard Progressive Matrices	103, (12), 86–130	−.54	<.01
80, (52),	37–336	WAIS-R FSIQ	117, (14), 81–138	−.40	<.01
83, (44)	41–259		117, (15), 81–138	−.46	<.01
236, (41)		WAIS FSIQ	118, (9)	−.08	n.s.
288, (48)			115, (8)	−.52	<.05

108, SD = 8) for a symbol-discrimination task, from 81 college students (Longstreth et al., 1985).[11]

Of the 24 available sets of results, 16 are significant, the range of correlations being from + .10 to − .61. Across all 24 results, the mean correlation is − .31 and the median − .39. However, as will be made clear in Section 5.3(b), there are sound grounds for rejecting the three sets obtained with the vibrator keys and when this is done the correlation increases to − .34 (median − .41). There are 12 sets of results for tasks involving lines or symbols, 5 for lights, and 4 for tones. Average correlations for these subgroups are − .33, − .28, and − .44, respectively. Further interpretation of these results is left until after the discussion of reliability and validity in the next section.

5.   RELIABILITY AND VALIDITY OF INSPECTION TIME (IT)

The various IQ tests used in the research summarized in Section 4 are widely available and, as set out in their respective manuals, have been shown to have acceptable reliability and to share considerable common variance among

[11]Longstreth et al. (1985) did not actually derive measures of IT, instead employing recognition accuracy as the dependent variable, so that their reported correlation is positive. However, their procedure follows the usual IT method, applying MCS and involving a backward mask, and their results conform to the typical negatively accelerating function that relates increasing SOA to increasing accuracy. Thus, their inclusion here in this way is justified. Average λ among the 13 high-IQ subjects represented in their Figure 2 is about 150ms, an outcome compatible with results for comparable samples in the 2-lines task (refer to Tables 2 and 3), bearing in mind that Longstreth et al. have analyzed their results for a 3-choice situation.

themselves and with other similar tests. The present section outlines several issues reflecting on the reliability of the different procedures and discrimination tasks used to measure IT. Alternative procedures have already been detailed in Section 3.2, together with a description of the 2-lines task and brief accounts of what is involved in the other tasks that have been applied. Some of these tasks are described more fully in what follows, because their characteristics are relevant to reliability. First, the equivalence of measures under different procedures and the stability of repeated measures with the same task and procedure is examined. This is followed by a discussion of subject variables that may, if operative, invalidate the measure obtained. The section concludes by considering evidence that IT provides an index of mental speed.

5.1 Measures of Reliability

(a) Different Psychophysical Methods

The MCS was adopted by Vickers et al. (1972) so as to interpolate λ from the cumulative normal ogive, and this procedure has been widely applied by Nettelbeck and coauthors (Nettelbeck, 1982, 1985a). Irwin (1984) has criticized this work on grounds (a) that λ is interpolated from that position of the psychometric function in the region of error-free performance, and therefore poorly defined; and (b) that λ has sometimes been determined by extrapolation beyond the range of target durations actually used in the study. Irwin's point is taken for establishing absolute values of IT. Nonetheless, as described in previous sections, differences from nonretarded–retarded comparisons, and from age comparisons, have generally been sufficiently large to establish reliable relative differences between such groups. Furthermore, it can be shown that measures of λ by MCS and by PEST are very similar. (PEST circumvents Irwin's criticism by directly measuring SOA at a specified level of accuracy within the steeper portion of the psychometric function, in the same way as the adaptive procedure favoured by Irwin). Thus, the two within-subject measures of λ from Nettelbeck (1985c) (see Tables 1, 2 or 3) had markedly similar distributions and were highly correlated ($r = .80$). Similarly, Nettelbeck and Wilson (1985, Study 2) found that measures from 7- and 11-year-olds by MCS under two different conditions and by PEST did not differ significantly. Within-sample correlations between PEST and the other two measures were moderately strong, with one exception; ($r = .68$ and .22 for 7-year-olds; $r = .62$ and .88 for 11-year-olds).[12]

While these two sets of results counter Irwin's criticism and suggest also that PEST is not particularly sensitive to essentially arbitrary specifications controlling the starting point, tracking rules and exit criteria within the pro-

---

[12]These correlations were not included in the published version of this study but are to be found in Wilson (1984, p. 120).

gram, the PEST procedure is not without its difficulties. Specifically, although performance within groups maintains reasonable relative stability at different accuracy criteria, the absolute size of estimates of IT under PEST can vary with the accuracy level selected. Nettelbeck, Evans, and Kirby (1982) obtained significantly longer average λ from two measures of SOA (75% accuracy) than from three estimates employing MCS. This result held within samples ($n = 10$) of university students and mildly retarded adults, even though correlations within samples were strong; for students, r ranged from .36 to .81 (mean = .61); for the retarded sample, r ranged from .65 to .84 (mean = .79).

Results from Nettelbeck (1985c) and Nettelbeck and Wilson (1985) that have confirmed close agreement between MCS and PEST (see above) were obtained for 85% level of accuracy, following Wilson (1984, Appendix 2.1). This experiment involving 15 university students found significantly longer λ estimated from SOA (75% accuracy) than from SOA (90% accuracy); (106ms and 84ms, respectively). The result was therefore very similar to Nettelbeck's (1982) significant difference between $\lambda = 113$ and 83ms using the same accuracy criteria, despite a correlation between measures of .62, from 56 university students doing the 2-lights task. However, Wilson also established $\lambda = 93$ms for SOA (85% accuracy), this outcome also being the average of the other two sets and therefore confirming the reliability of this particular estimate.

We may conclude from the foregoing that both MCS and PEST can result in equivalent outcomes, but that adaptive procedures do not necessarily result in more reliable measures of performance. This point is taken up again in the section that follows. We may note also that, whereas a second measure is usually necessary to test reliability with an adaptive procedure, split-half reliability is an option under MCS, providing that sufficient trials are taken. Thus, Nettelbeck (1973b) found $r = .78$ between two such internal estimates of IT from 24 university students. Irwin's (1984, Experiment III) adaptive procedure also permits comparison within a single session, because IT is estimated by averaging across durations (refer to Table 4).

(b) Test-Retest Reliability

MCS and PEST are equally satisfactory with respect to test-retest correlation, as may be seen from the various results collated in Table 4. Mean r is .76 from instances involving MCS, .71 for PEST, .78 for the three adaptive sets, and .75 overall. Combining data from repeated measures (including some shown in Table 4) but irrespective of task or the psychophysical procedure followed, Nettelbeck (1985a) found that average correlations within adult nonretarded and retarded samples and within children's samples at various ages were about .7. This result held, even after a period of 2 years (Nettelbeck

TABLE 4
Test-retest Correlations for IT, Estimated with Different Discrimination Tasks Using Different Psychophysical Methods

Author	Subjects	n	Task	Psychophysical procedure	r	Comment
Vickers et al. (1972)	University students	10	2-lines	MCS	.80	
Nettelbeck et al. (1982)	University students	10	2-lines	MCS	.56	Mean from 3 measures; range .39 to .81.
	University students	10	2-lines	PEST	.25	
	Retarded adults	10	2-lines	MCS	.75	Mean from 3 measures; range .64 to .84.
	Retarded adults	10	2-lines	PEST	.92	
Sen & Goswami (1983)	Children 6–11 years	48	2-lines	MCS	.57	Two conditions involving change to orientation of lines.
Raz et al. (1983)	University students	17	2-tones	MCS	.91	Recognition of "high" or "low".
Vernon (1983)	University students	50	2-lines	MCS	.80	
Irwin (1984, Expt. II)	12-year-olds	25	2-alphabet characters	adaptive	.78	
Irwin (1984, Expt. III)	Students	27	2-lines	adaptive	.87	Split-half.
Nettelbeck et al. (1984, Expt. 1)	University students	6	2-lines	PEST	.88	Dichoptic/binocular comparisons.
	Retarded adults	6	2-lines	PEST	.21	Dichoptic/binocular comparisons.
Nettelbeck et al. (1984, Expt. 2)	University students	8	2-lights	PEST	.60	Four ISI conditions; range .38 to .72.
	Retarded adults	8	2-lights	PEST	.47	Four ISI conditions; range .14 to .90.

Source	Subjects	N	Stimulus	Method	Reliability	Comments
Nettelbeck & McLean (1984, Expt. 1)	University students	16	2-lines	PEST	.59	Six successive measures; range .29 to .78.
	Retarded adults	16	2-lines	PEST	.59	Six successive measures; range .20 to .90.
Mackenzie & Bingham (1985)	University students	29	2-lines	adaptive	.66	Horizontal lines, screen placement varied.
Nettelbeck & Wilson (1985, Study 1)	8-year-olds	10	2-lines	PEST	.67	Four dichoptic/binocular comparisons; range .55 to .88.
	11-year-olds	10	2-lines	PEST	.62	Four dichoptic/binocular comparisons; range .43 to .91.
	University students	10	2-lines	PEST	.80	Four dichoptic/binocular comparisons; range .66 to .94.
Nettelbeck & Wilson (1985, Study 3)	7-year-olds	10	2-lines	PEST	.87	Retest after 2 weeks.
	12-year-olds	10	2-lines	PEST	.87	Retest after 2 weeks.
	University students	10	2-lines	PEST	.87	Retest after 2 weeks.
Nettelbeck & Wilson (1985, Study 3)	7-year-olds	10	2-lines	PEST	.58	Retest after 1 year.
	8-year-olds	9	2-lines	PEST	.85	Retest after 1 year.
	9-year-olds	9	2-lines	PEST	.52	Retest after 1 year.
	10-year-olds	8	2-lines	PEST	.74	Retest after 1 year.
	11-year-olds	9	2-lines	PEST	.80	Retest after 1 year.
	University students	10	2 lines	PEST	.90	Retest after 1 year.
Nettelbeck (unpublished)[a]	78-year-olds	20	2-lights	PEST	.53	Three successive measures; range .21 to .67.
Longstretch et al. (1985, June)	University students	81	3-alphanumeric symbols	MCS	.75	Different numbers of trials in the two sessions.

Note: [a] Reported by Nettelbeck (1985a).

& Wilson, 1985). Brand and Deary (1982) have reported that internal reliabilities of .8 have been typical of IT research at Edinburgh, the higher result probably reflecting the combination of retarded with nonretarded participants in some of these studies.

As may be seen from Table 4, most repeated measures have involved the 2-lines task, and results do suggest that this provides a highly reliable index of some basic attribute. The few examples for other tasks are equally promising (Irwin, 1984, Experiment II; Longstreth et al., 1985; Raz et al., 1985), except for the 2-lights task, where mean r for the two studies is .53 (Nettelbeck et al., 1984, Experiment 2; Nettelbeck unpublished, reported by Nettelbeck, 1985a), significantly lower than the mean of .77 for all other tasks ($p < .01$).

5.2 Subjective Variables

(a) Sensory Sensitivity and Concentration

Involving, as it does, very brief stimulus durations, the IT measure is vulnerable to diminished sensory sensitivity or to any lapse in concentration just prior to target onset. This is particularly so if occasional errors are made at longer durations where the probability of a correct response is high but where, as Irwin (1984) has stressed, the psychometric curve is least well-defined. Similarly, Brebner and Cooper (1985) have pointed to hypothetical instability in the measure, demonstrating that a 17% increase in λ is possible when only one additional error in 600 trials is made, if it occurs at a relatively long target duration.

One way of overcoming this difficulty is to include occasional long exposures, such that any error could only be caused by inattentiveness, and then to rescale the psychometric function, assuming that accuracy achieved at these exposures represents a ceiling, limited by distractibility rather than by perception. This has been done with data from retarded subjects, after confirming the presence of errors associated with poor concentration by recording eye movements (Nettelbeck, Robson, Walwyn, Downing, & Jones, 1986). However, this study found no evidence of lapsed concentration in the nonretarded sample. It should also be noted that, while revised estimates of IT among retarded subjects were shorter, poorly directed gaze in this sample at the time of target onset was only a minor contributory factor to measures of IT, which still remained substantially longer than those from nonretarded subjects.

To this time, there is little evidence available on the influence of individual differences in sensory sensitivity on IT, most studies assuming that it is sufficient to screen subjects by standard clinical procedures for normal visual acuity or auditory sensitivity. However, both Deary (1980) and Sharp (1982) have found a moderate correlation between acuity and IT ($-.45$ and $-.60$, respectively), but without this significantly influencing IT–IQ correlations.

Further, reduced optical efficiency with aging (Owsley, Sekular, & Siemsen, 1983) may in part be responsible for declining IT performance among the elderly. Although Sharp (1984) found a nonsignificant low correlation of only − .11 between visual acuity and IT, again without influencing the IT–IQ correlation (refer to Table 3), further research on this topic is necessary.

(b) Practice Effects

Evidence on practice effects in IT tasks is available from eight studies, included among those in Table 4, in which test-retest estimates have been made under the same conditions. Two studies have found no differences between two successive estimates (Irwin, 1984, Experiment III; Vickers et al., 1972). Three have reported improvement. First, Nettelbeck and Wilson (1985, Study 3) found about 17% reduction among both 7- and 12-year-olds, compared with 12% among university students; in the other two, Mackenzie and Bingham (1985) have reported 31% reduction for university students, and Irwin (1984, Experiment II) has reported 34% for 12-year-olds, but the larger reductions in these probably reflect the relative difficulty of their discrimination tasks, as already pointed out in Sections 3.1 and 4.1. Three successive measures have reduced λ by 30% among university students, compared with 24% in retarded adults (Nettelbeck et al., 1982) and 23% in elderly subjects (Nettelbeck, unpublished, reported by Nettelbeck, 1985a). Six successive measures have resulted in 30% reduction among both nonretarded and retarded adults (Nettelbeck & McLean, 1984, Experiment 1), with some indication of asymptotic performance in both groups by at least the fourth session. Even after this degree of practice the measures of λ within both groups remained substantially correlated. A reasonable inference at this time is that IT shows some sensitivity to initial practice, so that future research should consider longer periods of preliminary training to achieve measures of optimum performance. Nevertheless, although further work is required on this issue, we are justified in concluding that IT as measured so far is a relatively stable index of individual differences in time to make discriminative judgments, since relative improvement is approximately the same for groups of markedly different ages and intellectual abilities, with successive measures demonstrating good within-group stability.

(c) Response Strategies

Experimenters have previously been aware from subjects' reports that some subjects are able to achieve unusually high levels of accuracy at very brief target durations, by using subtle post-masking cues in the display which give rise to apparent movement or changes in brightness (Brand, 1984; Nettelbeck, 1982). With such subjects, then, the masking procedure sometimes fails to limit sensory input to the target exposures programmed, although under the usual methods followed there is no way of definitely ascertaining when this has occurred. Obviously, however, these instances introduce unspecified unreliability into IT measurement.

Mackenzie and Bingham (1985) have investigated the extent to which such strategies are employed, by questioning subjects after a test session about how they made the discriminations required. As shown in Tables 1 to 3, Mackenzie and Bingham found that 16 of their sample of 29 university students developed the strategy spontaneously, mean IT for this subsample being significantly shorter than among the 13 nonusers. No significant IQ differences were found between the two subsamples, however. Brebner and Cooper (1985) have essentially replicated these findings with a similar sample of university students, although this study did not measure IQ. However, 9 out of 16 of their subjects reported using an apparent movement strategy, with mean IT being significantly shorter among users.

Mackenzie and Bingham also attempted to instruct those subjects not initially employing the strategy to do so in future sessions. This was not effective, however, there being a significant increase in IT for this group in the session when the strategy was employed, and a subsequent decrease when the strategy was discontinued.

Thus, while an apparent movement strategy in the 2-lines task is not readily taught, something like 55% of subjects, at least from within university samples, may spontaneously adopt it, although how soon within a session or to what extent is not known. The effect of widespread adoption of this strategy would be to reduce any IT–IQ correlation, since IT becomes bunched around lower values among users. The problem may be overcome, however, with a discrimination which prevents this strategy, and part of the task devised by Longstreth et al., (1985, June) appears to do this. In this study, target stimuli were a capital O and a diagonal slash (/), both masked by Ø, the conventional symbol for zero in computer programming. Mean correct recognition scores across all SOA intervals were very similar (59 and 64%), and lower than for two other characters, capital C and U (70 and 84%), although only U was significantly higher. However, this outcome is consistent with more effective masking of the first two symbols; while, conceivably, postmasking cues may improve accuracy to C and U, this seems less likely for the others.

There is some evidence that individual differences in personality variables other than IQ can influence IT. Thus, Nettelbeck (1973b) found that, in a sample of 40 university students, individuals scoring at the extremes of personality dimensions measured by the Manifest Anxiety Scale and the Eysenck Personality Inventory had significantly longer IT than those scoring in intermediate categories. This study did not attempt to link personality variables to differences in response strategy. In a more recent study, however,

Brebner and Cooper (1985) have demonstrated the influence of what appear to be personality-related strategy differences. Brebner and Cooper predicted that, because adopting an apparent movement strategy would require less stimulus-analysis than attempting a discrimination of line-length, extraverts would use this strategy more than introverts. Subjects were 8 extraverts and 8 introverts, all university students. IT was measured in two conditions, one designed to involve more stimulus-analysis than the other because of longer delays following a warning signal that prepared the subject for target onset. Although there was not a general tendency for extraverts to adopt an apparent movement strategy, Brebner and Cooper found a three-way interaction between the personality variable, strategy use, and condition; the extraverted strategy users had significantly faster ITs than other subjects under the condition requiring less sustained attention prior to target onset. In view of the small samples involved, a replication is desirable. However, this outcome is not necessarily inconsistent with that from Nettelbeck (1973b), which did not permit an independent analysis of extraversion and neuroticism dimensions.

The possibility also exists that strategies can determine the accumulation of evidence in the IT task, and so influence outcome, although, as described in Section 3.1, the task was originally designed to prevent this from happening. Nonetheless, important differences have been found in the patterns of RT recorded from retarded and nonretarded adults doing the IT task (Lally & Nettelbeck, 1977; Nettelbeck et al., 1980). For nonretarded adults, RT to correct responses typically becomes faster with increasing SOA, approaching asymptote at a duration close to λ, and with overall error RT longer than that for correct responses. This pattern is predicted by the accumulator model (Vickers et al., 1972), since evidence for a decision accumulates more quickly while the target is present than after its offset. Among retarded adults, however, both correct and incorrect RTs have been found to be fairly constant across all target durations and therefore suggestive of deadline responding. Despite this, however, individual psychometric functions of accuracy against SOA conform to the theoretical normal ogive.

This pattern can be equated with the adoption of low criteria for responding (Lally & Nettelbeck, 1977), suggesting that retarded subjects take fewer samples when exposure is limited to make discrimination ambiguous. At this time, it is not known why some subjects adopt a deadline response strategy. This tendency may be linked to MA, since Smith (1985) has found similar evidence for deadline responding among about 10% of children aged 12–13 years, again without apparent effect on the psychometric function. Nor is it known whether such a strategy has any effect on IT.

(d) Adaptation and Noise

Vickers and Smith (1985) have drawn attention to difficulties for the interpretation of IT raised by results from their recent experiments, in which they have tested the influence of subjective expectancy and adaptation effects on discrimination. These experiments have found that, for a situation in which a subject has control over the number of inspections made in a discrimination task before a decision is reached, the early version of the accumulator model, described in Section 3.1, can substantially underestimate the actual response latencies measured. Vickers and Smith infer that this situation arises because of occasional inspections that make no contribution at all to the decision process. To understand the implications of this proposal for the interpretation of IT requires a brief digression into classical psychophysics.

The theory from which the IT measure is derived assumes that the sensory magnitude of the two simultaneously presented lines in the IT task can be represented as two normal frequency distributions. The mean of each distribution is equal to the actual length of that line, with each distribution having the same SD, representing neural noise (Vickers et al., 1972). The sensory magnitude at which these two hypothetical distributions intersect is termed the *point of indifference,* since at that value the sensory effect of both lines is the same. The early version of the accumulator model assumed that the point of indifference is always fixed at the intersection of the two distributions.

Vickers and Smith have proposed that, under some circumstances, the point of indifference may shift away from the point of intersection, thereby enhancing the relative discriminability of one line, while reducing that of the second line. It can be shown that a consequence of such a shift is a decrease in the overall accuracy of performance. Further, they point to evidence that inspections not favouring any particular outcome may arise from *variation in the degree* to which the indifference point shifts within an experimental session; in other words, the individual's performance may involve an *indifference region* (IR), representing a range of magnitudes of sensory effect. Both the position (i.e., mean value) and the width (i.e., range of values) of the IR are subject to variation as the individual adapts to changes in the *cumulative distribution* of sensory magnitudes experienced in previous trials. Such adaptation is held to be *automatic* and beyond strategic control. Applying a new version of the accumulator model which incorporates (a) the IR as a parameter of individual performance, together with (b) threshold for degree of caution (see Section 3.1), and (c) residual nondecision time (see Section 3.1), Vickers and coworkers have established close agreement between actual and predicted accuracy in discrimination tasks for which distribution parameters could be specified precisely (Vickers & Smith, 1985).

Since any inspection from within the IR makes no contribution to the decision process, it may be seen that, for any value of IR other than zero, the possibility exists that an initial inspection would not result in the correct response, no matter how easy the discrimination task. Such an occurrence would violate the fundamental assumption underlying the measurement of IT, that the initial inspection must favour the correct response (see Section

3.1). Furthermore, the proportion of trials in which a single inspection resulted in the correct response would decrease as the value of IR increased. To the extent that IR shifted from zero, this would inflate the estimate of IT. It is not yet possible to estimate whether this does occur in the IT task, and, indeed, the research referred to by Vickers and Smith has not involved the IT task. However, values for IR estimated from their experiments are such as to raise the possibility that, for some individuals, estimates of IT could be lengthened artefactually.

Vickers and Smith also query whether the lines-discrimination task commonly used is sufficiently easy to be beyond levels of internal noise for all subjects. They point out that the initial estimate of noise confirmed by Vickers et al. (1972) was an average for a group of student subjects, and that much higher individual levels have been recorded under some circumstances. It is certainly possible that levels of noise among retarded subjects could be sufficiently high to require a stimulus difference so large that eye movement would be necessary to input information. Attempts in Adelaide to resolve this question have so far been unsuccessful, largely because of problems in measuring λ among such subjects with high absolute accuracy.

We may note here that the question of whether IT could in some instances be confounded with noise is logically separate from the possibility of individual differences in IR. Nonetheless, the two parameters could interact. Thus, the effects on IT from a given value of IR would be greater where internal noise was higher.

5.3 Validity

(a) Equivalence of Visual Tasks

The initial rationale underlying the 2-lights discrimination task was that it is analogous to a limiting version of the lines discrimination from which one line had been removed altogether (Smith, 1978). One would predict, therefore, that measures of λ from the two tasks would be equivalent but, to date, support for this is equivocal. Exploratory comparisons between these tasks using results obtained by Wilson (1980) with lights, and Nettelbeck et al (1982) with lines, both following a PEST procedure, found no significant differences in λ within either groups of nonretarded or retarded adults. However, subsequent more stringent within-subject comparisons have been less encouraging. Thus, Nettelbeck (reported by Nettelbeck & McLean, 1984) found significantly shorter estimates with the lights task than with lines, among 10 mildly retarded subjects, although the correlation of .73 between tasks was strong. However, Edwards (1984) has not only found significantly shorter estimates with lights among 30 nonretarded adults (as shown in Table 3), but also a relatively weak correlation of .31 between the two versions. Shorter estimates with the 2-lights task may be the consequence of less effective masking in this version, a suggestion supported by lower estimates of test-retest reliability with this task, as remarked in Section 5.1(b). However, further research with adequate samples and involving MCS and PEST is necessary to establish whether these two tasks are equivalent or not.

Two areas of procedural uncertainty associated with recent attempts to develop video versions of the lines discrimination task may usefully be noted here. First, if a video screen is used instead of a tachistoscope to display stimulus figures, the refresh rate of the raster scan limits exposures to multiples of approximately 20 ms, and performance at other exposures can only be estimated by averaging (e.g., accuracy at 25ms can be interpolated from 75% exposures at 20ms and 25% at 40ms). Screen presentation may therefore result in less reliable estimation of IT than using a tachistoscope, although Mackenzie and Bingham (1985) have obtained a test-retest correlation of .66 with a video method (see Table 4). Second, unlike most tachistoscopes which permit independent control of luminance in different fields, video displays have fixed luminance. Since locus of masking can be influenced by the relative energy of target and mask (Turvey, 1973), it may be necessary to program covariation in target and mask durations when employing a video display to present the target throughout varying SOA, so as to ensure a target to mask energy ratio appropriate to achieving specific masking effects.

(b) Different Modalities

Brand and Deary (1982) have developed a procedure for estimating auditory IT, whereby the listener identifies the order in which two brief tones of markedly different frequency (770 and 880 Hz) and embedded between bursts of white noise are played separately, 1 second apart and with the duration of both tones varied together. IT is defined as the minimum tone duration at which the order of occurrence can be defined correctly. Although Deary (1980) found a correlation of .99 between this measure and visual IT for 13 subjects, this outcome was entirely due to the inclusion of two mentally retarded persons; with these excluded, the correlation was virtually zero. There are also grounds for interpreting measures by this procedure with caution.

First, Irwin (1984) has demonstrated that the degree of separation between the fundamental frequencies in this task varies with tone duration. This is because the amplitude consists of both the fundamental and various harmonics, the energy from these being more spread at shorter tone durations. Thus, at very short durations the task may be measuring different processes than at longer durations. Second, white noise does not appear to provide an adequate masking stimulus. Deary (1980) has reported an IT range (99% accuracy) of 6–160ms, but with 160ms representing an "outlier," since the two next longest measures were 15 and 20ms. This suggests that the mask employed was not effective. Irwin's (1984) results from 49 12-year-olds with this technique were markedly more widely spread but sharply positively skewed (mean for 71% accuracy was 196ms, median 16ms(?), SD = 340ms, skewness 2.34), suggesting that most children found the discrimination required very easy but that some encountered great difficulty. Following pilot work utilizing a sound-generating chip to produce a mask in which both target frequencies were rapidly alternated together with white noise, Edwards (1984) found markedly different results. However, as shown in Table 3, the range in λ was still substantially longer than was found with the 2-lines task, and the correlation between these two measures was low (though significant) (r = .39). Nettelbeck (1985c) has reported replicating these results with a different sample of 24 adults, so that there are some doubts about the reliability of this version of IT measurement.

An alternative task for measuring auditory IT has been used by Raz et al. (1983). One of a pair of tones classified as either high (870Hz) or low (770Hz) is presented for a brief, fixed duration, followed after a variable ISI by a masking tone. This task therefore avoids the problem raised by Irwin (1984) whereby degree of separation between fundamentals changes with varying duration. Since the effects of contralateral and ipsilateral masking in this task are similar (Massaro, 1970), and because SOA remains relatively constant with changing target duration (Raz et al., 1983), it can be concluded that masking is central, as is the case with the visual tasks described in Section 3.2. Further, although only two experiments involving small samples have yet been made with this task, it appears to result in high reliability (refer to Table 4) and estimates of IT that are compatible with those made with the 2-lines task from comparable samples. Thus, mean λ derived from Raz et al.'s data is 84ms, 142ms, and 255ms for their high, average, and low IQ samples, respectively.

Nettelbeck and Kirby (1983a) have pointed to problems with a measure of tactile IT. This task involved detecting which of two fingers was first stimulated by rapidly vibrating keys under the finger tips. Although correlations between this task and the 2-lights discrimination were significant (r = .75, .37, .32) for mildly retarded (n = 41), average IQ (n = 82), and above-average IQ (n = 59) groups respectively, many subjects complained that their fingertips quickly became numb, and values of λ obtained were certainly unexpectedly long. Edwards (1984) has confirmed this result (see Table 3), and found low, nonsignificant correlations between tactile IT and other measures in visual and auditory modes.

Auditory and tactile versions of the IT task have been assumed to be analogous to the 2-lines task, but without first determining that the discriminations involved were beyond normal levels of internal noise for those modalities. Since subjects are now known to lose sensitivity in the vibrator task as the session progesses, it has become obvious that the signal-to-noise ratio in this task will reach unacceptably low levels and result in unreliable measurements. This is an extreme example but it highlights the necessity of research aimed at establishing noise levels in modalities other than vision if reliable IT measures in those modalities are to be developed.

(c) Inspection Time (IT) as Mental Speed)

While results discussed in Section 5 generally suggest that IT provides a very reliable index of individual differences in accuracy, its validity as a measure of some fundamental limitation to the speed at which mental processes operate is problematical. Some research has indicated an association between IT and mental speed but other results have not been wholly consistent with this proposal. Nettelbeck (1985a) has discussed the issue, as it applies to studies comparing mentally retarded and nonretarded performance.

Nettelbeck and Kirby (1983b) found similar trends between IQ in the normal range (140 adults) and standardized measures of IT and choice RT (these measured in unrelated situations), consistent with the involvement of some common process. The correlation of .21 between nonstandardized measures of IT and RT was significant but low, as would be expected if RT includes additional processes not required by IT. A study by Hirons (1982) also supports the IT-as-speed idea. She compared IT in a 2-lights task with an alternative estimate of IT suggested by Vickers (1970), and defined as the difference between the mode and the fastest correct reaction from a distribution for 400 trials in a 2-choice RT task, following more than 800 practice trials. Among 14 university students, the two measures correlated .65.

These results, however, reveal nothing about the nature of speed indexed by IT. The following three studies attempted to address this by testing the degree of association between IT and various tests assumed to reflect different kinds of mental speed.

Wilson (1984, Experiment 2.1) tested 50 normal children aged 8 to 13 years for IT and performance on the Speed of Information Scale (essentially a number checking procedure) from the British Ability Scales. She found a correlation of − .53, reducing to − .38 with age partialled out. Moreover, the association was actually limited to 8- to 11-year-olds ($n = 30$, average within-cohort correlation = − .61), there being little correlation among the older children. A subsequent study (Wilson, 1984, Experiment 6) confirmed an MA interpretation of the earlier result, since no association was found within samples defined by MA. A correlation of only − .32 between IT and another pencil and paper test for perceptual speed (ACER speed and accuracy) reported by Tonisson (1982) from 66 deaf adolescents (mean age 15 years) supports Wilson's results. Clearly, stronger correlations than these would be expected if IT was predominantly a measure of processes shared by tests of perceptual speed as traditionally defined. Thus, a strong relationship between IT and perceptual speed may be limited to younger children.

Results from Edwards (1984) are consistent with this. Edward's study was planned within the framework of Cattell's theory about the structure of abilities and the nature of different kinds of speed within that formulation (Cattell, 1971; Hakstian & Cattell, 1978; see Section 2). Tests of primary abilities from the Comprehensive Ability Battery (CAB)[13] were selected with the aim of isolating different speed variables in association with different general capacities, as described by Cattell and outlined above in Section 2. Inductive Reasoning, Numerical Ability, and Spatial Ability were included, together with the Raven Advanced Progressive Matrices (APM), as tests loading on g_f; Verbal Ability and Mechanical Ability were used to define g_c; Speed of Closure, Perceptual Speed and Accuracy, and Digit Span (WAIS) were used to define g_v and g_s.[14] Associative Memory and Meaningful Memory were also included, to isolate *General Memory Capacity* (Hakstian & Cattell, 1978) since IT would be predicted to be independent from long-term retention. Although Edwards employed four versions of IT (2-lines, 2-lights, 2-tones, 2-vibrators), the account here is limited to the 2-lines and 2-tones tasks. (See discussion of validity in Sections 5.3 (a) and (b); the between-task correlation was highest for these (.39), though hardly sufficient to qualify them with confidence as equivalent forms.)

Results did not support a clear distinction between higher-stratum structures, only Speed of Closure and (less clearly) Perceptual Speed and Accuracy being separable from the other primary ability tests and APM, which were all moderately to strongly intercorrelated. Mean correlation among these other tests was .55, compared to .27 between these, Speed of Closure and Perceptual Speed and Accuracy, the last two being correlated .43. However, despite this strong evidence for a general factor, IT did not unambiguously conform to this pattern. Although both IT measures were moderately correlated with APM (see Table 3; multiple R = .47), and not with either of the two primary speed measures, IT was significantly correlated with only three of the other intercorrelated variables. Significant mean correlations between both measures of IT and other tests were − .40 (APM), − .40 (Associative Memory), − .34 (forward Digit Span), − .32 (Inductive Reasoning), the mean with all other tests being − .19. The small sample (n = 30) and the absence of a coherent distinction between different kinds of speed severely con-

---

[13]The relevance of the Comprehensive Ability Battery to this purpose was suggested by an early version of a study by Cooper, Kline, and Maclaurin-Jones (1986) which, however, used a different configuration of primary abilities to that described here.

[14]Although these two factors are theoretically discriminable, an examination of results from Hakstian and Cattell (1978) suggested that they could be difficult to separate in practice, although Spatial Ability (acknowledged to be factorially complex) might serve as a marker for g_v and Digit Span as a marker for g_s. This rationale was clouded, however, by Dempster's (1981) analysis of Digit Span as reflecting predominantly *speed of item recognition*, which he regarded as being determined by g_f.

strain conclusions from this study. At most, these results suggest that IT is associated with a more general capacity rather than with specific capabilities, and that IT is not related to perceptual speed or speed of closure, as defined by Cattell (1971). Nor do the results support an interpretation in terms of g_s. However, the reliability of this outcome is doubtful since Cooper, Kline, & Maclaurin-Jones (1986) have recently found a different pattern of correlations between IT and primary abilities measured by the CAB. Their study used a different configuration of CAB scales and, like Edwards, employed only a small sample ($n = 20$). While supporting Edwards' conclusion that g_s is not involved, they did find significant correlations between IT with both Cs and P.

The third study (Nettelbeck, 1985c) utilized Furneaux's model of problem solving in ability tests (see Section 2) to derive a measure of mental speed with which to compare IT. Briefly, Furneaux (1952, 1960) held that individuals differ with respect to any of three critical variables; (a) the rate at which mental processes operate to find a solution (intellectual speed); (b) the probability that an incorrect solution will be rejected (accuracy); and (c) the duration of persistence to find a solution before abandoning the problem (continuance). In these terms, if item difficulty is sufficiently low for all test takers to obtain the correct solution, then continuance and accuracy cannot influence outcome and individual differences in performance are limited to speed. Nettelbeck correlated two measures of IT from the 2-lines task (MCS and PEST procedures; see Table 3) with time to solve individually five items from the Raven Progressive Matrices (E-series). Analysis was limited to 30 university students who solved these items correctly. Solution speed was moderately reliable, the average correlation between items being .47. The average correlation between E-items and FSIQ (WAIS) was .49. The 10 correlations between items and the IT measures ranged from .24 to .51, and seven were statistically significant ($p < .05$); mean correlations with separate IT measures were .37 (MCS) and .31 (PEST). While consistent with the proposal that IT reflects intellectual speed, the outcome is less convincing than had been anticipated. In part, this may reflect error when timing items (a hand-held stopwatch was used), or limitations to Furneaux's model, which takes no account of guessing or differences in style of hypothesis testing on the way to a correct solution. The outcome may, however, also reflect subjective variables in the IT task, other than mental speed, as discussed already in Section 5.2. It is worth noting, however, that the IT–IQ correlation is not simply the consequence of time constraints in both IT and IQ tasks. Thus, a recent unpublished study, similar to that just discussed, but removing all time constraints to subjects' responses to Raven Progressive Matrices items, found a significant correlation of $-.34$ between IT and the number of items solved correctly (Nettelbeck & Vreugdenhil, 1986; $n = 25$ students; correlation between IT and FSIQ (WAIS-R) $= -.50$; for FSIQ and Raven score, $r = .58$).

6. CONCLUSIONS

Previous sections have reviewed results from some 29 theses and published articles that report direct investigations into whether IT is correlated with IQ. This is not a large number and, since method and outcome have varied considerably across these studies, to venture firm conclusions is a hazardous undertaking. Nonetheless, as behooves a reviewer, I will attempt to do so, asserting at the outset that there is a reliable relationship between IT and IQ. This is despite the apparent disparity between the levels of processing presumed to be involved in IT tasks and mental ability tests so that, based solely on the content of these two types of mental measurement, there is no reason to predict IT–IQ correlation. If this assertion is accepted, then two further questions pertaining to this correlation can be posed; first, is the correlation sufficiently strong to be of theoretical significance?; second, what does it mean?

Taken overall, the evidence is consistent with Brand's proposal that IT is related to a broad ability, rather than to more peripheral abilities limited to specific situations. Beyond about age 10 or 11, for example, IT does not bear much relationship to perceptual speed as traditionally measured in letter-number checking tests. With respect to verbal ability there is confusing contradiction, but a number of the available studies are procedurally flawed and, on balance, the evidence can be said to favour Brand's theory. However, there is clearly a need for further research into this issue; it may be that verbal ability tests are more sensitive to acquired knowledge than most of the other psychometric tests applied, and that IT is associated less with this factor than with, say, capacities for reasoning or comprehension. Results from Longstreth et al. (1985) are consistent with this idea. In addition to measuring IQ (Cattell Culture Fair Test), they scored 61 of their subjects on the Scholastic Aptitude Test (SAT). IQ and SAT correlated .48, and the IT–IQ correlation for this subsample (– .47) was virtually the same as for the larger group, as described in Section 4.3. The correlation between SAT and IT was nonsignificant (– .17), and partialling out SAT left an IT–IQ correlation of – .42, confirming that this relationship was independent of SAT. Multiple regression of IQ on IT and SAT resulted in R = .65, with both predictor variables making significant contributions to variance in IQ accounted for. Thus, the more specific abilities reflected in SAT, together with those processes represented in IT, predicted 42% of IQ variance.

Insofar as children are concerned, there is strong evidence for an assertion that IT shortens with cognitive development, at least until early adolescence. Hulme and Turnbull's (1983) results do not support Brand's prediction of stronger IT–IQ association at younger ages, but the issue is still open, since no study has directly addressed it by measuring IT within cohorts for samples with normally distributed IQ. No study except Hosie's (1979) has attempted to test a relationship between IT and g_f in a very young cohort. This result (Table 3) strongly supported Brand's theory, but the sample was too small to permit confident interpretation. (The 95% confidence intervals for this correlation are $-.38$ and $-.94$.) This study did, however, have a number of attractive procedural features, including associating lines of different length with highly discriminable colors so as to secure response reliability. It provides a useful model for a replication with a larger sample.

The best available estimate of the strength of association between IT and general ability across the full range of IQ is about $-.5$. First, the median of all correlations from adult samples, including those with retarded subjects, is $-.49$. Secondly, the uncorrected correlation among normal young adults (14 years and older) is $-.35$, which corrected for restriction of variability in IQ becomes $-.50$. This estimate has been made from 16 sets of results for which lines, visual symbols, or tones have been employed as stimuli (Brand, 1984; Cooper et al., reported by N. J. Mackintosh, personal communication, August, 1985; Edwards, 1984, two sets; Grieve, 1979; Irwin, 1984, Experiment III; Jensen, 1982, p. 120; Longstreth et al., 1985; Mackenzie & Bingham, 1985, strategy nonusers only; Nettelbeck, 1973, 1982, 1985c; Raz et al., 1983, Experiment II, two sets; Sharp, 1984; Vernon, 1983). Results not included when making this estimation are those where retarded and nonretarded have been mixed, or where there are specific grounds for asserting lower reliability than among those results included, according to foregoing discussion. The estimation has therefore been made from 529 measures of IT taken from 439 subjects. Descriptions of age and IQ are available for the majority of these, so that reasonable estimates are that ages have ranged from 14 to 52 years, and IQ from 81 to 142 (mean about 115, SD 10).

To inflate this estimate further by correcting for unreliability in the measurement of both variables could hardly be justified, given the range of IQ tests and different IT procedures employed. The point is that, despite some degree of test reliability and the attenuated and skewed distribution of IQ in most studies so far, the estimate advanced here suggests a sufficiently strong relationship to be of theoretical interest. This estimate has been possible without the necessity of applying multiple regression, unlike the situation with RT, where parameters that have been combined to achieve significant covariation with IQ have not always been the same across different studies.

Although it has been suggested that the pursuit of a mental speed–ability relationship is a wasted effort (Das, Kirby, & Jarman, 1979; Hunt, 1980), it seems that there is an association and it is important that we should ascertain to what extent and what it means. A variable which can possible account for about 25% of variance in IQ warrants the effort and resources required for a larger scale investigation of this relationship. My conclusion, then, is to support Mackintosh's suggestion for "a study of a large, representative sample of the population with normal mean and distribution of IQ, which employed factor analysis on a number of different IQ tests in order to discover which component or components were most closely related to inspection time" (Mackintosh, 1981, p. 529). This study should then be followed up by experimental investigations aimed at improving understanding about the nature of any relationships between IT and components of IQ.

To expand Mackintosh's suggestion, the order of subjects required to do even one such study adequately is such that collaboration between laboratories interested in this issue would be desirable. Such an arrangement should be feasible, however, given the wide availability of microcomputer technology, which could guarantee that a common procedure was followed by all research groups involved. Some preliminary developmental research would be required, however. Thus, the determination of method should extend beyond how IT was to be estimated, to include agreed procedures for personality screening, measuring sensory sensitivity, and for excluding the influence of strategies aimed at negating mask effectiveness (a topic discussed further below).

In addition to addressing the question posed by Mackintosh, such a project might also seek to clarify whether the same IT–IQ correlation is found at upper levels of IQ, as well as checking generalization to the retarded range. Neither of these matters can be said to be settled. Nettelbeck and Kirby (1983a) found that excluding 16 subjects with IQ > 115 from a sample of 96 near-normally distributed for IQ did not reduce IT–IQ correlation from $-.59$ in the main sample (average of two measures), but this is at best weak and indirect evidence for a ceiling to IT performance for above-average levels of IQ (Brand, 1984). The pattern of correlations in Lally and Nettelbeck (1977) was consistent with this idea but the distribution of nonretarded IQ was rectangular, not normal. Reanalysis of Vernon's (1983) data finds $r = -.29$ for IT and IQ 120 and below ($n = 24$), but the association beyond washes out, not so much because of convergence but because of a number of very long IT measures among high IQ subjects. The only evidence yet available on the second matter (see Section 4.2) suggests higher IT–IQ correlation within the mildly retarded range of IQ but this outcome was greatly influenced by Vernon's (1983) nonsignificant result in the nonretarded range; if this is not included then the outcome for both retarded and nonretarded ranges is virtually the same.

A sample of 300 young adults, selected in accordance with the full range of the normal distribution for IQ, would provide an adequate description of factors defined by a visual and auditory version of IT together with the 11 subscales of the WAIS for the 200 participants with IQs within ± 1 SD of the mean, while retaining 50 in each of two subsamples to check the effects of including more extreme IQ scores. This sample should be sufficient for both development and cross-validation, but procedural replications would be necessary for generalization to different populations, like children at a given age, or the elderly. In view of the effort and cost required to mount a project on this scale, psychometric tests selected would need very careful consideration. If the full CAB were used instead of WAIS, for example, the numbers required would increase considerably. It is not intended here to recommend either of these tests, although there would be advantages in using a complete instrument which provided a diversity of subscales and which had already been the focus of intensive research effort.

No conclusion can be reached regarding causation and, in view of signs of cognitive intrusion into IT performance, perhaps even at unconscious as well as conscious levels, it is certainly possible that intelligence is responsible for competence in IT tasks as well as in ability tests. The possibly extensively used strategy to detect apparent movement in some visual tasks poses a major threat to the successful demonstration of IT–IQ correlation, because individual differences in IT tend to collapse to some short common value, and some way around this difficulty must be found. The task devised by Longstreth et al. (1985) is promising, although how it might be checked against levels of internal noise is not clear. Alternatively, IT measures might be developed that were not dependent upon the backward masking method. Two potential alternatives in this regard are available (Vickers, 1970; Welford, 1971), although to this time their use has largely been restricted to comparisons between mentally retarded and nonretarded adults (Nettelbeck, 1985a). Moreover, both of these measures, which are derived from performance in conventional RT tasks, have the advantage of avoiding circularity that exists between noise and IT when measured with the backward masking procedure. (This arises because IT estimation relies on noise-free discriminative performance, but noise is defined in terms of variability in performance, allowing only a single inspection of sensory input). It is essential, however, that, before adopting any new method, it be found to match the considerable reliability of the current procedures. A useful future research strategy would be to examine within-subject performance in these tasks, together with current versions of IT and including also other tasks of phenomenal simultaneity and movement, commonly thought to reflect temporal limitations to input processing, as well as other threshold measures assumed not to do so. This would permit an examination of which measures were reliable, which converged and which did not, and may help advancement towards a more clearly defined IT construct.

As Vickers and Smith (1985) have pointed out (see Section 5.2(d)), the possibility exists that estimation of IT from the backward masking method is confounded, both by levels of internal noise beyond those anticipated and by individual differences in parameters reflecting unconscious adaptation-level. However, while such confusion would reduce the validity of IT as an index for speed of apprehension, it would not be expected to reduce reliability since the confounding variables are themselves held to be characteristic to the individual. In these terms, then, IT as currently measured may more appropriately be regarded as an index for the *efficiency* of activity associated with early central stages of perception, rather than as speed of apprehension. It would also seem advisable not to describe it as a measure of perceptual speed. However, to speculate further about what processes may be shared by IT and IQ tests serves no useful purpose, unless this has prospects for theoretical development. The suggestion by Hunt (1980), that allocation of "attentional resources" (pp. 466 ff.) may reflect strategic considerations of importance to an understanding of what constitutes intelligent behavior, seems intuitively plausible, and should lead to useful research with operationally defined attentional and strategic variables. However, as Brand (1984) has pointed out, whether the positive manifold among ability tests is attributed to "strategies in attention" or to *g* does not shift the level of explanation currently available; accounting for individual differences in terms of either construct essentially begs the question as to how such differences arise.

Vickers and Smith (1985) have referred to their recent progress with developing algorithms for simultaneously estimating several parameters of individual discriminative performance from the one set of data. Measures of degree of caution, residual nondecision time (see Section 3.1), and width of indifference region (see Section 5.2(d)) have conformed closely to predictions from a revised accumulator model but, so far, are limited to tasks for which difficulty, defined in terms of stimulus and exposure characteristics, is sufficient to virtually suppress the influence of individual differences in internal noise and IT. The longer-term aim of this work is to realize a similar degree of precision for situations where internal noise and IT can also be estimated, along with those measures already achieved. Until this is accomplished, however, the existing IT measures detailed in this chapter remain the most promising means for investigating a relationship between mental speed and intelligence. Nonetheless, the theoretical issues raised by Vickers and Smith do have important implications for the interpretation of IT research and the checks to future measurement that they have recommended, against extreme individual values for internal noise or adaptation-level, are advisable. A separate estimate of noise (Nettelbeck, 1973b; Vickers et al., 1972), or a test that λ did reliably result in virtually error-free subsequent performance, would provide a sensible adjunct to current procedures. Since changes in adaptation-level are manifested in stimulus and response-related sequential effects, response probabilities and latencies during the course of IT measurement should be recorded and examined for the presence of these effects (Vickers & Smith, 1985).

Foregoing discussion invites a comment on suggestions (a) that the IT measure might be developed to supplement conventional IQ assessment (Nettelbeck & Lally, 1976), or (b) that IT might provide a culture-fair test of intelligence, as an alternative to existing IQ tests (Brand & Deary, 1982). Although until now there has been little opportunity to evaluate these ideas, speculation about the second suggestion, in particular, has attracted world-wide publicity, both in the popular scientific press and in the general media (as summarized by Nettelbeck & Kirby, 1983b). Essentially, the assumption underlying (a) is that (i) IT can reliably reveal something about intelligence capacities that an IQ test cannot. The second proposal (b) rests on two additional assumptions: (ii) that whatever processes underly IT are dependent from cultural influences; and (iii) that IT provides a sufficient account for IQ.

Regarding assumption (i), it can be said that IT reflects an aspect of processing that is not immediately obvious from IQ test performance. This has been found to be of consequnce in a training situation involving mentally retarded persons (Nettelbeck, 1977; Nettelbeck, Cheshire, & Lally, 1979). However, the relevance of IT to intelligence rests entirely on the IT–IQ correlation, and it has not been substantiated for intellectual competence in any broader sense. Further, one cannot be certain that IT solely measures speed of apprehension, unconfounded by other variables and, while this is not critical to the assumption, it must limit the practical utility of the measure. Thus, conditions that would justify the adoption of suggestion (a) have not been realized, apart from the situation referred to.

As far as is known, no evidence is available about assumption (ii), but, irrespective of how simple a task appears to be, to the extent that cognitive strategies can be applied there exists a possibility of culture-related differences. In any case, this suggestion is not sustainable in the light of evidence reflecting on assumption (iii). Although there is shared variance between IT and IQ, it seems clear that adult intelligence, as measured by psychometric tests, involves much more besides processes engaged in IT. In fact, the degree of relationship found certainly could not support predictions about intelligence as currently measured with acceptable confidence; such predictions could be in error in either direction by the equivalent of about 13 WAIS-FSIQ points or more, in a third of all such cases.

While these speculations are not supported, however, one should not lose sight of the theoretical significance of the relationship between IT and IQ which emerges from examination of available data. Such speculation is peripheral to the main issue considered here and, as Egan (1985) has already argued, one may admit to procedural shortcomings in IT measurement without necessarily discounting findings from it; one should guard against throwing out the baby with the bathwater. The answer to the problem posed by Thurstone almost 50 years ago, and which has provided the focus for this review, seems to be "to a greater extent than has hitherto been appreciated." The questions raised by Brand about the strength and limitations of a relationship between speed of apprehension and cognition are still open.

7. SUMMARY

Inspection time (IT) is discussed in relation to Brand's theory that general intelligence can be understood in terms of the speed of initial apprehension of input. A rationale for measuring IT is described within the context of a theory of perceptual discrimination that incorporates temporal accumulation of evidence as a basic information processing operation. An estimate of IT (λ) is defined operationally as the minimum target duration at which performance in an easy task is virtually error-free. Various backward masking procedures in different modalities by means of which IT has been estimated are compared for reliability of outcome, the conclusion being that certain visual tasks requiring discrimination between 2-lines or 2-symbols, and an auditory version involving 2-tones, provide moderate to high reliability. Results from 29 direct investigations of a relationship between IT and IQ are summarized and compared in terms of sample characteristics and outcome. This examination finds important differences in method, with some studies procedurally flawed more than others, and considerable variation in outcome. Nevertheless, evidence suggests a correlation of $-.5$ between IT and IQ among normal adults, higher than has generally been found between IQ and laboratory procedures for measuring speed of information processing. Results from studies of children are not clear with respect to an IT–IQ correlation but strongly support the theory that mental speed increases with mental age. In broad terms, therefore, the outcome is consistent with Brand's theory but does not support speculation that IT might supplement or replace existing psychometric procedures. There is no clear evidence regarding the existence of a ceiling level beyond which mental speed does not increase, nor on the proposal that mental quickness at a young age is a sufficient condition for the subsequent development of high intelligence, but more than mental speed is clearly involved in adult IQ. Overall, these findings are accepted as justifying a large-scale project to develop improved procedures and to test further the nature of the IT–IQ correlation in samples at different ages with normally distributed IQ. What the IT–IQ correlation means is problematical. Attempts to link IT with different kinds of mental speed, as described by Cattell and others, suggest that IT does not reflect perceptual speed as conventionally defined but, instead, is associated with general intelligence. It is not clear to what extent IT reflects the outcome of neural efficiency, as Eysenck has suggested, rather than some fundamental rate determined by periodicity in processing. Despite face validity as an index for speed of input, there are signs that IT can be influenced by various subjective variables, some associated with personality differences, individual differences in sensitivity, concentration, level of noise within the perceptual system, and adaptation effects, that are thought to be beyond voluntary control. Other subject differences appear to reflect the adoption of different cognitive strategies and are presumed to be attributable to executive control. However, until procedures are realized whereby this structure–function distinction can be specified experimentally, it remains only a post-hoc description and cannot explain the IT–IQ association. The implications of these findings for future research are considered and various suggestions made throughout as to which directions seem likely to prove fruitful.

ACKNOWLEDGEMENTS

This chapter was prepared as part of a project supported by Grant No. A28315399 from the Australian Research Grants Scheme, and I wish particularly to thank Anthea Vreugdenhil for her unstinting help with preparation and collation of the manuscript. I am grateful to Chris Brand, Ian Deary, Charles Hume, N. J. Mackintosh, Glen Smith, and Tony Vernon for providing additional details concerning published and unpublished data, and to Carlene Wilson for permission to reproduce a figure from her doctoral dissertation. I am also grateful to Chris Brand for making it possible for me to read all of the Edinburgh theses referred to, and for very useful discussion about this material.

REFERENCES

Anderson, M. (1977). *Mental speed and individual differences in intelligence.* Unpublished thesis for the Honours Degree in Psychology, University of Edinburgh.

Beck, L. F. (1933). The role of speed in intelligence. *Psychological Bulletin, 30,* 169–178.

Berger, M. (1982). The "scientific approach" to intelligence: An overview of its history with special reference to mental speed. In H. J. Eysenck (Ed.), *A model for intelligence* (pp. 13–43). Berlin and New York: Springer-Verlag.

Brand, C. (1981). General intelligence and mental speed: Their relationship and development. In M. P. Friedman, J. P. Das, & N. O'Connor (Eds.), *Intelligence and learning* (pp. 589–593). New York: Plenum.

Brand, C. R. (1984). Intelligence and inspection time: An ontogenetic relationship? In C. J. Turner & H. B. Miles (Eds.), *The biology of human intelligence: Proceedings of the twentieth annual symposium of the Eugenics Society London, 1983* (pp. 53–64), Nafferton, UK: Nafferton Books.

Brand, C. R., & Deary, I. J. (1982). Intelligence and "inspection time." In H. J. Eysenck (Ed.), *A model for intelligence* (pp. 133–148). Berlin and New York: Springer-Verlag.

Brebner, J., & Cooper, C. (1985, June). *Personality factors and inspection times.* Paper presented at the second meeting of the International Society for the Study of Individual Differences, Sant Feliu de Guixols, Catalonia, Spain.

Cattell, R. B. (1971). *Abilities: Their structure, growth, and action.* Boston: Houghton-Mifflin.

Cooper, C., Kline, P., & Maclaurin-Jones, L. (1986). Inspection time and primary abilities. *British Journal of Educational Psychology, 56,* 304–308.

Das, J. P., Kirby, J. R., & Jarman, R. F. (1979). *Simultaneous and successive cognitive processes.* New York: Academic Press.

Deary, I. J. (1980). *How general is the mental speed factor in "general" intelligence?* Unpublished thesis for the Honour Degree (B.Sc., Med. Sci.) in Psychology, University of Edinburgh.

Dempster, F. N. (1981). Memory span: Sources of individual and developmental differences. *Psychological Bulletin, 89,* 63–100.

Dibner, A. S., & Cummins, J. F. (1961). Intellectual functioning in a group of normal octogenarians. *Journal of Consulting Psychology, 25,* 137–141.

Edwards, C. (1984). *Inspection time in three sensory modalities and its relation to measures of intelligence.* Unpublished thesis for the Honours Degree (B.A.) in Psychology, University of Adelaide, South Australia.

Egan, V. (1985, June). *Inspection time and strategies: Do high IQ subjects use special tricks?* Paper presented at the second meeting of the International Society for the Study of Individual Differences, Sant Feliu de Guixols, Catalonia, Spain.

Eysenck, H. J. (1953). *Uses and abuses of psychology.* Harmondsworth: Penguin.

Eysenck, H. J. (1967). Intelligence assessment: A theoretical and experimental approach. *British Journal of Educational Psychology, 37,* 81–98.

Eysenck, H. J. (1982). Epilogue: Is intelligence? In H. J. Eysenck (Ed.), *A model for intelligence* (pp. 255–259). Berlin and New York: Springer-Verlag.

Eysenck, H. J. (1984). Intelligence versus behavior. *The Behavioral and Brain Sciences, 7,* 290–291.

Felsten, G., & Wasserman, G. S. (1980). Visual masking: Mechanisms and theories. *Psychological Bulletin, 88,* 329–353.

Furneaux, W. D. (1952). Some speed, error, and difficulty relationships within a problem solving situation. *Nature, 170,* 3.

Furneaux, W. D. (1960). Intellectual abilities and problem solving behaviour. In H. J. Eysenck (Ed.), *Handbook of abnormal psychology* (pp. 167–192). London: Pitman.

Galton, F. (1883). *Inquiries into human faculty and its development.* London: Macmillan.

Grieve, D. (1979). *Inspection time and intelligence.* Unpublished thesis for the Honours Degree in Psychology, University of Edinburgh.

Guilford, J. P. (1956). The structure of intellect. *Psychological Bulletin, 53,* 267–293.

Guilford, J. P. (1965). *Fundamental statistics in psychology and education* (4th ed). New York: McGraw-Hill.

Hakstian, A. R., & Cattell, R. B. (1978). Higher-stratum ability structures on a basis of twenty primary abilities. *Journal of Educational Psychology, 70,* 657–669.

Heim, A. W. (1947). An attempt to test high grade intelligence. *British Journal of Psychology, 37,* 70–81.

Heim, A. W., & Batts, V. (1948). Upward and downward selection in intelligence testing. *British Journal of Psychology, 39,* 22–29.

Heim, A. W., Watts, K. P., & Simmonds, V. (1974). AH2 and AH3: Parallel tests of reasoning. *British Journal of Psychology, 65,* 493–503.

Hendrickson, A. E. (1982). The biological basis of intelligence. Part 1: Theory. In H. J. Eysenck (Ed.), *A model for intelligence* (pp. 151–196). Berlin and New York: Springer-Verlag.

Hendrickson, D. E. (1982). The biological basis of intelligence. Part II: Measurement. In H. J. Eysenck (Ed.), *A model for intelligence* (pp. 197–228). Berlin and New York: Springer-Verlag.

Hendrickson, D. E., & Hendrickson, A. E. (1980). The biological basis of individual differences in intelligence. *Personality and Individual Differences, 1,* 3–33.

Hirons, A. (1982). *The validity of inspection time and its relationship to mental retardation, incorporating measures of smooth pursuit eye movements.* Unpublished thesis for the Honours Degree (B.A.) in Psychology, University of Adelaide, South Australia.

Hosie, B. M. (1979). *Mental speed and intelligence: Their relationship and development in 4-year-old children.* Unpublished thesis for the Honours Degree in Psychology, University of Edinburgh.

Hulme, C., & Turnbull, J. (1983). Intelligence and inspection time in normal and mentally retarded subjects. *British Journal of Psychology, 74,* 365-370.

Hunt, E. (1980). Intelligence as an information processing concept. *British Journal of Psychology, 71,* 449-474.

Irwin, R. J. (1984). Inspection time and its relation to intelligence. *Intelligence, 8,* 47-65.

James, W. (1890). *The principles of psychology* (Vol. 1). New York: Holt.

Jensen, A. R. (1979). *g*: Outmoded theory or unconquered frontier? *Creative Science Technology, 2,* 16-29.

Jensen, A. R. (1982). Reaction time and psychometric *g*. In H. J. Eysenck (Ed.), *A model for intelligence* (pp. 93-132). Berlin and New York: Springer-Verlag.

Lally, M., & Nettelbeck, T. (1977).`Intelligence, reaction time, and inspection time. *American Journal of Mental Deficiency, 82,* 273-281.

Lally, M., & Nettelbeck, T. (1980). Intelligence, inspection time, and response strategy. *American Journal of Mental Deficiency, 84,* 553-560.

Lasky, R. E., & Spiro, D. (1980). The processing of tachistoscopically presented visual stimuli by five-month-old infants. *Child Development, 51,* 1292-1294.

Longstreth, L. E. (1984). Jensen's reaction-time investigations of intelligence: A critique. *Intelligence, 8,* 139-160.

Longstreth, L. E., Walsh, D. A., Alcorn, M. B., Szeszulski, P. A., & Manis, F. R. (1985, June). *Backward masking, IQ, SAT, and reaction time: Inter-relationships and theory.* Paper presented at the second meeting of the International Society for the Study of Individual Differences, Sant Feliu de Guixols, Catalonia, Spain.

Mackenzie, B., & Bingham, E. (1985). IQ, inspection time, and response strategies in a university population. *Australian Journal of Psychology, 37,* 257-268.

Mackintosh, N. J. (1981). A new measure of intelligence? *Nature, 289,* 529-530.

Massaro, D. W. (1970). Perceptual auditory images. *Journal of Experimental Psychology, 85,* 411-417.

McFarland, R. A. (1928). The role of speed in mental ability. *Psychological Bulletin, 25,* 595-612.

Muniz, J., & Lubin, M. P. (1985, June). *The relationship between psychometric intelligence and inspection time.* Paper presented at the second meeting of the International Society for the Study of Individual Differences, Sant Feliu de Guixols, Catalonia, Spain.

Nettelbeck, T. (1972). The effects of shock-induced anxiety on noise in the visual system. *Perception, 1,* 297-304.

Nettelbeck, T. (1973a). *An experimental investigation of some parameters affecting individual differences in perception.* Doctoral dissertation, University of Adelaide, South Australia.

Nettelbeck, T. (1973b). Individual differences in noise and associated perceptual indices of performance. *Perception, 2,* 11-21.

Nettelbeck, T. (1977). A skills approach to the vocational training of mildly retarded workers. *Australian Journal of Mental Retardation, 4,* 7-10.

Nettelbeck, T. (1982). Inspection time: An index for intelligence? *Quarterly Journal of Experimental Psychology, 34A,* 299-312.

Nettelbeck, T. (1985a). Inspection time and mild mental retardation. In N. R. Ellis & N. W. Bray (Eds.), *International review of research in mental retardation* (Vol. 13, pp. 109-141). New York: Academic Press.

Nettelbeck, T. (1985b). What reaction times time. *The Behavioral and Brain Sciences, 8,* 235.

Nettelbeck, T. (1985c, June). *Inspection time and IQ.* Paper presented at the second meeting of the International Society for the Study of Individual Differences, Sant Feliu de Guixols, Catalonia, Spain.

Nettelbeck, T., Cheshire, F., & Lally, M. (1979). Intelligence, work performance, and inspection time. *Ergonomics, 22,* 291–297.

Nettelbeck, T., Evans, G., & Kirby, N. H. (1982). Effects of practice on inspection time for mildly mentally retarded and nonretarded adults. *American Journal of Mental Deficiency, 87,* 103–107.

Nettelbeck, T., Hirons, A., & Wilson, C. (1984). Mental retardation, inspection time and central attentional impairment. *American Journal of Mental Deficiency, 89,* 91–98.

Nettelbeck, T., & Kirby, N. H. (1983a). Measures of timed performance and intelligence. *Intelligence, 7,* 39–52.

Nettelbeck, T., & Kirby, N. H. (1983b). Retarded-nonretarded differences in speed of processing. *Australian Journal of Psychology, 35,* 445–453.

Nettelbeck, T., Kirby, N. H., Haymes, G., & Bills, A. (1980). Influence of procedural variables on estimates of inspection time for mildly mentally retarded adults. *American Journal of Mental Deficiency, 85,* 274–280.

Nettelbeck, T., & Lally, M. (1976). Inspection time and measured intelligence. *British Journal of Psychology, 67,* 17–22.

Nettelbeck, T., & McLean, J. (1984). Mental retardation and inspection time: A two-stage model for sensory registration and central processing. *American Journal of Mental Deficiency, 89,* 83–90.

Nettelbeck, T., Robson, L., Walwyn, T., Downing, A., & Jones, N. (1986). Inspection time as mental speed in mildly retarded adults: Analysis of eye gaze, eye movement, and orientation. *American Journal of Mental Deficiency, 91,* 78–91.

Nettelbeck, T., & Vreugdenhil, A. (1986). *The IT–IQ correlation reflects more than task time constraints.* Unpublished raw data.

Nettelbeck, T., & Wilson, C. (1985). A cross-sequential analysis of developmental differences in speed of visual information processing. *Journal of Experimental Child Psychology, 40,* 1–22.

Owsley, C., Sekuler, R., & Siemsen, D. (1983). Contrast sensitivity throughout adulthood. *Vision Research, 23,* 689–699.

Raz, N., Willerman, L., Ingmundson, P., & Hanlon, M. (1983). Aptitude-related differences in auditory recognition masking. *Intelligence, 7,* 71–90.

Sen, A., & Goswami, A. (1983). Inspection time across developmental years and its relation to intelligence. *Indian Psychologist, 2,* 92–99.

Sharp, D. M. (1982). *Inspection time, intelligence and information processing theory.* Unpublished thesis for the Honours Degree (MA) in Psychology, University of Edinburgh.

Sharp, D. M. (1984). *Inspection time, decision time and visual masking: An investigation of their relationship to measured intelligence.* Unpublished thesis for the M.Sc. degree in Clinical Psychology, University of Aberdeen.

Smith, G. (1978). *Studies of compatibility and investigations of a model of reaction time.* Doctoral dissertation, University of Adelaide, South Australia.

Smith, G. (1985, June). *Individual differences in reaction time profile in inspection time tasks.* Paper presented at the second meeting of the International Society for the Study of Individual Differences, Sant Feliu de Guixols, Catalonia, Spain.

Smith, G., & Stanley, G. (1983). Clocking *g*: Relating intelligence and measures of timed performance. *Intelligence, 7,* 353–368.

Sternberg, R. J. (1977). *Intelligence, information processing, and analogical reasoning: The componential analysis of human abilities.* Hillsdale, NJ: Erlbaum.

Sternberg, R. J. (1984). Toward a triarchic theory of human intelligence. *The Behavioral and Brain Sciences, 7,* 269–315.

Stroud, J. M. (1955). The fine structure of psychological time. In H. Quastler (Ed.), *Information theory in psychology* (pp. 174–207). Glencoe, IL: Free Press.

Taylor, M. M., & Creelman, C. D. (1967). PEST: Efficient estimate on probability functions. *Journal of the Acoustical Society of America, 4,* 782–787.

Thorndike, E. L. (1926). *The measurement of intelligence.* New York: Teachers College, Columbia University.

Thurstone, L. L. (1937). Ability, motivation, and speed. *Psychometrika, 2,* 249–254.

Thurstone, L. L. (1938). Primary mental abilities. *Psychometric Monographs,* No. 1.

Tonisson, W. (1982). *On the importance of perceptual speed to language abilities in deaf adolescents.* Unpublished manuscript. [Research forms part of *Correlates of linguistic competence in congenitally deaf adolescents.* Unpublished doctoral dissertation, University of Queensland, Australia, 1985.]

Turvey, M. T. (1973). On peripheral and central processes in vision: Inferences from an informational-processing analysis of masking with patterned stimuli. *Psychological Review, 80,* 1–52.

Vernon, P. A. (1983). Speed of information processing and general intelligence. *Intelligence, 7,* 53–70.

Vickers, D. (1970). Evidence for an accumulator model of psychophysical discrimination. *Ergonomics, 13,* 37–58.

Vickers, D. (1979). *Decision processes in visual perception.* New York: Academic Press.

Vickers, D., Nettelbeck, T., & Willson, R. J. (1972). Perceptual indices of performance: The measurement of "inspection time" and "noise" in the visual system. *Perception, 1,* 263–295.

Vickers, D., & Smith, P. (1985, June). *The rationale for the inspection time index.* Paper presented at the second meeting of the International Society for the Study of Individual Differences, Sant Feliu de Guixols, Catalonia, Spain.

Welford, A. T. (1971). What is the basis of choice-reaction time? *Ergonomics, 14,* 679–693.

Wenger, L. (1975–1978). Unpublished experiments made in part requirement for a thesis (not yet completed) for the Ph.D. degree, University of Adelaide, South Australia.

White, P. O. (1973). Individual differences in speed, accuracy and persistence: A mathematical model for problem solving. In H. J. Eysenck (Ed.), *The measurement of intelligence* (pp. 246–260). Lancaster, UK: MTP Press.

White, P. O. (1982). Some major components in general intelligence. In H. J. Eysenck (Ed.), *A model for intelligence* (pp. 44–90). Berlin and New York: Springer-Verlag.

Wilson, C. (1980). *A developmental study of perceptual processing speed.* Unpublished thesis for the Honours Degree (B.A.) in Psychology, University of Adelaide, South Australia.

Wilson, C. (1984). *Developmental studies in timed performance.* Doctoral dissertation, University of Adelaide, South Australia.

Wissler, C. (1901). The correlation of mental and physical traits. *Psychological Monographs, 3,* (6, Whole No. 16).

CHAPTER 10

The Next Word on Verbal Ability[1]

Earl Hunt
The University of Washington

INTRODUCTION

Human language may well be evolution's most impressive intellectual feat. In most animals, intraspecies signalling is restricted to the communication of internal emotional states such as fear or sexual receptivity. A few species do use communication to identify specific threats or food sources. Humans can do all these things, discuss abstract or nonexistent beings, and even tell lies. Furthermore, our easily understood language is so complex that the much publicized "artificial intelligence" computers can only comprehend the simplest parts of our speech. A recent book on artificial intelligence offers a useful bolster to the human ego:

> an important aspect of intelligence is not that a genius can play the logical and mathematical game of chess but that people who are not considered to be very bright can talk, learn, understand, and explain their experiences, feelings and conclusions. Talking is incredibly complicated. A man with a low IQ is not stu-

[1]This chapter is a general review of the field of verbal comprehension. It includes brief summaries of studies my associates and I have conducted, supported by a variety of grants and contracts from the Office of Naval Research, the National Institute of Mental Health, and the National Institute of Education. The support received is gratefully acknowledged. Naturally, the opinions expressed are my own, and not those of the various sponsors. The chapter is also a summary of presentations made at the NATO Advanced Study Institute on Intelligence, Athens, in December of 1984, and at the British Psychological Society's Conference on Reading, Leicester, England, in April of 1986.

pid. He's incredibly intelligent compared to other animals and present-day computers.

(Schank & Childers, 1984, pg. 30)

This quotation captures several crucial facts about language. The most important fact is that the level of linguistic competence required to be even a somewhat marginal human is very impressive indeed. At the same time, the passage acknowledges the fact of variation in human ability. That variation is partly reflected in verbal competence. The ability to deal with language is related to, but not exactly the same as, a general ability to think well. Traditional intelligence (IQ) tests recognize this; virtually every IQ test (e.g., the Wechsler and Stanford-Binet tests) contains separate "verbal" and "nonverbal" scales. The distinction between verbal and nonverbal skills is hardly a discovery of modern psychology. In the *Odyssey,* Homer observed that not all men have the gift of eloquence. Many a classroom teacher has observed that not all have the gift of comprehension.

Individual differences in the ability to understand language (henceforth "verbal comprehension") are important in human life. Because formal instruction is largely verbal, individual differences in verbal comprehension are a major factor in determining who benefits from education. The benefits of being a good comprehender appear to extend outside the classroom. Sticht (1975) found that tests of reading and listening ability were among the best predictors of job performance in a variety of U.S. Army occupational specialties. The specialties tested included some (e.g., armored vehicle crewman) that are not usually considered to be highly verbal occupations. There are substantial individual differences in the skill with which people deal with their language, and these differences are important correlates of success in our society.

Traditionally the task of identifying those of high or low verbal ability has been regarded as a problem in personnel classification. An impressive set of tests has been developed to solve it. By and large, these tests are based upon face-valid samples of verbal performance. Vocabulary tests are given because vocabulary is obviously essential to linguistic competence. Paragraph comprehension tests provide small work samples of how well the examinee can comprehend a message. There is massive evidence showing that verbal comprehension tests of this sort do measure *how well* individuals can deal with important aspects of language. What the conventional verbal comprehension test does not do is to explain *how* some people achieve higher verbal competency than do others. The latter question can only be answered by using tests that are based upon a theory of how verbal comprehension is accomplished, and not upon a theory of how it is to be demonstrated.

Since this point is crucial, let us consider an analogy to a well known motor skill, typing. Typing competence can be measured by seeing how quickly and accurately different people type the same documents. The measurement procedure will identify good and bad typists, but will not explain why some people have typing skills and others do not. A finer analysis of typing shows that it depends upon a complex process of hand–eye–brain coordination. The muscle movements used to type a given character will depend upon the position of the typist's fingers before the character is to be struck. Typists typically read the scripts being typed several characters in front of the character currently being printed. Experienced typists may use information about likely character sequence, such as the high frequency triplet *ion,* to execute a sequence of movements as a single response. None of these actions is typing, but all of them are used in typing. Individual differences between typists could arise from individual differences in the ability to read ahead, differences in the ability to execute a sequence of movements, or individual differences in any of a number of other subsidiary processes of typing. Since efficiency in one of the subprocesses may compensate somewhat for inefficiencies in other subprocesses, observing that two typists type at the same speed does not ensure us that the two type in the same way.

Exactly the same arguments apply to attempts to understand individual differences in verbal comprehension. A well-designed work sample can identify good comprehenders. Explaining *why* some are better verbal comprehenders than others requires a theory of the comprehension process. The theory must identify the subprocesses of language understanding, and, ideally, it must specify ways in which these processes can be evaluated in isolation. Once such a theory has been developed, the next step is to locate populations that vary on global (worksample) measures of verbal performance. Further studies can then be conducted to associate global variation in competence with variations shown by the more theoretically understandable measures of subprocesses. Since 1970, experimental psychologists have attempted to do just this. Some of the key findings will be reviewed. Before the review can begin, though, the theoretical underpinnings of the approach must be made clear. The following section describes a theory of the human mind, with emphasis on linguistic analysis. Is it the correct theory? No one knows. Fortunately, though, many investigators are agreed upon the outlines of the model to be presented.

A Model of the Mind

Virtually all modern theories of cognition assume that the mind consists of two somewhat distinct information structures; a *working memory* that contains a relatively small amount of information about the current situation facing the thinker, and a *long term memory* that contains the facts that the thinker knows about the world. World knowledge can be divided into two types of information—*declarative knowledge* about facts, and *procedural knowledge* about the conscious and unconscious actions that are appropriate in particular situations. To give some flavor to the distinction, the knowledge that seeing the visual stimulus CAT is a signal to retrieve information about the concept "cat" is a piece of procedural information. My memory of the black cat that crossed my path when I went jogging on the morning of Friday the 13th is declarative knowledge.

Information in working memory and long term memory can be thought of as being stored in an abstract propositional code, rather than as a record of one's sensory coding of the environment. (The propositional code may contain some information about the sensory form of the stimuli, but that is another matter.) Working memory and long term memory are believed to be supplemented by modality specific buffer memories, or *channels,* that do contain memorial information that is closely tied to sensation. For example, it is generally believed that, during a conversation, people can recall the last four or five words that they have heard, but that information presented some time ago will be stored in a code that reflects the gist of the conversation but not the auditory sensations received by the listener. The theory assumes that the word "information" is stored in an auditory channel, and the gist "information" in the more abstract (propositionally coded) working memory.

The flow of information is assumed to be from the sensory system to the channels, and from there to long term memory, where procedural knowledge is used to produce semantically augmented codes that may be inserted into working memory information structures. The working memory structures are then available to provide a further cue for the procedural memory system. This scheme is shown in block diagram form in Figure 1.

To capture the flavor of the model, consider the internal events that might have been produced by the sight of a black cat early on the morning of Friday the 13th.

1. The sight of the animal places information in a visual channel.

2. The information on the visual channel activates long term information about "cats in general." Some of this information is placed into working memory, identifying the animal.

3. Working memory information activates further concepts about cats, including the semantically associated information about bad luck and, through it, recall of the declarative fact that it is Friday the 13th.

The point of this vignette is that the information structure contained in working memory constitutes an interpretation of an event. The interpretation will be influenced by the information already in long term memory, and, as the interpretation is formed, it will serve as a stimulus to activate other information in long term memory. In order to explain verbal comprehension,

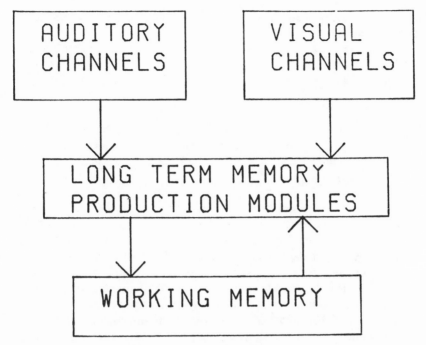

FIGURE 1.   A model of the flow of information during comprehension. See text for explanation.

one must explain how long term and short term information are molded together to create an event interpretation from a linguistic message.

The above account is a very broad-brush treatment of a model of the mind that is now the subject of intensive study in cognitive psychology. More formal treatments of these ideas can be found in Anderson (1983), Hunt and Lansman (1986), and Thibadeau, Just, and Carpenter (1982). The broad treatment presented here is sufficient to highlight the processes that appear to be essential in achieving the sorts of verbal competencies that people demonstrably do have. What are these processes, and to what extent do individual differences in them determine individual differences in general verbal competence?

Linguistic and Psychological Concerns

Linguists define a language as the (possibly infinite) set of well formed expressions that can be created by applying a finite set of rules to strings composed of symbols from a finite vocabulary. For example, the mathematical notation that students learn in high school algebra defines a language that has clearcut rules for constructing well formed expressions. Students recognize strings such as

(1) $a + x = 7 - y$

and

(2) $2(b + 2x) = 9y$

as being well formed because they can identify the elements in the lexicon (i.e., the elementary symbols), and they can use known rules of expression formation to recreate the strings. By the same token, students reject

*(3) $3(b)) = +$

as a well-formed expression because there are no language rules that permit the symbols in (3) to be combined in this manner. Mathematical theories of language that were popular in the 1950s and 1960s make language comprehension appear as if it depended upon a sequential analysis much like the one that might be used to analyze algebraic equations. In an extreme version of these theories, the comprehender first identifies the individual (lexical) items in a string, then conducts a syntactic analysis to determine where each lexical item appears in the structure of the string, and finally assigns meaning to a string by combining syntactical knowledge of its structure with semantic knowledge of the meaning of the lexical items, in isolation.

This process, which will be called the "pure linguistic approach," works well for the comprehension for artificial languages, including the important cases of algebra and computer programming languages. It is easy to show that the pure linguistic approach is not a good model of the comprehension of natural language. Numerous examples of its deficiencies will be offered below. The basic reason that the pure linguistic approach fails as a model of verbal comprehension is that, when humans comprehend language, their goal is to understand the situation in which the message is presented. The linguistic structure of the message itself is only one of several cues that they may use to do this. Perfetti, Beverly, Didonato, and Pertsch (1985) offered an excellent case in point, which has the advantage of being an actual example of an often hypothesized linguistic structure. A newspaper headline read

(4)   Police can't stop gambling.

Is this a comment on the police's inability to control criminals or their inability to control their own impulsive financial behavior? There is no way to know without understanding the situation to which the sentence refers.

A theory of verbal comprehension has to explain how messages such as (4) are understood, not how they are assigned linguistic structure. Therefore the pure linguistic model is not a model of the psychological process of comprehension. On the other hand, it is far from irrelevant. Certainly, some of comprehension is based on linguistic analyses. These analyses can be classified, loosely, as involving lexical processes, those involving single words, and syntactical-semantic processes involving groups of words. The linguistic model is a useful beginning point in examining how people apply their information-processing resources to word and sentence understanding. A psychological model must then be extended to pragmatic analysis of the message in the context in which it occurs. This is the point at which the linguistic model breaks down. And there is another problem, which is quite outside of linguistics.

A psychological theory of comprehension must explain how people cope with the real-time pressures inherent in comprehension. Understanding must keep up with the rate at which information is received. The demands are most obvious in listening, but are also present in reading. The lexical and syntactic processing of new input competes for resources with the syntactical, semantic, and pragmatic processing of old input. In addition, the processing of new input will be guided by the results of analysis of previously received fragments of a discourse.

Clearly, language comprehension is a complex process that depends on many subprocesses. There are marked individual differences in the overall ability to comprehend language. To what extent are they due to individual differences in the various subprocesses? Or in the ability of people to execute all the subprocesses at once? These are the questions that have to be addressed if we are going to understand individual differences in verbal ability instead of simply assessing them.

A Note on Terminology

A certain amount of jargon will be used in the remainder of this chapter. Unless otherwise indicated, the term "verbal comprehension ability" will refer to the ability measured by any of several written tests of verbal comprehension. Such tests typically include subtests of vocabulary knowledge, the ability to extract information from brief paragraphs, and (somewhat less often) the ability to recognize correct syntactical structures. Verbal comprehension tests can be thought of as work samples of reading. As has been noted, there is considerable evidence to show that reading comprehension is usually an excellent predictor of the ability to comprehend the spoken language (Palmer, MacLeod, Hunt, & Davidson, 1985; Sticht, 1975).

The term *high verbal* will be used to refer to a person who acheives a score in the top quartile of scores on a verbal comprehension test. A *low verbal* person will be defined as a person whose score is in the bottom quartile. Unless otherwise noted, the quartiles themselves will be defined relative to the population of United States university students. It is important to remember that university students as a group have considerably higher verbal comprehension scores than do members of the general population. A low verbal university student will have a score in the average range of the test scores in the high school population (Hunt, Lunneborg, & Lewis, 1975).

Throughout, "verbal ability" will refer to comprehension rather than production. One can easily imagine a person who is a high verbal, by the definition just offered, and is low in speech production. Unfortunately, the opposite case also occurs.

The remaining sections of this chapter will first present and illustrate particular aspects of the comprehension process, and then describe studies of individual differences in the process being described. Throughout, emphasis will be placed on whether or not a measure of a subprocess of verbal comprehension distinguishes between those who, globally, show high or low verbal ability.

LEXICAL AND SUB-LEXICAL PROCESSES

A language's lexicon is its collection of individual meaning-bearing elements—loosely, the word stems, suffixes, and prefixes. The vocabulary consists of the words constructed from lexical elements. The lexical items themselves are produced by combining perceivable but meaningless speech elements, such as phonemes and, in written language, graphemes. These will be referred to as sublexical elements. The sublexical elements are directly perceivable, but are not the smallest possible units of perception. In spoken language, the lexicon is developed from phonemes that are perceived as a unit, not as a combination of sounds, but the sounds in a phoneme can be perceived when they are presented alone. The graphemes of phonetically based written languages are similarly constructed of constrained letter groups that appear to function as perceptual units (Spoehr & Smith, 1973). Obviously, the individual letters can be perceived. In some cases, individual letters function as graphemes. They are made up of line patterns that can be seen separately but that are responded to as parts of a gestalt.

There are substantial individual differences in the ability to recognize and manipulate sublexical elements. My colleagues and I (Hunt et al. 1975) asked college students to judge the order of presentation of a pair of dichotically presented sounds that either were or were not sublexical units of speech. The experimental situation is shown diagrammatically in Figure 2(a). Figure 2(b) plots the results, showing accuracy in the perception of the order of presentation of phonemes (/bae/, /dae/ or /gae/) or nonspeech sounds (buzz, hiss, tone). High verbal students were better than low verbals at discriminating the order of speech sounds, but there was no difference in the discrimination of temporal order of nonspeech sounds. This result is consistent with the "analysis by synthesis" theory of speech perception, which maintains that

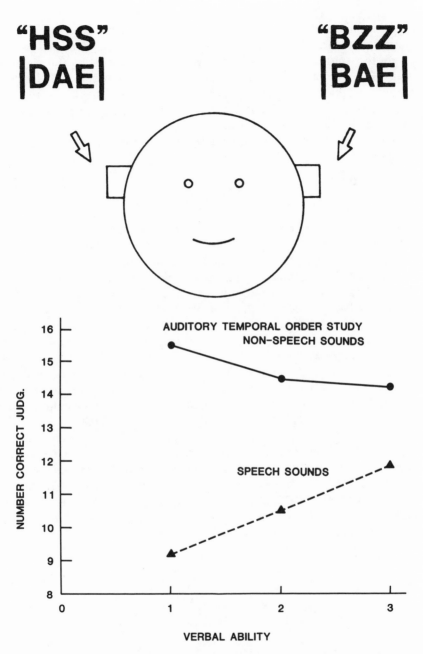

FIGURE 2. Verbal ability is related to the ability to perceive sub-lexical elements. The task (panel a) was to detect the order of dichotically presented speech or nonspeech sounds. High verbal people were better at detecting speech sounds than were low verbal people. There was no difference for nonspeech sounds.

phonetic units are perceived directly, by specialized speech processing brain systems that are at least partially isolated from the normal perceptual proces- ses for recognition of tones and nonspeech sounds in isolation (Liberman & Mattingly, 1985). Our results show that, across individuals, the efficiency of speech perception and nonspeech perception vary somewhat independently.

Frederiksen (1982) has reported a study of visual speech stimuli that is somewhat analogous to our study of verbal stimuli. High school students were shown strings of letters followed by a visual mask. A possible sequence would be

(5)   tmea

    ****.

The time between the onset of the letter string and the mask (stimulus onset asynchrony, or SOA) was varied systematically. Frederiksen estimated the rate of extraction of visual information from the stimulus by analyzing the improvement in report as SOA increased. (A rather complicated procedure was used to do this. No attempt will be made to explain it here.) Table 1 shows the change in rate of extraction of visual letter information as a func- tion of reading ability.

Juxtaposing Frederiksen's and our own results raises an interesting ques- tion. Are people who are sensitive to the perception of phonemes in spoken speech the same people who are sensitive to the perceptions of graphemes in written speech? While this question has not been fully studied, the data that are available suggests that they are. In our own work, high and low verbal students were identified on the basis of a written test, and then shown to dif- fer in aspects of speech-relevant auditory perception. In another study in our laboratory we found that tests of the comprehension of spoken paragraphs correlate as highly with tests of the comprehension of written paragraphs as the reading tests correlate with each other (Palmer et al., 1985). This is con- sistent with Sticht's (1975) finding that tests of the comprehension of written and spoken English are virtually interchangeable predictors of job perform- ance in the Army.

TABLE 1
Letter Identification and Reading Skill

Reading Group	Letter Identification Rate (Logistic Transform)
11–47th Percentile	364
48–77th Percentile	378
85–97th Percentile	406
98th Percentile +	443

Data from Frederickson (1982).

There is an important qualification to the general observation that reading and verbal comprehension go together. Some people do have reading-specific language disabilities (*dyslexias*), even though they appear, at least superficially, to have normal ability to comprehend verbal speech. Some writers have suggested that this is due to a specific deficit in manipulating visual information in memory. Such manipulation is a requirement in reading, since eye movements seem to move somewhat ahead of comprehension (Morrison, Giordani, & Nagy, 1977). Others have claimed that dyslexia is a reflection of weaknesses in general verbal comprehension that can be masked in verbal communication, but that cannot be in reading (Vellutino, 1979). There may be truth in both positions. Since reading depends upon visual analysis, the translation of visual information into language information, and the manipulation of language, failures in any of these component processes could produce a failure to read. No attempt will be made here to deal with this complicated clinical issue.

The term *lexical access* will be used to refer to the process of identifying an auditory or visual stimulus as a lexical unit. Several paradigms have been used to demonstrate individual differences in lexical access (Hunt, 1978; Hunt, Davidson, & Lansman, 1981). The *lexical* decision task illustrated in Figure 3 has proven to be particularly useful. A participant is shown either a word or a letter string that follows the orthographic conventions of English; e.g., CARD or CARG. The task is to identify the string as a word or a nonword. There is a correlation of − .4 between the time required for the word or nonword decision and verbal comprehension scores. The negative correlation is expected, because it indicates that slow lexical identification is associated with low verbal comprehension scores.

Does the lexical decision task really isolate the lexical access process? One can object that a word–nonword decision is a measure of a person's ability to identify a string as being in the lexicon, but that the decision is not analagous to normal lexical access because the decision can be made without retrieving word meaning. This does not seem to be a serious problem. The Hunt et al.

CARD   CARG

FIGURE 3.   The lexical decision task. Following a warning, a letter string is displayed. The observer must classify the string as a word or nonword. In the example CARD would be classified as a word if it were displayed. If CARG were displayed a nonword response would be made.

(1981) study included several other tests of various aspects of lexical retrieval. Among the measures taken were tests of the ability to identify words as different in form but same in meaning (e.g., bird–BIRD) and tests of the speed with which a noun could be identified as a member of a semantic category (e.g., Animal . . . Bear?). A factor analysis showed that the measures were tied together by a single "lexical identification" factor. These conclusions were reinforced in a larger study of reading in college students, which also identified a "word handling" factor and found that it correlated about .4 with a factor defined by scores on tests of reading comprehension (Palmer et al., 1985).

Lexical identification does not occur in a single leap, word meanings are retrieved over time. Furthermore, the deeper the meaning required, the more the high verbal individual separates from the low verbal. Goldberg, Schwartz, and Stewart (1977) demonstrated this using the stimulus matching paradigm illustrated in Figure 4(a). Subjects were presented with two words, and asked if they were "the same" by various criteria. For example, the words in the pair (DEAR DEAR) are physically identical, the words in the pair (DEAR DEER) are homophones, and the words in the pair (DEER ELK) are members of the same semantic category. Figure 4(b) shows the times taken by high and low verbal university students to make each sort of identification. Students in the high verbal category were faster at making identifications in all cases. The disparity between high verbal and low verbal students increased as the decision requirements became more complex.

Lexical access requires visual or auditory "scanning"; people seek out a target in the presence of irrelevant or conflicting stimuli. Scanning tasks are highly susceptible to practice effects. The difference in scanning speeds between practiced and nonpracticed participants may be as much as ten to one. The effect is quite general, having been observed when targets are defined by visual, auditory, or semantic characteristics (Fisk & Schneider, 1983; Poltrock, Lansman, & Hunt, 1982; Schneider & Shiffrin, 1977). Could the observed individual differences in lexical access simply be due to some people's having more practice with the language, and therefore having brought their scanning skills to a higher level of scanning efficiency? Practice undoubtedly does influence lexical access, for high frequency words can be accessed more rapidly than low frequency words. However, practice is unlikely to be the only reason for the observed individual differences. If high and low verbal students are given equivalent amounts of practice with an artificial lexicon, they still differ in their performance on the stimulus matching task (Jackson, 1980).

While this finding rules out an explanation of individual differences in lexical access based solely on differential exposure to lexical stimuli per se, two related explanations are still viable. People with high verbal comprehension skill may have developed superior techniques for detecting and storing the

(a) PHYSICAL IDENTITY   DEAR – DEAR

HOMOPHONE IDENTITY   DEAR – DEER

TAXONOMIC IDENTITY   DEER – ELK

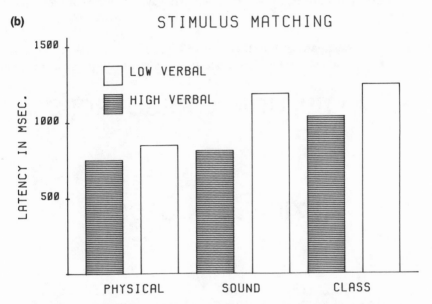

FIGURE 4. The stimulus matching task. Identity between items may be established at the physical, homophonic, or semantic levels. (Panel a) The disparity between high and low verbal ability students increases with the time required to make the match.

meaning of arbitrary linguistic stimuli. Some evidence to support this hypothesis will be presented subsequently. Assuming for the minute that the hypothesis is true, the high verbal students in Jackson's study may have produced better memorial representations of the artificial "verbal" stimuli than did the low verbal students, even though practice was equated in the two groups. It is also possible that good verbal comprehenders have superior pattern recognition mechanisms, and thus that they are better able to retrieve meanings than are poor comprehenders, even though both groups have equivalent representations of verbal stimuli in their memory. At present, there is no clearcut evidence favoring either of these hypotheses. Furthermore, the hypotheses themselves are not mutually exclusive.

What do these findings imply for the total process of comprehension? Let us consider three facts about lexical processing in general:

1. Lexical processing is compulsory. Language comprehension demands word identification.
2. Lexical processing approximates an automatic recognition process. To the extent that word recognition is completely automatized (in the sense of Schneider & Schiffrin, 1977) the act of recognition should exert minimal interference on concurrent mental tasks.
3. Individuals differ in the speed and efficiency with which they access their lexicon.

Figure 5 is a schematic of how these facts fit into the theoretical conceptualization of verbal comprehension. Each subprocess of comprehension must

ATTENTIONAL RESOURCES

LEXICAL PROCESSES

RESIDUAL RESOURCES

SYNTACTICAL AND SEMANTIC PROCESSES

PRAGMATIC PROCESSES

FIGURE 5.   A schematic of the competition for information handling resources during verbal comprehension.

complete for the use of a limited amount of information processing machinery, primarily working memory. Since lexical processing provides the raw material for comprehension (and since spoken words are ephemeral) lexical processing must be given high priority. To the extent that lexical access is rapid and efficient, its priority does not pose a threat to other subprocesses of comprehension, such as the manipulation of information in working memory. If lexical access processes are slow, and if they deliver imperfectly formed "products" (i.e., memorial codes for words) to the comprehension processes that follow lexical access, the entire act of comprehension may break down. There seem to be substantial individual differences in the speed and efficiency of lexical access. Given the same amount of text, and the same time to study it, the high verbal individual probably has a better quality of semantic information to work with as further comprehension is attempted, and is able to obtain the information at less cost.

Sentence Processing:
Syntactical and Semantic Aspects of Comprehension

A sentence is a string of lexical items that conforms to certain *syntactic* rules of well formedness. For example, one can imagine a simplified version of English in which all sentences were presented in subject–verb–object order. If comprehension followed the idealized linguistic model, the meaning of a sentence would be determined by discovering its structure, and then combining semantic knowledge about the individual lexical items with syntactic knowledge of the role that each item played in the sentence. The process can be illustrated by the analysis of expressions in a well known artificial language, common algebra. In algebra, the "sentences" are equations that must obey fairly simple rules for well formedness. The string

$$(6) \quad x + 2 * (y - 3) = z$$

is an assertion that the value of z is equal to the value of x plus two times the value of the quantity "the value of y minus three." The combined role of structure and semantics is illustrated by contrasting the interpretation of multiplication (" * ") in example (6) with its interpretation in example (7);

$$(7) \quad x + 2 * y - 3 = z.$$

Semantically, "*" always refers to the multiplication function, which maps any pair of real numbers into their product. The arguments for the multiplication function are determined by the structural role of " * " in an equation. The same point can be illustrated in natural language by observing that "John loves Mary" does not mean the same thing as "Mary loves John."

To take a somewhat more detailed set of examples, consider the following three sentences.

(8) * "Dog cat chased barked the the that."

(9) "The dog that barked chased the cat."

(10) "The cat that barked chased the dog."

Sentence (8) is gibberish, since it does not follow the syntactic rules of English. Sentences (9) and (10) are both "good English," since they have permissible syntactical structures. By combining the sentence structure with the semantics of the words, one can construct *propositions* from both (9) and (10). These are logical statements that express the meaning of the sentence. Assertions are usually written in a pseudomathematical notation that express the relations between terms that are intended by the sentence. The proposition stated in (9) is

(11) Chases((barks (dog,past)), cat, past),

and (10) is

(12) Chases (barks (cat,past),dog, past).

The propositional notation highlights the fact that the verb expresses a relation between the objects that are referred to in the sentence. Since verbs, like mathematical relations, can place (semantic) restrictions on their arguments, linguistic analysis breaks down if the syntactical analysis does not assign an appropriate entity to each argument of a verb. "John loves apple pie" is the basis of a linguistically plausible proposition, while "Apple pie loves John" is not, since only animate beings can be the subject of "loves". What the pure linguistic analysis is not concerned with is truth. "John loves apple pie" is an acceptable sentence even if John hates apple pie.

Although the idealized linguistic model will eventually prove to be inadequate to explain sentence processing, it is a useful vehicle for analyzing some miniature language understanding situations that have been designed to emphasize three important psychological points; the importance of working memory as a necessary part of comprehension, the existence of wide individual differences in speed and accuracy of sentence comprehension, even when the messages are of such low complexity that the idealized linguistics approach is an adequate model of comprehension, and the importance of individual differences in working memory capacity as a predictor of individual differences in verbal comprehension ability.

In *sentence verification* experiments, the participant is asked to determine whether or not a sentence correctly describes a picture. A simple example is shown in Figure 6. The speed and accuracy of verification is systematically related to the complexity of the proposition expressed by the sentence. For in-

PLUS ABOVE STAR

FIGURE 6. The sentence verification paradigm. The participant is shown a sentence or phrase, followed by a picture. The task is to determine whether or not the sentence accurately describes the picture.

stance, it takes longer to decide that the picture in Figure 6 can be described as "Plus not below star" than it does to verify the description "Plus above star" (Carpenter & Just, 1975; Clark & Chase, 1972). This phenomenon is not an artifact of the experimental situation, nor is it due to the fact that sentences expressing a complex proposition tend to be long. The time required to read sentences in text is a function of the number of propositions the sentence expresses, rather than the number of words involved (Kintsch & Keenan, 1973).[2]

Speed of sentence verification is correlated with verbal comprehension scores. This was first noted by Baddeley (1968), and has since been confirmed in several other studies (Hunt, 1978; Hunt et al., 1981; Palmer et al., 1985; Lansman, 1978; Lansman, Donaldson, Hunt, & Yantis, 1983). Statistically, sentence verification measures are associated with a proportion of the variance in verbal comprehension scores that is partially independent of the portion of variance associated with measures of lexical access (Hunt et al., 1981; Palmer et al., 1985). This shows that individual differences in syntactical-semantic processes stand apart from individual differences in lexical access. Put another way, there are two abilities; the ability to get at words and the ability to extract meaning from groups of words. They are related, but they are not the same.

---

[2]The relation between the time to analyze a sentence and the complexity of its propositions may break down in situations in which visual imagery is used to understand the sentence (MacLeod, Hunt, & Mathews, 1978). The interaction between visual imagery and linguistic understanding is an interesting topic in itself, but will not be explored here. Fortunately, it is also possible to arrange a sentence verification experiment in a manner that ensures that people rely primarily on linguistic strategies. (Kroll & Corrigan, 1981; Mathews, Hunt, & MacLeod, 1980). The remarks here are confined to studies in which it is reasonable to assume that linguistic strategies were being used.

The distinction between individual differences in lexical and syntactic-semantic processing can be made in another way. Suppose that high school and college students took tests of sentence verification speed and vocabularly knowledge. Scores on the two tasks would be positively correlated. However, the two can be broken apart by a universal, naturally occurring phenomenon: age. Figure 7 summarizes data from different experiments conducted in our laboratory, using two independent samples from the same population, University of Washington alumni who agreed to participate in a series of studies on changes in cognition over the working years. The left ordinate of Figure 7 shows vocabulary score as a function of age, in terms of the percentage of words correctly defined. We found, as have many others (Botwinick, 1977), that older people have vocabularies that are equal to or better than those of their younger counterparts. On the other hand, the speed of analysis of what are, after all, very simple sentences slows markedly with advancing age. These results are further evidence for the need to distinguish between measures of a person's lexicon and measures of a person's facility in sentence analysis. Both abilities are part of verbal comprehension, but neither defines comprehension ability.

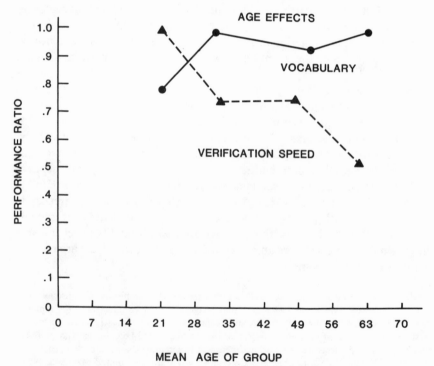

FIGURE 7. Vocabulary knowledge increases with age but speed of sentence verification decreases.

Since the ability to analyze a sentence is not perfectly correlated with measures of lexical access ability, the two processes must depend on somewhat different information processing structures. Working memory appears to be heavily involved in sentence analysis, but only minimally involved in lexical access. The case for working memory being involved in sentence analysis can be made on logical grounds alone. The syntax of natural languages permits the generation of strings that cannot be analyzed unless the comprehender can hold role assignment of a lexical unit in abeyance while other items are analyzed. Example 9 illustrates this. The processing of the main clause ("the dog chased the cat") must be interrupted while the relative clause following "dog" ("that barked") is analyzed. In other cases the first part of the string may appear to be analyzable with one structure, but that structure is disallowed by lexical items later in the string. The comprehender must fetch information back from working memory in order to derive the correct structure. Consider the "garden path sentence",

(13)   The horse raced past the barn fell.

The correct propositional structure for "The horse raced past the barn" cannot be extracted until the last word is detected. While garden path sentences are somewhat forced, they do occur in natural language and can be comprehended. Memory must be involved.

Direct observations of people's behavior during reading have provided indices of memory activity at key points during sentence analysis. Furthermore, activity in working memory appears to interfere with other, ongoing information processing. Constituent structures are contiguous words that are combined into a meaningful unit. For instance, the sentence "the red dog chased the black cat" contains as its constituents the agent (the red dog) and the predicate (chased (the black cat)). As shown, the predicate contains a constituent substructure. It appears that people store words in working memory more or less veridically, perhaps in an acoustic code, until they can identify constituents. The process of constituent analysis can interfere with ongoing perception. If a click is sounded during sentence processing, people tend to report clicks that were presented within a constituent as having occurred after it (Fodor & Bever, 1965). To illustrate, one would expect

(14)   The first (click) president spoke to the first lady.

to be heard as

(14′)   The first president (click) spoke to the first lady.

In terms of the model proposed earlier, the auditory portion of working memory serves as a holding area until the clause boundary is reached, at which time the clause is processed and moved into some more abstract code.

Only then is the auditory portion of working memory available for conscious reception of the sound of the click.[3]

Working memory may also be inferred by observing behavior during reading, where people can control the rate of input of information. Observations of eye movements during reading have shown that people pause when they encounter the end of a sentence. Presumably, the reader uses the pause to rearrange his or her working memory of the sentence just read, in order to extract the correct proposition. This has been called the "sentence wrap-up" effect (Just & Carpenter, 1980). As would be expected from this analysis, when people are queried for memory of the exact words they have just read, their memory is better for words within a sentence that they are reading than words across sentence boundaries, even when the total number of words to be recalled is held constant (Perfetti, 1985). This is consistent with the assumption that comprehenders store words until a sentence or similar constituent boundary is detected, and then replace the words by the proposition they express. There is no need to retain the exact words of a sentence in working memory once the proposition has been extracted.

In the studies just cited the role of working memory was inferred by noting how working memory involvement in comprehension appeared to preclude other activities requiring working memory. An alternative way to demonstrate the importance of working memory in sentence comprehension is to overload working memory with information that is irrelevant to comprehension, and then to show that the memory load interferes with comprehension. This has been done in studies by Baddeley and Hitch (1974) and Lansman (1978). A rather complex pattern of results has emerged.

Figure 8a shows Lansman's procedure. Her participants were first given a list of digits to remember, then verified sentences in a paradigm similar to that illustrated by Figure 6, and finally recalled the digits. A rather complex picture was observed. The presence of the memorization task increased sentence verification times, especially when the memory load was high (five or six digits to be remembered). However, the effect was almost entirely confined to an increase in the time required to verify the first sentence presented after the digits had been displayed. This is shown in Figure 8b, which displays sentence verification times as a joint function of the number of digits to be remembered, the position of the sentence relative to the memory task (immediately following or after one or more sentences), and the verbal ability of the

---

[3]The experiments on click perception have been criticized on the grounds that there may have been response biases to report uninterrupted constituents, and on the grounds that the effect could be produced by the participant's reorganizing constituent structures in memory at the time of recall. While response biases do exist, they cannot account for the entire effect. Even if the second point were granted, the studies would still demonstrate the major point being made here, that during comprehension constituent structures become constructed units in working memory. See Clark and Clark (1977) for a brief review of the issue and further citations.

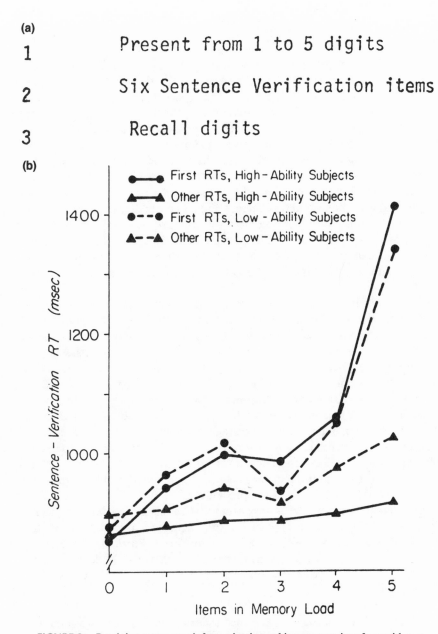

(a)

1   Present from 1 to 5 digits

2   Six Sentence Verification items

3   Recall digits

(b)

● — ● First RTs, High – Ability Subjects
▲ — ▲ Other RTs, High – Ability Subjects
● – – ● First RTs, Low - Ability Subjects
▲ – – ▲ Other RTs, Low – Ability Subjects

Sentence – Verification RT (msec)

Items in Memory Load

FIGURE 8. Retaining extraneous information in working memory interferes with sentence comprehension, but the relation is complex. Panel a illustrates how a memory and a sentence verification task were combined. Panel b shows the influence of a concurrent memory load on sentence verification. The effects are plotted separately for people of high and low verbal ability. Verification of the first sentence presented after the memory task is quite sensitive to memory load. The verification of subsequent sentences is much less sensitive to memory load.

367

participants in the experiment. A similar series of experiments by Klapp, Marshburn, and Lester (1983) produced essentially the same results. What this suggests is that the working memory space occupied by sentence comprehension is not identical to the space occupied by the digit memorization task. Thus, an analogy to a workbench shared between the two tasks is not appropriate. On the other hand, it does appear that attention can be fixed on only one of the tasks in working memory, and that, when a new task is introduced, some time is required for the comprehender to move attention from the working memory structures required for the first task (here, digit memorization) to deal with the second task (here, sentence comprehension). Both tasks compete for attention to working memory structures, but not for the space occupied by those structures. This phenomenon appears to be quite widespread, and can account for the data on competition between concurrent tasks in a number of fields in addition to language comprehension (Wickens, 1979).

These results introduce complexities into what at first seems a simple question; to what extent are individual differences in verbal comprehension determined by individual differences in working memory capacity? Clearly, some information about a linguistic message is held in memory while further information is being processed. The efficiency of the memory process will be determined by the amount of attention that can be devoted to it, but this will be determined by the amount of attention required by the comprehension process. The converse reasoning also applies; the amount of attention available for comprehension of an incoming message will be determined by the amount of attention required to maintain the memorial information needed to retain coherence in comprehension. Thus, a test of working memory capacity, in isolation, will be an imperfect measure of the availability of memory resources available during verbal comprehension.

Daneman and her colleagues have expanded on this idea to develop a technique for measuring the amount of working memory that is available in the context of language comprehension (Daneman, 1984). Participants read sentences aloud, to ensure that they must attend to each word. On demand, they must recite the last words of the sentences just read. A possible sequence of presentations is

(15) When at last his eyes opened there was no gleam of triumph, no shade of anger.

The taxi turned up Michigan Avenue where they had a clear view of the lake.

RECALL

Subject responds — anger, lake.

A person's "memory span while reading" is defined as the number of sentences that can be read while maintaining perfect recall. Memory span while reading is a better predictor of general verbal comprehension scores than is the conventional memory span test, in which a person is asked to recall letters, digits, or words without executing any concurrent task (Daneman & Carpenter, 1980). More impressively, memory span while reading can be shown to be an accurate predictor of a person's performance at those points in language comprehension at which working memory demands are highest. "Garden path" sentences such as example (13) provides a case in point. People with high memory spans while reading are better able to understand garden path sentences than are people with low memory spans (Daneman & Carpenter, 1983).

Studies of the role of working memory in the comprehension of isolated sentences probably understate its importance in normal discourse comprehension. Many of the propositions expressed in sentences in connected text can only be understood by reference to information in previous sentences. This is especially true if a sentence contains an *anaphoric* reference to items mentioned in previous sentences. Anaphoric references tax working memory, but at the same time they tie a text together by making explicit arguments shared by different propositions. Pronouns are good examples of anaphors, as in

(16)   John entered the restaurant. He was a tall and haughty man who had an appreciation for good food.

"He" in the second sentence refers back to John, connecting two separate propositions. Resolving anaphors requires a search of working memory for possible references. Resolution can be made difficult by increasing the amount of discourse between the referent and the reference. Compare (16) to

(17)   John entered the restaurant. The apple strudel looked particularly inviting. He was a tall and haughty man, who had an appreciation for good food.

Anaphoric references are still more difficult if there are semantically possible referents for a reference, as in

(18)   John entered the restaurant. The headwaiter approached quickly. He was a tall and haughty man who had an appreciation for good food.

compared to

(19)   John entered the restaurant. The hatcheck girl approached quickly. He was a tall and haughty man who had an appreciation for good food.

Daneman and Carpenter (1980) showed that memory span while reading is a predictor of the ability to resolve anaphoric references. Figure 9 depicts one of their results. This is particularly striking evidence showing that individual differences in the ability to hold information in working memory during language comprehension are important determinants of overall comprehension ability.

Understanding Words and Sentences in a Linguistic Context

Earlier, it was pointed out that the purpose of linguistic analysis is to discover the propositions expressed in a text. The purpose of verbal comprehension is to discover the propositions that describe a situation. The idealistic linguistic view (which no one seriously maintains) assumes that linguistic analysis precedes comprehension. It is easy to show that a comprehender's understanding of a situation can influence linguistic analyses. Compare

(20)   Mary heard a crash in the kitchen. She knew that John had a hand in the cookie jar.

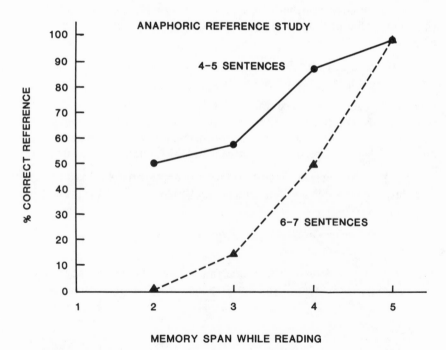

FIGURE 9.   Accuracy in resolving anaphoric references as a function of the distance between the anaphor and its referent and the level of performance on the "memory span while reading" test.

to

(21)   Mary spent all evening scrutinizing the account books. She knew that John had a hand in the cookie jar.

The contrast between these sentences could be presented as a special case of the resolution of lexical ambiguities, as in

(22)   The opera star took a bow.

compared to

(23)   The sailor stood on the bow.

In either case, some mechanism has to be described to explain how a comprehender knows which meaning to assign to the polysemeous word or phrase. The problem extends to the resolution of syntactical ambiguity. Perfetti et al. (1985) reported the newspaper headline

(24)   Council bill to protect squirrels hit by mayor.

The sentence structure of (24) is easily recovered, providing that the reader has the extralinguistic knowledge that mayors frequently attack bills, and seldom attack squirrels. A theory of verbal comprehension must explain how linguistic and world knowledge are combined to produce understanding.

Having an idea sensitizes a person to related ideas. This fact has been the basis of associationist theories of the mind at least since Aristotle (Anderson & Bower, 1972). In the case of verbal comprehension, the arousal of an idea in the early part of a text will facilitate the recognition of related ideas later in the text. This is one of the ways in which world knowledge can bias linguistic analysis. Example (25) is easily understood, because the predicate is semantically compatible with the subject.

(25)   Ivan the Terrible was cruel and despotic to his enemies.

Example (26) is harder to comprehend because naming the subject accesses semantic associations that are contradicted by the predicate.

(26)   Ivan the Terrible was kind and loving to his wife.

Responding to associations is an imprecise form of reasoning. There is nothing literally wrong with (26); it simply denies the semantic associations most Western readers have connected to "Ivan the Terrible." (There is some historical evidence for the sentence's truth!) It is easy to demonstrate, though, that recognition of one word primes the mind to recognize related words. Furthermore, priming depends upon the topic being attended to, and not solely upon the proximity of the priming word to the to-be-recognized word (Foss, 1982). Since most discourses are predictable, priming normally facilitates comprehension because it sensitizes concepts that, on a statistical basis, are likely to be referred to in the subsequent text. To what extent are there individual differences in the mechanism of priming, and individual differences in the relative weight that people place on priming or more precise linguistic analyses to determine meaning?

The lexical decision task is a useful vehicle for studying priming, since the lexical recognition of one word will facilitate recognition of semantic associates. For instance, presenting the word "Doctor" will speed recognition of the subsequent word "Nurse." The phenomenon has been replicated so often that it is beyond question. On the other hand, individual differences in sensitivity to priming effects appear to be small and unreliable. In one study in our laboratory (Palmer et al., 1985) we found substantial priming effects, averaged over subjects, but virtually no reliable individual differences. Naturally, this precluded our finding any relation between individual sensitivity to priming and other aspects of verbal performance. Results such as these suggest that the efficiency of the priming mechanism does not vary greatly across individuals.

An even stronger conclusion has been reached by Stanovich (1980), on the basis of a series of studies of priming by sentence context. In these studies, a sentence fragment is presented, followed by a target word. The sentence can establish a context that facilitates word recognition. An example is

(27)   CONTEXT → Ivan the Terrible was

TARGET   → cruel

Stanovich observed that fluent readers do not benefit from context more than beginning readers. If anything, the converse is true. It appears that weaker readers rely relatively more upon the nonspecific meanings reinforced by priming, while strong readers rely more on the precise definition produced by efficient lexical and syntactical-semantic processing.

Figure 10 shows some results that support Stanovich's argument. Skilled and unskilled grade school readers were asked to identify words, either alone, in the context of a list of related words, or in a context of a story. Skilled readers were faster than unskilled readers, but contexts made little difference. These data are particularly interesting because, in this study, context was established by a spoken sentence (Perfetti, Goldman, & Hogaboam, 1979). Apparently, Stanovich's argument applies to comprehension of both spoken and written speech.

The fact that "lower verbals" rely more on generalized context effects than do "higher verbals" was illustrated rather dramatically in a study by Gleitman and Gleitman (1979). Three groups of subjects—high school graduates not intending to go to college, college students, and Ph.D. candidates—listened to word strings and then explained what they meant. The linguistic structure and speaking intonations of the strings were created by taking a word triplet

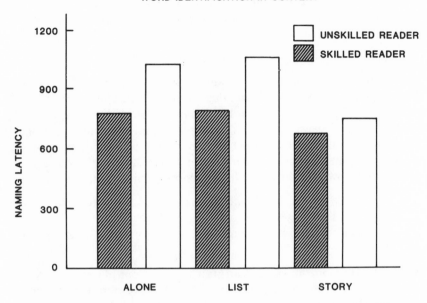

FIGURE 10.   Contextual priming effects as a function of level of reading skill.

and altering it either in phrasing or order. Such changes can drastically alter meaning. Everyone agrees that

(28)   black bird-house

is a dark house for birds. Somewhat more startlingly,

(29)   black-bird house

is a house, of undefined color, for a certain species of bird. But what is the meaning of

(30)   black house-bird.

My own favorite interpretation is "a canary dipped in ink."

The Ph.D. candidates were able to give interpretations that conformed to both the order and phrasing of the word string. The high school graduates were less able to do so. The pattern of their errors displayed a systematic bias toward conformity with the general context of the words: i.e., a distortion toward meaningful semantics by ignoring the precise order and phrasing of the linguistic stimulus. Some members of the high school group interpreted (30) as "black bird-house," disregarding the exact linguistic stimulus in order to react to semantic associations of its components.

Evidently people with generally higher verbal competence have a more precise picture of what the linguistic stimulus is. There is an interesting way to test this contention. Suppose a person encounters an unfamiliar word in a text. What does "glop" mean in the sentence

    (31)   Two glop three equals five.

This example is not whimsical. Vocabulary acquisition probably depends on learning from context much more than upon learning from explicit instruction (Miller, 1981). In the case at hand, most people will assume that "glop" means "plus," because "plus" fits the semantic and linguistic constraints of the sentence. Inferring the correct meaning is possible only if one knows English syntax, the meaning of other lexical items in the string, and the rules of arithmetic. Now consider the following, more complex example.

    (32)   The boyars hated Ivan because he had abrogated many ancient rights and privileges. The common people loved the tsar, both for his piety and because he had protected them against the harsh rule of the boyars.

What does the word "boyars" mean? Is it a singular or a plural term? As most readers will have guessed, boyars were medieval Russian nobles. How did you know?

People with high verbal test scores, and older children, provide better definitions from context than do low verbal people or younger children (Freyd & Baron, 1982; van Daalens-Kapteijns & Elshout-Mohr, 1981). In itself, this is not surprising, because inferring meaning from context requires an understanding of the restrictions imposed by context and, by definition, good verbal comprehenders are better at comprehension! The way in which the good comprehenders infer meaning is of more interest. Sternberg and Powell (1983) classified the cues provided by a context into external cues, provided by the unknown term's position in the sentence and the meaning of the words around it, and internal cues, provided by the structure of the word itself. In example (32), "boyars" are certainly animate and probably human, because the term must satisfy the semantic constraints on the subject of the verb "hated." The reference to "Ivan" as a "tsar" locates the boyars in history. The fact that the boyars had power indicates their position in society. These are external cues. In order to identify "boyars" as a plural term, internal cues must be used. To see this, note that example (32) would make sense if the singular term "Duke" were substituted for "boyars." However "boyars" is not capitalized, so it cannot be a proper noun, and the word ends in "s," which is the usual ending for an English plural.

Sternberg and Powell (1983) found that high school students, on the average, responded only to external cues, while college students responded both to internal and external cues. Taken together with the previous findings, the studies of how people extract word definitions from context provide further evidence that good comprehenders simply have a better idea of what the linguistic stimulus is than do poor comprehenders. Therefore, when comprehension is to be based on combining the information from linguistic analysis and general situational cues, the good comprehenders place relatively more weight on the linguistic analysis than do the poor comprehenders.

DISCOURSE COMPREHENSION

Comprehension is normally an attempt to understand discourse, not words or sentences in isolation. Purely linguistic theories are quite inadequate models of how people do this. Discourses cannot be understood without combined understanding of the linguistic structure of the message, the topic under discussion, and the role of the message in the overall situation. The latter is called the pragmatic meaning of the message. It can be quite different from the meaning that would be extracted solely by considering the information in the message itself. To coin a slogan, the meaning of the message may not be the meaning in the message. Shakespeare offers us an elegant example, Mark Anthony's funeral oration in *Julius Caesar*. Sentence by sentence, the oration is an explanation of why Brutus and Cassius had to kill the tyrant Caesar. Taken in context, it is a stunning denunciation of the assassins.

Walter Kintsch and Teun A. van Dijk have developed a model of discourse comprehension based on an extension of the idea of analyzing the propositions in a sentence (Kintsch & van Dijk, 1978; van Dijk & Kintsch, 1983). Their model extends the idea of propositional analysis to encompass discourses. For instance, the passage about Ivan the Terrible (Example 32) could be expressed by the proposition

(33)   And (Hate(boyars, Ivan = tsar,
            (attack (Ivan, rights of boyars))))),
         (Love(common people,Ivan,
            (and(pious,(Ivan),
               (protect(Ivan, common people,boyars)))))).

The central meaning of the text is expressed by the conjuction of two propositions, that the boyars hated Ivan and that the common people loved him. "Hate" and "love" are treated as propositions that require three arguments, an agent (boyars for hate, and common people for love), an object (Ivan in both cases), and a cause. The cause for hate is stated as a proposition about Ivan's attack on the boyar's rights, while the cause for love is a conjunction of two further propositions about Ivan's actions.

Kintsch and van Dijk refer to the propositional structure of a discourse as a *macroproposition*. The macroproposition must be built up piece by piece, by identifying the *micropropositions* in individual sentences and fitting them together. The actual construction of the macroproposition is assumed to take place in working memory. Since working memory will seldom be large enough to store all the micropropositions in a text simultaneously, micropropositions must be placed into the macroproposition selectively. What the comprehender must do is to keep in working memory those parts of the developing macroproposition that will be needed to fix new micropropositions into their appropriate place as they are identified.

The spirit of Kintsch and van Dijk's model can be illustrated by an informal analysis of example (32), the passage about Ivan. The various panels of Figure 11 show the progressive construction of a propositional form from the text. The first phrase ("The boyars hated Ivan") establishes the initial proposition (Figure 11a). In establishing the proposition, the verb "hate" is treated as a template for a particular propositional structure. This is consistent with several theoretical treatments of the representation of language semantics in memory (Norman & Rumelhart, 1975; Schank, 1972). Because the cause slot of the template is not filled by the phrase, a part of the developing working memory structure is left open. In terms of the theory, the goal of finding why the boyars hated Ivan will have been established in working memory, as a guide to subsequent processing of the linguistic message. The goal is satisfied by processing the next clause ("because he had abrogated their ancient rights and privileges") leading to the structure shown in Figure (11b).

The structure in (11b) is rather large. Suppose that it preempts virtually all working memory resources. If any more processing is to be done, something will have to be dropped. Figure (11b) also shows a substantial amount of cross referencing. This has been indicated by numbering each lexical item as it is encountered, but retaining the same number if two lexical items refer to the same semantic entity. Thus "Ivan (3)" appears twice, to indicate that the same Ivan is being referred to, and "boyars (2)" appears three times. The as-

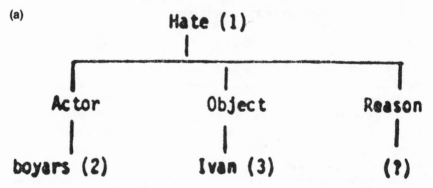

(a)

Hate (1)

Actor   Object   Reason

boyars (2)   Ivan (3)   (?)

FIGURE 11.   The sequential construction of a macropropositional representation of a discourse. See text for an explanation.

(b)

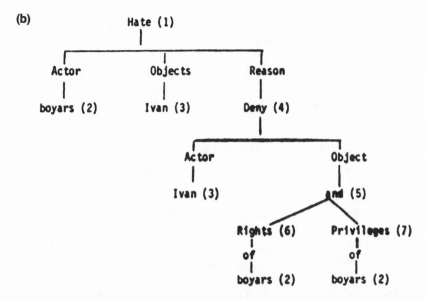

signment of reference numbers to the second and third appearance of the bo-yars term will have required a resolution of the anaphoric reference "their."

The second sentence ("The common people loved their tsar") cannot be processed until some room is made for it in working memory. Kintsch and van Dijk offer a variety of rules that comprehenders may use to compact the propositional structures in working memory. None of the rules is infallible, but all are useful when properly applied (van Dijk & Kintsch, 1983). One common rule drops propositions that are low in the hierarchy of proposi-tions. An example would be the proposition "pious(Ivan)" in (33), which is deeply embedded in the text macrostructure. Another is to retain proposi-tions that are linked to other propositions by extensive cross referencing. Note that Kintsch and van Dijk's rules could be executed by a production sys-tem machine, such as the one sketched in the section of cognitive theory. Ap-plication of the first rule, followed by processing of the first part of the sec-ond sentence, leads to the structure shown in Figure 11(c). Note the term "refer to LTM" in the "cause" position of "hate." This is a statement saying

(c)

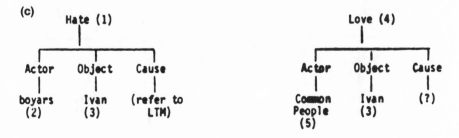

that the cause for hatred *may* have been stored in a long term memory structure, but is not now at the focus of attention. This point is discussed below. But first the analysis of the passage must be completed.

The question mark in Figure 11(c) indicates that the comprehender has established the goal of understanding why the common people loved Ivan. Parenthetically, it appears that finding causes for things is an important goal in human comprehension. The goal is realized by an analysis of the next phrase ("because of his piety and because he had protected them against the harsh rule of the boyars"), Figure 11(e). This is rather a mouthful, and would no doubt be comprehended in pieces. If working memory filled, something would have to be removed to make room for the final phrase ("protected them" . . ."). A candidate for removal is the entire structure concerning the boyars' hatred for Ivan, as this is a logical unit that is not required in order to comprehend the separately stated reasons for the people's love for Ivan (contrast Figure 11(d) to Figure 11(e)). Indeed, it could be argued that the final structure is itself too large for working memory. If so, what should be dropped? The most likely candidate is the structure relating to Ivan's piety, as this is both low in the hierarchy of propositions and not as tightly cross referenced to other terms in the macropropositional structure as is the proposition dealing with protection of the people.

The development of a working memory structure is a temporary stage in comprehension. In order to retain information for any length of time, propositional structures must be transferred to long term memory. Indeed, as shown in the diagram (and illustrated dramatically by studies of people with exceptional memorizing ability—Ericsson, 1985), long term memory is required as a supporting structure for working memory during comprehension, in much the same way that secondary storage systems (e.g., disks) are required in digital computer systems. What precipitates the transfer of information into LTM, and what rules are used to decide what is stored there?

The most parsimonious assumption to make is that transfer of information to long term memory is a random process over time, independent of the content of the information. Therefore, the only determinant of the probability of retention of information about a proposition will be the time that the proposition is resident in working memory. However, the time that informa-

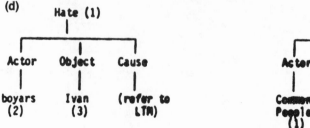
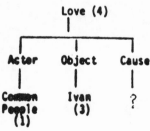

(e)

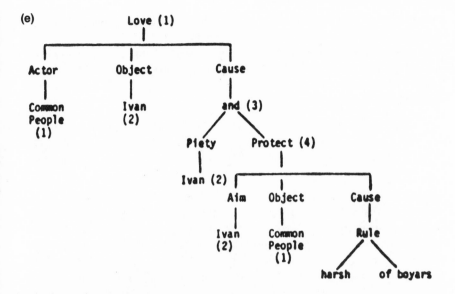

tion is resident in working memory will itself be determined by the role that the information plays in discourse comprehension. Propositions that are required to bind large sections of the discourse together will be resident in working memory for an extended period of time, and thus are almost certain to be stored in long term memory. In the illustration of Figure 11, the proposition "The boyars hated Ivan" has a long residency in working memory, and, thus, one would expect it to be recalled. There is experimental evidence for the expectation. Miller and Kintsch (1980) have shown that the probability of recall of a proposition in a text can be predicted by using the Kintsch and van Dijk model to analyze a proposition's residency in working memory during discourse comprehension.

It is worth noting that the Kintsch and van Dijk model stresses the influence of the comprehension task upon memory. If a recipient of a linguistic message were told to process that message in some way that did not require comprehension, such as counting words that began with "p," text structure should have little influence on memory.

The Kitsch and van Dijk model, and others like it (e.g., Sanford & Garrod, 1981) are compatible with the general theoretical position taken here. Models of comprehension can be realized by production systems. Comprehension will be guided by three different characteristics of the comprehender. These are the comprehender's possession of rules (productions) that identify the central points in a text, so that they are retained in working memory for some time; the total amount of working memory available; and the rate at which the comprehender transfers information from working memory into long term memory. To what extent are each of these processes significant factors in individual differences in verbal comprehension?

Daneman and Carpenter (1983) studied people's ability to integrate information across sentences. College students read a variety of cleverly worded paragraphs that contained references to previously presented information. An example is the "microstory"

(34) John heard a noise. He wanted something to defend himself so he went to the cupboard where he stored his baseball equipment. He found a bat that was large and brown and that flew out of the room when John opened the door.

The phrase "flew out of the room" can be placed in the propositional structure only if the comprehender has retained the lexical term "bat," so that its secondary meaning (small, flying animal) can be retrieved. If the surface structure has been replaced by a completely abstract semantic (or a long term memory reference to such a structure) that designates "bat" as "instrument for striking a baseball," disambiguation is more difficult. Daneman and Carpenter found that people with reading memory spans of five items or more correctly disambiguated 85% of the references, while people with spans of two or less correctly disambiguated only 49% of the references. Further experiments using other linguistic devices forcing information integration across sentence boundaries lead to essentially the same conclusion. Individual differences in the effective size of working memory appear to be a substantial source of variation in verbal comprehension, because of their interaction with rules for processing text. This result is particularly impressive because the participants in Daneman and Carpenter's studies were all undergraduates in a highly selective private university, and thus can be presumed to have had above average verbal skills.

Message comprehension is a cooperative process in which the message transmitter assumes that the receiver already has some relevant knowledge, identifies that knowledge, and then imparts some new information related to it. This is sometimes referred to as the "given-new contract"; the message first identifies information that the sender presumes the receiver already has, and then imparts a new piece of information related to the old information (Clark & Havilland, 1977). Comprehension depends upon the receiver already knowing the given, i.e., upon the receiver already having the vocabulary and concepts that will be used but not defined in the message. Technical writing is an excellent example of how comprehension depends upon this aspect of the given-new contract. The following introductory paragraph from an article in the journal *Science* makes very strong implicit assumptions about what the reader already knows.

(35) The crystal structures of four gene-regulatory proteins—the lambda cro protein, the NH2-terminal domain of the lambda re-

pressor, and the CAP protein and the trp repressor of *Escheria coli*
have been reported. Each of these proteins binds to its operator site(s)
as a dimer and forms a complex that is approximately twofold sym-
metric.

(Jordan, Whitcome, Berg, & Pabo, 1985).

Does this sort of communication only occur in academia? Hardly. Example
(36) is taken from the sports page of a daily newspaper;

(36)   Chicago hosts the LA Rams to determine the NFC's Super Bowl
representative. There will be no sideshows in this one but it doesn't need
any. Walter Payton running one way and Eric Dickerson the other is
plenty, and add to that The Refrigerator and friends snacking on Ram
quarterback Dieter Brock.

Seattle Times, Jan. 11, 1986, pg. D-1

Some people will understand one of examples (35) and (36), many people will
not understand either, and there may even be a few football-watching
biophysicists who understand both. There certainly are individual differences in comprehension that can be traced to individual differences in specialized vocabularies or individual differences in the content area of a
message. Technically, these could be said to be due to violations of the given-
new contract, the discourse producer has simply assumed something that the
receiver did not know. Studying the situations in which such breakdowns of
communication occur is not likely to tell us much about the psychology of
discourse *comprehension,* although it may tell us something about the
metacognitive demands of discourse *production.* That topic, however, is beyond the scope of the current article.

Schank (1982) has argued for a broader interpretation of the "given-new"
contract. He pointed out that linguistic messages are rarely, if ever, complete
thoughts. Instead, they remind the comprehender of a generalized situation
that is already known, and then specialize the general knowledge to a specific
case. To take a much used example, people in Western civilizations virtually
all have a "restaurant script" that describes how one obtains food in a com-
mercial eating establishment (Schank & Abelson, 1977). The restaurant
script contains a number of specialized scripts that refer to particular types of
restaurants. Thus, if one hears (in 1986) that

(37)   John paid $10.00 for a continental breakfast at his hotel.

one "knows," because it is part of the appropriate script, that John was probably greeted by a headwaiter, seated at a table, and presented a bill after having eaten breakfast. A very different set of assumptions (i.e., a different variety of the restaurant script) would have been evoked by "John paid $1.50
. . ." A child, less familiar with restaurant scripts, might not have realized the
differences in restaurants that is implied by a difference in price.

The knowledge that people have about general situations has variously been referred to as scripts, frames, and schemata. Although these terms have slightly different meanings, the distinction between them is not important here, so the more general term "knowledge structures" will be used. We all have committed a great many knowledge structures to memory, and we use them in our everyday comprehension. In fact, when people recall events discussed in a discourse, they may have trouble discriminating between information that was explicitly presented and information that would be included in the appropriate stereotypic structure (Bower, Black, & Turner, 1979; Locksley, Stangor, Hepburn, Grosovsky and Hochstrasser, 1984). Despite the possibility of such distortions, stereotypic knowledge structures are useful because they aid in organizing the incoming facts. In terms of the Kintsch and van Dijk model, the knowledge structure guides the comprehender in identifying the important propositions in the text, by alerting the comprehender to the propositions that are normally of central importance.

A number of studies have shown that the possession of appropriate knowledge structures accounts for the advantage that experts have over novices in recalling material within their field of expertise. A study by Spilich, Vesonder, Chiesi, and Voss (1979) illustrates the typical finding. In this study, participants listened to a "broadcast" of a fictitious baseball game. They were then asked to recall the key events. Figure 12 shows the number and type of propositions recalled by people who either did or did not have good knowledge of the game of baseball. The experienced baseball watchers had much better memory for propositions that were important in understanding the game (e.g., "A runner was tagged out at second base.") but did not have superior memory for propositions that were irrelevant to the game (e.g., "The umpire was tall.").

The idea that expertise guides construction of a macroproposition can be extended beyond the concept of an expert as a subject matter specialist, to include expert knowledge about discourse itself. The rules that Kintsch and van Dijk present for discourse comprehension represent a form of expertise. The rules assume that a discourse *generator* has followed certain rules in constructing a discourse. If the rules for generation have indeed been followed, the comprehension rules will construct an appropriate macroproposition. The expertise in the rules, though, is essentially a formulation of the expertise that Kintsch, van Dijk, and their colleagues had. To what extent do their rules of analysis represent psychological descriptions of people in general?

Brown and Day (1983) examined summaries of articles that had been prepared by people who varied widely in general verbal competence, from seventh grade students to college rhetoric teachers. The summaries made by the more experienced comprehenders closely conformed to those that would have been created by a "comprehending machine" programmed to use Kintsch and van Dijk's rules. Brown and Day's comprehenders had never re-

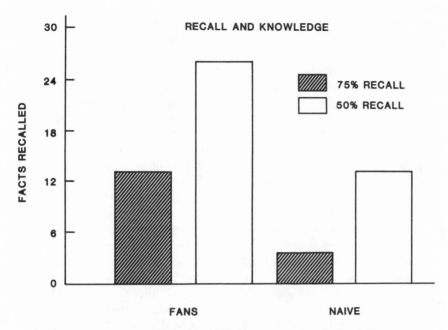

FIGURE 12.   Amount of information recalled from an account of a baseball game as a function of relevance of the information to the game and the comprehender's familiarity with baseball.

ceived explicit training in the Kintsch and van Dijk rules, so the results can also be used to argue for the psychological reality of the rules themselves.[4]

There are many situations in which a person does not need to demonstrate that he or she has understood a message until some time after the message has been comprehended. University examinations are a case in point; professors usually test students' comprehension of a lecture days or weeks after the lecture has been delivered. In terms of our normal functioning, then, the ability to store information presented in a discourse has to be considered part of effective verbal comprehension. On the other hand, the ability to remember is not identical to the ability to comprehend verbal messages. Dramatic cases of the dissociation between the two can be found in neuropsychological cases. Patients who have suffered damage to the hippocampus, a mid-brain structure that is evidently crucial for human memory, can comprehend discourse reasonably well as it is presented to them, but are quite unable to recall that they have participated in a conversation (or read a message) if they are tested

---

[4]A similar point has been made about discourse production. Elementary school children who are considered good writers provide explicit rules to identify coreferences, such as the use of the terms "Ivan," "he," and "the tsar" in example (28). The provision of explicit coreferences aids a comprehender using the Kintsch and van Dijk rules to extract the correct propositions from a text (Bartlett, 1984).

after doing unrelated activities. The amnesia apparently develops within minutes, and is permanent. It is as if the patients had lost the ability to consolidate information into long term memory in a retrievable forms. A similar but sometimes less dramatic syndrome is observed in Korsakoff's psychosis, a possible consequence of severe alcoholism (Kolb & Wishaw, 1980).[5]

Kintsch and van Dijk treat the storage of propositional information into long term memory as a probabilistic event. Information in working memory is moved into long term memory at a fixed rate, independent of the content of the information being stored. Important information in a discourse will be more likely to be remembered than unimportant information, because the central propositions in a text spend more time in working memory than do the less important propositions. Importance per se is not assumed to influence the storage process.

Dixon, Hultsch, Simon, and von Eye (1984) report a study that shows how individual differences in strictly verbal comprehension processes may interact with individual differences in effectiveness of memorization. The study was based on two separate observations. Scores on verbal intelligence tests decline very little over the adult life span. On the other hand, the ability to transfer arbitrary information (e.g., paired associates lists) from working memory into long term memory does seem to decrease with age (Carik, 1977). Dixon et al. reasoned that people of high verbal ability would use strategies that kept the main topics of a passage in working memory for a long time, and that this effect would be independent of age. Hence, high verbal subjects should be able to recall the central themes of a story regardless of their age, because all subjects would reach a performance ceiling for storing of such information. Memory for minor themes in a passage should be more sensitive to age, because the less important propositions, being in working memory for a shorter time, would be more sensitive to age-related losses in the effectiveness of memory consolidation. People of low verbal ability, on the other hand, should be less able to locate and retain in working memory the central theme of a passage, and hence should show age influences on memory for both central and peripheral themes.

Dixon et al. tested the ability to recall story information in people of high and low verbal ability. Their participants were from 20 to 60 years old. Figure 13 plots the recall of propositional information as a function of age, verbal ability, and level of importance of a proposition in the logic of the passage. The pattern of recall is exactly that anticipated by Dixon et al., and can be of-

---

[5]The nature of the memory deficit in both the hippocampal and the Korsakoff patients is complex. Both groups show a dramatic loss of the ability to recount details of an episode that they have experienced. This includes what would normally be called comprehension of a message. On the other hand, there is considerable evidence that these patients do record some information about events that they have experienced, even though they are unable to recall the events themselves.

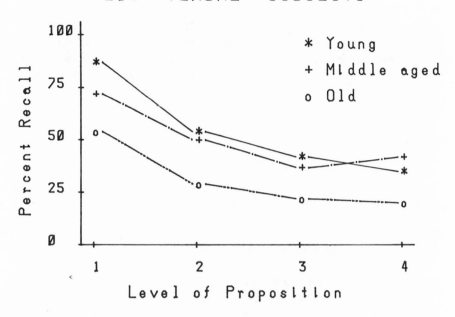

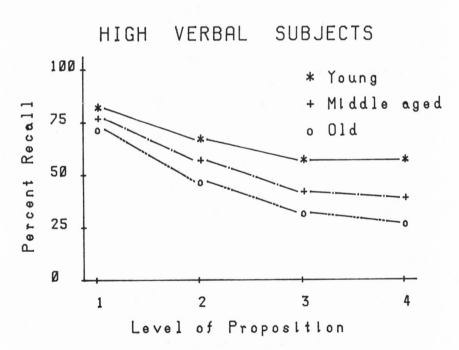

FIGURE 13. Recall of information from a text as a function of the propositional level of the information and the age and verbal ability of the comprehenders.

fered as evidence that there are individual differences in the capacity to consolidate information in long term memory, and that these differences do influence memory for verbal messages. The overall effect of variations in the memory process upon the retention of important information, however, will depend greatly on the strategy used to comprehend the message as it is received.

Pragmatic Comprehension

Van Dijk and Kintsch (1983) distinguish between a comprehender's internal representation of a linguistic message (the *text model*) and his or her internal representation of the situation in which the message is received (the *situation model*). When people develop a situational representation from a discourse, they often include in the representation both the information that is presented in the discourse and some information that is implied by it. Some of the inferences are based on knowledge structures about the situation being described, as was illustrated by example (37), the restaurant script. In other cases, the situational model will be amplified by representations that are based upon inferences from combinations of information explicitly presented in the discourse. For instance, if you are told

(38)   John had to go to three stores to find an aspirin yesterday.

it is reasonable to infer that John had a headache. Making such inferences to expand the situational model is an attention-demanding process, and must compete with the information processing resources required to construct the text model. The processing required for the text model must take priority, because text analysis has to keep up with text presentation. Thus, if "lower level" linguistic text processing is made difficult, the effects may first be seen in failures of pragmatic processing that depends upon drawing inferences from the text. This point will be familiar to anyone who has tried to understand a lecture on a difficult topic, delivered by a lecturer who speaks rapidly, or who has an unfamiliar accent.

Several studies of the role of inference in verbal comprehension provide evidence that pragmatic processing does have lower precedence than message analysis, and that the combination of processing priority and individual differences in various aspects of information processing will lead to characteristic individual differences in total comprehension. The studies in question utilize the fact that passage comprehension depends upon the use of information that appears in a passage, explicitly, and information that can be inferred from a passage by combining explicitly presented information with common knowledge. Example (39) illustrates this.

(39)   Downstairs there are three rooms: the kitchen, the dining-room and the sitting room. The sitting-room is in front of the house and the

kitchen and the dining-room face onto the vegetable garden at the back of the house. The noise of the traffic is very disturbing in the front rooms. Mother is in the kitchen cooking and Grandfather is reading the paper in the sitting-room. The children are at school and won't be home till tea-time.

Question (40) can be answered from information that is explicitly present in the text, while question (41) requires an inference

(40)   What is Mother doing? (cooking).

(41)   Who is being disturbed by the traffic? (Grandfather).

Figure 14 shows the results of a study in which people answered both inferential and verbatim questions (Cohen, 1979). The subjects varied in education (advanced degrees vs. high school diploma or less) and age (20s vs. over 65). Clearly, there are striking effects of both age and education. These are consistent with the view that better-educated people possess more efficient rules for constructing discourse representations in working memory, and that older people are slower in the "mechanics" both of moving information around in the mind and in consolidating information into long term memory. The effects are strongest on those questions that require inferencing, i.e., when the meaning of a discourse is largely determined by pragmatic infer-

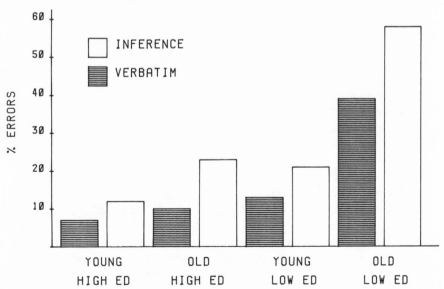

FIGURE 14.   Retrieval of information explicitly or inferentially presented in text as a function of age and level of education.

ences. Cohen's results have been supported and amplified upon in subsequent research (Cohen 1981; Light, Zelinski, & Moore, 1982).

CONCLUSIONS

What is verbal ability? The theoretical position taken here is that the "dimension" of verbal ability is the result of a somewhat correlated collection of skills. These skills depend upon a variety of more primitive psychological processes, including access to lexical memory, the ability to manipulate information in working memory, rapid consolidation of information into long term memory, the possession of knowledge about how to process discourse in general, and the possession of knowledge about the topic of the discourse being comprehended. Some of these primitive processes can be thought of as properties of the brain, closely linked to physiological processes. The efficiency of consolidation of information into long term memory is an example. Other processes, such as the use of restaurant scripts, are learned, and are highly culture dependent.

If the various verbal skills are distinct, why do psychometric analyses so consistently uncover a single dimension of verbal ability? It could be that all the primitive processes of language comprehension are derived from a single underlying brain process, and that the expressions of different processes are correlated across individuals for that purpose. There may be some truth to this, but it is an impossible proposition to prove or disprove.[6] The moderately high correlations between measures of different aspects of language comprehension could also be explained by interactions between them as they are developed. Being able to consolidate information into permanent memory rapidly would aid in the acquisition of lexical knowledge, and increasing one's vocabulary would increase one's ability to develop text and situation models, which could be used to increase lexical knowledge by defining new words in context. Since each subprocess of verbal comprehension encourages the development of the others, it is hardly surprising that, across individuals, the same people are usually good at different verbal comprehension tasks.

The concept of interaction between language skills is not confined to development. Similar interactions between skills occur in performance. Being better at one of the subprocesses of comprehension frees one's resources to attack the other processes. Throughout, the goal is total comprehension, a goal

---

[6]If a single underlying biological function, such as speed of neural impulse transmission, were the only factor determining individual differences in verbal comprehension, then measures of all aspects of comprehension would be perfectly correlated. They are not. Refer back to the discussion of the partial statistical independence of lexical access and sentence verification measures.

that is attacked until we have no more mental energy left. The argument can be summed up by an anecodote, which happens to be a true one. A husband and wife were discussing a book.

(42)   He: I'm not sure I know it.

       She: The Fascinating Woman? I've shown you excerpts.

For the sake of the marriage, one hopes she had. But only the highly verbal husband would realize what she claimed to have done.

REFERENCES

Anderson, J. R. (1983). *The architecture of cognition.* Cambridge, MA: Harvard University Press.

Anderson, J. R., & Bower, G. H. (1972). *Human associative memory.* Washington, DC: V. H. Winston.

Baddeley, A. D. (1968). A three-minute reasoning test based on grammatical transformations. *Psychonomic Science, 10,* 341–342.

Baddeley, A. D., & Hitch, G. J. (1974). Working memory. In G. H. Bower (Ed.), *The psychology of learning and motivation* (Vol. 8). New York: Academic Press.

Bartlett, E. J. (1984). Anaphoric reference in written narratives of good and poor elementary school writers. *Journal of Verbal Learning and Verbal Behavior, 23* (4), 540–552.

Botwinick, J. (1977). Intellectual abilities. In J. Birren & K. W. Schaie (Eds.), *Handbook of the Psychology of Aging.* New York: Van Nostrand Reinhold.

Bower, G. H., Black, J. B., & Turner, T. L. (1979). Scripts in memory for text. *Cognitive Psychology, 11* 177–220.

Brown, A., & Day, J. (1983). Macrorules for summarizing texts: The development of expertise. *Journal of Verbal Learning and Verbal Behavior, 22* (6), 1–14.

Carpenter, P. A., & Just, M. A. (1975). Sentence comprehension: A psycholinguistic model of verification. *Psychological Review, 82* (1), 45–73.

Clark, H. H., & Chase, W. G. (1972). On the process of comparing sentences against pictures. *Cognitive Psychology, 3,* 472–517.

Clark, H. H., & Clark, E. V. (1977). *Psychology and language.* New York: Harcourt Brace Jovonavich.

Clark, H. H., & Haviland, S. E. (1977). Comprehension and the given-new contract. In R. O. Freedle (Ed.), *Discourse production and comprehension.* Norwood, NJ: Ablex.

Cohen, G. (1979). Language comprehension in old age. *Cognitive Psychology, 11,* 412–429.

Cohen, G. (1981). Inferential reasoning in old age. *Cognition, 9* (1), 59–72.

Craik, F. I. M. (1977). Age differences in human memory. In J. Birren & K. W. Schaie (Eds.), *Handbook of the psychology of aging.* New York: Van Nostrand Reinhold.

Daneman, M. (1984). Why some people are better readers than others: A process and storage account. In R. J. Sternberg (Ed.), *Advances in the psychology of human intelligence.* Hillsdale, NJ: Erlbaum.

Daneman, M., & Carpenter, P. A. (1980). Individual differences in working memory and reading. *Journal of Verbal Learning and Verbal Behavior, 19,* 450–466.

Daneman, M., & Carpenter, P. A. (1983). Individual differences in integrating information between and within sentences. *Journal of Experimental Psychology: Learning, Memory, and Cognition, 9* (4), 561–584.

Dixon, R. A., Hultsch, D. F., Simon, E. W., & von Eye, A. (1984). Verbal ability and text structure effects on adult age differences in text recall. *Journal of Verbal Learning and Verbal Behavior, 23* (5), 579–592.

Ericsson, K. A. (1985). Memory skill. *Canadian Journal of Psychology, 39* (2), 188–231.

Fisk, A. D., & Schneider, W. (1983). Category and word search: Generalizing search principles to complex processing. *Journal of Experimental Psychology: Learning, Memory, and Cognition, 9,* 172–195.

Fodor, J. A., & Bever, T. G. (1965). The psychological reality of linguistic segments. *Journal of Verbal Learning and Verbal Behavior, 4,* 414–420.

Foss, D. J. (1982). A discourse on sentence priming. *Cognitive Psychology, 14* (4), 590–607.

Frederiksen, J. R. (1982). A componential theory of reading skills and their interaction. In R. J. Sternberg (Ed.), *Advances in the psychology of human intelligence. Volume 1.* Hillsdale, NJ: Erlbaum.

Freyd, P., & Baron, J. (1982). Individual differences in acquisition of derivational morphology. *Journal of Verbal Learning and Verbal Behavior, 21,* 282–293.

Gleitman, H., & Gleitman, L. (1979). Language use and language judgement. In C. J. Fillmore, D. Kempler, & W. S. Y. Wang (Eds.), *Individual differences in language ability and language behavior.* New York: Wiley.

Goldberg, R. A., Schwartz, S., & Stewart, M. (1977). Individual differences in cognitive processes. *Journal of Educational Psychology, 69,* 9–14.

Hunt, E. (1978). Mechanics of verbal ability. *Psychological Review, 85* (2), 109–130.

Hunt, E., Davidson, J., & Lansman, M. (1981). Individual differences in long-term memory access. *Memory and Cognition, 9* (6), 599–608.

Hunt, E., & Lansman, M. (1986). A unified model of attention and problem solving. *Psychological Review,* Vol. 93(4), 446–461.

Hunt, E., Lunneborg, C. L., & Lewis, J. (1975). What does it mean to be high verbal? *Cognitive Psychology, 7,* 194–227.

Jackson, M. D. (1980). Further evidence for a relation between memory access and reading ability. *Journal of Verbal Learning and Verbal Behavior, 19,* 683–695.

Jordan, S. R., Whitcombe, T. V., Berg, J. M., & Pabo, C. O. (1985). Systematic variation in DNA length yields highly ordered repressor-operator cocrystals. *Science, 230* (4732), 1383–1385.

Just, M., & Carpenter, P. A. (1980). A theory of reading: From eye fixation to comprehension. *Psychological Review, 87,* 329–354.

Kintsch, W., & Keenan, J. M. (1973). Reading rate as a function of the number of propositions in the base structures of sentences. *Cognitive Psychology, 5,* 257–274.

Kintsch, W., & van Dijk, T. A. (1978). Towards a model of text comprehension and production. *Psychological Review, 85*(6), 363–392.

Klapp, S. T., Marshburn, E. A., & Lester, P. T. (1983). Short term memory does not involve the "working memory" of information processing: The decline of a common assumption. *Journal of Experimental Psychology: General, 112,* 240–264.

Kolb, B., & Wishaw, I. Q. (1980). *Fundamentals of human neuropsychology.* San Francisco, CA: Freeman.

Kroll, J. F., & Corrigan, A. (1981). Strategies in sentence-picture verification: The effect of an unexpected picture. *Journal of Verbal Learning and Verbal Behavior, 20,* 515–531.

Lansman, M. (1978). *An attentional approach to individual differences in immediate memory.* Doctoral thesis, University of Washington, Seattle.

Lansman, M., Donaldson, G., Hunt, E., & Yantis, S. (1983). Ability factors and cognitive processes. *Intelligence, 6,* 347–386.

Liberman, A. M., & Mattingly, I. (1985). The motor theory of speech revised. *Cognition, 21* (1), 1–36.

Light, L., Zelinski, E., & Moore, M. (1982). Adult age differences in reasoning from new information. *Journal of Experimental Psychology: Learning, Memory and Cognition, 8,* 435–447.

Locksley, A., Strangor, C., Hepburn, C., Grosovsky, E., & Hochstrasser, M. (1984). The ambiguity of recognition memory test of schema theory. *Cognitive Psychology, 16*(4), 421–448.

Mathews, N. N., Hunt, E. B., & MacLeod, C. M. (1980). Strategy choice and strategy training in sentence-picture verification. *Journal of Verbal Learning and Verbal Behavior, 19,* 531–548.

MacLeod, C. M., Hunt, E. B., & Mathews, N. N. (1978). Individual differences in the verification of sentence-picture relationships. *Journal of Verbal Learning and Verbal Behavior, 17,* 493–507.

Miller, G. (1981). *Language and speech.* San Francisco, CA: Freeman.

Miller, J. R., & Kintsch, W. (1980). Readability and recall of short prose passages: A theoretical analysis. *Journal of Experimental Psychology: Human Learning and Memory, 6,* 335–354.

Morrison, F. J., Giordani, B., & Nagy, J. (1977). Reading disability: An information processing analysis. *Science, 196,* 77–79.

Norman, D. A., & Rumelhart, D. E. (1975). *Explorations in cognition.* San Francisco, CA: Freeman.

Palmer, J. C., MacLeod, C. M., Hunt, E., & Davidson, J. (1985). Information processing correlates of reading. *Journal of Memory and Language, 24* (1), 59–88.

Perfetti, C. A. (1985). Reading ability. In R. J. Sternberg (Ed.), *Human abilities: An information processing approach.* San Francisco, CA: Freeman.

Perfetti, C. A., Beverly, S., Didonato, L., & Pertsch, L. (1985). Parsing newspaper headlines. *Proceedings of the Psychonomic Society 26th Annual Meeting,* Boston, MA: Abstract 350.

Perfetti, C. A., Goldman, S. R., & Hogaboam, T. W. (1979). Reading skill and the identification of words in discourse context. *Memory and Cognition, 7,* 273–282.

Poltrock, S. E., Lansman, M., & Hunt, E. (1982). Automatic and controlled attention processes in auditory target detection. *Journal of Experimental Psychology: Human Perception and Performance, 8* (1), 37–45.

Sanford, A. J., & Garrod, S. C. (1981). *Understanding written language.* New York: Wiley.

Schank, R. C. (1972). Conceptual dependency: A theory of natural language understanding. *Cognitive Psychology, 3,* 552–631.

Schank, R. C. (1982). *Dynamic memory.* Cambridge: Cambridge U. Press.

Schank, R. C., & Abelson, R. P. (1977). *Scripts, plans, goals, and understanding.* Hillsdale, NJ: Erlbaum.

Schank, R. C., & Childers, P. C. (1984). *The cognitive computer.* Reading, MA: Addison-Wesley.

Schneider, W., & Shiffrin, R. M. (1977). Controlled and automatic human information processing: I. Detection, search and attention. *Psychological Review, 84,* 1–66.

Spilich, G. J., Vesonder, G. T., Chiesi, H. L., & Voss, J. F. (1979). Text processing of domain-related information for individuals with high and low domain knowledge. *Journal of Verbal Learning and Verbal Behavior, 18,* 275–290.

Spoehr, K. T., & Smith, E. E. (1973). The role of syllables in perceptual processing. *Cognitive Psychology, 5* (1), 71–89.

Stanovich, K. (1980). Toward an interactive-compensatory model of individual differences in the development of reading fluency. *Reading Research Quarterly, 16* (1), 32–71.

Sternberg, R. J., & Powell, J. S. (1983). Comprehending verbal comprehension. *American Psychologist, 38,* 878–893.

Sticht, T. G. (1975). *Reading for working: A functional literary anthology.* Alexandria, VA: Human Resources Research Organization.

Thibadeau, R., Just, M. A., & Carpenter, P. A. (1982). A model of the time course and content of reading. *Cognitive Science, 6,* 157–203.

van Daalen-Kapteijns, M. N., & Elshout-Mohr, M. (1981). The acquisition of word meanings as a cognitive learning process. *Journal of Verbal Learning and Verbal Behavior, 20,* 386–399.

van Dijk, T. A., & Kintsch, W. (1983). *Strategies of discourse comprehension.* New York: Academic Press.

Vellutino, F. R. (1979). *Dyslexia: Theory and research.* Cambridge, MA: M.I.T. Press.

Wickens, C. D. (1979). The structure of attentional resources. In R. S. Nickerson (Ed.), *Attention and performance VIII.* Hillsdale, NJ: Erlbaum.

Author Index

A

Abalan, F., 55, *60*
Abelson, R.P., 381, *391*
Ahern, S., 172, *173*
Aikens, H.A., 25, *60*
Albert, K., 53, *60*
Alcorn, M.B., 296, 319, 323, 324, 326, *344*
Amelang, M., 48, *60*
Amochaev, A., 173, *175*
Amthauer, R., 32, *60*
Ananda, S.M., 46, 47, *60,* 113, 168, *173*
Anastasi, A., 222, *235*
Anderson, J.R., 351, 371, *389*
Anderson, M., 25, *60,* 315, 316, 318, *342*
Arbitman-Smith, R., 71, *96*
Armstrong, S., 13, *19*
Arora, I., 113, *175*
Atkin, R., 222, *235*
Auble, P.M., 273, 285, *292*
Austin, S.V., 89, *96*

B

Baddeley, A.D., 363, 366, *389*
Bagley, W.C., 25, *60*
Baltes, P.B., 36, *60,* 247, *268*
Banbar, 55, *61*
Baron, J., 284, *292,* 374, *390*
Barr, A., 31, *60*
Barrett, P., 22, 41, 48, 51, 52, 58, *60, 61,* 114, *173,* 185, *198*
Bartlett, E.J., 383n, *389*
Batts, V., 297, *343*
Baumeister, A., 50, *64, 85, 96,* 177, 184, *198*
Beatty, J., 172, *173*
Beck, L.F., 297, *342*
Bell, P.A., 13, *18*

Bennett, G.K., 15, *18*
Berenbaum, S.A., 15, *19*
Berg, C.A., 272, 278, *292*
Berg, J.M., 381, *390*
Berger, M., 21, 26, 27, 28, *60,* 298, *342*
Bergman, K., 54, *64*
Berkson, G., 85, *96*
Bernstein, E., 25, *60*
Bernstein, M., 217, 278, *294*
Berry, J.W., 71, *96*
Bever, T.G., 365, *390*
Beverly, S., 352, *391*
Bieger, H.J., 32, *61*
Bilbro, W.C., 9, *19*
Bills, A., 306, 327, *345*
Binet, A., 23, *61*
Bingham, E., 302, 306, 308, 310, 314, 318, 323, 325, 326, 330, 336, *344*
Bisanz, J., 257, *268*
Black, J.B., 382, *389*
Blank, G., 103, 104, *173*
Blessed, G., 54, *64*
Blinkhorn, S., 77, *96*
Block, C.B., 279, *293*
Bobbitt, B., 39, *63,* 184, *199,* 248, 266, *269*
Bock, R.D., 220, *235*
Boies, S., 15, 19, 39, 65, 81, *99*
Boring, E.G., 1, *19, 64,* 107, *175*
Borkowski, J.G., 85, *96*
Botwinck, J., 13, *18,* 364, *389*
Bouchard, T.J., 8, 12, 18, *19*
Bower, G.H., 371, 382, *389*
Boyle, P.R., 86, 89, *98*
Braden, J.P., 113, *173*
Braden, W., 77, *97,* 185, *198*
Brand, C., 296, *342*

393

Subject Index